God, Gulliver, and Genocide

God, Gulliver, and Genocide

Barbarism and the European Imagination, 1492–1945

CLAUDE RAWSON

OXFORD
UNIVERSITY PRESS

2 92378

AUG 1 9 2004

OXFORD
UNIVERSITY PRESS

Great Clarendon Street, Oxford OX2 6DP

Oxford University Press is a department of the University of Oxford.
It furthers the University's objective of excellence in research, scholarship,
and education by publishing worldwide in

Oxford New York

Auckland Bangkok Buenos Aires Cape Town Chennai
Dar es Salaam Delhi Hong Kong Istanbul Karachi Kolkata
Kuala Lumpur Madrid Melbourne Mexico City Mumbai Nairobi
São Paulo Shanghai Taipei Tokyo Toronto

Oxford is a registered trade mark of Oxford University Press
in the UK and in certain other countries

Published in the United States
by Oxford University Press Inc., New York

British Library Cataloguing in Publication Data

Data available

Library of Congress Cataloging in Publication Data

Rawson, Claude Julien.
God, Gulliver, and genocide : barbarism and the European imagination, 1492–1945 /
Claude Rawson.
p. cm.
Includes bibliographical references (p.) and index.
1. Swift, Jonathan, 1667–1745. Gulliver's travels.   2. English literature—Irish
authors—History and critism.   3. Swift, Jonathan, 1667–1745. Modest proposal.   4.
Montaigne, Michel de, 1533–1592. Essais.   5. Satire, English—History and criticism.   6.
Difference (Psychology) in literature.   7. Genocide—Public opinion—History.   8. Public
opinion—Europe—History.   9. Religion and literature.   10. Genocide in literature.   11.
Indians in literature.   12. Racism in literature.   13. Aliens in literature.   14. Irish in
literature.   15. Poor in literature.   I. Title.
PR3724.G8 R38 2001   823'.5—dc21   2001033866

ISBN 0-19-818425-5
ISBN 0-19-925750-7 (pbk)

10 9 8 7 6 5 4 3 2 1

Typeset by Newgen Imaging Systems (P) Ltd., Chennai, India
Printed in Great Britain on acid-free paper by
Biddles Ltd., Guildford and King's Lynn

For George and Shelagh Hunter

PREFACE

When we say certain people 'ought to be shot', or exterminated 'from the face of the earth', we usually do so in the knowledge that we will not be thought to 'mean' it literally. It is a figure of speech, partially sanitized by the conventions of social usage. In this sense, it creates a protective fiction around itself, though this sometimes fails to do its work as a cordon sanitaire. We also create fully-fledged fictions (myths, stories, histories) of which the same might be said. They may fail to remain fictions, and be meant, or taken, for real. The victims in these stories may be whole peoples or groups of people, or even the whole of humanity, as when God said he would 'destroy man whom I have created from the face of the earth'. What God did to humanity, he has also urged humans to do to other humans. Sometimes the distinction is unclear as, on the human scale, the distinction between racial hatreds and a general misanthropy is not always clear, and humans have also used God's phrasing of their own accord.

The phrasing reverberates throughout Scripture and human history. It has been applied to the people of Israel and to their enemies, to conquered savages, the Irish, the poor, and the Jews of Nazi-occupied Europe. Its usage has ranged from the deadliest genocidal intentions, to satirical threats, fictional fantasies, and colloquial expressions of more or less undeadly irritation. We mean it, don't mean it, and don't *not* mean it, and this book is concerned with the spectrum of aggressions which inhabit the space between such figures of speech and their implementation, from the book of Genesis to the present day, but more especially in the period between the conquest of the Americas and the end of the Second World War. It examines a wide variety of authors and voices, chiefly Montaigne and Swift, but also Bartolomé de Las Casas and Jean de Léry, Oscar Wilde and George Bernard Shaw, and travel-writers and ethnographers from Columbus and Vespucci to Bougainville and Cook. Behind all these stand those mass-catastrophes in Genesis, the Deluge and the destruction of the Cities of the Plain, with their grim and quizzical relation to the mass-slaughters of human history, culminating in the Second World War.

More broadly, this book is about how the European imagination has dealt with the groups which it habitually talks about killing, and never quite kills off, because the task is too difficult or unpleasant, or the victims are needed for their labour, or competing feelings get in the way. It is concerned with the imaginative resonances of the idea of the savage, the 'other', not as simply noble or ignoble, but as a figure through whom we confront our own selves in an anguished self-implication too complex and 'conflicted' to be amenable to the customary reductive categorizations. We are obsessed with 'barbarians'. They are the 'not us', who do not speak our language, or 'any language', whom we despise, fear, invade, and kill; for whom we feel compassion, or admiration, and an intense sexual interest; whose innocence or vigour we aspire to, and who have an extraordinary influence on the comportment, and even modes of dress, of our civilized metropolitan lives; whom we often outdo in the barbarism we impute to them; and whose suspected resemblance to us haunts our introspections and imaginings. They come in two overlapping categories, ethnic others and home-grown pariahs, including some groups already mentioned: conquered infidels and savages, the Irish, witches, prostitutes, the poor, the Jews. This book looks afresh at how we have confronted the idea of 'barbarism', in ourselves and others, from 1492 to 1945.

The more considerable writers discussed in these pages have all been preoccupied with such questions, 'serving human liberty' in ways not always agreeable to a latter-day liberal conscience. They opposed oppression, but shared, and knew that they shared, in the impulse towards it. Montaigne and Swift spoke eloquently against colonial depredation and slaughter, and would have detested the

Nazis. But both sometimes contemplated the idea of mass-killing with an unsettling readiness not to repudiate or be shocked by it, and Shaw spoke baldly of the need to eliminate undesirable social groups. Swift's two great satires of extermination, *A Modest Proposal*, and the Houyhnhnms' project to exterminate their humanoid subjects 'from the Face of the Earth' in *Gulliver's Travels*, are directed against the victim, not the oppressor. The latter project is not implemented, but it is contemplated with seriousness, and with a detailed and unsettling anticipatory resemblance to what the Nazis actually did. A question posed by this book is how Swift, for example, is to be uncoupled, as he must, from the imputation of being an apologist for mass-slaughter while showing every sign of endorsing (or at least not disowning) the Houyhnhnm scheme.

This is a book about the Western imagination and Western perceptions, not the perceptions of conquered indigenous peoples, except as seen through Western eyes. Of necessity, it uses such terms as 'savages', 'natives', 'Indians', and 'Negroes' in ways which pertain to the times to which the discussion refers, and which are intended to reflect the European mentalities of those times.

I have taken the opportunity of this edition to correct some typographical and other errors.

ACKNOWLEDGEMENTS

Various parts of Chapter 1 appeared in the *London Review of Books*, August 1992, 10–12; *Modern Language Quarterly*, 53 (1992), 299–363, and (in the case a few wordings) *Eighteenth-Century Life*, 18 (1994), 168–97. Part of Chapter 3 (approximately one-third) was the Bateson Lecture (1999) and appeared in *Essays in Criticism*, 49 (1999), 101–31. Acknowledgements are due to the *London Review of Books* and its editor, Mary-Kay Wilmers; and to the editors (Marshall Brown, Robert Maccubin, and Stephen Wall) and publishers of the other journals (Duke University Press, Johns Hopkins University Press, and Oxford University Press).

The remainder of the book has not been published before, though parts of it began as papers to various universities and learned societies. My debt to those who sponsored these occasions or who participated in discussions is too considerable to specify in adequate detail. I do, however, wish to acknowledge particular debts to Frank Lestringant, who co-directed the Colloque France-Amérique XVI–XVIII Siècles at the Centre d'Études Supérieures de la Renaissance at Tours in 1992, where my first serious incursions into Montaigne were aired before an audience who knew more about the subject than I did; to Jonathan Lamb and Ian Higgins, directors of the David Nichol Smith Seminars at Auckland (1993) and Canberra (1996), where I was first encouraged to study *Gulliver's Travels* in the context of South Pacific travel narratives, and to Iain McCalman, Director of the Humanities Research Centre at the Australian National University, where, as a Fellow of the Centre, I spent two months in 1996 exploring that topic; to Paul-Gabriel Boucé, Suzy Halimi, and Serge Soupel, several of whose December colloquia in Paris were the trigger for some of the enquiries in this book; to Brean Hammond and Anthony Strugnell, successive Presidents of the British Society for Eighteenth-Century Studies, who invited me to give the Annual Society Lecture for 1998, where Chapter 4 of this book had its main beginnings; and to Sir Keith Thomas, President of Corpus Christi College, Oxford, who invited me to deliver the Bateson Lecture for 1999, and provided an early forum for some of the main arguments in Chapter 3. I am deeply grateful to Yale University, the National Endowment for the Humanities, and the John Simon Guggenheim Memorial Foundation for study leave and Fellowship support. I am also indebted to many libraries and their librarians and staff, chiefly the Yale University Libraries (including the Library of the Yale Center for British Art and the Lewis Walpole Library), the Bodleian Library, the British Library, the Cambridge University Library, the Warburg Institute, and the University of Warwick Library.

Many friends and colleagues, as well as members of my family, have given me guidance and information on specific points, often over many years, and in some cases have generously carried out time-consuming searches, or read parts or the whole of the book in typescript: Rolena Adorno, Yehuda Bauer, Michael Bell, Volker Berghahn, Linda Bree, Jim Carson, Kimberley Chrisman, Liza Cluggish, Gordon A. Craig, David Dabydeen, Karen Dalton, Laurence J. Davies, DeAnn DeLuna, Bronwen Douglas, Pascal Dupuy, Andrew Edmunds, Phyllis Gibson, John Gilmore, Antony Griffiths, Vincent Giroud, Jan Gorak, Robert Grant, Harriet Harris, G. J. Heuman, George Hunter, Shelagh Hunter, Frank Kermode, Georges Lamoine, Traugott Lawler, Frank Lestringant, Robert Mahony, Tina Mahony, Elisabeth Mårald, Donald Mell, Linda E. Merians, Jenny Mezciems, Andreas Mielke, Lori Misura, Sally Mooney, Jessica Munns, Max Novak, Ronald Paulson, Marjorie Perloff, Marcia Pointon, Judy Rawson, François Rigolot, Christa Sammons, Jeffrey Sammons, Nanette Stahl, Joan Sussler, Marianne Thormählen, Susan Vogel, Janet Whatley. The list is not exhaustive, and no mere listing can give an idea of the extent of the debt, or of my gratitude.

Last but by no means least, I owe special thanks to Kathie Hawtin, who gave extraordinary help, under difficult circumstances, in the final preparation of this book.

CONTENTS

LIST OF ILLUSTRATIONS

(Between pp. 206–207)

NOTE ON TEXTS AND EDITIONS USED

Montaigne

Essais, ed. Pierre Villey, rev. V.-L. Saulnier (Paris, 1988), 3 volumes, accompanied by English translations from *Complete Essays*, trans. Donald M. Frame (Stanford, Calif., 1965); *Journal de Voyage*, ed. François Rigolot (Paris, 1992).

Swift

Prose Works, ed. Herbert Davis *et al.* (Oxford, 1939–74), 16 volumes (abbreviated as *Works*). All quotations from *Gulliver's Travels*, unless otherwise noted, are from volume xi of this edition. References (e.g. IV. xii. 293) are to book, chapter, and page. *Poems*, ed. Harold Williams, 2nd edn. (Oxford, 1958), 3 volumes, and *Correspondence*, ed. Harold Williams (Oxford, 1963–5), 5 volumes. For letters up to July 1714, I have used the first volume of *Correspondence*, ed. David Woolley (Frankfurt, 1999), with page references to both editions.

Introduction

Swift's works are a meeting-house for some of the most troubling moral nightmares of European intellectual history in the last five hundred years: war, imperial conquest, the impulse to exterminate. His major satires, especially *Gulliver's Travels* and *A Modest Proposal*, contain remarkable prefigurations, not always attractive to a modern sensibility, of later fantasies and anxieties about these subjects, much as *A Tale of a Tub* stands as an advance-parody, as well as a brilliant exemplar, of some of the best and worst of the forms of modern writing.

This volume explores a series of stress points, moments of recognition, often charged with sexual tension and almost always with the menace of political or military force, which inhabit the European imagination in its sense of its encounter with the savage, from the period of the great Renaissance voyages collected by Hakluyt, De Bry, and others, to the *National Geographic* in the twentieth century. It is also concerned with the long-standing equivalence, or quasi-equivalence, of the savage 'other' and his domestic counterparts, helots, slaves, witches, whores, the poor, the mob, and those figures who have sometimes simultaneously combined the roles of alien and home-grown pariah, particularly the Irish and the Jews. The major focus will be on two writers, Montaigne and especially Swift, though some of their thinking on these questions goes back to the Old Testament and to classical authors, and some of the events I discuss as coming within the scope of their commentary occurred long after their lifetimes and include the Nazi Holocaust.

Both writers were, in their way, outraged by the injustices of conquerors, fiercely 'anti-colonialist' thinkers whose way of 'serving human liberty' derived from an authoritarian and conservative cast of mind. The writings of both are rich and complex repositories of traditions of political thought and ethnographic observation which go back to Plato and More, and to a vast body of classical and Renaissance writings from Homer onwards which is preoccupied with the idea of the barbarian or savage. Both examine with sophistication, and an exceptional intensity of self-implication, the old commonplace that this barbarian, whom Swift called Yahoo, is also, in the phrase from Conrad's *Lord Jim*, 'one of us'. And both have also set their own unmistakable and powerful stamp on later thought.

Both authors had an intense curiosity about other cultures, especially distant ones. Neither travelled very far, except in their reading, though Montaigne's *Journal* of a voyage to Italy, including his accounts of newly Protestant cities in Germany and Switzerland, of Holy Week observances in Rome, and of Jewish communities and rituals, suggest that he would have been an impressive field-ethnographer. His angle of vision remains Christian and European. A full recovery of distant cultures, including their responses to European appropriation, from an indigenous perspective, was largely outside his range, as of that of most men of his time, and of Swift's. Swift's writings are somewhat narrower than Montaigne's in ethnographic scope and detail. But he was widely read in the literature of travel and exploration. He owned the collections of Hakluyt and Purchas, and many individual travel narratives, as well as the standard sources of classical ethnography, Herodotus, Strabo, Pliny, and others. While working on *Gulliver's Travels* in the early 1720s, Swift reported to Vanessa, the young woman who loved him, that he had used a spell of bad weather 'to read I know not how many diverting Books of History and Travells', to which, in a letter to a male friend a few days later, he referred as 'an abundance of Trash'. But he evidently read it in large quantities. The breadth of this reading is reflected in countless phrasings and descriptions in *Gulliver's Travels*, and in some amusing mimicry of ethnographic discourse, though the main effect, especially in Book IV, is not, as in Montaigne, that of a particularized or comparative observation of individual peoples, but of a highly charged generic amalgam of 'all savage Nations'.

The Yahoos in *Gulliver's Travels* are a humanoid species in whom are embodied the collective features of this amalgamation. They have become a common name for the wilder, more uncivilized forms of humanity, and for savage and uncouth customs and behaviour. They are Swift's version of what we have sometimes chosen to call the 'other', whom we distinguish from ourselves and whose all too probable kinship with ourselves has always disturbed our consciousness, as well as our conscience. In our starkest thinking, he becomes 'our' representative, whether in a shameful sense, as in Swift, or a self-approving or self-exalting one, as when Rimbaud said, in two famous letters of May 1871, that 'je est un autre': a phrasing in which a statement of principled self-alienation is closely related to the declaration of a resublimated pariah status of 'je suis une bête, un nègre'.

The Yahoos are given a set of generic physical features, thick lips, flat noses and the rest, which are said to be the property of all those grouped in the category of 'savage', including especially, despite the inappositeness of the physical description, the Irish. The application of such descriptions to the Irish, down to flat noses, survived into the nineteenth century. It is part of an old English discourse about Ireland, assimilating the Irish to the generalized savage who, from the sixteenth century onwards, went under the name of 'Indian'. This declared kinship, subjected to ironic questioning and surprising variations, but never strictly repudiated, is a major theme of Swift's writings, with the Yahoos as its culminating embodiment.

The thick lips and flat noses are old signs of the 'not us', drawing on assorted features of this or that distant or conquered racial group. In one sense, they reflect the tendency, discussed mainly in Chapter 2, to treat the 'not us' as a single undifferentiated group, as the phrase 'common to all savage Nations', reverberating from Swift to Lombroso's 'tutti i popoli primitivi', implies. The English writers who listed specific facial and other features as descriptive of the Irish must have known, as a matter of daily observation, that the description did not generally fit. When Swift extends his perception of the Yahoos to the whole human species, including not only the English but the reader and author themselves, the literal inapplicability of highly specific physical details becomes even more pronounced. It is within this contradiction that Swift probes some of the interpenetrations of the 'us' and 'not us' which have haunted the European mind since ancient times, but perhaps most pressingly in the introspective aftermath of modern imperial depredations, beginning with the conquest of the Americas.

Swift is no ordinary proponent, however, of the notion of the 'savage in all of us'. The preoccupation with this is an old one. It includes Plato's reflections on the tyrant whose brutalities are equivalent to cannibal barbarism, and the anguished self-implication of Conrad's Marlow in the primitive rhythms of the African bush. Nor, on the face of it, would Swift be likely to endorse the strand in Montaigne's thinking which has led some readers to see him as an inventor of the noble savage. Swift was deeply read in Montaigne's writings. He shared Montaigne's indignation at imperial plunder and cruelty, and the denunciation of these at the end of *Gulliver's Travels* not only resembles, and probably derives from, a similar passage in the essay 'On Coaches', but exceeds it in angry eloquence. The atrocities of the invading adventurers against the 'harmless People' who are their victims are the same in both writers.

But Swift's 'harmless People' reflect none of Montaigne's compassion for suffering, or the Arcadian glow of Montaigne's evocation of the innocence of the New World: 'c'estoit un monde enfant'. Nor are they distinguished by the courage or ferocity of the Amerindian warriors of Montaigne's Brazil, Peru, or Mexico, an ambivalently admired prowess which coexists with the innocence, simultaneously complementing and undercutting it.

Swift's natives are, in that passage, 'harmless' only in order to bring out the viciousness of their invaders. The minimal acts of kindness associated with them are reported in the passive voice, as being experienced by the invaders rather than performed by the natives themselves. It is as though they had no active identity. If they too have complementary and undercutting *alter egos*, these are not Montaigne's proud warriors but the noisome Yahoos. And where Montaigne contrasts the atrocities of the French religious wars with the behaviour of Amerindian tribesmen, emphasizing difference in favour of the latter, Swift's project is to bring his 'civilized' compatriots into an unsettling equivalence with the savages, so that the European conqueror or English settler is just as Yahoo as the Yahoos of the bush or bog. Things are indeed sometimes worse 'on our Side of the Globe', but the point in Swift is to rub in the incriminating resemblance with our despised subgroup, not to highlight a depraved contrast with primitive virtue.

Nevertheless, as I argue in Chapter 1, there is a deep kinship in the fundamental outlook of the two writers. In the account of the brave Tupinamba, who ritually eat their dead enemy after killing him, and who are thus superior to the French who burn their own brothers alive, is to be found Montaigne's protest against the live burnings which were an appalling feature of the religious wars of Western Europe. The brave Indians do not do that. The whole tendency of his essay 'Des cannibales' (I. xxxi), is to emphasize that this is a European atrocity. And yet, in a passage inserted as an afterthought in the edition of 1588, at the end of the preceding essay, 'De la modération', we are told of Amerindian peoples who do the same thing.

The passage, as often happens in Montaigne, has little to do with any ostensible argument about moderation. It appears to have been strategically placed to disable an innocent reading of the account of the 'cannibals', without modifying this account within its own formal setting, thus having it both ways. It infiltrates into our reading an unillusioned sense that, for all the variety in human custom which Montaigne enumerates with studious and affectionate sympathy, human depravity remains a constant. And for all Montaigne's respect for cultural difference, his tolerance of alternative outlooks, and his friendship with some leading Huguenots, he was remarkably ready to harden his stance when some notionally tolerated or even admired behaviour by the 'other' occurred at home. The Huguenots represented for him a threat to stability and order comparable to that posed by Swift's dissenting sects, though the visceral sense of depravity that Swift saw in these unregulated representatives of our species was less overtly articulated in Montaigne's essays.

The Utopian counterpart or response to this vision of the human animal's subversive restlessness is the highly ordered and disciplined society, modelled on Plato and More, which Montaigne borrowed for his account of the Tupinamba polity, and from which Swift, drawing on the same sources and on Montaigne himself, invented Houyhnhnmland. These two ideal common-wealths have distinctly European and non-primitive origins, and for all their aura of principled native simplicity, both combine features of an 'advanced' and authoritarian civilization, a species of disciplined and conformist anarchism, with incongruous evocations of prelapsarian innocence.

The famous paradox of Montaigne's essay on cannibals, that the civilized Frenchmen are more savage and more 'cannibal' than the warrior tribesmen of Brazil, neither began nor ended with him. The idea that the tyrannical oppressor, or conqueror, is as savage as savages, or worse, already appears in Book I of the *Iliad*, in Plato's *Republic*, and in Aristotle's *Politics*. It recurs in the retort of some early Christians to their Roman persecutors, who said the Christians were cannibals because of the Eucharistic rite, to the effect that the Romans, who roasted their victims at the stake, were themselves the true cannibals, a charge remarkably and literally close to that levelled by Montaigne against the French in the religious wars. Yet it is with Montaigne that later applications of the formula of the oppressor as more savage than his imputedly savage victims have usually been associated, just as his essays on

Amerindians, written in scholarly meditation in his retreat in the Dordogne without the slightest element of field observation or any intention of crossing the Atlantic, are the starting-point of later discourses of Latin American cultural identity. His presence in those discourses, whether honoured or repudiated, is even more pervasive than that of the near contemporary figures of Caliban and Ariel, also mythologized beyond any possible imagining on the part of their creator, who appear in a play by Shakespeare which happens, unusually and at length, to cite Montaigne's essay 'On Cannibals' more or less verbatim.

It is not my intention to assert or debate the 'modernity' or otherwise of Montaigne (any more than of Swift), only to record the representative status he has acquired through readings, or misreadings, of his works in a major area of Western intellectual history. My interest in him, as in Swift, goes beyond the familiar issues of his contested idealization of the savage, and beyond contrary or complementary observations about his cultural relativism, or his racism or xenophobia or lack of these. The idea that the savage may be superior to his civilized conqueror, in Montaigne as in Swift (in whom it also surfaces from time to time in a sardonically muted form), is never the simple reductive formula which it usually becomes in the polemical discourses which are its natural home. It is arguable, moreover, that this idea, even in its most fervent proponents, exists under great if sometimes covert pressure from its own opposite; that it is undercut by assumptions of what might now be thought of as a radically Eurocentric kind; that anti-xenophobia feeds on elements of what it rejects; and that both derive from a network of unacknowledged perceptions and anxieties about actual kinship between the civilized spokesman and his savage subject. Both writers share an acutely distressed or resentful awareness of the deep untidy relationship between humankind and its own despised subgroups.

Montaigne and Swift are very different authors, the one thrusting and aggressive as the other was fastidiously tentative. But Montaigne was a formative figure in Swift's thinking, often tacitly taken for granted, and all the more deeply absorbed, I believe, for being little discussed. Beyond the differences of style and personality is a radical pessimism about the species, which is unillusioned about the human animal, of whatever race, in a way that is inclusive of both racism and anti-racism, to some extent participating in both. It assimilates all of us to our own despised subgroups, while not wholly condoning the contempt for these subgroups, and not wholly free from that contempt either.

Montaigne's insistence on the superiority of Amerindians to Frenchmen, as I suggested, is controlled by an ultimate sense in which the distinction is not allowed to stand up. Thus the French of the religious wars are more cannibal than the cannibals because they perform live torture while Indians eat their enemies dead, but Montaigne suppresses the fact that actual cannibal acts occurred in the religious wars, so that the barbarity he insists on in his own countrymen is not acknowledged in the one literal sense which would help to clinch his argument, and about which we know he knew. While the French are covertly protected from the full implications of the cannibal comparison, the superiority of the Amerindians in the matter of live burnings is surreptitiously compromised in advance by the additions to the preceding essay. What reads overtly as a stark contrast in favour of the 'savage' is in fact undermined by a subtext which attenuates both terms of the antithesis, covertly shifting some of the discredit from 'us' to the 'not us'.

The blurring of categories is an expression, in part, of Montaigne's enquiring openness of mind, willing to register every contradicting perception. This differs in style from Swift's more relentlessly focused enforcement of uncomfortable assimilations, and his aggressive practice of indeterminacies of inculpation. But we sometimes see in Swift the same opportunism of observation which leads to Montaigne's contradictions, and in Montaigne some traces of tactical point-making more readily associated with Swift. There is in particular a sense in both authors that the harmless native is finally neither harmless nor radically unlike his civilized invader, as well as the more obvious intimation that the invader or tyrant partakes of the savagery he imputes to barbarians.

Both Montaigne and Swift, in other words, treat the despised other, Indian or Irish, in ways which emphasize outlandish difference, for good or bad, but which actually encompass a knowing awareness of similarity to themselves that works in part as a radical inculpation of humankind as a whole. 'Indians' was the term, from the sixteenth to the eighteenth centuries, and even after that, which generically described the barbarians of other races, and it is known that the Irish, as described by English writers from Spenser to Swift, resemble standard accounts by European writers of the savage Indians of America. Montaigne's pluralistic ethnography, meditatively preoccupied with the whole range of ethnic variety, is also an assertion of common humanity through the particularities of cultural difference: he is a central figure in a long tradition of tentative anguished exploration, whose fullest fictional expression is Conrad's *Heart of Darkness*, of 'our' kinship with the barbarian opposite we conquer and despise.

Swift's mode is not that of nuanced tentativeness, but forcefully reductive. It equally encompasses similarity, within a similar range of contradictory perspectives, placing the savage old Irish on a par with Indians, and asserting, in compassion or contempt or both, a species of fellowship with them. That humanity is one which finds its common denominator not through Montaigne's or Marlow's introspective self-assimilations, but through the stripped down unaccommodated figure of the Yahoo. But the Yahoo is also a recognized allegory of the bog Irish, even while standing, more abstractly and absolutely, for the human animal as such.

This counter-logical intimation transcends the sometimes contested issue of whether the 'Whole People of Ireland' in the Fourth Drapier's Letter can reasonably be extended beyond the received definition of all Irish of British descent or a certain social level, to include the entire demographic range of the Ireland of Swift's day, as some nowadays claim. The latter view does not square with the

overt tendency of the group of pamphlets with which this resonant phrase is identified, and no wishful insistence is likely to
change that reality. The *Drapier's Letters* show an irritated determination to uncouple Swift's own settler class from the savage
or wild Irish, and to insist, contrary to the views of some ignorant
and patronizing English, that his own people do not share
the native outlandishness and appear very much like the English,
or better.

The idea that the wild Irish were also white, which drove Charles
Kingsley to apoplectic dismay, was not one to which Swift devoted
much interior questioning. But he had his own ways of dealing
with a fact which has recently been emphasized a good deal, that
the Irish and English are preoccupied with their differences from
one another precisely because of a recognition that they are,
racially and otherwise, very similar. One of these ways is the take-
it-or-leave-it portrayal of the Yahoos, encompassing 'Indians' and
Irish in a melting pot in which the whole human race is also given
an undifferentiated presence. Another is the trick in *A Modest
Proposal* of exploiting the old myth that the Irish (like Indians) are
cannibals, and applying it as much or more to the ruling group of
Anglo-Irish landlords, merchants, and bankers, as to the street riff-
raff of thieving and wife-beating native vagabonds. In that work, it
is again the conquerors or rulers of cannibals who are themselves
more cannibal than the savages they despise, a variation of
Montaigne's paradox, which also retains a variant of Montaigne's
ultimate reticence over a possible literalness in the imputation.
A Modest Proposal announces itself as a metaphor of political and
economic self-destruction, in the spirit of Stephen Dedalus's
description of Ireland as a 'sow that eats her farrow', even as it
tacitly skirts historical incidents of famine cannibalism among the
Irish poor, which might be thought of as tending to reinforce a
specific aptness of his fiction. The landowners and merchants of
A Modest Proposal show the ruling group assimilated to the
despised subgroup, while the Yahoos of *Gulliver's Travels* include
the whole of humanity in a reductive portrayal of that subgroup.

It is Swift's greatest achievement as the official 'inventor' of the Yahoo stereotype that he captured a mode of thinking which runs deep in the human psyche, and understood its unspoken assumptions and contradictions without facile assent or complacent repudiation. His work embodies a radical critique (radical in the sense of reaching down to roots) which refuses to shrink from the violence of its own thinking. It castigates the vulgar cruelties of racism without resorting or pretending to easy self-exculpations or the facile self-reassurances of the liberal conscience. His explosions of ethnic resentment do not pretend to be other than they are, but they include contempt for ethnic resentment and the inhumanities that flow from it, and their ultimate tendency is a diagnosis of human viciousness which is inclusive of all groups and wholly transcends ethnic difference.

In this study of the Yahoo stereotype in the European imagination, *Gulliver's Travels* occupies a central position, not only because of the exceptional completeness with which the Yahoo fiction anatomizes a vast range of largely unspoken and in some cases unspeakable assumptions, but also in a narrower and more specific sense, as the repository of many representative myths of the savage–civilized encounter: the cannibal question and mass-extermination (two interrelated themes fraught with enduring cultural reticences); the gunpowder issue, and its attendant narrative of the thunderbolt of an invader's first gunshot, typically presumed to have conquered a native people in a single instant of terror; the more metaphorically explosive issues of sexual perception and sexual encounter between invader and native; the death-dealing talk of xenophobic threats and the murderous genocidal realities which reach their ultimate monstrosity in the Nazi camps. There is a vast prurience, as well as an aura of unspeakability, about most of these issues, fraught with denial and self-righteousness. *Gulliver's Travels* is a work which looks before and after, combining a largely unspoken absorption of Montaigne, and a knowing exploitation of the commonplaces of early travel literature, with a harsh proleptic awareness of the later scenarios of oppression, with their complacencies and self-deceptions as well as their outright lying.

The book draws attention to some surprising connections. It raises questions which cannot be resolved but require continued reformulation, about the link between the language of punitive castigation (God destroying mankind 'from the face of the earth' in the Deluge), the *façons de parler* of personal or group hatred ('they ought to be shot', 'exterminate all the brutes'), and the stark realities of mass-killing. All share the same vocabulary, including a disposition to insert Old Testament resonances about eliminating the designated victim from the face of the earth, a biblical wording which has entered into many languages and will often be at issue in these pages. Such phrases usually express aggression towards some person or group, but not usually an actual intention to kill. A volatile combination of 'meaning it', not meaning it, and not not meaning it, enters into play, which varies with every example, may not ever be fully definable, and flirts elusively with its own literal content.

Literalism and the sanitizing or protective operations of fictions, ironies, and figures of speech are a theme of most sections of this book. The connections and disconnections between figures of speech and the realities or intentions they appear to be expressing are slippery (often deliberately evasive) and variable. The cases are always particular, and more than usually determined by context and tone, and I have returned a number of times to certain key phrasings in different contexts, or to the same statement from a variety of perspectives. I have done this in the belief that most generalizations on such questions are likely to be misleading, trusting instead to the more accurate lessons of a wide range of local approximations. I have also repeatedly revisited a number of Swiftian set-pieces (scenarios of conquest, accounts of gunpowder war), or key images (poisoned arrows, the flayed woman), some of which I have already discussed elsewhere, in the belief that such a cumulative and in some ways dispersed attention in renewed contexts throws more light on difficult and complex matters than attempts at a definitive discursive exposition.

Xenophobic defamations and deadly purposes generate their own euphemisms and reticences, their deceptions and self-deceptions, which are not always easy to distinguish from the fictive or ironic applications of a common vocabulary. Defoe's *Shortest Way with the Dissenters*, a parody of kill-speak, was taken straight both by the satirized aggressors and by their designated victims. *A Modest Proposal* does not really intend the killing and sale of babies, but it is an angry attack on the entire Irish population, not mainly a protest against English oppression of Irish victims. The murderous experiments, and the advocacies of extermination, in Sade's novels are 'fictions' which were only imperfectly, and perhaps accidentally, insulated from an element of practical implementation.

Fictions of extermination tend by definition to announce their disengagement from the practical sphere, and these disengagements are in some ways analogous to the protective insulation provided by ironies, metaphors, and those conventions of speech which are generally understood to disclaim their own literal content (as when someone is colloquially invited to 'drop dead'). The fact raises more questions than it answers. If the Yahoos represent a depraved humanity, how are we to interpret the Houyhnhnms' serious debate as to whether 'they should be exterminated from the Face of the Earth', especially when we recall that God expressed the same intention in the same language before unleashing the Deluge? or the fact that the Nazis used the same language, from Luther's Bible, about the Jews? or that Swift would have endorsed divine castigations, and might not have disapproved of their notional extension to the Yahoos, while not endorsing the Nazis, whose murderous activities he would certainly have classed with the human depravities that deserved the punishment in the first place?

There are no tidy answers to these questions. They are complicated by the fact that the languages of misanthropy and xenophobia often borrow from one another while intending different things. Both discourses draw naturally on beast analogies and animal insults, with calculated or inadvertent slippages in consistency or logic. The man–beast analogy often coexists, for example, with the idea that man is worse than beasts in uniquely human ways which triggered the beast analogy in the first place. Such slippages are found in Juvenal's fifteenth satire, where xenophobia and misanthropy interpenetrate, and where either or both seem teasingly undermined by the other, as well as by a self-disengaging excess of imprecation. They occur in sixteenth-century debates about savages, and in Swift's treatment of the Yahoos. But the fact that Yahoos are beasts to the Houyhnhnms and humanoid to humans, that humans are shamed by the analogy with them, only to be told, in case humans think they are better, that they are actually worse, does little to clarify or soften the implied call for their extermination, though that call is not (for the time being) enacted. But nor is it disavowed, and the fact that the story happens in a Utopian No-Place provides a formal or structured foundation for what, in everyday contexts, is our (normally justified) instinct not to suspend disbelief when we are told that someone ought to be shot.

The language of exterminating Yahoos from the face of the earth refers not to a particular ethnic group, but to a whole species, like God's drowning of humankind in a great flood, an event actively recalled in *Gulliver's Travels*. It is also language used, in Swift's own name and 'non-fictively', of beggars and other social nuisances towards whom his hostility was unmistakable, a fact which links him to everyone who has used the phrase 'they ought to be shot'. Swift knew the impulse to make deadly moral judgements, and to back them with calls for radical riddances. He knew he 'meant', or did not *not* mean, what he said. He thought it dangerous to assume that people understand rhetoric, 'and will not take *Hyperboles* in too literal a Sense', and that the bandying of death-dealing language sometimes turns out to be a 'desperate Experiment'. He understood the gap between saying that people deserved extermination and inflicting it on them, and that this gap was often ready to close, with fatal results. It is within the gap that his punitive language operates, and, like the rest of us, he was willing to utter devastating judgements without being inculpated in their implementation, even notionally and in a fiction. That is perhaps why the extermination of the Yahoos does not happen. He would, I think, have understood these velleities and shrinkings, as he would have felt that the aggressions are part of being a Yahoo, and deserved, at some level of moral adjudication, the punishment the Houyhnhnms contemplated for them.

That the Nazis also used the language of Genesis, or that Swift prefigured in fantasy, and in disconcerting detail, much of what the Nazis actually did, is a fact to be confronted. This does not make a Nazi of Swift, but it demands attention and invites appropriate discriminations as well as a recognition of a distressing analogy in the rituals of human expression. It may instead suggest something of his understanding of the potential for evil, and an uncanny prescience, both rejectionist and self-implicated. It also brings into focus an important aspect of Swift's self-acknowledged participation in many of the things he rejected. He brought himself within the scope of his own satire, and his resistance to much of what he would think of as the encroaching nastiness of a 'modern' future is often expressed with such inventive inwardness that it is not surprising that he should have been adopted as a formative example by many later writers, whose rejection of cherished standards of order and propriety he would have vehemently repudiated. He has in particular been seen as the *véritable initiateur* of that literature of cruel fantasy which goes under the name of 'black humour'. André Breton, who created the *Anthologie de l'humour noir* just before the outbreak of the Second World War, saw in him (correctly I think) an imagination playfully fascinated by the violent and the unspeakable, and willing to enter this territory beyond all obvious objectives of satirizing cruelty and condemning violence. He would not have wished to agree with such authors that nothing is forbidden to the imagination, but his imagination embraced many things he would have forbidden.

My hope is to open up this topic in a way that will uncouple Swift from the indignant diatribes of self-righteous post-colonial censors, as well as from the well-intentioned ministrations of 'liberal' sensibilities of the late Ph.D. era (which I date roughly from the end of the Second World War), performing the equal and opposite irrelevance of refashioning Swift into a benign upholder of favourite causes: democracy, the denunciation of slavery, anti-war protest, anti-colonialism, and doubtless also affirmative action, racial and sexual equality, and sensitive speech-codes. He spoke eloquently on some of these subjects, but the revisionist rectitudes of both groups are often as uncomprehending as the dismal colonial discourses they purport to replace. Swift has to be distinguished from what, in a different context, his cousin and biographer Deane Swift called 'these mighty softeners; these kind pretenders to benevolence; these hollow charity-mongers'. He is neither a benevolent defender of good causes, nor the demonic xenophobe or misogynist of some post-colonial opinion. Still less is he a holder, in Empson's phrase, of 'some wise balanced position between them'. He is not a figure of moderation, though he hated extremists, nor a Golden Mean fancier, though he might some-times speak approvingly of accommodations described by this phrase. He is an altogether more elusive and more eruptive figure, deeply authoritarian, and also a deeply implicated participant in unruly energies of the human mind which he simultaneously denounced and sought to control. He will not be understood through simplifying characterizations, but only in the volatile detail of his anxieties and allegiances, and his extraordinary sense, through these, of the culture of his day and its imminent trans-formations into that of our own.

I   Indians and Irish from
Montaigne to Swift

Catalogues of Conquest

At the end of *Gulliver's Travels*, Gulliver contemplates his 'Duty as a
Subject of *England*' to inform the Secretary of State of the countries
he has visited, 'because, whatever Lands are discovered by a Subject, belong to the Crown' (IV. xii. 293). He decides against doing
this for various reasons. Either the conquests would be worthless
(in the case of the tiny Lilliputians), or else the inhabitants might
defeat the invader, a prospect Gulliver contemplates with a certain
glee. 'I doubt', he explains, invoking a familiar American example,
'whether our Conquests in the Countries I treat of, would be as
easy as those of *Ferdinando Cortez* over the naked *Americans.*'
Moreover, some of the societies ought in his view to be civilizing us,
instead of the other way round. These reasons belong to familiar
debates about empire, and their implications, which are not as
simple as they might appear, are part of the subject of this book.

Gulliver then proceeds to a further reason, expounded in a
denunciation of imperial conquest which is a classic of the genre:

But, I had another Reason which made me less forward to enlarge his
Majesty's Dominions by my Discoveries: To say the Truth, I had conceived
a few Scruples with relation to the distributive Justice of Princes upon
those Occasions. For Instance, A Crew of Pyrates are driven by a Storm they
know not whither; at length a Boy discovers Land from the Top-mast; they
go on Shore to rob and plunder; they see an harmless People, are entertained with Kindness, they give the Country a new Name, they take formal

Possession of it for the King, they set up a rotten Plank or a Stone for a Memorial, they murder two or three Dozen of the Natives, bring away a Couple more by Force for a Sample, return home, and get their Pardon. Here commences a new Dominion acquired with a Title by *Divine Right*. Ships are sent with the first Opportunity; the Natives driven out or destroyed, their Princes tortured to discover their Gold; a free Licence given to all Acts of Inhumanity and Lust; the Earth reeking with the Blood of its Inhabitants: And this execrable Crew of Butchers employed in so pious an Expedition, is a *modern Colony* sent to convert and civilize an idolatrous and barbarous People. (IV. xii. 294)[1]

This belongs to a long line of summary invectives, prefiguring, for example, some indignant sarcasms of Conrad's *Heart of Darkness*. It is the fullest but not the only such statement in *Gulliver's Travels*: a briefer and more sharply sarcastic version is contained in Gulliver's account of human wars (IV. v. 246). Its mode of angry, sweeping summation has a prototype in several passages by Bartolomé de Las Casas, exposing Spanish atrocities in the Americas. In particular, Las Casas's *Short Account of the Destruction of the Indies*, the explosive *Brevísima Relación* (1552), contains several summary portrayals stressing large-scale extermination and depredation, towns, provinces, and kingdoms destroyed, the degenerate and reprobate character of the invaders, their greed for gold, their cruelty to gentle and innocent native populations, the sham of their 'pretending to be Christians' as they extirpate 'these pitiful peoples ... from the face of the earth'[2] (the latter a biblical phrasing which, as we shall see, plays a varied and significant role in Swift's writings, as well as in the history of human massacre).[3]

The *Short Account* was frequently reprinted, and translated into many languages.[4] It helped to fuel anti-Spanish propaganda by the Protestant powers and contributed to the formation of the 'black legend' of the Spanish conquest. The first English translation, *The Spanish Colonie* (1583), was included in the fourth volume of *Purchas His Pilgrimes* (1625), of which Swift owned a set.[5] But a particularly influential analogue to Gulliver's outburst, and perhaps a source, is an extended passage in Montaigne's essay,

'Des coches' ('Of coaches'), which is also a commentary on Spanish atrocities. It too is preceded by remarks about the unnatural 'ease' of the conquest, and continues:

Tant de villes rasées, tant de nations exterminées, tant de millions de peuples passez au fil de l'espée, et la plus riche et belle partie du monde bouleversée pour la negotiation des perles et du poivre: mechaniques victoires. Jamais l'ambition, jamais les inimitiez publiques ne pousserent les hommes les uns contre les autres à si horribles hostilitez et calamitez si miserables.

En costoyant la mer à la queste de leurs mines, aucuns Espagnols prindrent terre en une contrée fertile et plaisante, forte habitée, et firent à ce peuple leurs remonstrances accoustumées: Qu'ils estoient gens paisibles, venans de loingtains voyages, envoyez de la part du Roy de Castille, le plus grand Prince de la terre habitable, auquel le Pape, representant Dieu en terre, avoit donné la principauté de toutes les Indes; Que, s'ils vouloient luy estre tributaires, ils seroient tresbenignement traictez; leur demandoient des vivres pour leur nourriture et de l'or pour le besoing de quelque medecine; leur remontroient au demeurant la creance d'un seul Dieu et la verité de nostre religion, laquelle ils leur conseilloient d'accepter y adjoustans quelques menasses. (III. vi)

So many cities razed, so many nations exterminated, so many millions of people put to the sword, and the richest and most beautiful part of the world turned upside down, for the traffic in pearls and pepper! Base and mechanical victories! Never did ambition, never did public enmities, drive men against one another to such horrible hostilities and such miserable calamities.

Coasting the sea in quest of their mines, certain Spaniards landed in a fertile, pleasant, well-populated country, and made their usual declarations to its people: that they were peaceable men, coming from distant voyages, sent on behalf of the king of Castile, the greatest prince of the habitable world, to whom the Pope, representing God on earth, had given the principality of all the Indies; that if these people would be tributaries to him, they would be very kindly treated. They demanded of them food to eat and gold to be used in a certain medicine, and expounded to them the belief in one single God and the truth of our religion, which they advised them to accept, adding a few threats.[6]

Montaigne may himself, directly or through intermediary texts, be indebted to Las Casas, who was available in French translation, though the likelihood of his direct use is contested.[7] The issue must indeed be treated cautiously. A close analogue from Las Casas to the opening words of Montaigne's passage, resembling it in syntax and rhetorical cadence as well as in the enumerated details, occurs in the *History of the Indies*, which remained unpublished until 1875–6 and which Montaigne did not see: 'so much harm, so many calamities, so much destruction, so many kingdoms wiped out (*cuántas despoblaciones de reinos*), so many millions of souls ... perished'.[8] Such convergences seem to occur frequently on subjects of strong polemical urgency, and may reflect a received rhetoric and mode of thought rather than direct or even indirect derivation.

All these statements are strong protests against the cruelties of colonial conquest and tyranny. But none of them reflects any unequivocal rejection of imperial invasion or rule, or any simple opposition between unscrupulous predators and the purportedly 'harmless People' who are their victims. As Anthony Pagden and Tzvetan Todorov have both pointed out, Las Casas did not (at least in the 1550s) deny the legitimacy of Spanish rule in the Americas. He did not want the Indians liberated, but administered kindly and decently (in this he probably resembles Swift, in some moods, on the Irish natives). He believed that the indigenous peoples had voluntarily surrendered their sovereignty to the King of Spain. He would have resented the propagandist exploitation of the 'black legend' by the heretical Protestant nations hostile to Spanish power. Pagden says well that 'like many radicals, he was, in all respects but one, the staunchest of conservatives', who 'regarded all rebels as disrupters of "the common reason of man"'.[9] In this he resembles both Montaigne and Swift in their hostility to the disruptive innovations fomented by religious or political dissent.[10]

Despite the compassion they expressed for oppressed peoples, these writers show no strongly developed belief in 'racial equality' and no simple sense of the superior virtue of victimized races. This remains true even when, in the immediate context of anti-colonial polemic, the victims naturally occupy the moral high ground.

The idea of the noble savage, which Montaigne is sometimes said to have affirmed, or even invented, is not one to which, on the total evidence, any of these writers subscribed, any more than the Conrad of *Heart of Darkness* was to do.

Some complexities of Montaigne's treatment of American Indians are discussed later in the present chapter. The 'harmless People' of Gulliver's scenario of conquest are a generic distillation of the dozens of specific examples of gentle Indian peoples tortured and massacred by invading Spanish thugs, who appear relentlessly, region by region, in the pages of Las Casas's *Short Account*. In the total context of *Gulliver's Travels*, however, they are hardly representative of Swift's view of primitive peoples, conquered or unconquered. The Yahoos of Houyhnhnmland, expressly identified as an amalgam of 'all savage Nations' (IV. ii. 230), have been establishing throughout the fourth book an impression of ineradicable viciousness, neither innocent nor 'harmless'. In the penultimate chapter of Book IV, only a few pages before the mention of the 'harmless People', Gulliver, having left the fictitious land of the Houyhnhnms and arrived in the 'real' world of New Holland, or Australia, meets some naked savages ('Indians') 'round a Fire', one of whom shoots an arrow at him which he fears might be poisoned (IV. xi. 284), a particular mark of nasty barbarity in classical and Renaissance writers as well as Swift.[11] Ralegh gives a particularly vivid account, in his *Discoverie of Guiana* (1596), of the horrible torments caused by such missiles, and of the importance of antidotes, whose secret he was given by the 'Guianians'. Gibbon thought the use of poisoned arrows 'alone sufficient to prove the most savage manners', reporting it with contempt of Sarmatians, Scythians, Amerindians, and Sclavonians.[12]

There can be no innocent reading of the innocence of the 'harmless People' after that. A second look at the passage, with its strong charge of indignation at brutal invaders and its animated rendering of their cruelties, shows the 'harmless People' as having very little identity. They are recessive and somewhat lifeless figures, with almost no characteristics other than their harmlessness.

They are not once shown doing anything, if you exclude a general reference to the kindness with which they entertain their invaders. And even that is represented, grammatically, in the passive voice, so that the focus is all on the invaders, who *are entertained* with kindness, rather than on the invaded who do the entertaining. All the active verbs relate to the invaders: 'they go on Shore to rob and plunder; they see an harmless People, are entertained with Kindness, they give the Country a new Name, ... they murder two or three Dozen of the Natives, bring away a Couple more by Force for a Sample, return home, and get their Pardon.' It is as though the grammatical structure were itself designed to insinuate less the virtue of the natives than the viciousness of their tormentors, and there is an inescapable sense that the victims' decency and harmlessness are only introduced in order to intensify our perception of that viciousness.

After Gulliver's denunciation of empire, there follows a passage in which he exculpates the British from his devastating attack:

But this Description, I confess, doth by no means affect the *British* Nation, who may be an Example to the whole World for their Wisdom, Care, and Justice in planting Colonies; their liberal endowments for the Advancement of Religion and Learning; their Choice of devout and able Pastors to Propagate *Christianity*; their Caution in stocking their Provinces with People of sober Lives and Conversations from this the Mother Kingdom; their strict Regard to the Distribution of Justice, in supplying the Civil Administration through all their Colonies with Officers of the greatest Abilities, utter Strangers to Corruption: And to crown all, by sending the most vigilant and virtuous Governors, who have no other Views than the Happiness of the People over whom they preside, and the Honour of the King their Master. (IV. xii. 294–5)

We have no difficulty in reading this as angrily sarcastic, entirely consistent in spirit, if not in its literal surface, with what Gulliver said in the previous paragraph. The continuity is intelligible, however, only to the extent that we think of ourselves as following the modulations of a Swiftian voice. But the words are in fact spoken by Gulliver, who is by no means identical with Swift, though Swift's presence always hovers unsettlingly over what

Gulliver says. Gulliver is seldom, if ever, sarcastic in his own name. We are conditioned to take most of his statements as literally intended, and the redirection is all the more surprising because he is no longer the lover of his own country that he used to be. His statement taps into, and on Swift's part derides, a tradition of celebrating British imperial achievements as superior to those of other countries, whose many spokesmen include Hakluyt, Gibbon, Darwin, and Conrad.[13]

A tension between Swift's and Gulliver's meanings, and especially an uncertainty as to how to interpret Gulliver's in relation to his state of mind as the fiction shows it to be, remain unexorcized. Returning to his original concern about reporting the new lands to the government, Gulliver now adds that the countries he speaks of not only 'do not appear to have a Desire of being conquered, and enslaved, murdered or driven out by Colonies' but do not 'abound either in Gold, Silver, Sugar or Tobacco'. He concludes 'That no *European* did ever visit these Countries before me. I mean, if the Inhabitants ought to be believed' (IV. xii. 295). A passage in the first edition, subsequently deleted, and discussed more fully below (in Chapter 4), nevertheless speculates whether the Yahoos may not originate from a primeval English couple. This reinforces other suggestions that the Yahoos, that composite of all savage peoples, also represent all of 'us', and by extension implicates the 'harmless People' of the anti-colonial speech in a universal indictment of humankind.

Tensions, contradictions, inconsistencies, split purposes, the eruptive sense, painfully evident in many writers on colonial questions, of 'a plague on both your houses', are part of the subject of this book. In the two writers with whom I am mainly concerned in the present chapter, Montaigne and Swift, these often reside more in the texture of thought than in a formally articulated discursive substance. Indeed they are sometimes especially evident through being left unsaid. The gap between the 'harmless People' of Book IV, Chapter xii, and the vicious savages who throng the rest of Book IV, is never bridged. A silence of diffused inculpation hangs over it. This is not unlike the cultural reticence which hangs over unspeakable topics (like cannibalism, and the possibility that it might implicate 'us'), or unavowed or inadmissible purposes (like the wish to exterminate, and the idea that 'we', or a given speaker, might 'mean it' for real).

Unspeaking the Unspeakable

Montaigne's 'Des cannibales' (I. xxxi) is one of his most widely discussed essays. But one of its problematic features is, as far as I know, seldom addressed or even acknowledged, a fact which in itself is part of the problem it raises. It concerns a key passage, after the description of the Amerindian vengeance ritual, which demonstrates the Indians' observance of a brave heroic code, and the fact that, unlike the Scythians, they do not eat human flesh for food but 'pour representer une extreme vengeance'. Montaigne turns to his familiar comparison between 'savages' and Europeans, describing how Indians kill their victim before roasting him, in which they are alleged to differ from 'our own' practice, exemplified specifically here by the French religious wars (an alternative comparison, more prominent in 'Des coches', concerns Spanish barbarities against the Indians they call barbarian):

Je pense qu'il y a plus de barbarie à manger un homme vivant qu'à le manger mort, à deschirer, par tourmens et par geénes, un corps encore plein de sentiment, le faire rostir par le menu, le faire mordre et meurtrir aux chiens et aux pourceaux (comme nous l'avons, non seulement leu, mais veu de fresche memoire, non entre des ennemis anciens, mais entre des voisins et concitoyens, et, qui pis est, sous pretexte de pieté et de religion), que de le rostir et manger apres qu'il est trespassé. (III. vi)

I think there is more barbarity in eating a man alive than in eating him dead; and in tearing by tortures and the rack a body still full of feeling, in roasting a man bit by bit, in having him bitten and mangled by dogs and swine (as we have not only read but seen within fresh memory, not among ancient enemies, but among neighbors and fellow citizens, and what is worse, on the pretext of piety and religion), than in roasting and eating him after he is dead.[14]

From this Montaigne concludes that if the Indians and their ritual may be called barbaric by the rules of reason, they cannot be called barbaric 'eu esgard à nous, qui les surpassons en toute sorte de barbarie' ('in respect to ourselves, who surpass them in every kind of barbarity').[15] The question I wish to look into is that of the relation of Montaigne's remarks to the cannibal acts (literally rather than metaphorically understood) performed by his own compatriots in the wars of religion during which Montaigne lived and wrote (a similar question is posed, in the latter part of this chapter, in relation to Swift's *Modest Proposal*).

Montaigne's words do not make this clear, but the atrocities of recent memory, not only read about but witnessed, not between ancient enemies but among neighbours and fellow citizens, under the pretext of piety and religion, of which he speaks, did actually include cases of cannibalism. They were later to get a resonant poetic memorial in Agrippa d'Aubigné's *Les Tragiques*, not published until 1616. An especially famous case occurred in the Protestant city of Sancerre, which fell in 1573. D'Aubigné talks about *Sancerre affamee* (starving, under siege) in *Les Tragiques*, and in an early episode of the poem he reports the story of a mother eating her child at the siege of Jerusalem, which stands as the prototype of cases like that at Sancerre and another at the siege of Paris in 1590. D'Aubigné says that what seemed too horrible to believe in the ancient text, Josephus's *Jewish War*, has actually been witnessed in his own time, our senses belying its antiquity. He himself had been in Paris during the latter siege, which occurred after Montaigne's essay.[16] But several instances were reported before the essay, including the public sale and consumption of parts of mutilated Huguenots all over France, notably at Paris, Lyons and Auxerre during the bloody events following 24 August 1572, the start of the St Bartholomew's Day massacres, as reported in Jean de Léry's *Histoire d'un voyage fait en la terre du Brésil* (1578), who said there were thousands of people still alive to testify to these, and several books on the subject in print. Montaigne's passage speaks to the same effect of the atrocities, both seen and read about, to which he alludes. Léry's work is often assumed to be a source of Montaigne's account of the Tupinamba in 'Des cannibales'.[17] And the events at Sancerre itself had actually been witnessed by Léry and written up almost immediately after, in the *Histoire mémorable de la ville de Sancerre* (1574).

Montaigne could hardly be unaware of some of these events. It is not unlikely, as Géralde Nakam says, that Montaigne read the *Histoire mémorable* in particular, which is discussed in the *Voyage* and which, incidentally, also used Josephus's siege of Jerusalem as a narrative prototype: Protestant cities like Sancerre and La Rochelle thought of themselves as symbolic Jerusalems. The case of Sancerre evidently acquired an exemplary significance among contemporaries of all persuasions.[18] Léry cites cases of mothers eating children, and of famine cannibalism, from Old Testament and classical sources as well as from Josephus.[19] He also charts a progressive deterioration in eating habits before the ultimate decline into anthropophagy. Dead horses, asses, the blood of horses, cats, rats, mice, dogs, as well as herbs, wild roots (some poisonous), slate, soot, and the excrement of men and horses are resorted to before a cannibal act takes place. The scenario of dismal escalation is common in the literature of famine. Flaubert, who steeped himself in both classical and modern sources on the subject, was to offer a concentrated example in chapter xiv of *Salammbô*, and d'Aubigné reproduces a version of it.[20] Such accounts of what humans are reduced to by starvation bear a close relation to descriptions of the eating habits of 'savages' in their normal state.

Then, on 21 July 1573, the besieged of Sancerre witnessed the fulfilment of punitive prophecies from the Old Testament, that they who break the Law of God shall be reduced to eating their own offspring in a siege:

les enfermez dans Sancerre... ont veu commettre ce crime prodigieux, barbare et inhumain, perpetré dans l'enclos de leurs murailles. Car le vingt unieme de Juillet il fut descouvert et averé qu'un vigneron, nommé Simon Potard, Eugene sa femme, et une vieille femme qui se tenoit avec eux nommée Philippes de la Feüille, autrement l'Emerie, avoyent mangé la teste, la cervelle, le foye et la fressure d'une leur fille aagée d'environ trois ans, morte toutesfois de faim et en langueur.

those trapped in Sancerre ... saw this progidious, barbaric, and inhuman crime perpetrated within the walls of their own city. For on the twenty-first of July it was discovered and confirmed that a winegrower named Simon Potard, his wife Eugene, and an old woman who was with them named Phillippes de la Feüille, otherwise l'Emerie, had eaten the head, brain, liver, and viscera of their daughter, aged about three, who had indeed died of hunger and debility.[21]

They were virtually caught in the act, and Léry compares this to his Brazilian experience, just as in his Brazilian *Voyage* he was to recall Sancerre: 'Car combien que j'aye demeuré dix mois entre les Sauvages Ameriquains en la terre du Bresil, leur ayant veu souvent manger de la chair humaine, (d'autant qu'ils mangent les prisonniers qu'ils prennent en guerre) si n'en ay-je jamais eu telle terreur que j'eus frayeur de voir ce piteux spectacle, lequel n'avoit encores (comme je croy) jamais esté veu en ville assiegée en nostre France' ('For all that I have lived ten months among American savages in the land of Brazil, and often seen them eat human flesh (in so far as they eat prisoners taken in war), I yet never experienced such terror from them as when I saw this miserable spectacle, which (as I believe) had never yet been seen in France in a besieged town'). The formula of the unheard of is repeated with increments in the *Voyage*: 'choses non iamais auparauant ouyes entre peuples quels qu'ils soyent' ('things never before heard of among people anywhere'), possibly deriving from an insistent rhetorical routine of Las Casas and later exploited by Montaigne.[22] The comparison, like Montaigne's, is to the advantage of the Brazilians, but as I shall argue, it is a somewhat different comparison from Montaigne's.

The parents and the old woman were arrested and the father claimed to have been incited by the old woman, who died in prison the next day. The parents were of poor reputation, taken for

drunks, gluttons, and abusers of their children. They had married
à la papauté when the reformed Church would not marry them
without proof of the death of Mrs Potard's first husband. Potard
had also been a murderer and a horse-stealer. It seemed plain
therefore that they had acted not just from starvation but from a
depraved appetite: 'non seulement la famine, mais aussi un appetit
desordonné leur avoit faict commettre ceste cruauté barbare et
plusque bestiale' ('not only famine, but also a disordered appetite
led them to commit that barbaric and worse than bestial atrocity').
Thus the following punishments were deemed appropriate:

le dict Potard pere fut condemné à estre bruslé vif, sa femme estranglée, et
son corps, et celuy de la vieille qui fut deterré, bruslez aussi. Ce qui fut
executé le vingtroisieme dudict mois. Le mary et la femme et le corps de
ladicte vieille deterré, trainez de la prison sur une claye jusques au lieu du
supplice.

the said Potard, the father, was condemned to be burned alive, his wife
strangled, with her body, and the disinterred body of the old woman, to be
burned also. This was carried out on the twenty-third of the said month.
The husband and wife and the disinterred body of the old woman, dragged
from prison on a rack up to the place of torture.[23]

Montaigne might have agreed that the Potards were barbaric and
bestial (Léry's coupling of these categories is part of a paradox to
which I shall return), but the actual punishment inflicted on them
by the authorities of their own religious group in their own city
comes very close to what Montaigne was talking about in the
passage I quoted. If they were more barbaric than the Indians,
as Léry may be implying, their judges must appear even more
barbaric than themselves *in the precise sense* specified by
Montaigne, at least in the case of the father, who was burned alive.

Léry foresees that some might find 'ceste sentence trop rigour-
euse', and almost looks forward to Swift's Modest Proposer contemplating that 'it is not improbable, that some scrupulous People
might be apt to censure such a Practice (although indeed very
unjustly) as a little bordering upon Cruelty'.[24] Léry explains that
an example had to be set, so to speak, *pour encourager les autres*.

He reports an earlier case of 1438 (having three pages earlier said that nothing like this had been seen 'en nostre France', but perhaps he meant only 'en ville assiegée'), in which an old woman from a village near Abbeville kidnapped, killed, and salted little children as one does pigs. That old woman of Abbeville was also burned alive.[25]

Léry at this point draws on his ethnographic observations of Amerindians to remark that old women are the greediest of all cannibals: 'j'ay observé estant avec les Sauvages Ameriquains, que les vieilles femmes de ces pays là sont beaucoup plus friandes, appetent et souhaittent plus de manger de la chair humaine que les hommes, ny que les jeunes femmes et enfans' ('I have observed, while I was with the American savages, that the old women of those countries are much more edacious, and crave and desire to eat human flesh more than the men do, or the young women and children').[26] (pl. 1) The peasant woman of Abbeville, the old woman de la Feüille from Sancerre, and some child-eating old women described in Fynes Moryson's account of Irish famine during Tyrone's rebellion, conform to this pattern.[27] Whatever their factual status, they occupy an area of folkloric fantasy in which, so to speak, the grandmother and the wolf are one. Homer's Hecuba, declaring her wish to eat the raw liver of Achilles for his killing of Hector, may also include some such sexual typing (one of the innumerable variants of the predatory or 'cannibal' female), in a subtler or more muted form. She pointedly differs from Achilles in a closely parallel passage, in which he tells Hector that he wishes he had the stomach to eat him raw in vengeance but that, in effect, he cannot bring himself to behave in this fashion. The difference probably has at least as much to do with the fact that Hecuba is not a Greek as that she is an old woman, but the two intimations may be mutually reinforcing and are not easily separable. (Montaigne was familiar with the fact that the Greeks found cannibalism exceptionally repugnant, citing from Herodotus, in 'De la coustume', the story of Darius asking some Greeks 'what price would persuade them to eat their fathers' dead bodies.

They answered that there was no price for which they would do it' (I. xxiii)).[28] According to a later tradition, evidently first recorded by Euripides, Hecuba was metamorphosed into a bitch, and there is an old tradition linking rapacious wolves and dogs to the cannibal theme.[29] (An opposite and perhaps unusual gendering seems to apply to American 'Amazons', who, according to Thevet, do not eat the men they capture 'comme les autres sauvages', but burn them to ashes).[30]

Immediately after his brief digression on cannibal old women in Brazil, Léry returns to his Sancerre narrative. A famished man had asked him as early as 25 June whether he might be allowed to eat the buttock of a dead man without offending God 'en ceste extreme necessité', and the good pastor and ethnographer says the question seemed so odious that he told the man that even wolves are said not to eat each other: a conscious activation of the topos man is worse than beasts ('je luy alleguay les bestes pour exemple'). As to the woman of Abbeville, he had remarked with satisfaction that however famished she had been, it did not prevent the judges from sentencing her to be burned alive ('cela n'empescha pas ses Juges de la condamner d'estre bruslée vive').[31]

Thus Léry records cases in the fifteenth century as well as in his own time of people burned alive, in the manner Montaigne described as more barbaric than any Amerindian cannibal rite. In Léry, however, the punishment is inflicted for cannibal practices themselves. On these, in their French manifestations, Montaigne is silent. He uses a language and imagery which assert that the French are more barbaric than the Indians, and his references to roasting alive insinuate that they are more cannibal than cannibals, but in terms which, in the last analysis, dissociate themselves from a literal imputation. The language engages in an odd tug of war between literal and metaphorical usages. The opening declaration, 'Je pense qu'il y a plus de barbarie à manger un homme vivant qu'à le manger mort', implies that Indians eat dead men and Frenchmen eat live ones. But it is rapidly made clear that nobody eats live ones literally, and Montaigne's strong and vivid wording actually conceals the fact that the French, like the Indians though for different reasons, also ate dead bodies.

As the passage progresses, we only gradually realize that the live eating is not literal: this is not apparent in the language which describes the tearing of the victim's live flesh or the roasting of him bit by bit ('rostir par le menu'). The accumulation is in one sense appallingly real, registering in specific detail the burnings alive which characterized the French religious persecutions and caused Montaigne much anguish. Its rhetoric even has something of that play of horrified contemplation, that combination of fascination and recoil, which, in a more elaborate or extravagant form (as in Seneca's *Thyestes* for example) serves to neutralize the actuality of the unspeakable through unsparing excesses of utterance and a garish descriptive overkill. What Montaigne eventually offers, however, is not so much an overspeaking of the unspeakable as an unspeaking of it. It is only in the next variation, and then only after the reference to having the victim 'bitten' takes you another step in the direction of cannibal ingestion, that a decisive diversion is created, which suddenly makes clear that French bodies are not, in this discussion, being eaten by French people but by dogs and swine: 'le faire mordre', says Montaigne, 'et meurtrir aux chiens et aux pourceaux.'[32]

The proceeding, with its build-up of cannibal expectation concluding in a surprising retraction or withdrawal, suggests the extent to which, like many writers throughout the history of European letters, Montaigne shrinks from the idea of cannibalism in his own countrymen, but cannot leave the subject alone. The pay-off which reveals that the bodies are left to be bitten and mauled by dogs and pigs thus discloses that the remarks about the greater barbarity of eating one's victim alive ('il y a plus de barbarie à manger un homme vivant') are not literal, but a sidestepping of the cannibal issue into metaphor—a traditional manœuvre, in which troubling insinuations on this particular subject may be given their head without being taken for real.

The transfer of the ingestive charge from a cannibal context to one reminiscent of a more customary or quotidian fate of corpses in war brings to mind the repeated Homeric evocation of corpses left for food to dogs and beasts and birds of prey. Homeric scholarship sometimes entertains the notion that the gloating by heroes 'over the prospect of their enemies' corpses being the prey of carrion animals' may be a half-suppressed survival of what heroes did or wished to do to their enemies themselves.[33] The speech by Achilles to Hector to which I referred earlier is an evident survival of a cannibal taunt to the enemy, bearing a close relation to the kind of warrior-boast which Hans Staden reported from Brazilian Tupinamba: 'Cursed be you my meat ... vengeance on you for the death of my friends ... before sunset your flesh shall be my roast meat.'[34]

Achilles' speech to Hector is a variant or inversion of this type of heroic taunt, including in his case vengeance for the death of a particular friend, saying this is precisely what he would do (or outdo, since what he contemplates is eating Hector raw rather than roasted), if he could bring himself to behave in such a way. (The analogy is beguiling, in view of later, often unflattering, comparisons between Homeric customs and those of the New World). He speaks in response to Hector's proposed deal, whereby whichever of the two survived the contest would see to it that the other's body was not fed to the dogs. Achilles' words are:

No more entreating ... you dog ...
I wish only that my spirit and fury [*menos* and *thumos*] would drive me
to hack your meat away and eat it raw ...
no, but the dogs and birds will have you all for their feasting.

The implication is that he is not that kind of person (or that Greeks no longer do such things), so that the dog Hector will be eaten by dogs.[35] A secondary cannibal frisson in the formula that dogs will eat the dog is reinforced by the ancient fantasies already referred to, which falsely connect cannibalism (in the sense of eating one's own kind) with dogs and wolves; but it also removes the kind-eats-kind idea from humans to beasts. (Misconceptions about dogs in this context included later etymological fallacies that connected *cannibals* with *canis* in Columbus's mind, with *canaille*, especially favoured by Thevet, as well as with the Greek *kyon*, dog, and the monstrous Cynocephali).[36] If being eaten by dogs and birds is a diversion from or substitution for being eaten by one's fellow humans in those Homeric contexts, as some scholars have suggested, then Montaigne's surprising stylistic manœuvre makes a striking use of the resourceful slippage which this affords.

The manœuvre in Montaigne is especially remarkable because the fate of being left unburied, a prey to beasts, is often presented as a worst-case scenario (rather than second-worst, so to speak). That this is the normal assumption in Homeric epic is the point of Hector's plea to Achilles. It is in the same spirit, or a Christian variant of it, that Las Casas regularly insists on the atrocity of the Spaniards in throwing their Indian victims to wild dogs (a practice given vivid pictorial illustration in Theodore de Bry's *America*), and that Thevet (not often given to observations implying the superiority of Amerindian practices) praises his Indians for not leaving their dead to the dogs and birds, unlike some ancient peoples.[37] The peculiar force of Montaigne's apparent sliding, like that of Achilles' more overt rejection of the cannibal option, is that both speak of being thrown to the dogs as a *ne plus ultra* while actually turning away from something worse.

'Ils se sont entremangez'

Montaigne's hostility to the cruelties common in European tyrannies and wars, the various modes of torture and the burnings at the stake, are a recurrent theme in the essays. They come up again, unfavourably compared with 'cannibals' or other Amerindians in the essays on cruelty (II. xi) and on coaches (III. vi), which express a special revulsion against live torture: 'tout ce qui est au delà de la mort simple, me semble pure cruauté' ('all that goes beyond plain death seems to me pure cruelty'), a sentiment repeated in 'Couardise mère de la cruauté' ('Cowardice, mother of cruelty' (II. xxvii)). If one wants to boil and mutilate bodies in order to keep the people in line, or 'at their duty' ('tenir le peuple en office'), one should do it when the criminal is dead. Montaigne accepts the public use of keeping the people in line, and is prepared to coun-tenance what would be one of the worst nightmares for a Homeric hero: 'de les voir priver de sepulture, de les voir bouillir et mettre à quartiers, cela toucheroit quasi autant le vulgaire que les peines qu'on fait souffrir aux vivans' ('to see them deprived of burial, to see them boiled and quartered, would affect the common people just about as much as the punishments they make the living suf-fer'). He goes on to report that the people take an actual killing quite calmly, but react strongly to mutilations, even of insentient corpses. But what the French civil wars offer is a wholly new spectacle of live mutilations, gratuitously enjoyed without enmity or profit, *sans inimitié, sans profit*.[38]

Montaigne may, in later years, have hardened beyond the remark about keeping 'le peuple en office'. A passage in 'De l'utile et de l'honneste' speaks of the need sometimes to betray and lie for the public good, and a post-1588 insertion adds 'massacre': '[B] . . . Le bien public requiert qu'on trahisse et qu'on mente [C] et qu'on massacre' (III. i). When the 1588 or B text resumes, it adds a sarcastic comment, covering all cases, to the effect that such tasks should be left to the yes-men: 'resignons cette commission à gens plus obeissans et plus soupples.'[39] The addition is honourably in keeping with Montaigne's distaste for cruelty as well as falsehood, however publicly justified, and his disposition to keep his distance from *raison d'état*. Critics are at pains to distinguish the Montaigne of such passages from Machiavelli, but it is also recognized that such late passages show traces of Montaigne's involvement in public life in the 1580s, as Mayor of Bordeaux, and the impact on him of renewed outbreaks of civil war.[40] For all his breadth of spirit, and his admiration for some Protestant cultures (when well established and outside the range of civil conflict, as in some Swiss and German cities described in the *Journal* of his visit to Italy), Montaigne often thought of the Huguenots, within the French national context of his time, as disruptive innovators.[41] He may not have been altogether 'scandalized' by the famous massacre of French Protestants by the Spanish in Florida in 1565, about which (as Lestringant, following Chinard, reminds us) he certainly knew, and he remained silent also about the St Bartholomew's Day massacre of 1572, though there is a brief allusion in the *Journal de voyage*, which may originate with him or, alternatively, with his amanuensis. The two dates (24 August and 3 October) of the killings in Paris and Bordeaux are said to be missing from the copy of Beuther's *Ephemeris Historica* which served Montaigne as a daybook for important events (but this is inconclusive). It is sometimes suggested that the afterthought on the necessity and admissibility of massacre looks back to this national slaughter.[42] If so, though the thought is chilling, it still functions in Montaigne's hesitant and self-qualifying mode. The meditative guardedness, facing appalling possibilities with an open and critical mind, is in vivid contrast with the more explosively polarized ambivalence of Swift (whose intellectual connections with Montaigne are nevertheless considerable), radically hostile to extermination projects and murderous behaviour, but simultaneously capable of strongly charged extermination velleities of his own.

The simple comparison in 'De la cruauté' (II. xi), 'Les sauvages ne m'offensent pas tant de rostir et manger les corps des trespassez que ceux qui les tourmentent et persecutent vivans' ('Savages do not shock me as much by roasting and eating the bodies of the dead as do those who torment them and persecute them living'), perfectly expresses the official or 'prose' sense of the passage in 'Des cannibales'.[43] The superimposition of a cannibal metaphor for a worse-than-cannibal-but-not-cannibal outrage which occurs in that essay appears in a different form in 'Des coches', where Spanish atrocities in Peru and Mexico (including burnings alive in the name of religion, etc.) are capped by this comment on the intestine feuds among the Spaniards: 'Dieu a meritoirement permis que ces grands pillages se soient absorbez par la mer en les transportant, ou par les guerres intestines dequoy ils se sont entremangez entre eux, et la plus part s'enterrerent sur les lieux, sans aucun fruit de leur victoire' ('God deservedly allowed this great plunder to be swallowed up by the sea in transit, or by the intestine wars in which they devoured one another; and most of them were buried on the spot without any profit from their victory').[44] The anthropophagy of 'ils se sont entremangez entre eux' is no more literal than the image of the sea eating them up or of 'intestine' wars, referring to Spaniards being killed or condemned to death by Spaniards.[45] Montaigne himself makes clear in the previous sentence that many of the Spanish chiefs were executed by royal edict, the kings of Castille being justly offended by their conduct, and his readiness to use cannibal metaphors where there is little danger of literal meaning shows to striking effect.

In 'Des cannibales', by contrast, a literal sense was actually and historically in the offing. The cannibal metaphor of eating alive conceals a known cannibal practice through the last-minute diversionary detail of the dogs and pigs, signalling the return, or retreat, into metaphor. It does so in a manner which subverts the ostensible forensic thrust. The contrast is not, as the metaphorical surface suggests, between two cannibalisms. It is between cannibalism and something worse, which is itself falsely called cannibal, but which must at least be presumed to be preferable in some sense, in that it is not actually cannibal, in that it is speakable, whereas the actual unmentioned cannibalism of French sectarians is evidently not speakable. The metaphorical ascription of live eating to his countrymen makes it rhetorically appropriate for Montaigne to call them worse than cannibals. But the logic of the comparison with Amerindians would have been even more strikingly secured by pointing out that Frenchmen could be just as anthropophagous, *plus* the special discredit of live torture. The essay is, after all, dedicated to the project not only of defending

Amerindians from European imputations of barbarism, but of challenging the received idea that cannibal customs are 'barbaric' as such. Montaigne's ethnographic *donnée*, accepting cannibalism as a custom among others and denying its special status as a pariah depravity, is more radically 'demystifying' than anything in Léry, who is often severely critical of Amerindian mores and not above calling the cannibal Indians a 'canaille de sauuages'.[46] But his verbal sliding shows him more deeply locked into the very mystification he is purportedly defying.

This is remarkable not only because an open acknowledgement of events such as that at Sancerre would strengthen Montaigne's argument about the greater barbarity of Europeans. It would, additionally or alternatively, add force to his insistent affirmations of cultural relativism, enabling him to assimilate the starving victims of European wars to cases for whose allowability he cited classical precedents as well as humane common sense, and also to supplement these by vivid and thought-challenging modern instances. The essay is at pains to draw sympathetic attention to ancient examples. 'Chrysippus et Zenon, chefs de la secte Stoicque', and Juvenal's fifteenth satire, condoned survival cannibalism under famine or siege, and Montaigne makes a particular point of mentioning the example of 'nos ancestres' at Alésia.[47] These ancestors, one must suppose, were sufficiently distanced by time, by their status as a heroic example of Gallic nationhood, and by the authority of the classical text in which they are recorded.[48] It may nevertheless seem slightly anomalous that Montaigne's praise of Indians because their anthropophagous acts are committed for vengeance rather than nourishment should be followed, in the next paragraph, by an implicit defence of famine-cannibalism.

It might be argued that the more recent cases risked blunting, instead of sharpening, the indictment of European barbarity, by making his compatriots pitiable (as Juvenal found the Vascones pitiable) rather than vicious. But Montaigne's range of human sympathies was in general terms large enough to accommodate such varied feelings. Even if it had not been, the option existed, as for Léry, of presenting the cannibal act, in an Old Testament way, as itself a punishment for wickedness (a parallel exists in the biblical antecedents of *A Modest Proposal*);[49] or of treating the Sancerre episode and its perpetrators as especially disreputable in the way Léry himself had done in the *Histoire mémorable*; or of dwelling on the still more appalling cases (the sale of human fat and of mutilated parts at Lyons and elsewhere, the killing of a Protestant at Auxerre whose heart was then displayed, grilled, and eaten) which Léry had no difficulty in citing in the *Voyage* in the course of *his* version of the argument that 'we' are worse than the 'canaille de sauuages' who eat their enemies.[50]

Léry's reactions are more strongly marked and more polarized. Montaigne is diffident of entertaining strongly charged and simplifying judgements, a temperamental shrinking from catastrophic perspectives which may even extend to his normally obsessive distress at the atrocities of the religious wars: 'A voir nos guerres civiles, qui ne crie que cette machine se bouleverse et que le jour du jugement nous prent au collet, sans s'aviser que plusieurs pires choses se sont veuës, et que les dix mille parts du monde ne laissent pas de galler le bon temps cependant?' ('Seeing our civil wars, who does not cry out that this mechanism is being turned topsy-turvy and that the judgment day has us by the throat, without reflecting that many worse things have happened, and that ten thousand parts of the world, to our one, are meanwhile having a gay time?').[51] In this remarkable passage from 'De l'institution des enfans' ('Of the education of children') (I. xxvi), Montaigne for once omits a comparison between French civil strife and the behaviour of cannibals, but the latter are nevertheless in his mind, and mentioned in the previous sentence in another connection.

Montaigne's sensitiveness over the issue of French cannibalism may be seen as, in a certain sense, a counterpart to his obvious reluctance to denounce Amerindian rituals with the vigour of a Léry or Thevet. There is in his writings, as I indicated, a subdued acknowledgement of Amerindian barbarism, 'eu esgard aux regles de la raison', but no question of *canaille*.[52] This latter sensitiveness, however, takes quite different forms: moderation of reproach (combined with general sympathy) in the case of Amerindian cannibalism, but complete silence (combined with general reproach) over its French counterpart.

A difference from Léry's account in the *Voyage*, otherwise so similar in its description of Indian practices and in the broad tendency of its comparison with French behaviour, is Léry's much sharper sense of the boundaries between literal and metaphorical expression, and his readiness to speak literally where Montaigne will not:

apres qu'vn nommé Coeur de Roy, faisant profession de la Religion reformee dans la ville d'Auxerre, fut miserablement massacré, ceux qui commirent ce meurtre, ne decouperent-ils pas son coeur en pieces, l'exposerent en vente à ses haineux, & finalement le ayant fait griller sur les charbons, assouuissans leur rage comme chiens mastins, en mangerent?

After the wretched massacre of one Coeur de Roy, who professed the Reformed Faith in the city of Auxerre—did not those who committed this murder cut his heart to pieces, display it for sale to those who hated him, and finally, after grilling it over coals—glutting their rage like mastiffs— eat of it?[53]

Where Montaigne speaks of the French practice of eating their countrymen alive, only to unsay it with the disclosure that he means feeding them to the dogs, Léry's account of the Auxerre atrocity tells of the eating of the victim's heart by men, glutting their rage *like* dogs. Léry's dogs do not represent, as in Montaigne, a swerving away from, or cancellation of, an expected cannibal disclosure, but a heightened emphasis on the horror of French anthropophagous acts.

Another way of putting it is that Montaigne's dogs have the effect of retroactively making metaphors of his seemingly literal talk of human eating, while Léry's intensify his literalness on that point. It is the business of similes to explain themselves, but metaphors, which do not do so, are not normally used to obscure literal facts. In other words, there is nothing in the nature of metaphor as such which accounts either for Montaigne's extraordinarily graphic intimation of a supposed live eating, or for the startling redirection which follows. A possible intimation of the underlying state of mind may be found in Montaigne's prefatory assertion that his essays are open, simple, and unguarded, to the extent that his 'reverence publique' permits. Had he been living in a nation still under 'la douce liberté des premieres loix de nature' ('the sweet freedom of nature's first laws'), he would have portrayed himself entire and naked, 'tout entier, et tout nud', evidently like one of his own 'cannibals', as François Rigolot has suggested.[54] Despite this general sense of himself, there is no way of knowing how aware Montaigne was of the peculiar slippage he engaged in on the cannibal issue itself, but his stylistic manœuvre is familiar, in various guises, in the discourse of cannibalism at all periods, and presumably more often a matter of instinctual reticence than of deliberate concealment.

It is perhaps partly in response to these reticences, and to the verbal shuffling that habitually attends such questions, that the more baldly explicit Léry is anxious to make distinctions between literal and figurative utterance:

si on veut venir à l'action brutale de mascher & manger reellement (comme on parle) la chair humaine, ne s'en est-il point trouué en ces regions de par deçà, voire mesmes entre ceux qui portent le titre de Chrestiens, tant en Italie qu'ailleurs, lesquels ne s'estans pas contentez d'auoir fait cruellement mourir leurs ennemis, n'ont pu rassasier leur courage, sinon en mangeans de leur foye & de leur coeur? Ie m'en rapporte aux histoires. Et sans aller plus loin, en la France quoy? (Ie suis François, & me fasche de le dire) durant la sanglante tragedie qui commença à Paris le 24. d'Aoust 1572 . . .

if it comes to the brutal action of really (as one says) chewing and devouring human flesh, have we not found people in these regions over here, even among those who bear the name of Christian, both in Italy and elsewhere, who, not content with having cruelly put to death their enemies, have been unable to slake their bloodthirst except by eating their livers and their hearts? I defer to the histories. And, without going further, what of France? (I am French, and it grieves me to say it.) During the bloody tragedy that began in Paris on the twenty-fourth of August 1572 . . . [55]

This reference to the St Bartholomew's Day massacre immediately precedes the account of the selling and eating of human fat, hearts, livers, and other parts, in Lyons, Auxerre, and elsewhere. It shows Léry proleptically confronting the questions Montaigne faced, not only about the issues of barbarism, foreign and domestic, but about the issue of talking about them. Unlike Montaigne, it is literal cannibal acts by the French, not metaphorical ones, that he adduces as evidence of 'our' greater barbarity than that of 'savages'.

The particular form of Léry's insistence on a literal dimension, with its self-conscious evocation of Eucharistic debates, clearly hints at the Catholic doctrine of the 'real' presence ('manger reellement (comme on parle)') and is designed to identify Catholics with the savage raw-eating cannibals of America (not the Tupinamba admired by both Léry and Montaigne), a common feature of Protestant polemics. Like Montaigne, Léry put European behaviour under scrutiny, mentioning Italian cases ('Ie m'en rapporte aux histoires') as Montaigne mentions Spanish perpetrators in 'Des coches', but, like Montaigne, reserving the most painful strictures for his own countrymen. For Protestants like Léry, as not for Montaigne, Italians and Spaniards served as examples of specifically Catholic depravity, readily seen as outside the norms of civilized behaviour. Léry reported, in a later allusion to the regency of Catherine de Medici, that 'combien que i'aye tousiours aimé & aime encores ma patrie' ('much as I have always loved my country and do even now'), he finds the plight of the country so Italianized that he often regrets that he is no longer among Amerindian savages. When he turned to the French atrocities, he did so, as we have seen, in terms which imply a conscious determination to articulate the unsayable: 'Et sans aller plus loin, en la France quoy? (Ie suis François, & me fasche de le dire)'.[56] The words suggest an afterthought, real or rhetorical or both, emphasizing what seems a painful redirection in the train of thought, an unsuspected escalation literally and specifically registered. Montaigne's most notable redirection on the matter of French cannibalism is in the opposite direction, away from explicit disclosure of human eating to that of the dogs and pigs, and away from literalness to the use of cannibal language for non-cannibal events, among the French in 'Des cannibales' and the Spanish in 'Des coches'.

Good and Bad Indians

In Montaigne's project of exposing European barbarism as greater than that of the Amerindians, the issue of live torture as compared with anthropophagy is of cardinal importance. It is in any case a matter of rationally articulated convictions, although the issue is sometimes blurred by some sliding between literal and figurative usages. There is, however, an afterthought in which Amerindians are described as themselves widely given to live torture, which is part of a passage added to the ending of 'De la modération' (I. xxx) in the 1588 edition. Its placing, therefore, is immediately before 'Des cannibales' (I. xxxi), which maintains its contrary perspective in 1588 and after. The contrast is so startling as to suggest an element of deliberate challenge or shock tactics, although apparent 'inconsistencies' and multiple or even contradictory perspectives are a natural element in Montaigne's writings. Something more seems at work than the normal introspective serendipity of his style of meditation, letting his thoughts or his information take him where they will.

The named example is a Mexican one, but the account opens with generalized references to the new countries discovered in 'our time', which are all said to practise live torture, illustrating the universal assumption that God and nature are gratified by human killings, 'par nostre massacre et homicide', and that religions have universally embraced human sacrifice:

Et en ces nouvelles terres, descouvertes en nostre aage, pures encore et vierges au pris des nostres, l'usage en est aucunement receu par tout: toutes leurs Idoles s'abreuvent de sang humain, non sans divers exemples d'horrible cruauté. On les brule vifs, et, demy rotis, on les retire du brasier pour leur arracher le coeur et les entrailles.

And in these new lands discovered in our time, still pure and virgin compared with ours, this practice is to some extent accepted everywhere: all their idols are drenched with human blood, often with horrible cruelty. They burn the victims alive, and take them out of the brazier half roasted to tear their heart and entrails out.[57]

The passage is later than most of the passages on live torture I have cited, which are A passages belonging to the first edition. Any large-scale change in Montaigne's attitudes seems ruled out since Montaigne retained and does not seem to have gone out of his way to soften any of his earlier attacks on European torture, or his relative preference for the ritual roasting of dead enemies as practised by the Tupinamba of 'Des cannibales'.

The words recall what Europeans do to each other in 'Des cannibales', and also what Spaniards do to Indians in 'Des coches', down to the detail of live burning and removal of the half-roasted (*demy rotis*) victims from the fire. One does not read of Indians doing such things to each other, or at all, in either of the two other essays. The insertion belongs to the same edition (1588) as the addition of Book III as a whole, including 'Des coches', with which the insertion has other things in common. 'Ces nouvelles terres ... pures encore et vierges', for example, recalls other idealized Amerindian locations, especially the famous passage 'C'estoit un monde enfant', from the original 1588 text of 'Des coches', with its characteristic tension between lyrical evocation and brutal disclosure.[58]

Questions arise as to a possible motive for not including the passage in 'Des cannibales' or 'Des coches', and for placing it so conspicuously near 'Des cannibales' but not in it. The insertion's antithetical tendency might answer the first question, but only to raise the second more acutely. It was within Montaigne's range to consider alternative or contradictory perspectives within the same essay (*a fortiori*, one might suppose, in one dedicated to the relativism of values he was promoting in 'Des cannibales'). The passage has such a tenuous relation to the concerns of 'De la modération' that one is tempted to suppose that he was deliberately insinuating a connection with 'Des cannibales' while holding back from any formal assertion of this. One result is that a reader of the essays in their given sequence cannot proceed from 'De la modération' to 'Des cannibales' without a strong impression of the passage, damaging as it is to the Amerindians.

This means that the reader of 'Des cannibales' in the enlarged 1588 edition experiences an undermining disturbance or confusion, not unlike that of readers of the enlarged 1735 edition of *Gulliver's Travels*, whose naïve good-natured opening narrative is irreparably undermined by Gulliver's sour prefatory letter to Sympson, which gives an advance glimpse of more disenchanted perspectives. A strategic deployment of what may be considered in effect as prefatory additions creates, in both works, a disconcerting loss of orientation of a kind especially familiar to readers of Swift. The additions function in both authors as afterthoughts, creating a species of monitory voice-over, as if designed, once the book had been in circulation for some time, to adjust or complicate any future experience of reading it, perhaps in the light of perceived inadequacies in the book's original form or in the public reception of it. In both works, the pre-emptive intervention announces a loss of innocence. No reader of the 1735 *Gulliver's Travels* can take at face value the friendly and ingenuous Gulliver of the opening chapters to which readers had access in the first edition of 1726, just as no reader of 'Des cannibales' after 1588, who comes to it directly from 'De la modération', can take as unqualified Montaigne's portrayal of the Amerindian as noble savage.

An impulse is perhaps to be detected, in Montaigne as well as Léry (with his distinction between the raw-eating Ou-ëtaca Indians and the admired Tupinamba), to set up what eventually became something of a stereotyped pairing of 'bad' and 'good' cannibals (the latter idealized or patronized or both), which I have discussed elsewhere, and which developed into a familiar pattern in fiction, from *Robinson Crusoe* to Ballantyne, Henty, Kipling, and Conrad.[59] It seems to be an integral element, insufficiently studied, in the complex apprehension of ethnic alterity, and may answer to the same need as the tendency, also inadequately recognized, to insinuate into narratives of national or tribal conflict a subtext of tripartite rather than binary divisions, in which the favoured group confronts worthy as well as ignoble enemies: as Greeks confront Trojans as well as the Trojans' allies (the only true barbarians, a motley assortment of peoples effectively grouped as a *tertium quid*) in the *Iliad*, and as Romans confront Carthaginians as well as their riff-raff of tribal mercenaries from North Africa and Europe in Polybius.[60]

This was a pattern which Flaubert radically subverted in his account, based on Polybius, of the Punic Mercenary War. Romans are not much in evidence in *Salammbô*, but a sense of universal barbarism includes Carthaginians and mercenaries alike, and would have included anyone else: 'les bourgeois, c'est-à-dire tout le monde', as he wrote to Ernest Feydeau while composing the novel, saying it will vex (*embêtera*) them all, as Swift said *Gulliver's Travels* would 'vex the world'. Both authors target humanity, meaning their readers as well as their subject (Flaubert described his novel as a *Thebaid* which he was pushed into by his dislike of modern life), on a scale which transcends ethnic particularities while reporting these with bilious gusto.[61] Montaigne, much admired by both, had more tolerant sympathies, but a hard core of unillusioned contemplation of radical turpitude sometimes shows through the gentle surface.[62] He does not often, like Flaubert, obliterate ethnic distinctions in a sweeping misanthropic totalization, or divide mankind into uncompromisingly binary oppositions, like Swift's Houyhnhnms (good but literally utopian, i.e. non-existent) and Yahoos (humanoid, and all too human). The hints in Swift of good third parties (the Portuguese captain, the 'naked *Americans*', or 'harmless People' brutalized by European conquest), are of nugatory effect within the total economy of *Gulliver's Travels*, though academic rehabilitations, in the heyday of the Ph.D. era and its post-doctoral aftermath, have made a business of suggesting otherwise. Swift's harmless natives, as we have seen, exist only to set off the viciousness of colonial invaders: in themselves, both in Houyhnhnmland and outside it, they are malevolent savages.

Montaigne's naked Americans, on the other hand, are more like Houyhnhnms than Yahoos. Like the Houyhnhnms, they seem to derive from More's Utopians, inhabitants of Nowhere, which might signal an awareness of idealizing fantasy, though Montaigne maintains the fiction of their existence as he describes them, and seems partly to believe in it, while Swift made an even clearer point of signalling that the Houyhnhnms are regrettably outside the range of human possibility. Unlike Flaubert and Swift, Montaigne writes within the broad tradition of tripartite categorizations, in which there are two kinds of ethnic other, one good and one bad. This tradition may be said in an obvious sense to conform to empirical reality more closely than the simple (and I believe more exceptional) binary alternative, though it is itself formulaic and probably derives less from empirical fact than from the cultural and psychic needs of the perceiver. Montaigne's 'bad' savages differ from those of Swift or Flaubert not only in contrasting with 'good' ones where the later writers offer virtually no alternative, but in that they come over as an afterthought, countering a more dominant idealized portrayal. But modern analysts of the 'good' savage have detected racial slurs in that model as well as in its depraved counterpart, and it would be as much of a disservice to Montaigne to sentimentalize him in this regard as it would be to deny the radical decency of his vision (or Flaubert's or Swift's) of human exploitation and suffering.

Even in the new ending of 'De la modération' we are made aware that there are Amerindians and Amerindians. The insertion eventually focuses on the particular case of Mexico, itself very different from the Mexican matter appearing for the first time in the same edition, in 'Des coches'; while 'Des cannibales' concerns the Brazilian Tupinamba, as far removed from the ferocious and bloody Mexicans of 'De la modération' as they are from the advanced Mexican civilization of 'Des coches'. These distinctions have a certain explanatory force, but also a tendency to cancel out, in a manner characteristic of even the more good-natured perceptions of ethnic alterity. If there are Amerindians and Amerindians, there is also the sentiment that Indians are, after all, only Indians, and present-day descendants might be justified in feeling, about their portrayal in the essays, as some recent black readers feel about the Blacks of Conrad or especially of Harriet Beecher Stowe, notwithstanding the indubitable historical debt. The two perspectives coexist, more often than is realized, even in those who seem most disposed to repudiate ethnic stereotyping. Montaigne can say in 'Des coches' that Mexicans were more civilized and skilled than other Indian nations, 'plus civilisez et plus artistes que n'estoient les autres nations de là',[63] but there is a sense in the essay of broad racial generalization, mainly in praise. The new ending of 'De la modération' contains the less flattering flipside.

Its language likewise oscillates between the particular and an inclusive regional sweep which takes in the entire New World, mainly in shocked contemplation of atrocities, mixed with awe at Indian courage (a constant in Montaigne). It reports, in advance of Mexican examples, a practice of human sacrifices among the 'nouvelles terres, descouvertes en nostre aage' which is said to be very widespread. The impulse to define and limit the arraignment is challenged by an opposite emphasis on the ubiquity of the atrocities: 'l'usage en est aucunement receu par tout'. If 'aucunement' (here meaning 'somewhat' or 'to some extent' rather than 'not at all') suggests a limited scale, it is balanced by the wide sweep of 'par tout' and 'toutes leurs Idoles'. The total effect is anyway controlled by the opening declaration that a belief in the gods' pleasure in human sacrifice is 'universellement embrassée en toutes religions'. An effect familiar to readers of Swift, in which particular or well-defined cases are readily given wider applications than expected, and frequently assimilated to universal turpitudes, inculpating the whole of mankind in guilts that seemed only particular, is sporadically and informally in evidence, though Swift's exploitation of such paradoxical perceptions is in general more aggressively sustained. An irresolution on this point, which leaves the reader unsure, at the close of 'De la modération', of the exact reach of the accusation, is compounded by the transition from the Indians of essay xxx to those of essay xxxi. The ending of 'De la modération' (I. xxx) shows an *ex post facto* determination to undercut in advance (the paradox is inescapable) the Indian portrayal in 'Des cannibales' (I. xxxi), while letting the latter stand. It signals also that the cultural relativism exhibited in 'Des cannibales' is itself 'relative', not absolute, its bold principles subverted by a prior counter-assertion and thus, as we now say, problematized.

As the passage about Indians opens, we see people burned alive and removed half-roasted from the flames to have their hearts and guts torn out. On this point, the Indians of 'De la modération' are closer to the French than to the Indians of 'Des cannibales'. Nothing is said in the passage about cannibal acts which might have accompanied the human sacrifices, and a question arises as to why Montaigne seems kinder to Amerindian cannibalism than to Amerindian human sacrifices, some of which were certainly thought to include eating of the sacrificial victim in literal (as also in symbolic) ways. If the atrocities resemble European cases as mentioned in 'Des cannibales', then a reference to cannibalism in this context would risk implicating Europeans in the very activities from which Montaigne was evidently determined to dissociate them in that essay.

It is interesting also that Europeans are not mentioned at all in this particular account of the 'universality' of human sacrifice. Christianity preens itself on its freedom from sanguinary rites, but an awkward fact is that the most familiar ingestive ritual among Christians is one in which they eat their god, instead of offering human beings to Him.[64] As Freud pointed out, the idea that the Eucharistic sacrifice was a 'symbolic' re-enactment of literally ingestive tribal rituals (in Freud's version the killing and eating of the father by the Darwinian 'primal horde') did not originate with him, or even with Frazer.[65] The connection was available to a learned collector of customs like Montaigne, and Léry was willing to exploit it. Montaigne is silent here on eating rituals in which, in certain human sacrifices, a 'god' is consumed in the form of human flesh, and which bear an obvious relationship to Eucharistic practice, although, in the neutral tones of 'De la coustume' (I. xxiii), with its enumeration of the varieties of human customs, he speaks of a society 'où ils font cuire le corps du trespassé, et puis piler, jusques à ce qu'il se forme comme en bouillie laquelle ils meslent à leur vin, et la boivent' ('where they cook the body of the deceased and then crush it until a sort of pulp is formed, which they mix with their wine, and drink it'). This is an Amerindian example, taken from Gómara's *General History of the Indies* (though Montaigne does not, in this as in many other examples in this essay, identify either his source or the people in question). In the same essay, he cites the Greek repugnance at the idea of ingesting their fathers, and the greater revulsion of Indians (in this case from India) at the information that the Greeks cremated the bodies of their fathers.[66]

In such places, Montaigne will fall back on the relativity of usage, occasionally allowing an intimation of its relation to what he looks on as an absolute standard, adding after the example of Greeks and Indians 'Chacun en fait ainsi, d'autant que l'usage nous desrobbe le vray visage des choses' ('Everyone acts the same way, inasmuch as usage robs us of the true appearance of things'), just as he permits a glimpse in 'Des cannibales' of Amerindian barbarity 'eu esgard aux regles de la raison'. But his general disposition in the essay is non-judgemental, and its subtitle, 'de ne changer aisément une loy receüe', has an imperative connotation (captured by Florio, 'How a Received Law Should not Easily be Changed', but given a weaker force by some recent English translators, including Frame). In this spirit, cannibal practices in the broadest sense are flatly reported merely as one of the ways of life: 'Icy on vit de chair humaine; là c'est office de pieté de tuer son pere en certain aage ... ' ('Here they live on human flesh; there it is an act of piety to kill one's father at a certain age ... ').[67]

Such enumerations of strange customs had become a common literary routine, stimulated by the rediscovery of antiquity and the discovery of America and of a new route to the East. A certain neutrality is built into the genre, over and above Montaigne's conviction, which he was not the first to hold, that the customs of others are described as 'barbarian' merely because they are different from ours.[68] Montaigne is rightly regarded as doing more than 'collectionner des faits'. But his practice of 'comparing and judging' leads him less to the assertion of absolute standards than to a deepened sense of the relativity of morals, and his conservatism persuaded him of the unwisdom of changing or rejecting established customs.[69] In the 'Apologie de Raimond Sebond', he returns to the eating of deceased fathers, granting that the idea is repellent, but explaining its significance and raising the question of European burial practices, which leave corpses for food to beasts and worms:

Il n'est rien si horrible à imaginer que de manger son pere. Les peuples qui avoyent anciennement cette coustume, la prenoyent toutesfois pour tesmoignage de pieté et de bonne affection, cherchant par là à donner à leurs progeniteurs la plus digne et honorable sepulture, logeant en eux mesmes et comme en leurs moelles les corps de leurs peres et leurs reliques, les vivifiant aucunement et regenerant par la transmutation en leur chair vive au moyen de la digestion et du nourrissement. Il est aysé à considerer quelle cruauté et abomination c'eust esté, à des hommes abreuvez et imbus de cette superstition, de jetter la despouille des parens à la corruption de la terre et nourriture des bestes et des vers. (II. xii)

There is nothing so horrible to imagine as eating one's father. The nations which had this custom in ancient times, however, regarded it as testimony of piety and good affection, trying thereby to give their progenitors the most worthy and honorable sepulture, lodging in themselves and as it were in their marrow the bodies of their fathers and their remains, bringing them to life in a way and regenerating them by transmutation into their living flesh by means of digestion and nourishment. It is easy to imagine what a cruelty and abomination it would have been, to men saturated and imbued with this superstition, to abandon the mortal remains of their parents to the corruption of the earth and to let it become the food of beasts and worms.[70]

Montaigne speaks with an impressive understanding of the religious meaning of the cannibal custom, the piety of affording the father an honourable sepulchre, the absorption of the father's flesh and its transmutation into that of the descendants, the belief in the power of physiological processes of digestion and nourishment to achieve this transmutation, revivifying and regenerating the dead. He covers himself by speaking of 'superstition', but the sympathetic intelligence with which he attempts to enter into pagan perspectives is considerable, and the completeness with which any mention of the Eucharist is excluded in this context will seem remarkable to many readers. Here, as in other places, he avoids dangerous European analogies which Léry, who is in general less indulgent to savage cultures, would have no compunction in bringing out, though their 'prima-facie' appositeness to Montaigne's argument in 'Des cannibales' is obvious.

As the account in 'De la modération' continues, women are flayed alive, their blood-soaked skins used to make clothes and masks. This is a spectacular and violent variant of a technology which goes back to Scythian tribes described by Herodotus, and looks forward to *Gulliver's Travels* and the cannibal Ireland of *A Modest Proposal*, as flayed women look forward to the 'Digression on Madness'.[71] There is also an unsettling gaiety about these proceedings, in which the victims go to their death not only soliciting alms for the sacrifice but singing and dancing with the celebrants:

A d'autres, voire aux femmes, on les escorche visves, et de leur peau ainsi sanglante en revest on et masque d'autres. Et non moins d'exemples de constance et resolution. Car ces pauvres gens sacrifiables, vieillars, femmes, enfans, vont, quelques jours avant, questant eux mesme les aumosnes pour l'offrande de leur sacrifice, et se presentent à la boucherie chantans et dançans avec les assistans.

Others, even women, are flayed alive, and with their bloody skins they dress and disguise others. And there are no fewer examples of constancy and resolution. For these poor people that are to be sacrificed, old men, women, children, themselves go about, some days before, begging alms for the offering at their sacrifice, and present themselves to the slaughter singing and dancing with the spectators.

The transition from constancy and resolution to the examples which illustrate these virtues is not what most readers would expect. The old, the women, and children, singing and dancing before their own ordeal, enact a scenario not of steadfast endurance but of perverse and painful tribal festiveness. The pretended parable of courage under duress turns into a disturbing account of irrational gaiety and collective masochism, which seem to belong to the psychopathology of orgiastic immolation and of which Montaigne's homespun gloss gives no adequate account.

To this information taken from Gómara, Montaigne adds an anecdote from the same author in which envoys from the King of Mexico inform Cortez that their monarch sacrifices fifty thousand people a year, waging war with his neighbours to provide exercise for the youth of the country and to supply himself with prisoners to sacrifice. Fifty men were sacrificed all at once in another town in honour of Cortez's arrival, and Cortez was offered five slaves from Indian nations he had conquered. He was told that if he was a fierce god, he should eat them and be given more; if a kind god, they offered incense and feathers; and if a man, he should accept some birds and fruit: 'si tu és un Dieu fier, qui te paisses de chair et de sang, mange les, et nous t'en amerrons d'avantage; si tu es un Dieu debonnaire, voylà de l'encens et des plumes; si tu es homme, prens les oiseaux et les fruicts que voicy.'

This pay-off confers a species of quirky wisdom on the Mexicans, hardly foreseeable from the appalling information supplied so far. It has something of the anecdotal power which concludes 'Des cannibales', where another Amerindian displays an even greater sagacity on matters of royal behaviour, although he doesn't even wear breeches. In both, the mood is raised by a closing surge of moral sanity. In the case of 'Des cannibales', however, this comes over as the natural extension of a discourse whose general argument was itself dedicated to demonstrating the superiority of

Indian culture. In 'De la modération', on the other hand, it is made to round off a description of Amerindian carnage which is not only shocking in its own right, but also closer, in some details, to Montaigne's portrayal of Europeans than of Indians in 'Des cannibales' and elsewhere. Unresolved incongruities attach to this passage, both in its internal relations and in its relation to 'Des cannibales'. Montaigne's placing of the passage immediately before that essay, an afterthought which acts as a pre-emptive strike, seems designed to bring the incongruity into relief, undermining what follows, not to the advantage of the Europeans, but to a revised perception of Amerindians as hardly superior, and to the general discredit of the human race.

This broadly targeted misanthropic disenchantment is not Montaigne's habitual or most characteristic state of mind. It is reflected in a stylistic manner whose implications are diffusely guilt-inducing, with an uncertainty on the reader's part as to who, exactly, shall scape whipping. It aligns Montaigne's manner in such places with the either-way-you-lose character of Swift's style and with the general mood of *Gulliver's Travels*. Swift was not given to redemptive surges of anecdotal uplift of the kind which characterizes the terminations of both essays, though the final chapter of *Gulliver's Travels* contains a scenario of ruthless colonial depredation which is written with the Spanish conquests in mind (specifically 'those of *Ferdinando Cortez* over the naked *Americans*') and which resembles in several details the account in 'Des coches' of European thugs invading and betraying a well-disposed and welcoming native population.[72]

Montaigne's essays sometimes end with anecdotes. They have an open-ended quality more suited to his discursive idiom than any conclusive summation would be, inviting rather than foreclosing reflection on their resonances and implications. 'De la modération', in particular, has a power to disconcert because the parable of moral wisdom in its concluding detail is incongruous with the rest of the portrayal of Indians in the paragraph as a whole, and because that portrayal is in turn incongruous with what follows in 'Des cannibales'. In this it differs from the ending of 'Des cannibales', where moral wisdom is what much of the rest of the essay leads us to expect, although, as I have argued, a reading of this essay is itself made problematic by the close of 'De la modération'; and also from the ending of 'Des coches', where suicidal loyalty and courage rather than wisdom or sanity are the subject of the anecdote, picking up a thread of characterization of Amerindians which runs through most of Montaigne's writings on that subject.

The added ending of 'De la modération', with its large-scale inculpations, its ambivalent pay-off, its unresolved incongruities with 'Des cannibales' as well as within itself, its mixture of admiration and disgust for 'savages', and its unofficial or subtextual intimations that, in their savagery at least, savages (including the 'civilized' savages of Mexico and Europe) are more or less at one with the whole human race, is one of the puzzles of Montaigne studies.[73] Its disconcerting effects derive largely from the stark suggestiveness of unglossed anecdote, rather than from the continuous pressure of aggressively guilt-inducing energies which we associate with Swift's ironic manner.

Montaigne's usual style is more genial, more relaxed, and less defensive. Its aggressions are sporadic rather than continuous. But some of its stress points achieve in local power something of the unpredictability, the harsh conflict of categories, the unsettling indeterminacies which Swift was to build into the normal fabric of his style. In essays dealing with pain and violence, Montaigne gives voice to a feeling of unappeased disturbance, of floating irresolution and generalized guilt. The final anecdote of 'De la modération', starkly unmoralized, projects (as the endings of 'Des cannibales' and 'Des coches' do not) a weird coexistence of murderous habits and flower-power sagacity; and the singing and dancing of the sacrificial victims introduces a disconcerting gaiety, which has little to do with the 'constancy and resolution' it is said to illustrate, and which does nothing to relieve the hideous grimness of the narrative of their fate. Swift knew the power of surreal flashes of festiveness in a context of pain, as when in the *Short View of the State of Ireland* (1728), a work expressing his own blend of pity and contempt for a colony of 'savages' nearer home, he sarcastically answered those who claimed Ireland was in a flourishing condition by saying that, if so, 'it must be against every Law of Nature and Reason; like the Thorn at *Glassenbury*, that blossoms in the Midst of Winter'.[74] A queer menace, an atmosphere of disturbing significances hovering undeclared, attaches to what is normally an image of religious exaltation and joy, closely comparable to the process by which the tidiness of Montaigne's parables and pay-offs is violated by an eruptive gaiety or sanity, difficult to accommodate within the prevailing tendency of his discourse.

Utopians, Tupinamba, Houyhnhnms, Yahoos

The famous passage summarizing the culture of the Tupinamba, which was to be cited more or less word for word in the *Tempest*, expresses ideals very close to those embodied in the Houyhnhnms:

C'est une nation, diroy je à Platon, en laquelle il n'y a aucune espece de trafique; nulle cognoissance de lettres; nulle science de nombres; nul nom de magistrat, ny de superiorité politique; nul usage de service, de richesse ou de pauvreté; nuls contrats; nulles successions; nuls partages; nulles occupations qu'oysives; nul respect de parenté que commun; nuls vestemens; nulle agriculture; nul metal; nul usage de vin ou de bled. Les paroles mesmes qui signifient le mensonge, la trahison, la dissimulation, l'avarice, l'envie, la detraction, le pardon, inouies. Combien trouveroit il la republique qu'il a imaginée, esloignée de cette perfection.

This is a nation, I should say to Plato, in which there is no sort of traffic, no knowledge of letters, no science of numbers, no name for a magistrate or for political superiority, no custom of servitude, no riches or poverty, no contracts, no successions, no partitions, no occupations but leisure ones, no care for any but common kinship, no clothes, no agriculture, no metal, no use of wine or wheat. The very words that signify lying, treachery, dissimulation, avarice, envy, belittling, pardon—unheard of. How far from this perfection would he find the republic that he imagined.[75]

That last phrase suggests not that the Indians are unlike Plato's Republic, but that they surpass it on its own ground, and the irony is similar to that in which the horse-shaped Houyhnhnms outdo in perfection any rational ideal devised by men. It is in this spirit that Montaigne regrets that Lycurgus and Plato had not had knowledge of these Amerindians, and that Gulliver more aggressively suggests that instead of trying to invade the Houyhnhnms, we would profit more by their sending 'a sufficient Number of their Inhabitants for civilizing *Europe*' (IV. xii. 293–4).

The idea in Montaigne is not only the expression of a common tendency to describe and measure the American Indian against values and expectations of a classical or classicizing kind, but part of a sustained subtextual play, throughout the essay, with the fact that the original meaning of the Greek word *barbaros* was 'one who did not speak Greek' and therefore included all non-Greeks.[76] It is with this linguistic fact in the immediate background ('car les Grecs appelloyent ainsi toutes les nations estrangieres'), that the essay begins with Pyrrhus' discovery that the powerfully disciplined army of the Roman barbarians is 'not at all barbarous', and all but closes with the observation that the poetry of the Cannibals is 'tout à fait Anacreontique' ('altogether Anacreontic') and that their language had a pleasing sound, 'retirant aux terminaisons Grecques' ('somewhat like Greek in its endings':[77] the supposed affinities of Indian languages with Greek was becoming a commonplace, though the pointed linguistic irony of calling them barbarian is not always exploited in Montaigne's sharply focused way).[78]

It would be nice to think that the learned author of the *Critical Remarks on Capt. Gulliver's Travels* (1735), whether or not he was Arbuthnot, might have been remembering this passage when he remarked, 'what can be more evident, than that the *Houyhnhnm* Language was perfectly understood by the ancient *Greeks*, as the *Irish* (which has the nearest Similitude of Sound and Pronunciation to that Language) is intelligible to many curious Persons at present?'[79] There is evidently a joke about Irish speech, perhaps to the effect that it is all Greek to him.[80] The essay is a mock-learned demonstration that the Houyhnhnms were a real people, well known to the ancients. But whether or not it shows a perception of the connection between the Houyhnhnms and Montaigne's good Indians, Montaigne's description of the Greek-resembling Indian language is a reinforcement of the feeling that these Indians derive, as do Swift's Houyhnhnms, from an amalgam of Golden Age primitivism and the austerely disciplined and highly structured civilizations of Lycurgus' Sparta, Plato's *Republic* and *Timaeus*, and More's *Utopia*.

Montaigne said he regretted that Lycurgus, as well as Plato, had not known of the Amerindians, just as, in their complementary primitivist splendour, the Indians also surpassed all poetical descriptions of the Golden Age, 'toutes les peintures dequoy la poësie a embelly l'age doré'.[81] Gulliver wished the Houyhnhnms could come over to civilize Europe (IV. xii. 294), and they too combine a prelapsarian innocence with elements of a morality and social organization which derive from Lycurgus' Sparta and the ideal states of Plato and More. Socrates and More are two of the six heroes of a '*Sextumvirate* to which all the Ages of the World cannot add a Seventh' (III. vii. 196) reported by Gulliver in Glubbdubdrib. Gulliver spoke of Houyhnhnm principles as in conformity 'with the Sentiments of *Socrates* as *Plato* delivers them; which I mention as the highest Honour I can do that Prince of Philosophers' (IV. viii. 268), and the influence of Spartan ideals of conduct, on Swift as on the other authors, is well established.[82] Montaigne's description belongs in this tradition, and he drew on it as deeply as on the live or written testimonies of New World travellers, in his invention or imagining of the Tupinamba Utopia—as much, in appropriate Morian terms, a no-place as a good place.

The political and social ideas embodied, with individual variations, in the tradition within which all these authors wrote had become sufficiently current, as an 'alternative' ideology if not as a dominant one, to render specific attributions of influence unnecessary and perhaps misleading. Each writer had read his predecessors, and each had absorbed the climate of thought. But Montaigne's paragraph, which blends many of the standard ingredients with some more recent descriptions of Amerindians (themselves partly based on amalgams of Golden Age fantasy and of Platonic or Morian civilization), has exceptional power and comprehensiveness, and acquired a kind of anthology status for Shakespeare and others. Such traditional elements of Houyhnhnm culture as the absence of letters, laws, commerce, or clothes, as well as of a vocabulary for lying and other irrational or unsocial activities, all occur in Montaigne within the space of a hundred words. (Even their dwellings, as I shall suggest, are not dissimilar). Other and more general elements, like simplicity of life, the freedom from false needs, the diet of plain, slightly insipid (*un peu fade*) food, and the health and longevity are in evidence in both societies:[83] Gulliver in Houyhnhnmland is fed plain food which he thought 'at first a very insipid Diet' and which ensured that he 'never had one Hour's Sickness' in that country (IV. ii. 232).[84] The Houyhnhnms have no diseases, and die of old age (IV. ix. 273, 275), live a life which is tranquil and undisturbed by passion, and perhaps resemble even more closely the summary portrait of Brazilian Amerindians in the 'Apologie de Raimond Sebond':

Ce qu'on vous dit de ceux du Bresil, qu'ils ne mouroyent que de vieillesse, et qu'on attribue à la serenité et tranquillité de leur air, je l'attribue plustost à la tranquillité et serenité de leur ame, deschargée de toute passion et pensée et occupation tendue ou desplaisante, comme gents qui passoyent leur vie en une admirable simplicité et ignorance, sans lettres, sans loy, sans roy, sans religion quelconque.

What they tell us of the Brazilians, that they died only of old age, which is attributed to the serenity and tranquillity of their air, I attribute rather to the tranquillity and serenity of their souls, unburdened with any tense or unpleasant passion or thought or occupation, as people who spent their life in admirable simplicity and ignorance, without letters, without law, without king, without religion of any kind.[85]

The last words are a variation on a sequence often used in disparagement of Indians, who were alleged to lack the letters *f*, *l*, or *r* and to be thus disabled from saying faith, law, and king (in Spanish, Portuguese, or French).[86] They might almost be used to describe the Houyhnhnms, though Swift himself could never make such a statement except in disparagement, as Montaigne evidently could. Consider the remark about Ireland in 1720, that 'Whoever travels this Country, and observes the *Face* of Nature, or the *Faces*, and Habits, and Dwellings of the *Natives*, will hardly think himself in a Land where either *Law*, *Religion*, or *common Humanity* is professed'.[87] This is (perhaps) said more in sorrow than in anger. But it is not offered as an object of admiration, as the absence of law and religion are noted with admiration of Montaigne's Indians. The description was of a kind which could, whether for Montaigne or Swift, be applied to even less edifying examples. That latter role, in *Gulliver's Travels*, belongs to an altogether different species, the Yahoos.

An interesting example of this form of split is the fact that although Montaigne's Amerindians practise polygamy, in *Gulliver's Travels* it is the Yahoos and not the Houyhnhnms who, 'like other Brutes, had their Females in common' (IV. vii. 263). As Paul Turner suggests, there may be an ironic allusion to Plato's *Republic*, where it is envisaged that 'these women [the female guardians] shall all be common to all the men', since 'there is no denial that the community of women and children would be the greatest good, supposing it possible'. Socrates responds to objections by saying that 'feasibility' would have to be established, and he is talking, in Utopian or No-Place terms, of a highly specialized set of persons. Turner says the irony resides in the fact that 'this "Utopian" arrangement is normally practised in European society'. But this assimilation of European mores to unregulated animal wantonness is, I suspect, uncoupled from any reflection on Socrates, whom Swift and Gulliver both revered. Neither resembles the structured character of the social arrangement, or the 'as if' status of the Republic in which such a custom would take place, though Plato was attacked for what De Quincey called an 'Otaheitian carnival of licentious appetite'.[88] Swift's Houyhnhnms followed Plato in believing that it was (with minor exceptions) wrong 'to give the Females a different kind of Education from the Males'. The reference seems to be to the education of children in common rather than in the family. The downbeat explanation is the human example. Since 'one Half of our Natives were good for nothing but bringing Children into the World ... to trust the Care of their Children to such useless Animals ... was yet a greater Instance of Brutality'. The Houyhnhnms were strictly mono-gamous, and the matrons abstained from sexual activity after achieving their quota of one child of each sex. Mating extra-maritally was only permitted to replace a lost child, if the wife was 'past bearing' (IV. viii. 268–9).[89] It is variously evident that Swift would not have shared Montaigne's tolerance of the Amerindians' sexual arrangements. It was easier for Montaigne than for Swift to integrate such arrangements notionally within a polity described as being like or better than Plato's, even though it differs sub-stantially from Socrates' plan.

In Montaigne, the dual role is embodied in the same people, their 'barbarian' dimension frankly conceded in 'Des cannibales' and elsewhere, though the principal emphasis is on their some-what paradoxical nobility. The noble savages he has conceived, with their tranquillity and serenity, their admirable simplicity and ignorance, and their freedom from letters, laws, king, or religion, nevertheless abide by codes of conduct and of government which, as we have seen, belong to the highly structured ideals of an advanced civilization. The paradox which brings together evoca-tions of the Golden Age as well as of Plato's *Republic* is not uncommon in the Utopian imagination. Swift's Houyhnhnms, whose serene unlettered ignorance is quite as marked as that of Montaigne's Tupinamba, but whose failure to strike the reader as 'primitive' is equally marked, do in fact show a similar blend. There is an extraordinary irony in the fact that when Gulliver first arrives in Houyhnhnmland, he 'takes out some Toys, which Trav-ellers usually carry for Presents to the savage *Indians* of *America*' (IV. ii. 228). Even the Houyhnhnm dwelling, 'a long Kind of

Building, made of Timber, stuck in the Ground, ... the Roof was low, and covered with Straw', to which we are here introduced before we know who the inhabitants are, is in some details reminiscent of Montaigne's description: long buildings, covered with barks of great trees, resembling our barns, whose covering hangs down to the ground (I. xxxi).[90] It is hard, in hindsight, not to believe that a subtextual intimation of specific resemblance is being offered, complementing the main or official irony, in both authors, to the effect these natives are not savage at all.

The likeness highlights a paradox about the blend of the Utopically civilized and the virtuously innocent primitive. The effortless coexistence of the two vividly illustrates the degree to which the paradoxical fusion has taken place. Their 'primitive' qualities take second place both to their supreme rationality, and to the more dramatically sketched alternative primitivism of the Yahoos, a textbook example of *ignoble* savagery. Since they belong to a fictional Utopia or No-Place, a matter whose wider implications will be considered in the following chapters, the Houyhnhnms come with no barbaric residues like cannibalism to be explained away.[91] Even so, they have most of the primitive features listed in the summary passages I quoted from *Essais* I, xxxi and II, xii, including strong lineaments of a prelapsarian innocence uncorrupted by exposure to depraved human ways. This is conventionally emphasized by their incomprehension of Gulliver's clothing, and of any reason 'why Nature should teach us to conceal what Nature had given' (IV. iii. 237). The nudity of Amerindians was from the start a commonplace of the discourse of discovery and conquest, whether as a sign of innocence or of savagery, and perhaps occasionally as a value-free descriptive fact. Gulliver spoke generically of the 'naked *Americans*' (IV. xii. 293).

Montaigne's Amerindians were naturally naked and also, in 'Des cannibales' and even in parts of 'Des coches' (which was largely concerned with their capacity for an advanced civilization), carried their own strong prelapsarian glow. Not only were they naked, but they were not even hairy, and moreover made sure to shave off any growth of hair much more cleanly than 'we' do.[92] The *Letter* to Soderini, by or derived from Vespucci, published *c.*1505 and translated (from the Italian) into Latin in Martin Waldseemüller's *Cosmography* (1507), describes the Ameridians (of, roughly, Venezuela) as practising total depilation 'except the head, because they consider bodily hair an ugly thing'.[93] Thevet and Léry later mention that depilation of facial and body hair was practised by women as well as men. This seemed especially noteworthy to Thevet, since hairiness was expected of savages. He wrote a whole chapter 'Against the opinion of those who consider savages to be hairy'. Lévi-Strauss, in *Tristes Tropiques*, a book suffused with admiration for Léry, cited some Spanish testimony of 1525 in which the Indians' lack of beard, and their habits of depilation, were used as evidence of savagery, along with cannibalism, the absence among them of a judicial system, their nakedness, and their eating of fleas, spiders, and raw worms. As Whatley points out, hairiness is a standard feature of 'the Wild Man of European myths'.[94] This may explain the sense of aberrancy: savage if hairy, unnatural (therefore savage) if not, a double bind worthy of Swift, but which the Yahoos, whose features are said to be 'common to all savage Nations', are in fact spared. They are very hairy, hairier even than Gulliver at first thinks of as human, for he hopes the Yahoo beast 'might direct me to the Cabbin of some *Indian*' (IV. ii. 230; i. 223–24). So far removed were actual Indians from this stereotype that they found the beards of the invaders puzzling and frightening.

Gunpowder Magic

Beards were not the only part of the story of what Gulliver called the 'easy' victory 'of *Ferdinando Cortez* over the naked *Americans*' (IV. xii. 293). The official account was of Spanish arms and valour. The truth seems to be that Cortés's letters were self-aggrandizing

and tendentious, that Spanish atrocities and treacheries on and off
the battlefield were extraordinary, and that the Mexicans, though
weakened by division within their own empire, resisted fiercely
and inflicted heavy losses on the Spanish, forcing them, in Inga
Clendinnen's words, 'to level much of the city they had sought to
preserve'.[95] A much mythologized factor in the victory were the
Spanish horses, 'formidable creatures of power whose fame had
run ahead of them'. They were unfamiliar in America, and terri-
fying. An account, recorded in Sahagún's *Florentine Codex*, of the
force and terror of their impact, bears a grimly ironic resemblance
to Gulliver's gleeful fantasy of what the Houyhnhnms might do to
a European invader (IV. xii. 293). Above all were the muskets and
cannons, against which non-explosive weaponry and mere courage could not ultimately prevail.[96]

If the conquest was not 'easy', the Spanish account prevailed,
even among those, like Montaigne and Swift, who found it dis-
honourable, and there were revisionist versions. One of the best
known is the passage in 'Des coches', not very different as a
factual summary from Columbus's own descriptions, in which
Montaigne lists three factors which explain how it was that such
brave peoples were conquered by Spanish riff-raff: gunpowder,
and the unfamiliar sight of bearded men on horseback, in a land
where beards and horses were as unknown as explosives, so that
the conquerors seemed fierce gods shaped like centaurs, and able
to direct lightning which killed the native inhabitants from afar,
causing a 'juste estonnement'.[97]

Swift does not expound this triad explicitly, but it is part of the
received mythology of Amerindian conquest, and Montaigne's
'Des coches' maintains a strong subtextual presence in Gulliver's
speech. Swift did, moreover, ring his own variations on the theme
of hair, horses, and gunpowder. The Yahoos, classic types of the
hairy savage, are the antithesis of the smooth-skinned Indians,
and the idea of natives being cowed by the invaders' horses is
gleefully overturned by Gulliver's fantasy of the horse-shaped
Houyhnhnms repelling would-be European conquerors with

emphatically equine force: 'overturning the Carriages, battering the Warriors Faces into Mummy, by terrible Yerks from their hinder Hoofs.' Gulliver caps the entire upside-down scheme by suggesting that far from conquering the Houyhnhnms, he wishes they could instead 'send a sufficient Number of their Inhabitants for civilizing *Europe*' (IV. xii. 293–4).

These reverse symmetries are not conspicuous to most readers, and provide at best a subtextual or even fortuitous piquancy. But the issue of gunpowder terror is prominent in *Gulliver's Travels*, notably in two scenes which are dramatically insulting to Gulliver as a representative of European civilization (II. vii. 134; IV. v. 247), and the standard scenario of surprise by explosion is comically acted out in Lilliput, when Gulliver fires one of his pistols in the air: 'Hundreds fell down as if they had been struck dead.' This episode is benign. Gulliver had come without hostile intent, and had prepared the Emperor for the shock, with no thought of frightening him into any sort of submission (I. ii. 36–7). He surrenders his pistols to the Emperor, begging him to keep the ammunition away 'from Fire; for it would kindle with the smallest Spark, and blow up his Imperial Palace into the Air'. The pistols are part of a portable machinery which also includes Gulliver's noisy timepiece and seems mainly a playful imagining of how an Englishman would appear and sound to a people six inches tall. This includes a sense of technological wonder, but seems less concerned with the superiority or menacing power of European technology, than with the difference in size. The effect of the gunpowder is comparable in kind to that of the collective dazzle of Gulliver's sword over the Lilliputian army: 'immediately all the Troops gave a Shout between Terror and Surprize; for the Sun shone clear, and the Reflexion dazzled their Eyes, as I waved the Scymiter to and fro in my Hand' (I. ii. 36).

This has a playful poetry about it, and the comedy of the pistols was perhaps already becoming a traditional script. An escalation of it, reported by Sheldon Dibble, seems (or was believed) to have occurred on one of Cook's approaches to Hawaii, when not only the white men's firearms but their cigars were said to have been taken for volcanic manifestations of deity (and their clothes for folds in their skins, with the pockets as doors, opening anatomical cavities full of treasure. A final irony was that some red water-melons from Monterey, which Cook's men were eating, were supposedly mistaken for human flesh).[98] To impress in this way, and indeed to use firearms to suppress native hostility, seemed acceptable to Cook and to his chroniclers in ways which would normally seem repellent to Swift or to Montaigne.

Certainly the initial defeat of the Amerindians, aided by the shock of guns, beards, and man-horses, was part of the emotional furniture of the story of empire. Echoes of it reverberate throughout the eighteenth century, not only in Swift, but also, in an updated form, in Bougainville's *Voyage autour du monde* (1771), at a time when the main thing to be said about the story was that it no longer applied: the Indians (in this case the *Indios bravos* of the river Plate) spend their life on horseback, drink themselves into a stupor, steal livestock from Spanish properties, and practise highway robbery, murder, and slavery. The days are gone, says Bougainville, when a single Spaniard could put a thousand Indians to flight: 'le temps n'est plus où un Espagnol faisait fuir mille Américains.'[99]

Bougainville's account may be set beside a comparable passage in the journal of one of his men, Charles-Félix Fesche. It describes the same or a similar group, though without the fully orchestrated sense of historical reversal which culminates in Bougainville's last sentence. But in a later entry on the *Sauvages* of the Strait of Magellan, which contains a comparison between them and the Indians of the River Plate, Fesche does report that they showed no surprise at seeing the Frenchmen's guns or hearing them fired.[100] The Tahitians, who are the main subject of Bougainville's *Voyage*, were a more complex case: both Bougainville and Fesche, on arrival in Tahiti, report firing sky-rockets which caused terror and then admiration among the natives, though this did not prevent a Frenchman's pistol being stolen, perhaps while the paradisal blandishments of the celebrated Cytherean welcome were taking place (later the natives asked to hear some gunfire).[101]

The use of explosives to impress, or at least probe, the natives is already evident in Columbus's first voyage. The *Diario* of this voyage, transcribed by Las Casas, shows Columbus aware, on the little island of Guanahani, of natives who are not acquainted with arms, have no iron, and cut themselves on his sword through ignorance (11 October 1492). Later, on Hispaniola, he orders 'a lombard and a spingard to be fired', records the friendly king's astonishment at their force, and the fact that 'when his people heard the shots they all fell to the ground', exactly like the Lilliputians with Gulliver's pistol. He informs the king, who is at war with the Caribs (who have 'no knowledge of iron or of steel'), that the 'sovereigns of Castile would order the Caribs destroyed' (26 December 1492; a similar friendly show of force is put on a week later, on 2 January).[102] This situation, with many variations, had a long history, which takes in Captain John Smith in 1624, and both Bougainville and especially Cook were conscious of its potential, as well as its agonizing moral implications.[103]

The mythography of colonial confrontations is rich with accounts of the supposed magic of gunfire, of which Gulliver's experience in Lilliput is a comic replay. Robinson Crusoe is from the beginning very conscious of gunpowder magic: 'upon the Noise or Report of the Gun, a thing I have some Reason to believe those Creatures had never heard before', he is struck by the 'horrible Noises, and hideous Cryes and Howlings' he has provoked. A little later, shooting at 'a great Bird', he causes similar panic among the fowls, and marvels at having let off the 'first Gun that had been fir'd there since the Creation of the World'. The novel has several scenes of astonishment and terror (as well as injury) spread among the natives by this means.[104] There are also accounts of ironic demystifications and reversals. The process seems to have begun afresh with each encounter. An ironically pre-emptive example occurred in Manly Cove in Sydney Harbour in 1788, when a young Aborigine, after being frightened by the explosion of a pistol ball which perforated his shield, asked if a 'pistol would make a hole through him', but evidently believed that his own weapons would do it better.[105] The belief was, one might say, technologically innocent, but the superiority of spears to firearms as a technology received validation when it was recognized that a 'tribesman could throw four spears in the time it took to reload a flintlock'.[106] In 1770, Cook found his firearms surprisingly slow to impress local resistance, though when he took possession of 'New South Wales' in the name of the king on 21 August, he laid on a ceremonial of small arms fire, having discarded his cannons on the Barrier Reef: thus, says Robert Hughes, 'by the slap of muskets echoing across a flat warm strait, Australia was added to the British Empire'. Inevitably, as time went on, the Aborigines learned to exploit the weapons of the invaders, and Hughes's account reads like a replay of Bougainville on the *Indios bravos*: 'Aborigines stole guns and learned how to use them; they made devastating attacks on sheep and cattle, harassed miners, killed horses and burned homesteads.' Typically, it was Conrad's *Heart of Darkness* which took this pantomime of colonial might to its most exquisite distillation of 'lugubrious drollery', with its French warship 'firing into a continent' ('and nothing happened'), or the 'pilgrims' with their Winchesters 'simply squirting lead' into the bush. A parallel bit of demystifying occurs from the direction of the same bush, as 'the arrows came in swarms. They might have been poisoned, but they looked as though they wouldn't kill a cat.' Nevertheless, gunpowder magic, 'the thunderbolts of that pitiful Jupiter', was how Kurtz tamed the natives, and became their 'adored' despot.[107]

This is the lowered actuality of imperial reversal, whose ideal counterpart is the wishful fantasy of Houyhnhnms battering European invaders 'into Mummy'. The 'Indians', whether of America or the South Seas, are hardly heroic, as in Montaigne. Swift would have expressed little admiration for the real-life versions, whose protagonists from savage nations clearly came into the category he described as Yahoos, though a residual satisfaction at European come-uppance would have to be set against the menace of unruly natives getting out of hand. Such ambivalence is the stuff and texture of Swift's thought. But it is clear that in the grim comedy of gunpowder war, as in much else, *Gulliver's Travels* looks before and after. The allegorical thrust of Book I into politics is quite deadly, but not much of it is evident at this early stage, and the Lilliputians in any case correspond, in that allegory, to a European state rather than to its conquered victims. By the time Gulliver has a chance to display technological machismo, it is in Brobdingnag, where Gulliver's size is no longer a threat, and where the noise of his pistols would have been unlikely to impress. What comes into question, as he boasts to the king of the power of gunpowder, is his morality, or that of the civilization he represents, whose nastiness the King of Brobdingnag is quick to despise (II. vii. 134). Size now acts ironically in reverse, since the king is as much bigger than Gulliver as Gulliver was than the Lilliputians, and the idea of explosives capable of destroying the Brobdingnagians' enemies suggests very powerful technology indeed. Gulliver is not allowed to try it, and is heard with horror. In offering gunpowder know-how, Gulliver is not threatening, any more than he was in Lilliput, only ingratiating himself, and his gunpowder proposals translate into diplomacy of the classic rather than the gunboat kind. By the time he gives a similar account to the Master Houyhnhnm, he is past all diplomacy, but as the Houyhnhnm will not believe what Gulliver says humans get up to in battle, Gulliver smiles smugly 'at his Ignorance' and proceeds to yet another of his entranced descriptions of gunpowder war (IV. v. 247).

In the last passage, there is a shocking pay-off. The huge carnage described by Gulliver takes place 'to the great Diversion of all the Spectators'. The story has come a long way from the playful comedy of Gulliver's pistols, and the idea of 'diversion' itself, in such a context, represents a significant darkening of the moral landscape.[108] The gunpowder passages, moreover, are not mainly concerned with excesses of empire, like Montaigne's essays on America. Gunpowder is, for Swift, the expression of a radical human depravity, while Montaigne thought the invention of it

was of not much account.[109] These passages are part of the run up
to the attack on colonial conquests in IV.xii, as well as the particular sarcasm about the 'ease' of Cortez's victory, though they are
principally an exposure of human cruelty wider than, if inclusive
of, such conquests. When Gulliver comes to consider and rule out
the idea of reporting his discovered territories to the government,
the ironies of the gunpowder threat, and of the intended victims'
reversal of that threat, are an important detail, but only a detail, in
a more comprehensive anatomy of human wickedness and the
punishments it deserves.

Fynes Moryson and the *Intelligencer*

For all their differences of emphasis, Montaigne was a formative
figure in Swift's outlook and thought. The relation of Swift's
writings to Montaigne's essays should not be emphasized at the
expense of other writers in the classical and humanist tradition of
which both authors formed a part. The importance of Plato and
More is attested by Gulliver himself, and Swift was also well read in
the literature of travel, whose style is mimicked by Gulliver. But
Montaigne was a natural part of the reading of any educated person of Swift's time and cultural disposition. 'Nobody required an
introduction' to Montaigne during the lifetimes of Swift or his
patron Sir William Temple, in whose household Swift 'was certainly encouraged to read' his essays, according to Swift's biographer Irvin Ehrenpreis, who repeatedly speaks of the influence of
Montaigne on the writings of both men, and of resemblances
between Montaigne's and Swift's styles of composition and
modes of thought. Even hostile witnesses perceived a resemblance, John Evans, Bishop of Meath, remarking in a letter of
28 February 1718 on one of Swift's sermons that 'it was somewhat
like one of Montaigne's essays ... making very free with all
orders and degrees of men amongst us—lords, bishops, &c.—men
in power'.[110]

Swift evidently knew Montaigne from an early date, citing him with genuine familiarity in letters as early as 1704 and as late as 1730 (and even later in one of his printed works, *The Advantages Propos'd by Repealing the Sacramental Test*, 1732). He evidently made Vanessa read him. When, in *Cadenus and Vanessa*, a group of babbling women come to bore her with their chatter, '*Vanessa* held *Montaigne* and read, Whilst Mrs. *Susan* comb'd her Head' (ll. 372–3).[111] Swift's friends Pope and Bolingbroke cited Montaigne in letters to him, in a manner which confirms that familiarity with the *Essais* was taken for granted in his circle.[112] Swift is known to have owned a copy (in French) from at least 1715, and probably earlier, until the time of his death. According to the Earl of Orrery, Thomas Sheridan, Swift's friend and the co-author with him of the *Intelligencer*, was in 1736 engaged 'at his leisure hours [in] giving us a translation of Montagne'.[113]

The *Intelligencer*, which provides indirect evidence of a Swiftian reticence comparable to Montaigne's, was a periodical mainly but not exclusively of Irish interest. It ran to nineteen more or less weekly numbers between May and December 1728, with a longish interruption in the summer, and a single further number in May 1729. It was written by Swift and Sheridan, a clergyman, schoolteacher, and man of letters, and grandfather of the playwright. It includes at least two of Swift's important works, his critique of the *Beggar's Opera* in No. 3, and a reprint of the *Short View of the State of Ireland* in No. 15, perhaps the single most eloquent of his Irish writings, and close in time and subject-matter to *A Modest Proposal*. It belongs to the period of Swift's most intensive involvement in Irish affairs, three years after his pamphleteering in the *Drapier's Letters* defeated the project of 'Wood's halfpence', two years after *Gulliver's Travels* (which has an important Irish dimension),[114] and a year before the *Modest Proposal*. Swift probably contributed about ten numbers and Sheridan nine, with one number of uncertain authorship.

It has been recognized for some time that No. 18 by Sheridan (late November 1728), in James Woolley's words, 'foreshadows the

Modest Proposal by quoting ominously from Fynes Moryson's seventeenth-century account of the English oppression of Ireland: it led to the eating of babies.' Moryson was an English official who helped to suppress Tyrone's rebellion and whose *Itinerary* (1617) was an account of his life and travels, which Swift may or may not have read. But he would certainly have read his own collaborator's account, and the particular issue in which it occurs, moreover, opens with a proposal for public celebration of Swift's birthday on 30 November, in gratitude for his services to Ireland. (According to newspapers, 'the Birth-day of that memorable Patriot M.*B. Drapier*, the great Deliverer of this Kingdom' was indeed marked with bells from St Patrick's Cathedral, where Swift was dean, and with illuminations, bonfires and 'Healths...drunk by the Populace'.)[115]

Sheridan then launches into his cannibal story, as one 'untoucht upon before [not strictly true], by those who Writ against *Wood*'s Half-pence, which I have read in an *English* Historian of great probity, and Truth'. '*Fines Morrison*... was Secretary of State to the Lord *Monjoy*, our chief Governour, in the Reign of *Queen Elizabeth*', says Sheridan, so he 'had the best oportunity, of knowing the State of this Nation at that time.' An Irish rebellion had to be quelled. It was led by ringleaders of English extraction, a pattern which seems to have remained consistent in Irish history to the time of Parnell and of Yeats (or at least a perceived pattern, since Sheridan, following Spenser, was wrong about the English origin of some of the leaders). A decision was made in England to flood Ireland with base coin, subduing the rebels by ruining the economy, a trial run, Sheridan implies, for the more recent project of Wood's halfpence, which Swift, writing as the Drapier, had defeated. The kingdom was 'reduced to Famine, in so much, that all the publick Roads were strowed with Dead Carcases of miserable Wretches, whose Mouths were Green (as the Author expresses it) with their last meal of Grass'.[116]

Sheridan's intention is to maximize the pathos, and he simplifies the situation, both in respect to Fynes Moryson, and by comparison with any use Swift came to make of the cannibal story. For this passage, which precedes the cannibal revelation, insinuates an impression of the Irish as cattle, who eat grass. It is not innocent. Even those English writers who wrote compassionately about the Irish had a strong tendency to think of them as subhuman or bestial. Moryson's own text gives a harshly specific account of outlandish consumptions which goes some way beyond Sheridan's suggestion of vaguely bovine victims passively grazing to death: 'no spectacle was more frequent in the Ditches of Townes, and especiallie in wasted Countries, then to see multitudes of these poore people dead with their mouthes all coloured greene by eating nettles, docks, and all things they could rend up above ground.'[117] The feverish energies seem a lot more like the Yahoos eating roots and tearing their food with their teeth than like crushed defenceless paupers after 'their last meal of Grass'. Sheridan's pastoralized version also omits the non-vegetarian elements in the diet of the starving Irish, 'unsavourie birds of prey,... Horseflesh, and other things unfit for mans feeding', to which the Yahoos feeding on the 'Flesh...of Asses and Dogs, and now and then a Cow dead by Accident or Disease', and generally on the 'corrupted Flesh of Animals' (IV. ii, vii. 229, 261), are closer in general tendency than anything Sheridan is willing to quote.[118]

It is interesting that the starvation diet described by Moryson strongly resembles the tribal eating habits of primitive peoples, including Amerindians, as described by (often unfriendly) European observers. There was an established rhetoric which assimilated 'savage' eating habits to the diets of impoverished populations, and to the outlandish foods consumed, often as a prelude to cannibalism, in states of siege or of starvation at sea. Thevet disgustedly describes his American savages as eating wild beasts, rats of all sorts and sizes, large toads, and crocodiles, as well as wild roots and herbs. A less exotic or more European counterpart is Léry's account of the diet of horses, blood of horses (also a reputed Scythian and Irish food), cats, dogs, rats, mice, as well as herbs and poisonous roots, consumed by the starving citizens of Sancerre: a description of which Swift offered a simplified generic model in *Intelligencer*, No. 19, the immediate successor to Sheridan's essay on Moryson, in which he asserted 'that *Rats*, and *Cats*, and dead *Horses*, have been bought for *Gold*, in a Town besieged'.[119] The essay is one in which the economic situation of the Irish is compared to that of '*wild Indians*', except that 'the *Indians* enjoy the Product of their own Land'. Swift's agenda here is not principally to make ethnic points but to complain that Ireland is so short of money that, like Indians, the Irish may be forced 'to truck and barter'. But likening the Irish to Amerindians was common practice, whether on the subject of their sorry plight or their savage ways, and a powerful haze of ambivalence as between pity and scorn is a licensed feature of many writings on such themes. More highly charged examples will be considered later.

Agrippa d'Aubigné, perhaps the most compassionate of all commentators on the calamities of the French religious wars, has a formulation which provides the operative link between compassion and contempt:

> Car pour monstrer comment en la destruction
> L'homme n'est plus un homme, il prend refection
> Des herbes, de charongne et viandes non-prestes,
> Ravissant les repas apprestez pour les bestes;
> La racine douteuse est prise sans danger,
> Bonne, si on la peut amollir et manger;
> Le conseil de la faim apprend aux dents par force
> A piller des forests et la robbe et l'escorce.

For, to show how in destruction man is no longer a man, he nourishes himself with herbs, carcases and uncooked meats, snatching meals fit for beasts. The doubtful root is taken without hesitation, good if it can be softened and eaten. The counsels of hunger teach strength to teeth, for ransacking both the husks and the barks of forests.[120]

Hunger drives people to eat food fit for beasts and gives them the animal strength, for example, to bite the barks of trees, with some of the same ravenous energy Fynes Moryson was to perceive in the rending and gnawing of the starving Irish. 'L'homme n'est plus un homme': the perception readily shades into what gets said about savages, and into the censorious horror Léry expresses when a citizen of Sancerre experiences so much as a cannibal thought.

Léry was not alone in thinking that cannibalism might not be condoned even for survival, Montaigne's invocation of the Stoics and of Juvenal being (on this as on other points) almost certainly a minority view.[121] The more common doctrine, summarized by Anthony Pagden, held that 'every man who ate—even for survival—foods which were, by their nature, inappropriate to his species was guilty of an act of self-defilement'. This applied as much to the mores of conquered savages as to starvation victims in Europe, throwing the two into a poignant symmetry. 'The Church in Peru made an effort to punish anyone found eating lizards or fleas "or licking the plates off which they eat".' The Catholic Church seems no longer to hold this position. At the time of the Andes air disaster in 1972, it was concerned to reassure the survivors that the eating of their dead comrades had been entirely legitimate under the menace of starvation, though it also had to disabuse them of any notion that their cannibal acts had a Eucharistic significance.[122] But in the sixteenth century, whether in Spanish America or in Europe, the idea that starvation precipitated a reversion to tribalism or bestiality was commonplace among both Catholics and Protestants. For all d'Aubigné's tenderness over the suffering victims of civil war, a Protestant version of the same thinking seems present in 'L'homme n'est plus un homme' and undoubtedly animates Léry's responses at Sancerre.

Moryson was well within this tradition in expressing not only pity but a form of disgust. His words are well within the traditional territory of ethnic slurs based on savage eating habits and outlandish foods,[123] territory familiar in the discourse of Amerindian conquest, and as old as ethnic divisions, whose memorable fictional manifestations include the Yahoos and, over a century later, the Unclean Eaters (*mangeurs de choses immondes*) of Flaubert's novel, *Salammbô*. Flaubert's example is of interest, because this pathetic and disgusting tribe, one of the few invented details in the closely researched local colour which Flaubert used for his

North African setting, is both a named people among others, though not like the others historically attested, and through its unusual and unlocalized name, a vaguely universal type of humanoid untouchable. This may be compared to the way in which the Yahoos simultaneously evoke the Irish (the resemblances between them and the Irish as portrayed in Swift's non-fictional writings at the time are a commonplace of Swift studies)[124] and stood officially for the detritus of a human race stripped of polite or rational accretions.

The ethnic slur of unclean eating is, in both cases, at once tribe specific and an expression of distaste for the whole human species, an outlook Swift and Flaubert had in common in ways and to a degree probably not matched by other writers. As so often, Swift went a step further in the invention of unnaturalnesses. The Yahoos, in addition to their 'normal' habits of obscene eating, take the forbidden consumption of food 'inappropriate to [their] species' into an unusual domain of trans-specific perversion. For example, 'they would privately suck the Teats of the *Houyhnhnms* Cows' (IV. ix. 271). The habit seems related to, but should not strictly be confused with, the episodes of the Brobdingnagian monkey who took Gulliver 'for a young one of his own Species' and 'held me as a Nurse doth a Child she is going to suckle', and of the Yahoo female who wishes to mate with him, which seem designed to suggest that the human creature is both biologically close to species it considers inferior, and even more specifically akin to the Yahoos (II. v. 122; IV. viii. 266–7). Something of the same impression is generated in the cannibal episode in chapter xiv of *Salammbô*, where starvation and cannibal transgression engender some unnatural lusts, but the strangely moving power of Flaubert's scene differs greatly from the tart satiric reductions to which Swift subjects the Yahoos on this matter. Swift put a quizzically perverse spin on the theme of unclean eating, in a portrait of an unaccommodated humanity designed as of general import, but drawing its particulars from images of Irish as well as Amerindian savages.

Fynes Moryson, a century before Swift, was registering harshly mixed sentiments about the Irish, which he, like Swift, inherited from the general tenor of English commentary on Ireland, including Spenser's *View of the Present State of Ireland*, whose title prefigures that of Swift's own *Short View*. These are difficult and problematic feelings, not usually amalgamated with the sentimental simplicity of a Sheridan and not often fully and openly acknowledged. Pity for oppressed races is seldom free of contempt on the oppressor's side. If Moryson's contempt was at best subtextual, Swift's was overtly aggressive, and he did not need Moryson to teach him anything in that line. The savage Yahoos not only resemble Swift's descriptions of the savage Irish in non-fictional contexts, but Swift elsewhere, both before and after the *Intelligencer*, reported on Irish eating habits (including the Irish/ Scythian habit of drinking the blood of horses) in the highly charged blend of pity and disgust which is part of a received discourse, usually more concerned with cultural point-making than dietetic discriminations.[125]

Moryson's remark about mouths green with grass-chewing has another highly charged subtext, embodying an old contradiction. It anticipated Swift's mock-rhetoric in *A Modest Proposal*, in which the Irish are spoken of both as herds of cattle and as cannibals, and activates a famous unresolved equation in the literature of cultural or ethnic defamation. Part of the trick is to describe the victim as bestial, and then to instance cannibalism as a sign of this, even though the example of animal behaviour initially registered might not even be carnivorous, let alone cannibal. Secondly, the insinuation of cannibalism as subhuman or bestial, in a familiar rhetorical slippage, runs against an opposite perception, often used in denunciations of humans as a species, that it is humans who, in the entire animal kingdom, are alone inclined to cannibal acts. Dog don't eat dog. The famous tag that man is a wolf to man, found in Erasmus, Rabelais, and others, usually means not that man eats man as wolf eats wolf, but that man eats man as wolf eats sheep or lambs.

There is a traditional association of wolves with the para-cannibalisms of human exploitation and cruelty, readily invoked in adaptations of the myth of Lycaon from Plato to d'Aubigné, or the Iliadic idea of the king who devours his people, which reappears in Erasmus and More, and in d'Aubigné's denunciation of kings who 'Du troupeau domesticq sont les loups sanguinaires'.[126] It is the usage of Las Casas, when he speaks of the Spaniards as resembling wolves (or lions or tigers) eating sheep or lambs, a common image for Amerindians, used with great pastoral tenderness in his vocabulary, and of Léry, speaking of Protestants fleeing from Catholic persecutors.[127]

Like other cannibal-related imagery, dogs and wolves were used to illustrate extremes of cruelty or exploitation, in sexual and parental as well as economic and political contexts, whether or not cannibal activity was also involved in a literal sense. Its frequency in French sixteenth-century writing seems striking.[128] In the domain of political metaphor, d'Aubigné imagines the villages of France overrun by wolves and foxes, in a context which evokes not only general cruelty and oppression, but the brutalizing of victims by their reduction to obscene eating practices ('L'homme n'est plus un homme', and its hint of man becoming, as in the proverb, a wolf to man). Villages are devastated, their houses destroyed and emptied, and perhaps even literally taken over by beasts: 'Les loups et les renards et les bestes sauvages / Tiennent place d'humains, possedent les villages'.[129]

Léry, schooled by Eucharistic quarrels and thus more alive than most to the figurativeness of figurative language, described the cannibal Ou-ëtaca Indians as 'comme chiens & loups', meaning not that dogs and wolves ate each other but that these Indians ate their meat raw, like beasts. When he described the anthropophagy of the Catholics at Auxerre, who ate the grilled pieces of a Protestant's heart, 'assouuissans leurs rage comme chiens mastins', his point was that they tore into their prey like enraged mastiffs. When he had to make himself clear to the *quidam* at Sancerre who asked if it was permissible *in extremis* to eat the buttock of a dead man, Léry, repelling the 'demande...odieuse', had no hesitation over the zoological facts: 'je lui alleguay les bestes pour exemple, et les loups qu'on dit qui ne se mangent l'un l'autre.'[130] That wolves do not eat each other seems to be the view of modern zoologists, as is the old perception that humans are the main if not the only eaters of their own kind, so that, running against the rhetoric which says cannibals are bestial, is an opposite tradition, that humans are worse than beasts, who do not eat their own kind. Its most powerful early expression is Juvenal's fifteenth satire.[131]

This version of the topos man-is-worse-than-beasts seems to merge with a more general complaint about man's inhumanity to man. When Erasmus, in his discussion of the adage *Dulce bellum inexpertis* ('war is sweet to those who have not tried it'), applied it to warfare, and to the modern horrors of gunpowder war especially, he seems to have deliberately revised Juvenal in intimating that the deeper and more appalling human atrocity was not cannibalism (those, so to speak, were the good old days), but the new evils of hellish artillery (gunpowder was commonly spoken of as the invention of the devil). A similar point is made in a passage of Boileau's eighth *Satire*, specifically imitating Juvenal's fifteenth, but replacing cannibalism by gunpowder war.[132] Montaigne applied this topos in a better-known way, equally aware of Juvenal, whom he cites on a related matter in 'Des cannibales', but going on to articulate the famous paradox that Europeans with their wars and civil wars are more savage than the savages and more cannibal than cannibals. Montaigne is not the first to say this, even in the discourse of Amerindian conquest, and the cultural *tu quoque* which equates the tyrant or conqueror with the cannibal barbarian or worse is found in a rudimentary form in Homer's 'people-devouring king' (*demoboros basileus*), more fully in Plato, and later still in the dialogue between early Christians and their persecutors, where it partly revolved around the issue of Eucharistic practices, as it came even more strikingly to do at the time of the Amerindian debate.[133]

Indians, Irish, and the Scythian Myth

The association of imputations of bestiality and of cannibalism was problematic, but only in a strict logic abstracted from the actual energies of defamatory practice. European commentators like Thevet had no difficulty in calling Indians bestial (non-rational, unclothed, subhuman, eating wild roots, making mourning noises like dogs and cats), as well as cannibal. Indeed Thevet stumbled on the idea that their cannibalism made them worse than beasts, without noticing that it also proved them to be human.[134] (There was also a table-turning or antithetical dis-course, which described the oppressors of Indians, or of French Protestants, as worse than beasts, analogous to the reversal which portrays the Homeric or Platonic tyrant, or the persecutors of Christians, or the sixteenth-century conquerors of cannibals, as the real eaters of men).[135]

In the cannibal allegory of Swift's *Modest Proposal*, a similar coexistence of bestiality and cannibalism is effortlessly pre-supposed, Swift's idea of the Irish as bestial, or subhuman, the so-called *mythe animal*, being reflected in a vocabulary of breeders, saleable commodities, carcases, and 'a Child, *just dropt from its Dam*'.[136] The built-in cannibal imputation was assisted by an ancient notion, found in the Greek geographer Strabo and in English writers, as well as Las Casas, that the Irish were literally anthropophagous. They were said to be descended from the Scy-thians, whose cannibal habits are reported as early as Herodotus, and who are deemed by a tendentious etymology to be the ancestors of the modern *Scoti* or Irish.[137] Amerindians were also said to be descended from the Scythians, who in the Renaissance often stood as the type of absolute barbarian.[138] As Lestringant pointed out, Montaigne distinguished their cannibalism, derived from a 'seul appétit bestial', from the ritual vengeance of the Tupinamba.[139] Montaigne's own words were gentler, 'pour s'en nourrir'. A page earlier in 'Des cannibales' he compared the

Scythian and Tupinamba habit of burning or cutting to pieces false prophets, evidently without disapproval (the passage is discussed in Chapter 4), and in general does not seem to treat Scythians any worse than many other peoples whose customs differ from 'ours'.[140] In 'Des destriers', 'Of war horses' (I. xlviii), he records the habit of drinking the blood of horses, under necessity at war, a common perception of the Irish diet in Swift's time and earlier.[141]

The savage or cannibal Irish are featured in English writers like Spenser and Camden, and there are significant parallels between English descriptions of the Irish and European descriptions of Africans and Amerindians, a standard colonial discourse.[142] Sir John Temple, father of Swift's patron, spoke of them in 1646 as 'living like beasts, biting and devouring one another', a common and perhaps intentional telescoping of the notions of bestiality and a specifically human worse-than-bestiality.[143] This language gets straight into the Yahoos of *Gulliver's Travels*, whose physical characteristics are also expressly said to be those 'common to all savage Nations' (i.e. flat face, depressed nose, large lips, wide mouth, etc., IV. xii. 230), traceable more or less indiscriminately to Amerindian, African, and Asian stereotypes, as described in numerous travel narratives, except of course that the Yahoos are not cannibal. A writer of 1836 even reported the Irish as having depressed noses.[144] In particular, the Irish were described in ways which were 'point by point...paralleled in writing about the American Indians', including bestiality, cannibalism, the Scythian parallel, modes of dress, building, and warfare, and their animal war-cries. Many New World explorers, including Ralegh and Drake, also had experience of Irish affairs. England's colonization of Ireland taught lessons applied in the New World, just as the Spanish experience in America had guided English behaviour in Ireland. Cromwell's ideas for Irish rule seem to have been influenced by the Spanish treatment of Indians, and he sold many Irish into West Indian servitude. (There is an allusion in *A Modest Proposal* to Irishmen selling 'themselves to the *Barbadoes*'). Sometimes the identification carried opposite sympathies.

Richard Brinsley Sheridan's *Pizarro* (1799), with its several political targets, has an Irish subtext. The persecuted Amerindians are in part an allegory of the Irish, with the conquistadors driven out at the end. But the harsh view seems to have remained dominant.[145] An Englishman in 1652 said 'we have...Indians in Cornwall, Indians in Wales, Indians in Ireland'. There is some evidence, though 'accurate only up to a point', that Ireland was seen as 'an eastern extension of the New World, with the Gaelic Irish cast as the local Red Indians'. Fynes Moryson spoke of it as a 'famous Iland in the Virginian Sea'.[146] A totally innocent version of what seems to be the same confusion, in reverse form, was reported by an American sea-captain, encountering the son of a *Bounty* mutineer on a small Pacific island as late as 1808. The young man asked him, 'where is America? Is it in Ireland?'.[147]

Swift inherited this tradition, in which, more often than not, the comparison worked to the discredit of both parties. His own assimilations of Irish and Indians, in *Intelligencer*, No. 19, seem at first sight to be an exception, since they have to do with Irish poverty and English exploitation and register compassion for an Irish predicament said to be even worse than that of the Indians. He says that those Irish emigrants to America who have not 'Dyed miserably in their Passage' are likely to be settled by the English in the 'Tract of Ground, which lyes between them, and the *Wild Indians*', as the Romans included 'some barbarous People...in their Armies, for no other service, than to blunt their Enemies Swords'. This use of the Irish 'as a Screen between his Majesty's *English* Subjects and the savage *Indians*' was again noted about two years later in the 'Answer to the Craftsman'.[148]

The bitterness about the oppression of the Irish natives is real.[149] But it is sparsely expressed, and usually mixed with gruff contempt for their laziness and ignorance, and the squalor of their mode of life. The victimization Swift took most to heart was that of the *colons* or settlers. He complained in *A Proposal for the Universal Use of Irish Manufacture* (1720) of ministers and other officials who 'were apt, from their *high* Elevation, to look *down* upon this

Kingdom, as if it had been one of their *Colonies* of *Out-casts* in *America'*. Needless to say, this passage is not protesting at the analogy of Irish and Amerindian, but deploring the fact that the English settlers in Ireland were being treated, not like Indians, but like the Dissenting or criminal riff-raff who fled or were transported to America. The American comparison occurs in a different form in *A Letter to the Lord Chancellor Middleton*, dated 26 October 1724, where he complains of people from England who know little more of Ireland 'than they do of *Mexico*; further than that it is a Country subject to the King of *England*, full of Boggs, inhabited by wild *Irish Papists'*, and who think 'it were better for *England* if this whole Island were sunk into the Sea'. Edward Said thinks Swift is complaining that the Irish natives are being caricatured in the same way as 'African and Asian peoples' are today, but he does not quote the whole statement. The concern, also expressed a few days earlier in the *Letter to the Whole People of Ireland*, dated 13 October, is not mainly over any slur on the natives (or even the idea that they should be 'sunk into the Sea') but over the fact that people like himself are being confused with them.[150] The distinction Swift insists on in both passages, incidentally, tends strongly to reinforce the view that the much-debated 'Whole People' does not include the natives, about whom the *Letter to Middleton*, rebutting the opinion that Ireland is overrun by wild Papists, says reassuringly that they are 'as inconsiderable, in Point of Power, as the Women and Children'.[151]

It is true that as early as the *Proposal* of 1720, and *a fortiori* in the later Irish tracts, Swift also registers complaints about the conduct of the settlers themselves, an evolution reaching its peak in *A Modest Proposal*. But the Amerindian parallel remained, even in that work, mainly concerned with the natives, and when he mimicked the callous references to them as *'our Savages'*, he was pointing out aspects of their way of life (e.g. that their 'Children are seldom the Fruits of Marriage', and their indifference to the fact) which he and others viewed as typical examples of Irish barbarism. Swift referred to 'the savage old Irish' in his

correspondence, distinguishing them from the English population of Ireland.[152] Such passages are not far, in either sentiment or
idiom, from Thevet's references to 'nos sauvages', though the
humane and generous commitment of Swift's Irish writings sets
him off from Thevet's callous obtuseness.

As to Indians, Swift unfailingly refers to them as 'savage' or
'wild', from the time when the author of the *Mechanical Operation
of the Spirit* (1704), a correspondent of 'the *Literati* of *Tobinambou*',
referred to the 'wild *Indians*' as devil-worshippers, to the Irish
writings of 1728–30. In *A Modest Proposal* the Irish love of their
country is actually said to fall short even of '*the Inhabitants of*
TOPINAMBOO', and neither they nor the Tupinamba would have
much grounds for satisfaction at any of these comparisons.[153]
Locke had used the same instance, citing '*Tououpinambos*' from
Léry to make a point about ideas of numbers among 'Americans'.
This typical, and typifying, choice of the Tupinamba as generic or
representative reflects a habit which goes back to the early sixteenth century and survives into the twentieth, as is frequently
seen in verbal and visual depictions of Indians from both South
and North America.[154] Montaigne himself is evidence of this
habit. Like Locke, he evidently got much of his ethnographic
information from Léry, and it may be that, though he never used
the name in his essays, the 'Tupinambization' of the Amerindian
was reinforced by the classic status of 'Des cannibales' in the literature of empire and the history of ethnography. For example,
when Bougainville first landed in Tahiti on 6 April 1768, and heard
'Indians' playing the flute and slowly singing '*une chanson sans
doute anacréontique*', he was almost certainly remembering, perhaps a touch sardonically, Montaigne's Indians, transplanted to
a South Sea paradise, a 'charming scene, worthy of the brush of
Boucher'.[155]

The pathos of the victimized Irish of *Intelligencer*, No. 19, serves
mainly, in fact, to bring out the viciousness of their English
exploiters, as that of the 'naked *Americans*' or the 'harmless People'
at the end of *Gulliver's Travels* is more concerned to expose the

European invaders than to extol or even describe the invaded (IV. xii. 295–6). Elsewhere in *Gulliver's Travels*, the Yahoos, who resemble both Indians and Irish, offer little scope for kind feelings towards subject races. When the Modest Proposer invokes the cannibal expertise of 'a very knowing *American* of my Acquaintance in *London*', in what might be thought of as an ironic variant of Montaigne's conversations with Amerindians in Rouen, and of the point in 'Des cannibales' that the Indians have more to teach Europeans than vice versa, the evidence similarly suggests that neither the American teacher nor the Irish pupil has any reason to feel flattered.[156]

If the Yahoos have both Irish and Indian associations, they are not, like the Irish of *A Modest Proposal*, actually cannibal, though they do eat disgusting foods. *Gulliver's Travels* does no more than flirt with the cannibal theme. Thus Gulliver, helped by the Sorrel Nag in Houyhnhnmland, makes things of Yahoo skin, as humans do with the skins of beasts, engendering a crypto-cannibal *frisson*. This comes into its own in *A Modest Proposal*, where it is suggested that if the proposal of eating the babies were adopted, then the manufacture of such by-products as 'admirable *Gloves for Ladies*, and *Summer Boots for fine Gentlemen*' would become possible. In *Gulliver's Travels*, the allegory of using Yahoo skins is presented as a matter of what men do to beasts, while in the *Modest Proposal* it is what humans do to humans (and what the Scythians were said to do in Herodotus).[157]

At this point, one misconception should be cleared up. *A Modest Proposal*, contrary to uninformed perceptions, is not predominantly concerned with what the English do or might do to the Irish, but with what the Irish do or might do to themselves. The allegory asks to be translated into various ironies about the self-destructive political, social, and economic behaviour of the Irish, but the core of the imagery goes back to the old imputation of Irish cannibalism. Fynes Moryson, of whom Swift was at the very least recently made aware or reminded, had painfully opened up a literal dimension of this, just as the cannibal acts under siege in the French religious wars opened up a literal potential in Montaigne's argument that Europeans are more cannibal than the cannibals. How Swift and Montaigne responded to this potential is of great interest.

Immediately after his reference to the green-mouthed corpses, Sheridan says Moryson reports 'a very horrible Fact; too horrible indeed to mention' which he then proceeds to mention (unmentionability is a common theme in the not inconsiderable literature of cannibal behaviour, and Sheridan's phrases are limp with a fussy sensationalizing speechlessness worthy of Poe). But the facts are strong, even in his version:

a poor Widow of *Newry*, having six small Children, and no food to support them, shut up her Doors, Died through despair, and in about three or four Days after, her Children were found Eating her Flesh. He says farther, That at the same time, a discovery being made of Twelve Women, who made a practice of stealing Children, to Eat them, they were all burned, by order of *Sir Arthur Chichester*, then Governour of the *North* of *Ireland*. He likewise tells us, that the poor Butchers, and other Trades-men, who could not afford to part with their goods, at such Rates as the Army would have them, were daily Dragooned by them. That the poor Soldiers were also ruined for not being able to Buy their Cloathing here, they were obliged to be supplyed from *England*, at double Rates.[158]

This focuses on several Swiftian preoccupations about the Irish condition, and the irony of being forced to buy English clothing 'at double Rates' has an oblique aptness to Swift's castigation of the Irish (in *A Modest Proposal* and in earlier writings) for voluntarily buying English clothes instead of those of Irish manufacture.[159]

Sheridan's use of Moryson is the consistently simplifying one of portraying the Irish as victims, while Swift's agenda in the *Modest Proposal* was to inculpate them in their own misfortunes, a difference which the example of clothes illustrates with a fortuitous neatness. Sheridan goes on to give the story a fairy-tale ending. 'The good Natured, and Compassionate *Author*' is reported as saying that the Queen quickly 'put a stop to the base *Coin*' which was the cause of all the distress. In just this way did the 'Noble

Spirited DRAPIER' save his country from a later invasion of base
foreign coin. Therefore he should not be forgotten, but celebrated
on his birthday (for good measure, the birthday of 'the Great and
Glorious *King William'*, another saviour of the Irish, in this case
'from *Popery* and *Slavery'*, but underappreciated of late, also gets a
plug from Sheridan).[160]

The amiable Sheridan is more benign than Moryson in one way
and than Swift in another. His fairy-tale ending was a good deal
less straightforward in real life. James Woolley points out that
the Queen moderated the grant of coinage 'only slightly', and
Moryson gives a sour account of the outcome from the perspective of 'the Queene's servants' (even Sheridan let some of this
through). Most revealing is the unusual graphic frankness of
Moryson's portrayal of the cannibal acts, very different from
Sheridan's bland pathos. He speaks of

a most horrible spectacle of three children (whereof the eldest was not
above ten yeeres old), all eating and knawing with their teeth the entrals of
their dead mother, upon whose flesh they had fed twenty dayes past, and
having eaten all from the feete upward to the bare bones, rosting it continually by a slow fire, were now come to the eating of her said entralls in
like sort roasted, yet not divided from the body, being as yet raw. ...
Captaine Trevor & many honest Gentlemen lying in the Newry can
witnes, that some old women of those parts, used to make a fier in the
fields, & divers little children driving out the cattel in the cold mornings,
and comming thither to warme them, were by them surprised, killed and
eaten, which at last was discovered by a great girle breaking from them by
strength of her body, and Captaine Trevor sending out souldiers to know
the truth, they found the childrens skulles and bones, and apprehended
the old women, who were executed for the fact.[161]

This is not incompatible with, but in atmosphere quite far
from, Sheridan's 'good Natured, and Compassionate *Author'*.
The old child-eating women come over as more wicked than
wretched, and the children eating and gnawing at their mother's
entrails, 'not divided from the body, being as yet raw', have
something of the malign energy one later finds in the children of
Lord of the Flies or *John Dollar*. Woolley is right, and indeed a bit

cautious, when he says 'Sheridan distorts Moryson's account in some details'.[162]

When Swift came to write *A Modest Proposal* less than a year after Sheridan's paper appeared, he went beyond Sheridan and Sheridan's version of Moryson in his own way. This ironic fantasy, as is well known, argued that the sale for human consumption of small Irish children would rescue the economy, please the Irish nation, and prevent *'the Children of poor People in Ireland, from being a Burden to their Parents or Country; . . . making them beneficial to the Publick'.* It would 'be a great Inducement to Marriage', putting a stop to abortions, and making men 'as *fond* of their Wives, during the Time of their Pregnancy, as they are now of their *Mares* in Foal, their *Cows* in Calf, or *Sows* when they are ready to farrow; nor offer to beat or kick them, (as is too *frequent* a Practice) for fear of a Miscarriage'.[163] The passage is in some ways reminiscent of the young man in Yucatan who boasted, in Las Casas's *Short Account*, of working hard to make 'the local women pregnant so that they would fetch a higher price as slaves'.[164] Both register the brutal degradation of living under oppressive conditions, and both are concerned with the brutalities of using people as objects of trade. Las Casas's monster, however, is a profiteering Spaniard, not a victim. Las Casas's fury at this man goes with a huge compassion for the oppressed group, of which there is little sign in Swift, whose tendency is to regard the degradation as inherent in the victim, and as in some ways self-inflicted.

The cannibal metaphor extends to all levels of Irish society, indicted in all sorts of ways for behaviour that is self-destructive on a scale which simultaneously suggests that cannibalism is in line with their natural bent, and that it is the only remedy likely to find general acceptance, all others having already been proposed (by Swift among others) and rejected. The Irish in this definition include the Anglo-Irish *colons*, the commercial and political classes who resented their rulers in London almost as much as they despised the native rabble (in a situation replayed in this century among the Europeans in colonial Kenya, and in Algeria under

French rule). Swift sees himself as implicated in the predicament of the *colons*, and he shares many of their prejudices as well as hating their guts, along with those of the English bosses and the savage natives.[165]

The remarks about the latter, which are his fullest articulation of the beast imputation, are, as I have already suggested, a particularly pointed description of the domestic and family mores of the Irish poor, whose 'Children are seldom the Fruits of Marriage, *a Circumstance not much regarded by our Savages*'. Most of Swift's details of degraded parental behaviour and bad family habits were staple items of anti-Irish rhetoric.[166] The language mimicks the ethnic slurs of the more highly placed, but these include Swift himself many times over, and the mock-compassion for beggary in the *Proposal*, often mistaken by modern readers, is in fact a sneering impersonation of boneheaded and insensitive establishment planners mouthing sugared platitudes. Swift had a strong distaste for this species of phony benevolence, his real feeling about beggars being that they are fit 'to be rooted out off the Face of the Earth'.[167] This language was previously used of the Yahoos (IV. ix. 271–3), and earlier still of mankind itself by no less an authority than God (Genesis 6: 7), who proceeded to implement the idea in a great death by water, a matter I return to in Chapter 4.

'*Our Savages*', for whom the Proposer expresses tenderness, treat their children worse than their '*Sheep, black Cattle*, or *Swine*', because they have not yet picked up the idea of making children profitable. The cash-nexus is merely a homogenized extension of tribal greed of a kind familiar in Swift, who was fond of viewing 'modern' refinements as archetypal extensions of primitive depravity. 'Our *Scythian* Ancestors' fathered not only the Irish cannibals, but the *True Criticks* of *A Tale of a Tub*, a phenomenon of modern intellectual life he took pleasure in tracing to primeval slime.[168] Savages are savages, Irish and Indian and town and country. Amerindians, one of them an acquaintance of the Proposer, are living in modern London, not only replaying in an ironic mode the Indians in Rouen of 'Des cannibales', but evoking

perhaps the London gangs of home-grown savages called
Mohocks, about whom Gay wrote a play, who, as Swift told
Archbishop King, 'every Night cut some body or other over the
Face; and commit a hundred insolent Barbarities'. Swift compared
them to the Irish *Houghers*, gangs of lawbreakers who began
slaughtering cattle in the Connaught countryside in 1711 (the year
Gulliver entered Houyhnhnmland) and who have been proposed
as a not implausible source for the Yahoos.[169] American acquain-
tances can, at all events, be called upon for expert advice as to the
age at which children taste best and are most nourishing, 'whether
Stewed, Roasted, Baked, or *Boiled'*, the Proposer adding, from his
own experience of European refinements, evidently unexplored
by the 'American', that he thinks 'it will equally serve in a *Fricasie,*
or *Ragoust'*.[170]

England, often reproached by Swift for its treatement of Ireland,
is only marginally a target in *A Modest Proposal*. It is twice referred
to at the end, when the Proposer says his scheme has the particular
advantage that,

as it is wholly new, so it hath something *solid* and *real*, of no Expence, and
little Trouble, full in our own Power; and whereby we can incur no Danger
in *disobliging* ENGLAND: For, this Kind of Commodity will not bear
Exportation; the Flesh being of too tender a Consistence, to admit a long
Continuance in Salt; *although, perhaps, I could name a Country, which would
be glad to eat up our whole Nation without it.*[171]

The double sarcasm about England is bitter, but it is also offered as
an afterthought, subsidiary to the main point, which has to do
with the special commendability of the proposal to the Irish, just
the kind of thing they can do by themselves and carry out suc-
cessfully and profitably.

Sheridan's crude and well-meaning little essay hardly accounts
for this network of intensities in *A Modest Proposal*. Its routine
pathos does not reappear in Swift, except as the mock-pathos of
the Projector, surveying the 'melancholly Object' of 'the *Streets,*
the *Roads,* and *Cabbin-doors* crowded with *Beggars* of the Female
Sex', or parading his objection to cannibalizing older children on

the grounds that the meat of males is too tough, that the females are more useful as breeders (an idea which may derive from perceptions about Amerindian practice), and that 'some scrupulous People might be apt to censure such a Practice (although indeed very unjustly) as a little bordering upon Cruelty; which, I confess, hath always been with me the strongest Objection against any Project, how well soever intended'.[172]

But if Swift unsimplified Sheridan, what did he do about Sheridan's simplification of Moryson? The animus against the Irish that drove him to the exasperated version of the cannibal slur that is *A Modest Proposal* can only have been strengthened by literal evidence of so shocking a kind as is revealed even in the sentimental rendering by Sheridan: strengthened in the suggestion that this is what the savages do anyway, or (equally pertinent) that the whole Irish nation is driving its poor to such things. (The perception of Irish self-destructiveness, whether malevolently, neutrally, or compassionately conceived, was routinely expressed in cannibal terms, from Spenser's scheme for subduing them in such a way that they will 'quicklye Consume themselves and devour one another', to Stephen Dedalus's description of Ireland as 'the old sow that eats her farrow').[173] If Swift consulted Moryson's original, he would have found a note of contemptuous horror, akin to his own feelings, and in line with the general run of comments by articulate Englishmen like Spenser or Camden. If he allowed no trace of either Moryson's or Sheridan's literalism, it cannot be from any access of tenderness to anyone likely to come under the purview of his satire.

The cannibal imputation has been a staple of ethnic defamation since as far back as Homer. There is a corresponding pudeur over imputations of it to oneself or one's own people in any literal sense (it is said that even tribes known to practise ritual cannibalism are given to denying it and to imputing the practice to their neighbours, a matter which is a prominent theme in Melville's *Typee*).[174] This may help to explain why cannibal metaphors, e.g. to describe cruel or exploitative behaviour, are felt to be powerful, but seldom allowed to get out of hand through unduly literalizing implications. Swift's fable, showing the Irish to be fit for a cannibal economy, is perhaps the most uncompromising use of the cannibal slur ever directed at them in modern times. There is no sign of a desire to moderate or soften the attack, but although the evidence of literal enactment offered obvious reinforcement to the fable, Swift made sure that the metaphorical boundaries were not crossed.

A similar phenomenon may be observed in Montaigne, arguing that Europeans are more barbaric than the barbarians. At the very moment when he asserts that it is better to eat a dead man than a live one, he almost pointedly stops short of saying that eating their own people is what his countrymen do, notwithstanding recent cases of the kind reported by Léry in his books on Sancerre and on Brazil, the latter of which evidently influenced Montaigne's thinking about Amerindians (as it later became part of the ethnographic formation of Lévi-Strauss).[175] Montaigne's relation to Léry may have been similar to that of Swift to Moryson in that the lesser author in each case provided the explicit examples which the greater refused to exploit. It is one of history's symmetries that Sheridan, who mediated Moryson to Swift, may also have devoted himself to a translation of Montaigne, and is likely to have had conversations with Swift about him.

2   The Savage with Hanging Breasts
Gulliver, Female Yahoos,
and 'Racism'

'A young Female *Yahoo*...inflamed by Desire'

One day, towards the end of his narrative about the land of the Houyhnhnms, Gulliver is, as we would nowadays say, sexually harassed by a female Yahoo, one of those bestial humanoids who live in the country of the rational horses. It is an 'exceeding hot' day, and he asks his Houyhnhnm 'Protector', the Sorrel Nag, for permission to bathe in the river:

He consented, and I immediately stripped myself stark naked, and went down softly into the Stream. It happened that a young Female *Yahoo* standing behind a Bank, saw the whole Proceeding; and inflamed by Desire, as the Nag and I conjectured, came running with all Speed, and leaped into the Water within five Yards of the Place where I bathed. I was never in my Life so terribly frighted; the Nag was grazing at some Distance, not suspecting any Harm: She embraced me after a most fulsome Manner; I roared as loud as I could and the Nag came galloping towards me, whereupon she quitted her Grasp, with the utmost Reluctancy, and leaped upon the opposite Bank, where she stood gazing and howling all the time I was putting on my Cloaths.

This was Matter of Diversion to my Master and his Family, as well as of Mortification to my self. For now I could no longer deny, that I was a real *Yahoo*, in every Limb and Feature, since the Females had a natural Propensity to me as one of their own Species: Neither was the Hair of this Brute of a Red Colour, (which might have been some Excuse for an Appetite a little irregular), but black as a Sloe, and her Countenance did not make an Appearance altogether so hideous as the rest of the Kind; for, I think, she could not be above Eleven Years old. (IV. viii. 266–7)

One of the effects of this episode, which has many resonances and *frissons*, is that it reverses the standard scenario of courtship (perhaps to be perceived as a Western or 'civilized' one), in which it is the male who makes the passes.[1] The Yahoo girl's youth ('she could not be above Eleven Years old') also reverses a more recent scenario of our culture, in which it is the adult rather than the child who is expected to do the molesting. Swift perhaps did not have this second scenario in mind, but there seem to be further piquancies. As has recently been pointed out, Irish legislation of 1710, dealing with rape, decreed that carnal knowledge of a female under twelve, even with her consent, was a felony, punishable by death.[2] The female would-be rapist would thus, in Swift's Ireland, be inflicting capital punishment on her victim. Twelve is also 'the marriageable Age' in the old Utopian Lilliput (I. vi. 62), and the age at which Yahoos, like slaves in the West Indies, were deemed 'fit for Service', unlike asses, who, more efficiently, could be used at the age of five (IV. ix. 273).[3] Eleven was evidently a defining date, violating most available codes.

The female Yahoo's youth is variously significant in the configuration of sexual imaginings in the story, and connects with that of other characters who show a sexual interest in Gulliver, including the Maids of Honour in Brobdingnag. The story has attracted the attention of those who are interested in Swift's psychobiography. The pattern of a reluctant male parrying the advances of a lustful female has been seen as a replay of some essential features of Swift's relations with Vanessa, as portrayed in *Cadenus and Vanessa*, a poem published a little before *Gulliver's Travels*, in the same year. And secondly it has been suggested that the Yahoo's tender age 'may be an allusion' to 'the extreme disparity in age' between Swift and Vanessa, 'who, though nearly 25 years his junior, fell in love with Swift. ... Gulliver's experience in the river seems almost like a grotesque parody of Vanessa's pursuit of Swift to Ireland (1714) and his discouragement of her sexual advances.'[4]

If biographical allegories are present at all, I assume they can only be a kind of impish assimilative tease, a joke so private that only intimates, possibly only the author himself, would be expected to identify it. Swift's other great love, Stella, whom he recalled first seeing 'at Sixteen, The brightest Virgin of the Green', was also considerably younger than Swift. The Yahoo female's extreme precocity would be a crude transformation of anything Swift ever imputed to either woman, and the pattern of teasingly eroticized teacherly avuncularity which Swift developed with both women is wholly outside the scope of the Gulliverian treatment. The odd concession that the Yahoo girl's 'Countenance did not make an Appearance altogether so hideous as the rest of the Kind', which Gulliver seems to attribute to her tender years, is hardly in the class of Swift's compliments to Vanessa's or even Stella's charms, but it is as much gallantry as Gulliver can afford, or ever proffers, to a Yahoo 'Brute'. It also echoes, whether knowingly or not, an idiom of sexual encounters with savages, as we shall see. The Yahoo's hair, 'black as a Sloe', may recall Stella's, 'blacker than a raven', but the special point that the Yahoo is not red-headed has nothing to do with Stella, and is a sarcasm for which Swift had prepared the ground on the previous page: 'It is observed, that the *Red-haired* of both Sexes are more libidinous and mischievous than the rest' (266).[5]

This bit of folklore about redheads had already been invoked in the poem 'The Author upon Himself' (1714), where Swift spoke scurrilously of the Duchess of Somerset and her red hair (ll. 1, 55). A legend existed that Judas, who supposedly had incest with his mother, was red-headed, which is held to explain the connection with lechery.[6] Characteristically, the Gulliverian 'Brute' isn't even red-haired, such is the concupiscence of that humanoid species. This is not a slur on females, or women. The real-life Vanessa, in a poem published the same year as *Gulliver's Travels*, was also much younger than the real-life Swift, and lusted after him, and since the Gulliverian episode has been seen as an allegory of that relationship, it seems apposite that she is never called a 'brute' or shown to behave like one, while the men around her are expressly cast in that role. She had the advantage of Swiftian tutoring, which enabled women to be as equal to men as Swift believed women were capable of being, and her lust for her tutor is balanced by a stand-offishness towards other beaux, whom she dismissed as having no 'Judgment, Knowledge, Wit, and Taste', which, 'she offer'd to dispute, / Alone distinguish'd Man from Brute'. Swift makes Vanessa report other women's predilections for 'A Dog, a Parrot, or an Ape, / Or some worse Brute in human Shape'.[7]

When Swift made Vanessa say these things about oafish suitors, he was replicating what she said to him in a letter of June 1722 about the guests of 'a great lady' she had been visiting:

their form's and gestures were very like those of Babboons and monky's they all grin'd and chatter'd at the same time…one of these animals snatched my fan and was so pleased with me that it seased me with such a panick that I apprehended nothing less than being carried up to the top of the House and served as a friend of yours was but in this one of their owne species came in upon which they all began to make their grimace's.[8]

Vanessa is alluding to the episode where the Brobdingnagian monkey carries Gulliver off 'to a Roof that was next to ours' (II. v. 122). As Harold Williams noted, the letter suggests that Vanessa had seen drafts of Book II and probably Book IV of *Gulliver's Travels*, and another scholar has argued that Vanessa's words show her early recognition of 'the resemblance of Irish society to that of the Yahoos'.[9] It is one of many places, in the writings of Swift and those who thought like him, where the brutishness of the savage Irish is seen to rub off on polite ruling groups. In Vanessa's letter, Yahoos of both sexes are in question, and the would-be ravisher of Vanessa is clearly male. Vanessa is no brute, but he is, and, as in the poem, the brutes would seem to be of both sexes, whom Vanessa evidently thinks of as ape-like Yahoos. In the world of *Gulliver's Travels*, the Yahoo brute who lusted after Gulliver, as Vanessa lusted after Swift, is both bestial and human, all too human.

That is Gulliver's special point. The girl's brutish lust is to mate with a human, a traditional litmus test of biological kinship: 'now

I could no longer deny, that I was a real *Yahoo*, in every Limb and Feature, since the Females had a natural Propensity to me as one of their own Species.'[10] I believe this episode was expressly planted by Swift to indicate that Gulliver's, and 'our', identity with the Yahoos is an objective fact of the narrative, and not merely a distorted projection of Gulliver's misanthropy. The Yahoos are also 'brutes' in the same sense as the natives of the African bush are to Kurtz or to Marlow in *Heart of Darkness*, eliciting the same troubled suspicion of radical kinship, and the same outbursts of murderous rejection. When Kurtz exclaims, in the famous delirious postscript, 'Exterminate all the brutes!', he is replaying a grisly commonplace of the literature of empire, ubiquitous in fiction as well as in the narratives or polemics of exploration and conquest, and manifested in the debate in the Houyhnhnm General Assembly as to 'Whether the *Yahoos* should be exterminated from the Face of the Earth' (IV. ix. 271).[11] Swift is appropriately but incompletely distanced from this idea. It is what several English writers proposed to do about the 'savage Irish' and corresponds with due obliquity to Swift's own explosions of rage against such groups as the nation's representers, or fat Irish women who wear English clothes, or bankers, or beggars, who ought, in velleities articulated in Swift's own name, to be shot, or hanged, or rooted out from the face of the earth.

This opens up a particular feature of the Yahoos, observed from another perspective in Chapter 1, that they are on the one hand a type of 'all savage Nations', specifically Irish savages and their recognized analogues, the Indians of America, inferior to 'us', and at the same time generically human, 'ourselves'. 'I observed, in this abominable Animal, a perfect human Figure; the Face of it indeed was flat and broad, the Nose depressed, the Lips large, and the Mouth wide: But these Differences are common to all savage Nations' (IV. ii. 230). Three things may be noticed: the teasing slippage between what is true of savages and what is generic to humankind; the idea that 'all savage Nations' look the same, with flat noses, thick lips, and so on; and the adoption, in a frame of generalized portrayal, of a markedly specific idiom of ethnographic observation, a parody of field-observation, as it were, in no particular field. When the Yahoo girl forces her attentions on Gulliver, and we are told that 'This was Matter of Diversion to my Master and his Family, as well as of Mortification to my self' (IV. vii. 267), it is hard not to sense a note of quasi-scientific curiosity in their amusement. There may also be a teasing echo of what humans sometimes do in Swift when contemplating obscene horrors: bombings and maimings in gunpowder wars, for example, enacted 'to the great Diversion of all the Spectators' (IV. v. 247).

But the analogy is only partial. There is a hint of malice, more Swift's than the Houyhnhnms', or at least of derision, in the Houyhnhnms' diversion. In the episode with the female Yahoo, the Houyhnhnms are not enjoying or applauding cruelty, but entertained, almost as anthropological observers, by a mildly surprising if not wholly unexpected piece of outlandish behaviour. Gulliver appears to them somewhat like the African fireman in *Heart of Darkness*, of whom Marlow says, not without admiration (in both senses), 'to look at him was as edifying as seeing a dog in a parody of breeches and a feather hat, walking on his hind-legs'. There is an overlapping of perspectives, in which the Houyhnhnm view of Yahoos as beasts merges with the book's other intimations that they are humanoid and their homologue Gulliver actually human. It probes, and exploits with satirical finesse, some of the man–beast analogies found in the travel-writers' crude efforts at ethno-zoology. A seventeenth-century traveller to Central America, Alexandre (or 'John') Exquemelin, found it 'delightful to see the female monkeys carry their little ones upon their backs, even just as the negresses do their children', or to watch them administering medication to their wounded, which caused 'in me great admiration, seeing such strange actions in those irrational creatures'.[12]

The prim Houyhnhnms sometimes seem to practise a form of *Nil Admirari*, but the master Houyhnhnm, on first observing Gulliver changing his clothes, had shown similar 'Signs of Curiosity and Admiration' (IV. iii. 237). It is the pleasurable wonder of the scientific observer at the quiddity of his material. On the sexual episode, the diversion strikes a less genial note. Though the passage also shares an ethnographic flavour with Exquemelin, it raises somewhat different aspects of the man–beast analogy. Part of the comedy for the Houyhnhnms is that of observing a trained circus animal, having previously been acquainted only with his counterpart from the bush. Since natives and animals are seldom entirely separate in the minds of ruling groups, this shades for the reader into another type of humour, reminiscent of a later vaudeville, which deals in the antics of a domesticated black sambo abruptly returned to a jungle habitat—remembering always that 'sambo' is here a white European male, 'our' representative. The equivocating and protracted tease, which assimilates humankind to its own despised subgroups, as well as to humanoid or animal analogues, is a Swiftian signature.

The Savage with Hanging Breasts

We know, at all events, that the Yahoos were deliberately drawn after some notion of a generic primitive. Throughout Book IV, they are presented in a series of *National Geographic* glimpses, the women carrying their infants on their backs (IV. ii. 230), with long hair hanging down and hanging breasts:

The Females . . . had long lank Hair on their Heads, and only a Sort of Down on the rest of their Bodies, except about the *Anus*, and *Pudenda*. Their Dugs hung between their fore Feet, and often reached almost to the Ground as they walked. (IV. ii. 223)

The last detail might seem a flourish of Swiftian caricature, or a wild flight of misogynistic body-hatred, but it is a standard travel book portrayal. Buffon was later to identify 'long and flabby' breasts as a definitional feature of the savage in the wild.[13] But travel-writers long before Swift provided examples of grotesquerie equal to or exceeding the description of female Yahoos. These are so frequent as to constitute a trade jargon, and, since Swift is sometimes associated with a highly charged recoil from the female body, it is useful to compare a fairly substantial sampling. Some pre-Gulliverian analogues include Heylyn's *Cosmographie* (1652), on Brazilians whose breasts came down to their knees; Richard Ligon (1657), on African slave women in Barbados: 'their breasts hang down below their navells, so that when they stoop at their common work of weeding, they hang almost down to the ground, that at a distance, you would think they had six legs'; Vincent le Blanc, in *The World Surveyed* (1660), on breasts slung over the shoulders; and a comment by Woodes Rogers about Indians of the Amazon region in *A Cruising Voyage Round the World* (1712), that it was 'a question whether the Women's Hair or Breasts be longest.'[14]

An especially large group of examples concerns the much mythologized and much maligned Hottentots. Hottentots were considered, along with Australian aborigines, to be the lowest specimens of humanity. Both peoples, unsurprisingly, have strong connections with the Yahoos. The Hottentots, as the default pariahs of travel-books, are a natural, well-documented source of *Gulliver's Travels*, and the Yahoos are near neighbours of the savages of Australia (New Holland), who try to kill Gulliver when he is expelled from Houyhnhnmland (IV. xi. 284). Buffon had Hottentots in mind when he discussed 'a savage man and an ape... viewed together'.[15] In the words of Sir Thomas Herbert, the people of the Cape were 'an accursed Progeny of *Cham*'. Herbert, whose *Travels* Swift owned in the first edition of 1634, and annotated with exuberant contempt, added that: 'The women give suck, the Vberous dugg stretched over her naked shoulder.' John Nieuhoff's *Voyages and Travels, into Brasil and the East-Indies*, which Swift also owned, again writing on Hottentots, says the women have 'long breasts... and when they are suckling their Infants, [their breasts] hang backwards over their shoulders'. Nathaniel Crouch's *English Acquisitions in Guinea & East-India* (?1686) describes a Cape people neighbouring the Hottentots: 'They carry their sucking Infants under Skins upon their backs, and their

Breasts hanging down like Bagpipes, they put them up with their hands that they may suck them over their Shoulders'. Closer to Gulliver's time, Francis Leguat, in a *New Voyage to the East-Indies* (1708), and Daniel Beeckman (1718), say that Hottentot women had 'nasty Duggs,...com[ing] down as low as their Navels', and 'long flabby breasts, odiously dangling down to their waist; which they can toss over their shoulders for their children to suck, whom they generally carry on their backs'.[16] Since the resemblance of humans to apes was seen, from Aristotle to Linnaeus, to include 'two pectoral [as distinct from ventral] mammae', breasts readily became a focus for the traditional ape analogies in descriptions of savages, and Hottentots seem to have been special beneficiaries. 'Naturalists' are reported to have held the view, which is not without its own folkloric embellishments, that the breasts of female apes were 'undesirably flabby and pendulous, resembling Hottentots', even though in reality 'apes have small, unremarkable mammae'.[17]

There is a freakish folkloric subtype. The narrator of Schouten's *Relation of a Wonderfull Voyage* (1619) says that, on Hoorn Island, 'the women were very unsightly both in face and bodie,...their brests long hanging downe to their bellies like lether satchels', an image varied to 'money bags' by William Lithgow about the Irish in 1620. The comparison with pouches, satchels, and similar objects recurs in many later texts, including several in South Pacific locations, where the Yahoos live, such as J. R. Forster's description in 1774 of old women whose breasts 'are flabby, broad, like an empty leather-bottle', and half a century later, Dumont d'Urville, on 'their dry dugs, pleated and pendent, [which] resemble old pouches' ('leurs mamelles sèches, plissées et pendantes, ressemblent à de vieilles besaces'). There were folkloric associations between breasts and bags, suggesting abundance, of which these images are a grim negative variant.[18]

The commonplace of hanging breasts is pictorially represented in the illustrations to de Bry's famous *Great Voyages* (pl. 1). Bernadette Bucher's Lévi-Straussian study of these illustrations, which is known in English under the title *Icon and Conquest* (1981), was originally published in French as *La Sauvage aux seins pendants* (1977). The verbal accounts, perhaps predictably, exceed the visual in grotesquerie, but Bucher's plates of South American and South Sea examples are representative of habits of mind shared by the travel-writers. The tradition continued well beyond the Renaissance voyages collected by de Bry. Once again, Hottentots get a lot of attention, in images included in Guy Tachard, *Voyage de Siam* (1686) and S. de la Loubère, *Du Royaume de Siam* (1691), and illustrations such as *Hottentot Woman of the Cape of Good Hope* by Moritz Bodenehr (1692) and those of others, several of which also show the woman carrying a child on her back. The illustrations of Peter Kolb's influential *Present State of the Cape of Good Hope* (published in German in 1719 and translated into Dutch in 1721 and English in 1731) and its translations show similar features.[19] They are also present in eighteenth- and nineteenth-century depictions of Australian and other South Pacific peoples by Thomas Watling, Augustus Earle, and others. The convention has continued in photography (pl. 2), including that of the *National Geographic*.[20]

The series of voyages published from the 1590s onwards by Theodore de Bry and his sons, with their collection of pictorial images, were in some ways the *National Geographic* of their day, except that engravings and woodcuts allowed even more scope for mythologizing than the 'realistic' selectiveness of the photographer's camera.[21] Indeed some photographic examples are especially striking since they only allow limited scope to the artist's powers of imaginative distortion and are consequently especially revealing about their selective agendas, which are not always disparaging in the mode of de Bry and his successors. Claude Lévi-Strauss, who started Bucher on her research, published about twenty photographs of bare-breasted indigenous Brazilian women in the sixty-three plates in *Tristes Tropiques* (1955), no more than a quarter of them belonging to the hanging type. Some of these, and many others, are reproduced in his recent book, *Saudades do Brasil* (1994), and include examples which don't belie de Bry's portraiture, and some almost lyrical studies of full-breasted young women, taken from what is self-consciously conceived as the Brazil of Léry and Montaigne. The captions to many of the photographs confirm an affectionate delight in these Indian peoples, especially their women and (usually female) children. In one picture, there is a long-breasted young woman with a puppy (*chiot*) nestling over her genitals and two with a small monkey on their head (a 'savage' counterpart to the fine ladies' lapdogs and pet monkeys of elegant drawing-rooms, a theme to which I shall be returning). Another caption speaks of the attraction of the Nambikwara people, despite their detestable reputation ('l'attrait qu'exerçaient les Nambikwara, nonobstant leur réputation détestable'), as largely due to their very young and graceful women.[22]

The feelings evoked by such captions are strongly reflected in the pictures themselves, which include not only an extensive collection of Nambikwara women and girls, but several women from Amazonas, old and young, with their pleasure in personal ornaments, and a dozen or so Tupi-Kawahib women. Even the photographs most strongly tending to the grotesque suggest a respect and affection for the subjects generally absent from the sixteenth- and seventeenth-century voyagers. You will not find in Lévi-Strauss anything like Bucher's plate of 1618 from an appendix to a report of Spilbergen's navigations, which shows the woman with breasts like leather pouches mentioned by Schouten and referred to earlier. This was a model for a somewhat doctored de Bry illustration of a *Kava Festival on Hoorn Island* (1619). In the 1618 illustration there is also a curiously aged child, one of many suggestions of the more or less monstrous in this tradition of portraiture, which disappears in the de Bry version.[23]

There were less extravagant ways of representing native women. The Vespuccian *Mundus Novus* (*c*.1502) and the *Letter* to Soderini (*c*.1505), as if pre-empting later accounts, both made a point of the fact that the lustful Amerindian women he encountered, and who are said to have been eager to offer themselves to him and his companions, did not have 'sagging breasts', despite frequent child-bearing.[24] As if to illustrate this, a late sixteenth-century engraving of *Vespucci 'Discovering' America* shows a solemn and unsexual Vespucci coming upon a figure of America as an eager, full-breasted, Germanically blonde female on a hammock (pl. 3), the antithesis of the many savages with hanging breasts in the verbal accounts of later travellers, and the illustrations of de Bry.[25] The Vespuccian remark suggests that as early as the beginning of the sixteenth century exceptions to the stereotype were thought to call for comment. This was still true a year or so before *Gulliver's Travels* appeared, when Defoe's *New Voyage Round the World* spoke of a South Pacific island queen: 'Her Breasts were plump and round, not flaggy and hanging down, as it is general with all the *Indian* Women, some of whose Breasts hung as low as their Bellies; but Sitting as Beautifully up, as if they had been lac'd up with Stays round her Body and below her Breasts, she had a broad Piece of a Skin of some curious Creature ... wrapped round her very tight ...'[26]

Half a century later, John Webber, who went as draughtsman on Cook's third voyage (1776–80), painted the Polynesian Princess Poedua in 1777, whose torso has the dignified and sensuous amplitude of a European tradition of portraiture typically reserved for goddesses and great ladies (pl. 4). J. R. Forster reflected, in his *Observations* (1778), that the shape of breasts, as perhaps with Defoe's Queen, was an issue of social rank in Tahiti itself: 'the gentle constriction of the upper part of the body, by the finer sorts of cloth in which the O'Taheitean women of quality gracefully wrap themselves, contributes likewise to keep the breasts high, and to prevent their flaccidity and pendulous state.' The description conforms with Webber's Poedua. Forster thought that it was not suckling practices, but 'the greater relaxation of the body in the women of the lower class, who are ... more exposed to the air and sun, being constantly naked above the waist', which contributed to the 'pendulous' state, though he thought women of some South Sea islands were less affected by this phenomenon than 'negroe-women'.[27] In this too his view seems confirmed by

Webber's portraiture, for if Poedua was a special case by virtue of her rank, his *Woman of New Holland*, carrying a child (pl. 5, also 1777), may stand as a less idealized representation, with a mannish face, but with a strong maternal body otherwise free of grotesquerie. New Holland (Australia) was said to be near Gulliver's Houyhnhnmland, and was the site of one of his Cousin Dampier's major voyages. The portrait shows a young mother with full hanging breasts and a child on her back, a more wholesome version than the grimly Rabelaisian verbal versions of the travel-writers.[28] The perception represented by this image, as by the Vespuccian accounts, also lies behind some more 'realistic' portrayals of native women, many of them carrying a child on their back, as natives (including sometimes fathers) are supposed to do. Examples are some New Guinea women by Diego Prado de Tovar in the early seventeenth century, or the strong-breasted Brazilian and Black women by Albert Eckhout in the 1640s, or a Californian woman in an illustration from George Shelvocke's *Voyage Round the World* (1726), published the same year as *Gulliver's Travels*.[29] These 'wholesomer' portrayals, however, sometimes bring unpleasant surprises. Eckhout's young *Tarairiu Woman* (1641), who exudes a sensuous maternal serenity, is carrying on her back not a child, but a basket with a human leg sticking out, evidently destined for a cannibal meal (pls. 6–7).[30]

But the tradition of hanging breasts, often (but not always) designed to degrade rather than idealize the native women, was a potent one. It survives in twentieth-century travel-writing, fiction, and poetry. Graham Greene's *Journey Without Maps* (1936) describes West African Kru women 'with their long hanging breasts uncovered'. Young girls, not just mature women, have 'dark hanging breasts', and the report does not simply register disgust: 'It was curious how quickly one abandoned the white standard. These long breasts falling in flat bronze folds soon seemed more beautiful than the small rounded European breasts.'[31] A similar expression of sexual arousal occurs, with a peculiarly explicit schematism, in Barry Unsworth's novel, *Sacred Hunger* (1992), whose setting is the slave-trade in the years 1752–65, and in which a major protagonist, Matthew Paris, is, like Gulliver, a ship's surgeon. The commercial unwisdom of purchasing 'women with dugs to their knees' comes up for comment more than once. In an episode involving Kru traders, a commercially undesirable woman with 'dugs down her belly' is paired with a young girl, 'hardly out of puberty, with high, small breasts and a thin down of pubic hair' (they turn out to be mother and daughter). Mr Barton, the first officer, thinks she is likely to be a 'hot little bitch', though he himself 'would rather rattle the older one. I like 'em matoor, they knows more tricks'. The prurient interest of the 'drop-breast woman' (at this point she is called 'full-breasted, with high muscular haunches, and slender legs') matches that of the unformed girl's, the hag's and the nymphet's, mother and daughter evidently projected as equally or comparably desirable.[32] The pairing is a replay of Greene's, and also of Gulliver's, whose Yahoo nymphet is the iconographic counterpart of the other females, whose 'Dugs hung between their fore Feet'.

Gulliver's Yahoo admirer is no more than eleven and we are not told anything about her breasts. In this she is unlike the general run of Yahoo females, and in fact conforms to a pattern in which the grotesquerie of hanging breasts, while commanding a special charge of attention, is countered by less spectacular, and less unappealing, examples. One variant, in the iconography of Cook's voyages, might be Webber's portrayals of the New Holland mother and the handsome full-breasted Princess Poedua, where the differentiation reflects differences of social rank rather than age. The Gulliverian episode is one in which the hag is countered by a nymphet rather than a princess. This Swiftian pattern is a downbeat version of a traditional one. It is remarkable how often reports of the pendulous grotesqueries of old women are juxtaposed with idealized stereotypes of youthful beauties. Richard Ligon, the mid-seventeenth-century writer who thought slave-women's breasts were so long that they looked as if they had six legs, also wrote of 'pretie young Negro Virgins . . . their breast round, firme, and beautifully shaped'. 'The Young Women have really fine breasts, but those of the old ones are flabby, broad, like an empty leather-bottle' is how Johann Forster put it in 1774. In a journal entry of 23 January 1941 in Nigeria Patrick White offered a version of the classic contrast between old black beggar-women, 'naked to the waist, with disgusting dugs' and 'young girls, apple-breasted and beautifully balanced'.[33] The photography of Lévi-Strauss's *Saudades do Brasil* also moves within the full range from hag to nymphet.

The image of the savage with hanging breasts has long been a staple of the *National Geographic*, a fact arrestingly brought out in Elizabeth Bishop's poem 'In the Waiting Room'. This tells of an episode when Bishop, aged almost seven, sees a copy of the magazine, on a visit to the dentist with her aunt. The magazine is full of the usual subjects, a volcano, cannibal doings ('A dead man slung on a pole— "Long Pig," the caption said'), and 'black, naked women' with 'horrifying' breasts.[34] The poem goes on to trace a gradual realization that she, her aunt (whose shocked voice she hears, only to realize it came from her own mouth), and the people in the magazine, are bound to one another by 'similarities' which amount to a deep sense of human oneness:

> What similarities—
> boots, hands, the family voice
> I felt in my throat, or even
> the *National Geographic*
> and those awful hanging breasts—
> held us all together
> or made us all just one?

The poem is at the opposite pole from Swift's treatment of Yahoo women in a superficial sense: it accepts rather than deplores a common humanity. But this common humanity, a Yahoo humanity, is one which Swift also recognizes, and asserts with a comparable intensity of awareness.

Such recycling or repetition of details, or even of specialized images, is typical of the ethnographic as much as of the topographical material in the literature of exploration, discovery, and conquest. It reappears in later anthropological studies, which report the deliberately induced elongation or distortion of breasts among peoples in many regions of the world, to improve efficiency in suckling, and as marks of beauty and maternal fecundity, even in young women. The recurrent analogy with bags or satchels, for all its grotesquerie, may itself correspond to ideas of richness or fertility: breast-shaped money boxes (and wine-cups) are traditional in several European countries. In some African or South American cultures, long hanging breasts are also associated with sorcery and witchcraft, much as in the depiction of hags and witches in medieval and Renaissance Europe, a mark of the profound ambivalence surrounding this motif.[35] Spenser's Duessa, whose 'dried dugs, like bladders lacking wind, Hong downe, and filthy matter from them weld', and who derives from Alcina in Ariosto, is representative of countless hags and witches. Both of them are seductive sorceresses who appear beautiful until unmasked, and both go back to the whore in Revelation 17: 16. A striking visual example is the figure of Old Age in Hans Baldung Grien's *The Ages of Man and Death* (pl. 8). In Baudelaire's hell, when Don Juan goes there, the women are displaying their hanging breasts and wailing. The most inventively extravagant imagery of the descriptions of savages can be matched in accounts of European women, as when the sixteenth-century Venetian courtesan Veronica Franco was described as having breasts so low that she could paddle a gondola with them (an allegation belied by one contemporary portrait of her).[36]

Swift's own whore, in 'A Beautiful Young Nymph Going to Bed', acquires the added grotesquerie of having to remove, at night, 'the Rags contriv'd to prop/Her flabby Dugs and down they drop' (ll. 21–2). In Fielding's *Amelia* the bawd Blear-Eyed Moll's 'vast Breasts had long since forsaken their native Home, and had settled themselves a little below the Girdle'. In a letter of 2 October 1939, Patrick White described the madam of a brothel in Halifax, Nova Scotia, as dressed 'in flowered chiffon with a bust reaching to her knees'.[37] The hag is never far away from the whore, or the earth mother, though earth mothers are not much in evidence in Swift. The presence of this grotesque iconography in descriptions of older whores and bawds outside primitive settings is an insistent and resourceful version of the ancient uneasy equation between the barbarian and the domestic mob, or 'race' and 'class'.

Hottentots and Irish

The Irish were traditional candidates for this equation. As early as 1620, William Lithgow brought them into the stereotype by reporting that Irish women suckle their children in the accredited breast-extending ways, and as a result have extravagantly long breasts from which money-bags could be manufactured by a good tanner, a detail significantly close to the accounts of Hottentots already cited. They

carry their Infants about their neckes, and laying the dugges over their shoulders, would give sucke to the Babes behinde their backes, without taking them in their armes: Such kind of breasts, me thinketh were very fit, to be made money bags for East or West-Indian Merchants, being more then halfe a yard long, and as wel wrought, as any Tanner, in the like charge, could ever mollifie such Leather.[38]

This grotesquerie, recently re-fantasticated in Hilary Mantel's *The Giant, O'Brien*, has many analogues, and may have helped to suggest the Modest Proposer's idea that from the skins of Irish infants could be made 'admirable *Gloves for Ladies*, and *Summer Boots for fine Gentlemen*', though that particular fantasy also has other connections.[39] The suckling posture described by Lithgow, which occurs repeatedly in descriptions of Hottentots and others, was sometimes said to flatten noses. The Yahoos, like 'all savage Nations', seem to have got their 'Nose depressed' by constant pressure of their face against their mothers' shoulders in infancy (IV. ii. 230). This explanation for the flat noses of savages was current before Swift, and was still in circulation in Buffon's time.[40] It is a curiosity of such mythologies that even flat noses have been attributed to Irish people.

The Yahoo resemblance to Hottentots is well established.[41] Its particulars include such folkloric commonplaces as the frequently reported Hottentot ritual of urinating on people, their supposed lack of language, the fact that (as the *Encyclopédie*, following many travellers' accounts, reported) they liked to eat *viandes infectées*, the equivalent of the corrupted flesh of animals which is part of the Yahoo's staple diet, and the habit of Hottentots and Bushmen of using poisoned arrows (not strictly a Yahoo practice, but one attributed by Gulliver to the neighbouring tribe among which he finds himself on first leaving Houyhnhnmland). Diderot urged the Hottentots to rebel by using their poisoned arrows against their oppressors.[42] Crouch's account of the Hottentots' near neighbours on the Cape might almost have come from *Gulliver's Travels*, though there is no evidence that Swift owned the book:

Both Sexes make coverings for their heads of Cow-dung mingled with a little stinking Grease, and besmear their Faces therewith; which makes their Company insufferable if they get the Wind of you; They eat rotten mouldy Biskets fit for nothing but the dunghill, y'ea they will devour what a hungry Dog in *England* would refuse... These Brutes devote themselves to Idleness, for they neither spin nor dig;... their Faces are ill favoured, most of their Noses flat;... their Skins very tawny; swift they are of foot, and will throw Darts and shoot Arrows very dangerously.[43]

The accusation of idleness is commonplace, the Irish being said by Lithgow, for example, to have this characteristic, which is routinely ascribed to the whole international class of natives, and which J. M. Coetzee has identified as a particularly salient item in the Dutch accounts of Hottentots in Southern Africa.[44] This view of natives, which is more fully discussed in Chapter 3, replicates a parallel discourse about the lower orders at home, and it is apposite here as elsewhere to recall the double status of the Irish natives, as both colonized savages and domestic underclass.

The Hottentot dimension of the Yahoos is heightened by the fact that analogies between Hottentots and Irish was a staple of English writing about the Irish. The extract from Lithgow (1620) is an early example of implicit assimilation. In 1634, Thomas Herbert was quite explicit when, immediately after his own account of the Cape women suckling over their shoulder, he added that their 'apishly sounded' language is hard to pronounce, 'being voyced like the Irish'.[45] In the final quarter of the eighteenth century, Lord Chief Justice Clonmell complained that the English treat the Irish 'as the Dutch do the Hottentots', and the Irish behave 'as the Hottentots do'. 'A man in station, in Ireland, is really like a traveller in Africa, in a forest among Hottentots and wild beasts.' Clonmell, an Anglo-Irishman from Tipperary, complains of English oppression, but harps on the Hottentot analogy in a way that testifies to its character as an established sore point: the term is repeated at least seven times in two short paragraphs of his diary.[46] As late as 1886, the Irish were being compared to Hottentots in *Punch* and other journals. In that year Lord Salisbury said the Irish were as incapable of self-government as Hottentots, and in 1892 Sidney and Beatrice Webb thought both races equally repellent.[47] Swift was actively aware of the analogy, writing from 'Wretched Dublin, in miserable Ireland' to one correspondent that he would have to go 'to the Hottentots' to 'match' Irish behaviour, to another that 'would prefer living among the Hottentots' rather than in Ireland, and to a third that he believed 'the people of Lapland, or the Hottentots, are not so miserable a people as we'.[48] In *A Modest Proposal* the people of Lapland had been paired with those of Topinamboo, i.e. Montaigne's cannibals, as superior in patriotism to the Irish, in an extension of an anti-Irish jibe to Anglo-Irish ruling groups. A similar extension was made by Thomas Sheridan in *Intelligencer*, No. 2, after Swift had nearly been run over by the coach of a country squire called Abel Ram. Ram was not sufficiently apologetic when Sheridan remonstrated with him, and Sheridan exclaimed 'what a *Hottentot* have I been talking to!').[49]

The equations between Hottentot and Irish and between Hottentot and Yahoo are received lore, and naturally interpenetrate deeply with the Yahoo–Irish equation, widely perceived in the time of *Gulliver's Travels* and in its long afterlife.[50] It is not surprising that the Yahoo women have hanging breasts. This image of unpleasant femininity, naturally associated with past (and sometimes even present) child-bearing, often acquired secondary associations of the monstrous or unnatural. There is a subtype, represented in de Bry, of androgynous old women with long hair and masculine features, including a powerfully emphasized musculature. This motif persists from the earliest phases of the *conquista*. Columbus reported on 9 January 1493 sighting three sirens jumping out of the sea, who were not as beautiful as usually depicted because their faces had something masculine about them.[51] Columbus also spoke of warrior-women,[52] and it is part of the classicizing fantasy endemic in the literature of early American discovery that tribes of warrior-women named Amazons were deemed to occupy various territories.[53]

The androgynous version also had a powerful survival in portrayals of witches. It occurs in Hans Baldung Grien's *Old Age* (pl. 8) and in descriptions of female criminals and prostitutes, who are in turn often assimilated to 'savages'. The mixture of the rancid maternity of hanging breasts with masculine features is summarily captured in the *Dunciad*, a poem dedicated to Swift, with its description of Eliza Haywood, 'With cow-like udders, and with ox-like eyes'. She has 'Two babes of love close clinging to her breast', an icon of the native mother, carrying not one but two babies, and suggesting the morals of a whore (II. 164, 158). This gets all the stereotypes in with a concentration of which Pope was master. The 'ox-like eyes' are a milder and subtler prefiguration of the bullish features of the sixty-four-year-old malefactress in the study by Lombroso and Ferrero, *La Donna delinquente: La prostituta e la donna normale* (1893), who is described as having 'muscoli del collo esagerati come nei buoi', 'neck-muscles, exaggerated as in oxen'.[54]

The prostitutes which are discussed with lurid obsessiveness in nineteenth-century medical and sociological treatises are the descendants of the hags and witches of earlier centuries. Separately or together, the hanging breasts and masculine features haunt the pages of Lombroso. The billowingly mammalian old whore of his nowadays much-reproduced plate, *Polisarcia in Abissina* (pl. 9), taken from Ploss and discussed below, may be set beside the prostitute and criminal labelled 'Z', who has 'an exaggerated frontal angle, such as one notes in savages and monkeys (*che è proprio dei selvaggi e delle scimmie*); while the jaws and lip— indeed her whole face is essentially virile (*in tutto il volto un tipo essenzialmente virile*)'. Ploss's compendium, which is critical of Lombroso's views on the moral and physical degeneracy of prostitutes, nevertheless noted that masculine or asexual features were common in women in societies where their social status was low, including 'primitive peoples and...the habitually under-nourished and overworked sections of civilised communities'.[55] Such equations readily introduce notions of 'perverse' sexuality, a staple of portrayals of Amerindian or other natives (imputations of sodomy and incest were, as we shall see, common), and may also be associated with stereotypes of cruel and rapacious old women in accounts of Amerindian cannibal rituals and some 'metro-politan' variants (in sixteenth-century France, for example; or, to the extent that Ireland could be considered a 'home' rather than a conquered or savage territory, in Irish famines;[56] or among the criminals and prostitutes of Lombroso and Ferrero). Some of these are Swiftian themes, but Swift expressly absolved the Yahoos of 'unnatural Appetites' and does not in *Gulliver's Travels* deal in ravenous ogresses.

The androgynous hag also came into political demonologies. As late as the 1790s, an anti-Revolutionary caricature, *The Hopes of the Party or the Darling Children of Democracy* (1798) shows Democracy with a man's bearded face, and vertical breasts with nipples pointing downwards (as in some de Bry examples, but more misshapen and not symmetrical). On Democracy's lap are Charles

James Fox (left) and John Horne Tooke (right), and all three are wearing *bonnets rouges*, the badge of hardline revolutionary radicals.[57] Swift would have liked this image, with his strong views on the mutual interpenetration of anarchy and tyranny. Herd leaders, among the Yahoos, were 'always more *deformed in Body*, and *mischievous in Disposition*, than any of the rest' (IV. vii. 262).

The Hottentot Venus

The nuclear motif of hanging breasts has many forms, including variants emphasizing a fertility and a rich maternal amplitude. The earliest surviving prototypes are Venuses of Willendorf, Laussel in the Dordogne, Dolni Věstonice in Moravia, and Lake Baikal in Siberia, which provide evidence, from *c.* 25,000 –13,000 BC, of a 'Late Stone Age Mythology in which the outstanding single figure was the Naked Goddess', usually with an emphasis 'on the breasts, sexual triangle, and buttocks'. The suggestion is of a rich and benign fecundity, often conveyed by the heavy and asymmetric character of the pendent breasts.[58] A much later image reproduced by Joseph Campbell shows a peasant featured as a mother goddess with a cartographic globe as her body from neck to thigh, and large breasts hanging benignly over the world's continents, with a Cupid sucking at one of them. More stylized versions, of breasts elegantly pointing downwards, are common in African and Australian aborigine art.[59] These are not part of Swift's imaginative world.

The pendent breasts may be full or worn and wrinkled, sharply and elegantly stylized, or ample and amorphous like those of the Willendorf Venus, or, in the downbeat version, of Fielding's Blear-eyed Moll. The Hottentot Venus, who was a public spectacle in London and Paris from 1810 to 1815, and has become a topic of recent concern, seems to have belonged somewhere between the two.[60] Hanging breasts are part of, or an extension of, a general pattern of exhibiting what Bucher refers to as a 'hypertrophy of the sexual organs'. The topic is typically fraught with prurient curiosity, which may be assumed to be common to many portrayals, stylized or realistic, monstrous or normal, Swiftian or unSwiftian. The Ploss compendium reports genital 'enlargements' (and excisions) among many peoples.[61] In a well-known article 'Black Bodies, White Bodies', Sander Gilman explored a preoccupation with hypertrophy of the genitalia among African women, including especially Hottentots, in nineteenth-century art and socio-medical literature. He pointed out that some anatomical distortions deriving from the manipulation of the labia, nymphae, and other genital parts were considered in some tribal cultures to enhance beauty.[62] Such induced distortions in turn contributed to European conventions of portraying primitives, which dwelt to the point of caricature on enlarged genitals, buttocks, and breasts.

Some anatomical distortions were 'natural' to certain groups, rather than the product of manipulation. Sartje Baartman, known as the Hottentot Venus, became a widely exhibited and publicized example of the enlarged posterior mainly associated with some Southern African peoples. She is nowadays best known pictorially through the profile of her by Jacques Christophe Werner (pl. 10), based on a watercolour of 1815 by Nicolas Huet le Jeune, and first published in 1824.[63] She was evidently of Bushman rather than Hottentot stock, two Southern African distinct peoples often spoken of interchangeably under either name. I use these terms, rather than the indigenous Khoi for Hottentots and San for Bushmen, for the same reason as J. M. Coetzee does in *White Writing*, because European perceptions are my subject and these are the terms in circulation.[64] Baartman has her own connections with the theme of hanging breasts, and with that of the female Yahoo's sexual interest in Gulliver, though her most widely known and most spectacular characteristic was her steatopygic or protruding posterior. She also represents a significant and specialized moment in a long history, going back at least as far as Columbus, of importing specimen natives from conquered or distant lands. She was brought to London from South Africa in 1810, and was exhibited for commercial profit in London and Paris until her death in 1815, one of those freakish spectacles of empire of the kind Gulliver had hoped to bring back from Lilliput and Blefuscu.[65] Gulliver himself became for a time such an exhibit in the fairgrounds of Brobdingnag. The two-way traffic between *Gulliver's Travels* and this cultural by-product of empire is further illustrated by the tradition of calling freakshow dwarfs Lilliputians, as notably in the case of the Aztec Lilliputians who aroused interest and controversy in England in 1853–4. The Hottentot Venus belongs, as Richard D. Altick says, among those 'successors to Omai, the American Indian chiefs, and the other lionized dark-skinned London visitors'.[66]

There were two important differences. Unlike these 'noble' antecedents, the 'successors' were perceived as 'savages who had lost their nobility'.[67] They also came to attract scientific rather than sentimental interest, as well as enormous popular curiosity and wide coverage in the public prints, including pictorial coverage. Some fifteen prints about her, not including the two images just discussed, are recorded in the British Museum between 1810 and 1824, by William Heath, George Cruikshank, Rowlandson, and others (pls. 11–12). Many of these derive from an aquatint poster by Frederick Christian Lewis, published on 18 September 1810, to advertise the show. (There is also a remarkable pen and ink drawing of her face by Rowlandson).[68] Nearly all of these satirize the voyeuristic obsession with her posterior, which had become a popular sensation in both London and Paris. A similar fad was revived in Paris in 1829.[69] In 1838, a new 'Hottentot Venus' was exhibited in Hyde Park, and, as we shall see, became involved in an episode of Brobdingnagian bizarrerie.[70] This anatomical peculiarity was not mentioned in the *Encyclopédie* entry on Hottentots, and seemingly seldom observed before Baartman was put on exhibition in London in 1810. Among the infrequent earlier reports is one in John Ogilby's *Africa* (1670), which says of the 'Kaffers or Hottentots': 'Most of them have their Bellies long and wrinkled, with Buttocks sticking out'.[71] A few years before Baartman, in 1801 and 1803, some drawings of Hottentot women were made, showing a scientific interest in steatopygia.[72] But widespread popular and medical interest apparently began around 1810. The Hottentot Venus became the subject of a post-mortem by the French anatomist Georges Cuvier, first published in 1817.[73] The event is an extension, or marks an escalation, of the increasingly scientific character of voyages of exploration in the late eighteenth century, with the exotic specimen being studied in-house rather than on location, in a metropolitan laboratory.

The genitalia of Hottentots had, on the other hand, long exercised European imaginations. Males were widely reported to have only one testicle as a result of ritual surgery, during which it was said that the patient was urinated on.[74] The principal peculiarity of Hottentot women was a large genital apron or *tablier*, widely reported, notably in the *Encyclopédie*, as a racial characteristic, and which chiefly interested Cuvier as the most celebrated topic in natural history (reports of it go back to the seventeenth century).[75] The feature was hidden from view. Cuvier even failed to notice it when she agreed to be painted in the nude, and did not know she had it until after her death. Another French anatomist, Henri de Blainville, who conducted a live examination of her on 18 March 1815, some nine months before her death, confirmed that it was invisible in her standing position, but could be seen from behind, hanging between her thighs, when she bent down or was walking: a grotesquerie which is not without visual homologies with the ancient stereotype of the hanging breasts. Ovington was expressly told in 1689 that the protruding 'Female Parts were cut in the Fashion of small Teats hanging down'. Blainville's observations are reported in the third person, as though by someone transcribing from his dictation or notes. Both Blainville and Cuvier were inclined to think of this apron not as a separate organ but as abnormally enlarged nymphae. Cuvier said Baartman had kept this feature hidden between her thighs or deeper down, an observation consistent with Blainville's exasperated experience of her *pudeur*, as she shrank from his prying into her genitalia.[76]

By contrast, the *Encyclopédie* had affirmed that Cape women were willing to display their apron to anyone who had the curiosity or intrepidity to ask, setting up the prurient freakshow on location, rather than in the shows of London and Paris, a transfer in the opposite direction to that of the scientific drift to the metropolis. Earlier travellers confirm the *Encyclopédie*'s observation, one of them, Ambrose Cowley, reporting in 1686 that in a Hottentot village outside the Cape Settlement he was able to see the 'Hottentot apron' for the price of twopence.[77] But metropolitan science retained the last word, placing Baartman's apron and the genitalia of other women on permanent exhibition in the Musée de l'Homme, whose ownership of them has recently been disputed by South Africa, but where they remain (though removed from exhibition in the 1980s) along with the somewhat later brain of the famous anatomist Paul Broca.[78] It was Cuvier who, in his post-mortem, made the formal presentation of Baartman's genitalia to the Academy. An irony on this subject is recorded by Stephen Jay Gould: 'in three smaller jars, I saw the dissected genitalia of three Third-World women, and neither Broca's penis nor any male genitalia grace the collection.' Or as Elizabeth Alexander, who has presumably read Gould, put it:

> Her genitalia
> will float inside a labeled
>
> pickling jar in the Musée
> de l'Homme on a shelf
>
> above Broca's brain.

The words purport to be spoken by Cuvier in 1825, when Broca was one year old. Baartman's brain was in fact also preserved.[79]

But Baartman's other special characteristic, immediately and strikingly visible, and medically referred to as steatopygia, 'protuberance of the buttocks', aroused a prurient interest among both scientists and the public. Cuvier and Blainville said it consisted not of muscular but of elastic and wobbly substance. Van der Post attributes to it the function of storing 'a reserve of valuable fats and carbo-hydrates against dry and hungry moments'.[80] But Blainville loses himself in paroxysms of wonder both over the fatty wobbliness and the sheer size of the buttocks. Really enormous, he calls them: 'ses fesses sont réellement énormes'. They tremble and shimmer when she walks, and flatten and massively overflow when she sits. He lingers over their measurements and their line of declivity, their breast-like contours ('irrégulièrement mamelonnées'), the 'grande intumescence' they form at the base of her trunk, and the deep, wide, and oblique furrow in which they terminate. Cuvier was more restrained, but he too reported the vibrations of her buttocks and their 'masse... élastique et tremblante'.[81] And it is he who acquired a posthumous reputation for being voyeuristically implicated. Elizabeth Alexander's poem imagines Baartman saying:

> Monsieur Cuvier investigates
> between my legs, poking, prodding,
> sure of his hypothesis.
> I half expect him to pull silk
> scarves from inside me, paper poppies,
> then a rabbit. He complains
> at my scent.[82]

In a recent play by Suzan-Lori Parks, which both cites and travesties Cuvier's autopsy report extensively, Baartman is represented as the lover of Cuvier, himself portrayed as an old masturbator aroused by her copious black flesh, and scorned by his equally depraved peers for his disreputable amour with a Black. He is referred to throughout as the Baron Docteur (he was ennobled only in the last year of his life), a name which gives him something of the sleazy sinister shadowiness of Baron Samedi in the Haiti of Graham Greene's *The Comedians* (1966).[83]

The scientific interest in her was itself perceived as a showbiz phenomenon, inseparable from the spheres of public spectacle and the theatre of parliamentary politics. In William Heath's *A Pair of Broad Bottoms*, one of two English political caricatures of 1810 reproduced by Altick, and punningly connecting her steatopygia with the current unfulfilled expectation of a new Broad Bottom Ministry, Richard Brinsley Sheridan, the dramatist and Member of Parliament, is shown scrutinizing her buttocks with a pair of callipers (pl. 11).[84] In a print of 1811 by George Cruikshank, *The Examination, of a Young Surgeon*, the wall of the examination room at the Royal College of Surgeons is adorned with pictures, including one of the Hottentot Venus, arrayed behind the table at which a disreputable group of elderly examiners is sitting (pl. 12).[85] There are a number of prints in which framed portraits or statues of her are featured as part of the background of the composition, a reflection of her status as a cultural icon at the time. Her pipe-smoking even gets into these pictures within pictures, including the one in *The Examination*. In George Cruikshank's *Double Bass* (1811), her portrait stands behind a trio of musicians and shows her with feathers on her head, cavorting with a smoking pipe in her hand while her huge rear is used as a drum; in Rowlandson's *Exhibition at Bullocks Museum of Bonepartes Carriage Taken at Waterloo* (1816), her portrait is prominent among the exhibits; George Cruikshank's *The Court at Brighton à la Chinese!!* (1816) shows a statue of her inscribed 'Regency Taste!!!!!' on its base; and in William Heath's *All the World's a Stage* (1824), a portrait of her hangs behind the armchair in which George IV sits nursing his gout.[86]

At least four of the six pictures within pictures, as well as *A Pair of Broad Bottoms* and more than half the other prints, show her smoking or holding a pipe.[87] Smoking was traditionally connected with savages, and reported of Hottentots at least as early as Peter Kolb, who says mothers smoked the narcotic *dacha* while nursing. Smoking and breast mythologies also came together when the grotesquerie of making bags out of breasts acquired a tobacco pouch variant, supposedly 'sold in great quantity on the Cape of Good Hope'.[88] The Modest Proposer would have found the idea

appealing. Lithgow, who described Irish women in 1620 as hanging-breasted, in an image still actively remembered in Hilary
Mantel's recent novel, also spoke of the Irish fondness for tobacco,
and Irish pipe-smoking, in a familiar iconography of nineteenth-
century caricature, was depicted in a similar way to that of the
Hottentot Venus.[89] An irony about Baartman's much caricatured
pipe is that Blainville reports that she did not smoke but chewed
tobacco, and both he and Cuvier speak of her fondness for *aqua
vitae*.[90] Lithgow and Lord Clonmell spoke of Irish drunkenness,
the latter comparing it to that of Hottentots, but this was another
routinely reported savage trait.[91] It is also striking that many of
the images portray her as coal black, although Cuvier described
her as yellowish-brown and Blainville says she was light brown
over most of her body and a darker brown in some parts.[92]

Baartman's notoriety was widespread, and the prurience about
her was hardly confined to scientists. A ribald ballad telling the
'story of the Hottentot ladie and her lawful knight who essaied to
release her out of captivitie' proclaimed:

> A rump she has (though strange it be),
>   Large as a cauldron pot,
> And this is why men go to see
>   This lovely Hottentot.[93]

The Hottentot Venus provided a real-life activation, on metropolitan rather than exotic territory, of the sexual excitations of
gigantism, to which travel-writers, as well as Gulliver and perhaps
Swift, were traditionally susceptible. At her public displays, she
was pinched and prodded by visitors, and there seems even to have
been an extra fee for touching her.[94] In November 1810, at a
hearing to stop the exhibition, on grounds of indecency as well as
cruelty, it was reported that she was 'clothed in a light dress,
resembling her own complexion, and made in such a manner that
she appeared to be naked'. The Attorney-General made a point of
adding that her clothes 'exhibit all the shape and frame of body',
again 'as if naked'.[95]

The attempt failed on the supposed grounds that Baartman's show was voluntary and that she was paid for it, though the court was told that 'it was impossible for anyone to hear her deep sighs and observe the sullenness of her manner, and not be convinced that she was acting contrary to her inclination'. The ballad affirmed that 'in this land of libertie'

> No one can show another's tail
> Against the owner's will,

but concluded that 'looking to her latter end, Delights the Hottentot'.[96] A month earlier, Hendrick Cezar, the entrepreneur who first exhibited her in Piccadilly, wrote to the *Morning Chronicle* asserting that she had 'as good a right to exhibit herself as an Irish giant or a dwarf'.[97] Cezar's remark may be an allusion to the giant Richard Byrne (d. 1783), the subject of Hilary Mantel's *The Giant, O'Brien*, and in many ways a proleptic male Irish counterpart to the Hottentot Venus: a 'flabby-fleshed' and bibulous unfortunate who was exhibited in London, stalked for his skeleton by the surgeon John Hunter, and ended up as an exhibit at the Royal College of Surgeons.[98] Cezar's pairing of giants and dwarfs taps into an enduring two-way traffic between *Gulliver's Travels* and the world of popular exhibitions and freakshows.[99]

A print of uncertain date satirizing the prurience about Baartman, which Gilman sees mainly as an expression of it, has become widely known through Gilman's various recyclings of his discussion of her.[100] It is entitled by him *The Hottentot Venus*, though the original image goes back at least as far as an English print of 1797 by Richard Newton, which predates the Baartman fad[101] and does not target Hottentots (pls. 13–14). In both versions the man is sitting incongruously in an armchair in the open air, with his dog beside him, peering through a telescope into the rear of a black woman, who is bending over on a raised piece of ground a short distance away and perhaps defecating in mockery of him, in a sophisticated variation of Hottentot-inspired Yahoo behaviour. The telescope suggests a pun on the planet Venus, and, but for the anachronism, might have been thought to intimate, in the words of Thomas Harris's *Hannibal*, 'an astronomer locating a black hole'.[102] The joke would be fully in Newton's spirit.

The telescope additionally suggests, even more than Sheridan's callipers in William Heath's print of 1810 (pl. 11), that a 'scientific' prurience is being derided, a suggestion more appropriate to the Baartman case than to that of Newton's negress, where the voyeur cannot manage his scientific paraphernalia and seems merely a drooling example of white men's obsessions with naked black women. The well-dressed dog-faced observer is evidently a studious elder, and, if the German image dates from after Blainville's medical examination in 1815 or Cuvier's autopsy report of 1817, the joke might be directed at the prurient curiosity of one of these anatomists. But the presence of a picture of Baartman on the wall in *The Examination, of a Young Surgeon* (1811) shows that medical curiosity about her had started early (pl. 12). The disreputable looking elders who are assessing the young surgeon are spiritual cousins of both Newton's and the German imitator's male figure. The main point, however, is to ridicule the voyeurism, adapted, in the German version, to the popular sensation of Baartman's public exhibition, though Gilman, who notes neither the astronomical jokerie nor, more important, the man's animal face or the woman's obvious contempt for him, sees it mainly as an 'erotic caricature of the Hottentot Venus'. The description of the voyeur as 'a white, male observer' seems hardly adequate to the satirical register of the portrait.

The later image is more widely known than Newton's print, and the occasion for some current preoccupations. Prevailing accounts of it are anomalous and unreliable. The woman is not steatopygic, merely fat, and does not resemble conventional portrayals of Baartman (not surprisingly, since the original image has nothing to do with her). The labelling of it as *The Hottentot Venus*, which does not originate with Gilman, is either a deliberate super-imposition on the part of the later artist, or a simple mistake by some later interpreter.[103] Gilman's date, in 'Black Bodies', *c.*1850, is also anomalous. The garments are obviously anachronistic. It is not easy to see why the Hottentot Venus should surface in a caricature forty years after her years of notoriety (1810–17), even though occasional public appearances of steatopygic women are recorded in the intervening years, including 1829 and 1838. In both *Difference and Pathology* and *Sexuality*, Gilman still speaks of this as a 'midcentury' caricature, though the caption to the plate itself now says it is 'from the beginning of the nineteenth century', as does Eduard Fuchs.[104]

The words from the dog's mouth are 'ganz schwarz' ('totally black'). The words under the telescope are 'Total finster' ('totally dark'), another astronomical pun, alluding to an eclipse of the moon, which is the title of the print which is the immediate source of the image. On the signboard, the first three lines, under magnification, clearly read 'Es giebt viele Dinge zwischen Himmel und Erden' ('there are many things between heaven and earth'), and the remaining lines seem indecipherable. It is clearly a near variation of a well-known passage from a German translation of *Hamlet*. The Schlegel-Tieck translation, somewhat more literal, is: 'Es giebt mehr Ding' im Himmel und auf Erden, Als eure Schulweisheit sich träumt' ('There are more things in heaven and earth, ... Than are dreamt of in your philosophy').[105] While, therefore, the German print adds little visual substance to Newton, except for reversal from left to right and 'restoring' the proper direction of the telescope, it adds a good deal of verbal elaboration. In Newton there are no words by the telescope or from the dog's mouth, and the signboard merely reads 'MANTRAP' above some non-verbal squiggles.

The later image is an adaptation of Newton, either German, or possibly French deriding a perceived German voyeurism.[106] Assuming that there is no earlier version than Newton's of the common image, there are some iconographic analogues or sources, including an etching published in 1794, believed to be based on a lost drawing of *c.*1734 by Hogarth entitled *The Complicated R——n*. This shows the painter Jonathan Richardson the

Elder with a telescope looking through the anus of his son, who is reading Virgil, and whose classical learning the father is seeking to absorb in this way.[107] More remotely, it also seems icono-graphically related to Hogarth's *The Punishment inflicted on Lemuel Gulliver by applying a Lilypucian fire Engine to his Posteriors* (1726), where the fire engine not only has the function and appearance of a clyster but visual associations with the telescope (highly apposite to the role of microscopes and telescopes in Swift's imagining of big men and little men). This 'punishment' was inflicted for Gulliver's 'Urinal Profanation of the Royal Pallace at Mildendo', an act which might be said to have Hottentot as well as Rabelaisian prototypes.[108] Newton knew his Hogarth, and his work includes at least one political cartoon, *A Proclamation in Lilliput* (1792), inspired by *Gulliver's Travels*: Gulliverian images were in fact not uncommon in both erotic and political caricature in this period.[109] But while these analogues have in common an iconography of telescopes and posteriors, they are wholly without the sexual satire both of *The Full Moon in Eclipse* and of the 'German' image.

David Alexander has recently described this as 'one of Newton's most absurd schoolboyish prints', which seems a shade censorious for a vivid satirical statement by a talented and successful young artist, who died the following year at the age of twenty-one. *The Full Moon in Eclipse* satirizes a species of cross-racial prurience which was to be spectacularly exploited by the exhibition of the Hottentot Venus from 1810 onwards, but which must already have been a matter of public awareness thirteen years earlier. No special point about Hottentots is being made in Newton's original print. The Negress's bottom is merely large, but not strictly speaking steatopygic, whereas the later picture may contain a faint hint of the distinctive upward curve also displayed in the post-mortem profile of Baartman (though not in the original watercolour) and in many of the caricatures. If so, the suggestion is vestigial, and may be attributable to a bulge in her pulled-up clothes, and the curve may be mainly a caricaturists' flourish anyway. The photographs in Ploss suggest that this curve was not an especially common feature of the nevertheless quite distinctive steatopygic protrusion, of which there is no evidence in Newton either way.[110] It seems that the exhibition of Baartman in London and Paris was exploiting a sexual fad about black women with ample parts which was already sufficiently widespread to generate satires of male voyeurism on the subject as early as 1797, when neither Baartman nor even steatopygia had reached the consciousness of the public. The steatopygia, apparently not often mentioned until then in accounts of Hottentots, was revealed as an accentuated or enhanced version of something which was already exercising sexual imaginings, and which may even have influenced the dress fashions of white women for several decades before 1810.

This steatopygous Venus appears iconographically as a negative and hypertrophied counterpart of the famous Callipygian (beautiful bottomed) Venus, or Vénus Callipyge, whom Evelyn described in 1645 as 'that renowned piece of Venus pulling up her smock, and looking backwards on her buttocks'. This statue, possibly 'a restored copy of a Hellenistic original', was then in Rome and is now in Naples. It was much admired in the eighteenth century, and widely reproduced in bronze, marble, plaster, ceramics, and in miniature versions on Wedgwood products.[111] The statue is the centrepiece in Rowlandson's satirical composition, *The Exhibition 'Stare' Case* (pl. 15, c.1811), and is repeatedly alluded to in Sade (*Aline et Valcour*, *La Philosophie dans le boudoir*, and *Histoire de Juliette*, for example, in accounts of the attractions of posteriors and the virtues of sodomy).[112]

The profile of the Hottentot Venus accompanying Cuvier's autopsy was not published with his article of 1817, but in a reprint of it in the *Histoire naturelle des mammifères*, by Étienne Geoffroy-Saint-Hilaire and Cuvier's brother Frédéric. It is a lightly clothed reworking by Jacques Christophe Werner (pl. 10) of the nude watercolour by Nicolas Huet le Jeune, one of three artists from the Jardin du Roi commissioned by Cuvier to portray her in 1815.[113] Cuvier's objective was scientific accuracy, but a suggestion may be detected, in Werner's reworking of the protruding posterior, more clearly than in the 'German' image, of the slight upward lift which may or may not derive from a by then well-established tradition of caricature, though the grotesquerie is minor in comparison. It also gives a hint of large and somewhat pendulous breasts, but not of the impression these evidently made on both Cuvier and Blainville, and it is clear that her steatopygia merged readily with the traditional preoccupation with hanging breasts. Cuvier reported that she kept her breasts raised and pressed under her garments, but that, left to themselves, they were massively pendulous ('montrèrent leurs grosses masses pendantes'). Henri de Blainville, in his report of a live examination, spoke of her breasts as 'très grosses, extrêmement pendantes', descending to the elbow-line or just above the navel.[114]

She also had a reputation for libidinous behaviour, and was reported to have thrown herself forcefully, like Gulliver's female Yahoo, at a man she coveted, but Blainville is said to have doubted this particular allegation.[115] From the point of view of the present discussion, it is the fact that the allegation was made that is of interest, not whether it was true. That it seems to have been untrue reinforces a sense of the automatic introduction of such suppositions in scenarios of colonial encounters, even in an inside-out version like hers, played out on a European stage rather than on the site of invasion. By the same token, it highlights the deep typicality of Gulliver's account, even in details which in themselves already bear a marked Swiftian stamp. Cuvier also reports that she allowed herself to be painted nude in 1815 in Paris, shortly before her death.

Cuvier's anatomical examination was meticulously scientific, but he was still actively intrigued by the old and much-canvassed notion of a relationship between Hottentots and the orang-utan. Blainville similarly compared this woman with the lowest of human races, the Negro race ('la dernière race de l'espèce humaine, ou la race nègre'), and with the highest species of apes ('la première des singes, ou l'orang-outang'), and found her head and facial features closer to the latter. Cuvier also spoke of her simian features and noted the 'brutal appearance' of her face. He thought the genital apron distinguished her from apes, but that the enlarged rear, which according to recent travellers was common to the whole Bushman nation, was close to that of apes.[116] Gilman reports, on the other hand, that the apron and similar genital peculiarities came to be used as arguments for a 'polygenetic' view of black people.[117]

These observations did not stand in the way of either scientist observing that she spoke some Dutch, and a little English, and a few words of French. Blainville said she pronounced Dutch and English very well. Perhaps all orang-utans are like that. The irony is picked up in Elizabeth Alexander's poem, which makes Baartman say of Cuvier:

> He complains
> at my scent and does not think
> I comprehend, but I speak
> English. I speak Dutch. I speak
> a little French as well, and
> languages Monsieur Cuvier
> will never know have names.

The suggestion that Cuvier did not know these things, despite the fact that his report is the source of the information, belongs to a nowadays familiar gesturing. Presumably, Alexander read it in Gould. It is a symmetrical counterpart to the scientists' insistence on Baartman's animality, even as they note her intellectual and social skills. Thus, in addition to her linguistic abilities, Cuvier reported that she had an excellent memory, and Blainville that she had a very sweet voice, and seemed kind, gentle, and timid, though capable of stubbornness and of a reluctance to have her genitals scrutinized (even for money, of which she was fond) by Blainville, to whom she took a spirited dislike. The response might be thought not only human rather than apelike, but fully civilized.[118]

Cuvier's and Blainville's definitional preoccupations tapped a tradition of enquiry both into the nature of the human animal and into racial taxonomies in which *Gulliver's Travels*, as we shall see, also shows a marked interest.[119] The idea of Hottentots and Negroes as providing the missing link, or at least a median position, between humans and apes (a compliment also extended to the Irish) was in circulation in the travel-book background to *Gulliver's Travels*. It was expounded in John Ovington's *Voyage to Suratt* (1696), while their kinship to monkeys, their tendency to 'mixe unnaturally' with the great apes, 'the resemblance they bear with Baboons, which I could observe kept frequent company with the Women' and the tendency of bearded satyr monkeys to 'fall foul on the *Negro* Women' possibly with the Negroes' consent, are reported at least as early as Herbert, and in the second and third editions of Wafer's *New Voyage to the Isthmus of America* (1704, 1729), which Swift possessed in the first edition of 1699, and by many others.[120] How the Hottentot Venus with her orang-utan features and her alleged lust for white men might fit into this scenario, or where it placed the white men themselves, taxonomically speaking, is not gone into in the reports. But it is even possible that the earliest inclusive name given by seventeenth-century Dutch settlers in South Africa to Hottentot and neighbouring peoples, *Bosmanneken* or bushman, was paradoxically intended to indicate a simian rather than human identity, since, as Stephen Jay Gould points out, the term 'was a literal translation of a Malay word ... *Orang Outan*, or "man of the forest"' (this etymology was already well known to Buffon). Gould cites a case in which this 'equation of Bushman and animal became so ingrained that one party of Dutch settlers, out on a hunting expedition, shot and ate a Bushman, assuming that he was the African equivalent of the Malay orang', a teasing reversal of traditional cannibal roles, exceeding sexual selection, indeed passing the love of women, as a mode of species identification.[121] But sexual selection was doubtless more usual, and a parallel from Voltaire's *Candide* is discussed below.

Cuvier did not speak in such terms. He expressly disclaimed inferring racial characteristics from the Hottentot Venus's peculiarities, though this was because he had not seen enough examples to exclude the possibility of individual characteristics, and he clearly believed in the cruel law which seemed to condemn to perpetual inferiority those races with lowered and compressed crania.[122] He thought that her movements were apelike, and that her lips jutted like an orang-utan's. He did not consider the genital apron to be simian, because the nymphae of monkeys were in general barely visible, but the protruding buttocks definitely resembled those of monkeys, and were (unlike the genital apron) common to the whole Bushman nation. He did not consider her a Hottentot. (The *Encyclopédie*, on the other hand, though not mentioning steatopygia, had reported that the *monstrueuse difformité* of the apron was common to all females from the Cape region.)[123] The *OED* entry on steatopygia shows that this feature has continued to be attributed to Hottentots by Darwin and others, as well as to Bushmen, and that ancient evidence has survived of steatopygic groups in Egypt, Greece, and elsewhere. The Ploss compendium cites further European and other examples. Laurens van der Post reports speculation that the Bushman was related to an ancient North African and Paleolithic Iberian people, and notes that there are similarly shaped figures in the caves of Lascaux (a remarkable steatopygic figurine of the Late Stone Age, 'La Polichinelle', was found in Grimaldi on the Riviera).[124] Cuvier perceived other apelike features, as well as some resembling dogs and other carnivores. He spoke in particular of her prominent snout, even more protruding than the Negro's. On some aspects of her bone structure he commented baldly 'ce sont tous là des caractères d'animalité.'[125]

Like Lombroso on prostitutes, Cuvier noted 'l'apparence brutale de sa figure', remarking for good measure on her negroid jaws and lips and her mongoloid cheekbones and flat nose. The *Encyclopédie* said the Hottentots had their noses artificially flattened in infancy, because prominent noses were regarded as a deformity, an interesting variation on the manipulation of genitalia reported by Ploss and others: more traditionally, the flat nose was regarded as characteristic of non-white peoples, or, as Gulliver put it, 'all savage Nations'. It was used as a racial test in South Africa under apartheid.[126] But Cuvier thought it right to add that her shoulders, back, and chest had grace, her paunch was not excessive, her thin arms well made, her hand charming, and her foot pretty (indeed, 'fort joli'), an odd appearance of offbeat gallantry in scientific discourse, though it is, as I will suggest, characteristic in travelbooks about natives. Even the churlish Blainville reported that her upper limbs were reasonably well made, with the shoulders swollen by the cellulo-fatty substance he also found interesting in the buttocks, and with a well-made forearm. The hands, which Cuvier found charming, Blainville merely called very small, with fingers which were unremarkable.[127]

He is, in his curious way, not unaroused. We have already seen that although Cuvier, as the more famous figure, became mythologized as pruriently implicated in his relations with the Hottentot Venus, it was Blainville's report which showed an unusually warm engagement with the idea of her fat wobbly flesh. But even Cuvier's paragraph cannot end without a reference to the Venus's knee, which was fat and crooked ('gros et cagneux'), somewhat outdoing Swift's affectionate deflation of Stella as 'one of the most beautiful, graceful, and agreeable young women in London, only a little too fat'.[128]

The Bum Shop

Lombroso and other medical writers show a penchant for relating enlarged erogenous parts among tribal peoples, including outsize cases like the Hottentot Venus, to the pathology of prostitutes whose genitalia were reportedly swollen by infection or disease. (Hottentot cases had also been compared by Lombroso and Ferrero at the outset to the voluminous genitalia of female chimpanzees.) Prostitutes were assimilated to savages, especially to Hottentots or Bushmen, seen by Ferrero as the nadir of primitive lechery.

According to Gilman, the assimilation extended to anatomical features. Prostitutes were accorded a posterior iconography parallel to that of the black Venus, again in medical treatises, as in a sketch of 1905 of an Italian prostitute with steatopygia, cited by Gilman from a work by Abele de Blasio, a student of Lombroso.[129] The anatomical configuration evokes that most stiffly artificial of eighteenth-century fashions, the hoop-petticoat and its analogues and derivatives, giving them, as you might say in hindsight, an unsuspected and raffish aura of neo-primitivism.[130]

The hoop-petticoat was, throughout the eighteenth century, surrounded by a series of sexually charged paradoxes. In one of its variant shapes, it simulated pregnancy, as Fielding and others remarked, and could also, it was said, be used to conceal that condition.[131] In some examples its armatures conceal the body's actual shape, but also simulate some provocative anatomical contours, like the Hottentot Venus's or a steatopygous prostitute's rear, excessive and exotic and forbidden to the quotidian imagination and to the touch: the constant prodding to which Sartje Baartman was later subjected is evidence of the craving, on a cultural scale. Another variant of the hoop resembles not a presumed exotic anatomy, but a Tahitian mode of dress, used in gift-bearing ceremonies, which employed large quantities of bark-cloth rather than a scaffolding of whalebone. The wearer stands at the centre of a very wide circle just below her breasts, with drapes descending to just above her ankles. Several portrayals of this exist, including watercolours by Webber (1777) and P. J. de Loutherbourg (1785), and some appeared in print. Two women thus attired were bringers of gifts to Captain Cook on 5 September 1777, before his departure from Tahiti. An engraving of Webber's *Habit of a Young Woman of Otaheite Bringing a Present* was included in various editions of Cook's *Voyages* and the writer of the entry for that day gives an elaborate description, remarking on the 'resemblance to a hoop-petticoat', a resemblance confirmed by images of English and French hoop garments from the 1740s to the 1770s (pls. 16–17). Further cloth was wrapped round the outside 'being five or six yards in circuit', and the weight was a severe strain on the women. The ceremony was rare, and 'we never saw it practised upon any other occasion'. The cloth was presented to Captains Cook and Clarke, along with hogs, fruit, and other gifts. It was not normal attire, and was worn for a necessarily short time. But the image was drawn by more than one artist, reproduced in book form, and seen by English ladies.[132] It is a case, not exactly of life imitating art, but of the primitive coinciding, presumably in unawareness of the fact, with metropolitan fashion at its ostensibly least primitive.

A modern historian of fashion reports that 'After 1810, numerous fashion engravings show evening toilettes with more sharply defined waists and fuller backs'. He had in mind the 'reappearance of the corset' in England in 1810, rather than the fact that the Hottentot Venus went on display in that year. The passage is cited in a programme note to a production of *Venus* (1996), a play about the Hottentot Venus by Suzan-Lori Parks, evidently under the impression that 'back' refers to buttocks.[133] The play is concerned with the erotic appeal to white males of the black woman's enlarged posterior, and the note is tendentiously designed to reinforce this thesis, but its suggestion of a link between decorous fashion and a *louche* primitivism is not out of place. The erotic appeal of anatomical and sartorial features of 'savages' is reflected in other fashionable adornments. There are many images in which the protruding rear is featured in conjunction with feathered hair-ornaments evoking the headgear of an Amerindian or South Pacific warrior.[134] Such feathered headgear is later found adorning the Amerindian woman who symbolizes America in the frontispiece of the first issue of Andrés Bello's *Repertorio Americano*, a Spanish American independentist journal published in London from 1826.[135]

Long before the Hottentot Venus was exhibited in 1810, the caricaturist Miss Hoare of Bath, daughter of William Hoare, who painted Pope, drew a naked European woman with Jayne Mansfield breasts and a steatopygic rear closely corresponding to the Hottentot–Bushman stereotype. The caricature is entitled

A Modern Venus: or a Lady of the present *Fashion in the state of Nature*, and is designed to show how a woman would look if modern garments really represented the contours of the body, with the implication that the glamorous sexiness was really an impossible fantasy fostered by dress fashions. It dates from 1785 and was engraved on Horace Walpole's instructions and made into a print in 1786. Walpole showed it to the Countess of Upper Ossory, describing it as 'a Venus of the present hour in her *puris non naturalibus'*. What this meant may be gauged by juxtaposing the drawing with Lady Ossory's response, which exposed the anatomical fiction, as it were, by the paradoxical process of clothing it (pls. 18a–c). Her sketch showed the same figure fully dressed and hatted in the modern fashion.[136] According to Diana Donald, the print of 1786 'provides a playful visualization of the physique suggested by the "pouter pigeon" fashion of the 1780s, with its puffed out bosom and rump'.[137] In the present context, what seems remarkable is Miss Hoare's evocation of a rear closely resembling that of steatopygic Hottentots, as though the extremes of sartorial artifice had been designed to reproduce some of the more unromantic contours of savages, in an unacknowledged tribute to their sexual attraction. Her drawing even has the upward curve of the rump which is later found, as a caricaturists' flourish, in depictions of the Hottentot Venus. The stereotype of hanging breasts, or even of their magnified reincarnation in the 'grosses masses pendantes' which Cuvier reported in Sartje Baartman, is transfigured into something we would more readily associate with a silicone implant.

Horace Walpole dictated as an addition to the caption, found in both the drawing and the print, the couplet: 'This is the Form, if we believe the Fair, Of which our Ladies are, or wish they were.'[138] A few months later, on 4 May 1786, he expressly suggested that modern dress mimicked primordial forms: 'our fine ladies seem to copy [nature], at least the ancient symbols of her; for though they do not exhibit a profusion of naked bubbies down to their shoe-buckles, yet they protrude a prominence of gauze that would cover all the dugs of alma mater.'[139] He was alluding not to the long-breasted hags of Gulliver and the travellers, nor even to some analogue of the Willendorf Venus, but to the many-breasted Diana of Ephesus, a figure used to illustrate Nature, as Joan Sussler points out, in eighteenth-century art treatises (see Hogarth's *Boys Peeping at Nature*, 1731).[140]

Walpole owned a print entitled *The Bosom Friends*, by George Stubbs's son George Towneley Stubbs, published on 28 May 1786, which not only illustrates Walpole's point about bosoms but took in the concomitant phenomenon of cork-inflated posteriors and feathered headdresses. Bosom friends became a term for the wool or flannel used to inflate bosoms. In *The Inconvenience of Dress*, also by Stubbs, the enlarged bosom and bum create comic discomforts (pls. 19–20). Another print, *The Bum Shop* (1785), perhaps by Rushworth, shows these devices in the various stages of being fitted on several women. Stubbs's amplified ladies bear a remarkable resemblance to Max Beerbohm's blousy madam with slightly negroid features who befriends the author of *Mrs. Warren's Profession*, and who evidently achieved similar ample contours on the profits of her calling, without any accessories from the bum shop.[141] The idea or fantasy of the bum shop was to provide, as decorous beauty aids, all the gadgetry used long ago by the ageing whore in Swift's 'Beautiful Young Nymph' (the rags to prop her 'flabby Dugs', the bodice to 'Press down the Lumps, the Hollows fill'), in order to transform herself from a hag to the pride of Drury Lane.[142] It can be thought of as the social mechanism by which society women could pass notionally from one primitive stereotype to the other, from the savage with hanging breasts to the amply endowed enchantress from the bush or island paradise. Not everyone at the time can have been conscious of the connections to which I am drawing attention. But Miss Hoare, Walpole, and some of the artists and caption-writers clearly were, and their testimony establishes some contemporaneous awareness of primitivist tendencies in elaborate styles of dress where we might least expect them.

In the 1790s, looser styles became fashionable for a time, partly in response to revolutionary sentiment. Dressing *à la sauvage*, while attracting similar accusations of indecency and lewdness, seems to have been associated with the abandonment, rather than an accentuated use, of stays, corsets, and paniers, or hoops. As Lawrence Stone has said, 'in their very different ways, both fashions reflected an identical desire to advertise sexual attractions', but it is arguable that the hoops and corsets tap a deeper source in primitivist fantasy than fashions which emphasized the unfettered body and an element of see-through nakedness. Softer corsets without whalebone came into use in the early 1800s,[143] and it appears that protruding rears of the kind which the hoop-petticoat or panier provided at various stages throughout the eighteenth century did not become fashionable until some time after Sartje Baartman went on show in 1810. But the point was quickly taken, judging by the print *Fashionables Comparing Notes with the Hottentot Venus*, which shows the pipe-smoking Baartman wondering what 'some folks sees in me that's so beautiful', while ladies with and without artificial posteriors are comparing themselves with her.[144] An early Victorian commentator, Mrs Charles Matthews, writing in the *Memoirs* of her husband over twenty years later about the prurient interest aroused by the Hottentot Venus in 1810, opined that the Hottentot Venus's status as 'a curiosity' (her use of the term may be closer to that of *curiosa* than she intended) was due to the fact that bustles had not been in use in that year, English women of that time wearing 'no shape but what Nature gave and insisted upon... without whalebone or buckram to distort or disguise it'.[145] It is not easy to imagine her comments about de Blasio's Italian prostitute had she lived to see her in 1905. Her perception of the relationship between the Hottentot Venus's contours and the sartorial scaffoldings of modern fashion, and therefore between primitive sensuality and the modern structuring of hoops and bustles, was the symmetrical and negative obverse of that of the caricaturist Miss Hoare in 1785. Some medical dictionaries to this day describe steatopygia as the 'Hottentot bustle'.[146]

There is a sense in which the connection perceived by Mrs Matthews is tenuous. In hard sociological terms, it is no more than the registering of a social *fait divers*. As Andreas Mielke has forcefully stated, and as the history of fashion abundantly demonstrates, the Baartman craze can hardly be said to have initiated styles of dress with pronounced posteriors.[147] But her comment does in its own way embody an important intuition. In the progress from hoop-petticoats and the Modern Venus and the bum shop to the Hottentot Venus and the perceived connection between the excitements of her exhibition and the emergence of the Victorian bustle, a relationship was working itself out between primitivist fantasies and the social comportment and sartorial designs of European society. That this was a longstanding phenomenon, for which Baartman provided a particular momentary focus, is testimony to the unspoken ways in which the sexual interest in savages penetrated and governed the aspirations and fantasies of those who thought themselves their betters. The prurient imaginings of travellers and invaders about the sexual features of natives answered to patterns in the evolution of metropolitan fashion, as though the Swiftian connection between the Yahoos of the South Pacific, neighbouring the wilds of New Holland, the polite society of 'brutes' in *Cadenus and Vanessa*, and the household of Vanessa's hostess, the great lady, had demonstrated itself on another plane.

In Lombroso's *La Donna delinquente*, the wheel comes full circle in a startling plate which juxtaposes enlarged posteriors of the Hottentot Venus type with an Abyssinian prostitute's massive hanging breasts, perhaps a more spectacular case than any recorded in de Bry's *Voyages*, though not out of line with Cuvier's comment in 1817 about the breasts of the Hottentot Venus herself. The plate, entitled *Polisarcia in Abissina. Cuscinetto Posteriore in Africane*, which comes from a part of the book not included in the English translation published as *The Female Offender* in 1895 and often reprinted, also includes as its fourth item ('d') a portrait of a young African mother with the caption *Donna selvaggia che porta un bambino sul dorso, come in tutti i popoli primitivi* ('savage woman carrying a child on her back as in all primitive peoples') (pl. 9)—a passage strikingly analogous, in its phraseology and mindset, to Swift's account of the Yahoos' resemblance to 'all savage Nations' and which made a point of taking in the practice of 'carrying [children] on their Backs'.[148]

This detail evidently became another generic typification of the primitive, and was used to explain the phenomenon of hanging breasts (as in the passages cited earlier from Herbert and Nieuhoff), as well as the flat noses and thick lips and other distortions of the countenance, which were attributed, in Gulliver's words, to the infants' 'nuzzling with their Face against the Mother's Shoulders' (IV. ii. 230). The habit of typifying savages as carrying their children may suggest that civilized people have it done by others, or, when nursing is also involved, are not limited to these basic activities.[149] In a conversation in Mantel's *The Giant, O'Brien*, a man says he has heard of a type of fairy with 'tits so long and supple that they can fling one over their shoulder so the babby can suck on it, which is a great convenience to them when they are labouring in the fields', at which someone asks 'Whoever heard of gentlefolk that labour in the fields?'. This bit of folk whimsy is the prelude to the Giant's story of a young nursing mother on the road to Galway who comes to grief by agreeing to suckle a wicked queen's child.[150]

Perhaps gentlefolk also felt themselves to be above (or did not want to be observed in connection with) grossly animal behaviour. Animals are presumably the norm, in this thinking, but the role is sometimes reversed, as when Alexandre Exquemelin expressed his delight at female monkeys carrying 'their little ones upon their backs, even just as negresses do their children', full of wonder at 'irrational creatures' acting like humans, somewhat as the Houyhnhnms were quizzically amused in reverse by Gulliver and the female Yahoo. Lombroso's young mother is an indistinct portrait, with none of the grotesquerie of the others. She has graceful contours but something of a mannish face, like Webber's

'Woman of New Holland', also carrying a child (pl. 5), though this mannishness is not so pronounced as in some of de Bry's hanging-breasted grotesques and many of the European prostitutes in Lombroso's own study. In Lombroso's Abyssinian prostitute ('a'), hanging breasts come without mannish features, but bring together the primitive and the prostitute, in a work principally concerned with prostitution in European cities.

Matings with Strangers

Gulliver is repelled by the young Yahoo, though 'her Countenance did not make an Appearance altogether so hideous as the rest of the Kind' (IV. viii. 267), as handsome a compliment as any human is likely to get from him by this stage of his travels. The compliment replicates a remark about one of the Brobdingnagian Maids of Honour, among whom the 'handsomest' was 'a pleasant frolicksome Girl of sixteen' (Stella's age, in an important poem).[151] She would sometimes set Gulliver 'astride upon one of her Nipples; with many other Tricks, wherein the Reader will excuse me for not being over particular' (II. v. 119). Such fantasies attached themselves to the rears of Hottentot women, one of the real-life approximations to gigantism available in a modern context. A French traveller of the 1780s claimed to have seen Hottentot children riding on their mothers' posteriors. The idea resurfaced as a satirical fantasy in more than one caricature of Baartman herself: Williams's *Neptune's Last Resource* (1811), where the Duke of Clarence as Neptune begs to be allowed to 'ride triumphant' on her rump, pocketing her money, and the punning *Love and Beauty* (1822), where a winged cupid is riding on Venus's rump. A later real-life replay, involving the steatopygic rear of a post-Baartman 'Hottentot Venus' exhibited at Hyde Park in 1838, is described in the memoirs of T. E. Crispe. He recounts being taken to a fair at the age of five, where he was 'placed a-straddle, and holding to a girdle round her waist—the almost sole article of her apparel—I plied a toy whip on the flanks of my beautiful jade, who, screaming with laughter, raced me round the circle'.[152]

Crispe found the episode more agreeable than Gulliver, who was 'so much displeased' that he asked not to see 'that young Lady any more'. But there is a distinct note of sexual excitation behind his comically grudging compliment, and such episodes of back-handed gallantry belong as much as hanging breasts to the erotic furniture of travel literature. Instances include Vespucci's report that lustful Amerindian women, with their clean shapely bodies, 'are not as revolting as one might think', his account of inde-scribably 'barbarous' ceremonies in a native village, 'where they offered us their women, and we were unable to fend them off', and Cuvier's account of the selected graces of the monstrous Hottentot Venus, with her graceful chest, charming hand, and pretty foot. Johann Forster's somewhat confused broodings on apes, Negroes, and the fair sex, noted below, may be a marginal case. But Graham Greene on the 'long breasts falling in flat bronze folds', which he came to prefer to the 'white standard' in these matters, and Barry Unsworth's Mr Barton, who prefers the mother with hanging breasts to her delicately proportioned young daughter, because he likes them 'matoor', provide, as we have seen, further illustrations of the sexual charge in descriptions of the purportedly repellent, whether in hags, nymphs, or nymphets. There is an evident prurience in the idea of the 'not as revolting' as expected, of embraces impossible to 'fend off', and indeed of the hanging breasts themselves. In *Memoirs of a Woman of Pleasure*, Fanny is startled to see that 'the venerable mother Abbess' of her brothel, whose ill-coloured breasts 'swagged down, navel low at least', could arouse the lust of a handsome horse-grenadier 'moulded in the *Hercules*-style'. Sade was later to write of the attractions of the ugly, as evidence of the relativity of beauty, as sexually stimulating to jaded tastes, and as in some sense 'natural' in their own right.[153]

A prurience about strange matings, or matings with strangers, as well as a generalized curiosity about the sexuality of the 'other', is comically recognized in *Gulliver's Travels*, where sexual confrontations of some sort occur in every voyage except perhaps the third. This, as Boucé has remarked, is in spite of the fact that Laputian women are highly sexed and fond of strangers.[154] But Book III is about countries where the people, however bizarre in their behaviour or circumstances, are of normal human size and appearance. Where there are considerable differences in size, as in Lilliput and Brobdingnag, folktale giants as well as travel-books are part of the background. Sexual fantasies about giants are extensively reported in psychoanalytic literature, though the present discussion is concerned with accounts not usually encumbered by inward-looking self-perception, either about the sexual encounter itself or in the narrator's consciousness of reporting it. Gulliver's account of the Brobdingnagian maids, their skins 'so coarse and uneven, so variously coloured when I saw them near, with a Mole here and there as broad as a Trencher, and Hairs hanging from it thicker than Pack-threads', and nipples on which Gulliver could be set 'astride' (II. v. 119), has a later analogue in the 'scientific' prose of Ploss's anthropological compendium, which, in a section on ageing women, tells of 'yellow and even brown discolorations ... , and ... a peculiar redness, almost copper', and 'wart-like thickenings and isolated bristly hairs sprout[ing] out'.[155] The visual relativity of Gulliver's human perspective of giantesses is readily adapted, and perhaps even derived, from purportedly sober ethnographic reporting, each with its own charge of sexual feeling, both repelled and fascinated.

Ploss's section on the 'anthropological aspect' of middle-aged women homes in on an 'Abyssinian matron', twice photographed, and showing perhaps the nearest visual counterpart to the verbal grotesqueries of the travel-writers or Gulliver himself, the breasts 'mostly pendent ... like a bag incompletely filled with sand':

In many cases the pendent character of the colossal breasts assumes enormous dimensions, and the woman can hold them up only with a certain amount of effort [pl. 2]. The large knotty areolae and the likewise big and shapeless nipples do their share in making the sight anything but a pleasant one.... Instead of the youthful smoothness, there appear all manner of roughnesses and knots: Often, too, the nipples are much lengthened and thickened, so that they protrude from the big knotty areolae almost like a finger.[156]

What Ploss describes as 'anything but a pleasant' sight must, in its entranced particularity, be set beside Blainville's and Cuvier's half-rhapsodic contemplation of the Hottentot Venus's enormities. Like much of Gulliver's ethnography, this is offered as a generalized portrayal, with a ghoulish particularity which in this instance corresponds to features of Gulliver's giantesses. Where Gulliver is concerned with the disproportions of gigantism, Ploss's compendium is concerned with a generic portrayal of 'the middle-aged woman', strongly focused on native women in general, though, as in this example, instancing particular individuals. It comes almost as a surprise that Ploss is not primarily concerned with the particular case. On this, as on other topics, Swift has a keen intuition of the workings of generalized description in expressing highly specific observations, and his mock-ethnography, directly mimicking other travel-books, extends to future cases like Ploss's, including (and in its way partaking of) their sexual curiosity and a palpable predilection for the avowedly unappealing.

It is a truism that anthropologists and ethnographers are not necessarily free of the pruriencies of travel-writers or authors of exotic fictions. Sexual disgust and sexual arousal are closer to one another than most people admit, and a sexual interest in members of despised underclasses, homegrown or foreign, has its own long history. In contemplating the erotic behaviour of alien peoples, 'scientific' curiosity readily combines with some non-scientific impulses. The sexuality of natives is a staple of our imaginings about ethnic difference, including those which, for example, report, or impute, polygamy, promiscuity, incest, or sodomy, as well as quotidian lust, to savages. These imputations were common in accounts of Amerindians from the time of Columbus and Vespucci, as well as in reports of other lands, in which Swift was widely read. They feature extensively in the ethnography of

Herodotus, Strabo, and Pliny. Gilman cites a twelfth-century
Jewish traveller describing a people 'at Seba on the river
Pirhon ... who, like animals, eat of the herbs that grow on the
banks of the Nile and in the fields. They go about naked and have
not the intelligence of ordinary men. They cohabit with their
sisters and anyone they can find ... And these are the Black slaves,
the sons of Ham.'[157]

The passage is hardly a Swiftian source, but it shares several
generic features with accounts of Hottentots by Herbert,
Ovington, and Beeckman, and with Gulliver's description of the
Yahoos. Swift's idiom again impishly sports a technical air of
ethnographic reportage (bordering on the zoological as Exquemelin observing maternal monkeys bordered on the ethnographic). 'Those Animals, like other Brutes, had their Females in
common', the Master Houyhnhnm tells Gulliver (IV. vii. 263),
speaking as a member of another species, but effectively engaging
by proxy, as the reports of Gulliver and of Swift himself do more
directly, in analogies of savages with 'brutes' which are a feature of
Gulliver's Travels and endemic in the vocabulary of racial difference. The specific equation of sexual promiscuity with animals is
at least as old as Herodotus. The phrase resembles Herbert's remark
about the Hottentots and Troglodytes, 'a whole Tribe commonly
keeping together, ... coupling without distinction', which
precedes the reference to their unnatural mixing with apes, but it
is again apposite to notice the generalizing drift of Swift's 'like
other Brutes' and the odd extension of the language of a particular
ethnography to a much wider generic coverage.[158]

The words have little of the *Encyclopédie*'s overt censoriousness
as it affirms that 'la communauté des femmes ... est un excès que
toutes les nations policées ont en horreur', though Swift's real
feelings doubtless had more in common with this sentiment than
with the ethnographic openness, with its potential for lyricism, of
Montaigne or Diderot.[159] Just before the mention of Yahoo polygamy, for example, the master Houyhnhnm informs Gulliver that
the principal employment of a Yahoo leader's favourite 'was to *lick*

his Master's Feet and Posteriors, and drive the Female Yahoos *to his Kennel'*, a more sarcastic formulation than that of any dispassionate scientific observer. But the sarcasm is in Swift's voice-over rather than the Houyhnhnm's voice, and much of the account mimics an idiom of anthropological observation, ostensibly or partially free of declared sympathies, as the Houyhnhnm describes the rituals of herd leadership among the Yahoos:

He had heard indeed some curious *Houyhnhnms* observe, that in most Herds there was a Sort of ruling *Yahoo* (as among us there is generally some leading or principal Stag in a Park) who was always more *deformed* in Body, and *mischievous in Disposition*, than any of the rest. That, this *Leader* had usually a Favourite as *like himself* as he could get, whose Employment was to *lick his Master's Feet and Posteriors, and drive the Female* Yahoos *to his Kennel*; for which he was now and then rewarded with a piece of Ass's Flesh. This *Favourite* is hated by the whole Herd; and therefore to protect himself, keeps always *near the Person of his Leader*. He usually continues in Office till a worse can be found; but the very Moment he is discarded, his Successor, at the Head of all the *Yahoos* in that District, Young and Old, Male and Female, come in a body, and discharge their Excrements upon him from Head to Foot. (IV. vii. 262–3)

The anthropology or zoology of kingship seems to have been a topic of travel-narratives and fictions. Passmann cites from Purchas a *Treatise of Brasil*, in which a grimly ugly Ape-king is shown being tended by an ape page. The detail, as well as the generic style, are reflected in the straight-faced mock-ethnography of the Houyhnhnm's account.[160]

The final item in the Houyhnhnm's description is a replay of Gulliver's first account of the Yahoos, when they 'began to discharge their Excrements on my Head' (IV. i), repeating travel-book reports of Hottentot and simian urinating and defecating rituals, notably in the ceremonies of marriage and genital surgery. T. S. Eliot's King Bolo receives similar attentions from his bodyguards, without even being 'discarded'. That monkeys do it too, in books Swift possessed, is part of the point which links Yahoos, Hottentots, and apes. Dampier's *Voyages and Descriptions* (1699) describes the monkeys of Campeachy scattering 'their Urine and Dung about my Ears'; and Wafer, whose *New Voyage and Description of the Isthmus of America* (also 1699) Swift owned, also spoke of monkeys 'pissing down purposely on our Heads', as well as citing (in the second and third editions) a Royal Society observer's account of monkeys which 'are very leacherous, and often fall foul on the *Negro* Women'.[161]

But the passage about the selection of the Yahoo leader shows the detail elevated or transferred to the status of a tribal rite. It is the solemn foolery of ascribing a ritual character to what is in fact described as an unbridled collective incontinence, which supplies the air of scientific reporting, whereas the earlier episode had registered a strong sense of the traveller's shrill discomfiture. What is captured is something of the stance (later exemplified in Gilman's medical and anthropological texts) of the ostensibly value-free scientist negotiating prurient material. The detachment does not survive extended exposure in either case. Gulliver seems both horrified and fascinated that, unlike 'other Brutes', a 'She-*Yahoo* would admit the Male, while she was pregnant', one of the practices which distinguished them from all other 'sensitive Creatures', so that their humanoid ways end up as worse than those of brutes (IV. vii. 263). He seems to be repeating Pliny, who says that few animals other than women have coitus when they are pregnant. Ploss's compendium reports many societies where 'coitus with a pregnant woman is most strictly forbidden?[162] On the other hand, the Yahoos do not go in for other 'unnatural' practices, which, we shall see, distinguish them from 'us', to our disadvantage.

Polygamy and lax sexual mores, bordering on free love, are ubiquitous travel-book topics. Among Amerindians, they are reported as early as the 1490s.[163] Polygamy is specifically a custom of Montaigne's cannibals, who in other ways resemble the virtuous, but monogamous and distinctly undersexed, Houyhnhnms, as well as of the Tahitian paradise later described by Bougainville and Cook.[164] Montaigne's essay has left very strong marks on *Gulliver's Travels*, as we have seen, and the Tupinamba had in any case become, long before Montaigne, the model for European conceptions of the savage, whether noble or ignoble. They are named, in more than one text of Swift, and in defiance of geographical or chronological propriety, as the locally representative or generic type of the savage.[165] I suggested in Chapter 1 that Swift took from Montaigne's cannibals elements of the Houyhnhnm commonwealth, and relegated polygamy and other savageries to the common pool of Yahoo depravities as Montaigne would not have done. The long loose hair of Yahoo females is a feature of Tupi women, as portrayed by Vespucci, and in the illustrations to many accounts of American voyages, though the location of their country is in the South Seas.[166]

Sexual come-ons by native women are widely featured, and the Yahoo female may be seen as a downbeat version of those Tahitian beauties who freely offered themselves to Bougainville's men. How Swift would have responded to their narrative is not pleasant to imagine. Closer to the spirit of *Gulliver's Travels* is a scabrous account in Thomas Phillips's journal, reporting on an African slaving voyage of 1693–94 (but not published until the 1730s), which spoke of 'negroe women, who talk'd to us mainly smutty English words, making lascivious undecent gestures with their bodies, which were all naked, excepting a little clout about their waste, hanging down to the middle of the thigh, which they would often take up to shew us their merchandize'.[167] Bougainville's *Voyage round the World* appeared in 1771, almost half a century after *Gulliver's Travels*, and South Sea paradises like his *Nouvelle Cythère* are perhaps a later and more idealized stereotype, whose English counterparts and contemporaries (or immediate successors) were the various South Sea islanders (including Tahitians) of Cook's voyages, though Cook himself resisted the blandishments, much as Gulliver did, particularly deploring the New Zealanders' habit, induced by 'commerce with Europeans', of offering their women to his crews.[168]

Reports, or fantasies, of 'native women's sexual hospitality' popularly suggest South Sea paradises nowadays, but they go back a long time in the literature of conquest and reappear in Victorian fictions of empire. An example occurs in the African setting of Rider Haggard's *She*. The Amahagger woman Ustane offers herself to the hero Leo, by kissing him 'publicly' on the lips, according to a custom in which if the man 'kissed her back it was a token that he accepted her, and the arrangement continued till one of them wearied of it'. The hero, looking 'slightly astonished', nevertheless 'returned the embrace' on the supposition that this people 'followed the customs of the early Christians'. But the Amahagger have a sexual code, free but responsible and socially functional, which is admired in the novel with the usual dose of Montaigne-and-water, laced with a flourish of Victorian worldly wisdom: 'It is very curious to observe how the customs of mankind on this matter vary in different countries, ... and what is right and proper in one place wrong and improper in another ... there is, even according to our canons, nothing immoral about this Amahagger custom, seeing that the interchange of the embrace answers to our ceremony of marriage, which, as we know, justifies most things.'[169] (Leo and Ustane become lovers until the sorceress She disposes of the latter. The custom, as usual, has its dark side, and when another Amahagger woman is rebuffed by the servant Job, a grim cannibal punishment is planned, narrowly averted by the narrator's timely firing of a pistol).[170]

The Victorian episode brings home, on a plane of extravagant fantasy, the lesson that the offering of women, on their own initiative or by their menfolk, was not always an expression of pure sensuality or erotic generosity, and was seldom free of trouble. Vespucci reports girls being brought to his boats as part of an ambush, and, as if in explicit commentary on this, the late sixteenth-century engraving showing Vespucci being welcomed by a sexy blonde America shows cannibals preparing a meal in the background, rather as Eckhout's pleasantly sensuous woman is portrayed carrying a human leg instead of a child on her back (pl. 7).[171] Even in Tahiti, commercial or political purposes were often involved, and sexual blandishments were sometimes accompanied by treachery or theft.[172] European reactions varied, from the friendly responsiveness of some of Bougainville's men to the denunciation of Tahitian vice by post-*Bounty* missionaries. For example, a European might resent the 'refusal to traffic in [sexual] favours' on the part of one tribe as a 'want of sociality', and to praise it in another as a noble refusal to prostitute their women, except unmarried girls of the lower class, as Dumont d'Urville did in the 1830s in disparagement of Melanesians and in praise of the Polynesian Maori, evidently a display of racial preferences on his part.[173] Bernard Smith has said in *Imagining the Pacific* that the 'market in sex in the South Pacific was established as a result of Cook's voyages', with generally amiable consequences, but with some collateral damage through the importation of syphilis into the region, on which Gulliver, or his author, would certainly have been pleased to report. (Cook was repeatedly exercised by worry about the transmission by his men of venereal diseases to the island populations).[174]

It is sometimes overlooked that *Gulliver's Travels*, and especially its Fourth Book, is a story of the South Pacific, though it exhibits a peculiar time-warp, discernible in many eighteenth-century writings, in which references to the savage and the primitive are permeated with American examples and motifs, where Hawaiians or Tahitians or inhabitants of New Holland and New Zealand were regularly called Indians, and where even wigwams are occasionally found in the South Seas.[175] As early as de Bry, the term 'Indians' had extended to Canary Islanders, Africans, Micronesians, Polynesians, and natives of the Magellan Archipelago. But at that time America was still the dominant focus of colonial expansion and exploration, and the later survival of American examples and images in non-American locations is perhaps more striking because this was no longer so. The mindset of Montaigne, and evocations of his locales, survive in arresting ways, as when Bougainville noted, on first landing in Tahiti, that the flute-playing and singing 'Indians' were 'doubtless' engaged in an 'anacreontic' song.[176] And this mindset, including its ironies and indignations, is as strong a shaping force on Swift's travel-fiction as the sites of the *Voyages* of Dampier, whom Gulliver called his cousin, and whose South Sea travels provide the nominal location of the voyage to Houyhnhnmland.

Grim warnings about the seductions of exotic temptresses go back as far as the *Odyssey*, and there are purported eyewitness reports of Amerindian examples as early as 1500. Vespucci's published writings are insistent that Amerindian women copulated with Christians whenever they could.[177] The unpublished 'familiar' letters to Lorenzo di Pierfrancesco de' Medici (a cousin of Lorenzo the Magnificent) also hint at the lechery of native women, but more reticently.[178] The published 'letters' of *c.*1502 and 1505 may have been editorially spiced with 'pornographic' additions. For example, the *Mundus Novus* says the women were so lustful that they used poisonous animal stings to swell their husbands' members to a monstrous thickness and shape, so that many of them eventually rotted away. The *Letter* to Soderini announces that 'decency bids us pass over the wiles they employ to satisfy their inordinate lust'. Both works stress the women's lack of bodily shame, their fleshy well-formed bodies, and (as we saw) the rarity of 'sagging breasts' among them.[179]

It is perhaps in conformity with these accounts that, as I have suggested, the later engraving of Vespucci *'Discovering' America* (pl. 3) depicts America as an inviting full-breasted beauty, evidently eager to offer herself to the stiff and priggish Florentine. Bucher cites one of de Bry's plates, in part 10 of the *Great Voyages*, showing 'the *conquistadores*, with Vespucci leading, as slightly ridiculous beneficiaries' of the favours of Amerindian women. Cross-cultural couplings are a theme of the literature of the *conquista*, already present in the accounts of Columbus's voyages, and de Bry's illustrations sometimes treat these in more or less derisive mode. Another image shows some Spaniards 'on the island of Curaçao trying to seduce three giantesses', and giants early became part of the sexual comedy of narratives of colonial encounter. John Ogilby's *America* gives an exuberant account of mustachio'd giantesses making gross passes at the Dutch surgeon Henrick Haelbos in 1643, 'their Husbands giving consent thereunto',[180] a Rabelaisian fancy which gets replayed in the tart episode of Gulliver among the Brobdingnagian maids of honour (II. v. 119).[181] Giants were common in travel literature since the *Odyssey*.[182] Vespucci reports an Isle of Giants (Curaçao), sighting and describing the females before the men, though not offering sexual disclosures on this occasion.[183] Travellers, from Magellan's companion Pigafetta (who reports giantesses with 'teats half a yard long') to John Byron, the poet's grandfather, claimed to have seen giants in Patagonia: these seemed to be 'good' giants, unlike their Odyssean prototypes, and there were other examples of good giants, present and past, some of whom even acquired a Rousseauistic nobility.[184] Frankenstein's monster, whose story was the result of a suggestion by the poet Byron, has some features of this, accompanied by an atmosphere of lurid fears of miscegenation. The more or less genial extension of giant fantasies to the sexual sphere may go back to Odyssean ogre-enchantresses as well as to Rabelais, but in any event it is obvious that even in this somewhat specialized aspect *Gulliver's Travels* draws on the literature of travel.[185]

The Spanish are often portrayed as exploitative sexual aggressors, not only in de Bry but in their own accounts.[186] They were in fact sometimes boastful about it, like Cuneo, or the scoundrel in Yucatan denounced by Las Casas for impregnating the local women for profit.[187] On the other hand, the British are usually to be found behaving with punctilious correctness, as when they decorously ask 'through an emissary from the governor for the hand of ... Pocahontas'. Sir Walter Ralegh in Guiana self-consciously established an image of the chaste empire-builder, imposing sexual restraint in a shaming propagandistic contrast to Spanish behaviour.[188] This sexual variant of an idea of British is best, famously asserted by Gulliver in the sphere of colonial administration in the final chapter, is consistent with the Dutchman de Bry's Protestant bias and his agenda of discrediting the

Catholic imperial powers. It evokes the patriotism of Hakluyt, a set of whose *Voyages* Swift possessed, and who was an acquaintance, admired model, and frequent source of de Bry and his sons. Hakluyt's declaration that 'liberty...can only be found under the English flag' is the prototype of a long line that includes Gulliver and goes on to Gibbon, Darwin, Conrad, and others, as we have seen. Gulliver's praise of the British Nation's 'Caution in stocking their Provinces with People of sober Lives and Conversations' (IV. xii.294) taps into an established discourse with its own applications in the sexual subsphere, and his recoil from the female Yahoo is a dyspeptic and jaundiced advance-version of the principled abstinence of Cook.[189] Bougainville was a French version of this stereotype of the good colonial administrator or flag-bearer (each country of course had its own, and Diderot expended on these questions some ironies less stinging than Swift's). But the scenes described in Bougainville's Tahitian chapters, which may not have been very different in practice from what befell Cook's own companions, reinforce the usual mythologies of things being ordered differently in France.

Needless to say, such mythologies, including the simple scenario of native women offering themselves to the European invader, or being offered by their menfolk, are seen from a European angle of vision. They are shaped by the conqueror's perspective, and include elements of personal fantasy and cultural self-inflation, as well as forms of national point-scoring. The complex social realities of inter-ethnic encounters, involving not only sexual confrontations, but conflict and dispossession, are not usually brought into view, any more than are the perspectives of invaded populations and the social tensions created within them. A fully-rounded understanding of the 'politics of contact', including the internal politics of the bestowal of women and changes in the generational power-contest between young native men and tribal elders, of the kind undertaken in the Australian context by the historian Henry Reynolds, seems virtually non-existent in older travel-writing, and wholly outside Swift's field of vision.[190]

Going Native

If the episode of the female Yahoo opens the door on a well-established theme of interracial mating, Gulliver's rejection of her ensures that it cannot develop, as his revulsion from the Brobdingnagian breasts, or his passing up of whatever opportunities may have been offered by the Lilliputians' admiration for his imposingly proportioned phallus, ensure that nothing approaching miscegenation is going to occur, despite some coy innuendo.[191] 'Going native', or, in the parlance of Cook's day, 'turning Indian', a process usually identified with taking a native woman, was a fairly common phenomenon, which does not appear to have acquired, even as late as the 1770s, that aura of hushed voices and averted eyes with which it is associated in some nineteenth-century fictions. Gulliver's experiences are in any case sufficiently curtly arrested, on this as on most other topics, to make any development into novelistic density unthinkable.

His rejection of all foreign females is eventually extended to his own wife and is not 'racist' in any ordinary sense. It is a generic rejection of humanity as a whole. When he is appalled 'that by copulating with one of the *Yahoo*-Species, I had become a Parent of more' (IV. xi. 289), it is to his wife and children that he refers. By the end his preference for the company of his horses is an aspiration not so much to join a master-race as an alien species. He does speak with approbation of a form of colour-discrimination, practised by the Houyhnhnms:

among the *Houyhnhnms*, the *White*, the *Sorrel*, and the *Iron-grey*, were not so exactly shaped as the *Bay*, the *Dapple-grey*, and the *Black*; nor born with equal Talents of Mind, or a Capacity to improve them; and therefore continued always in the Condition of Servants, without ever aspiring to match out of their own Race, which in that Country would be reckoned monstrous and unnatural. (IV. vi. 256)

This Houyhnhnm 'racism', though specifically based on colour, is in fact an issue of rank or class rather than race, in a more specific sense than is usual in the common perception that racial discriminations are in themselves an extension of class conflict. Immediately after this account, Gulliver tells the Houyhnhnm about the 'altogether ... different' arrangements of '*Nobility* among us', including lewd morals, sickly constitutions, and the habit of marrying people 'of mean Birth' to improve a family's finances or physical constitution (IV. vi. 256–7). These arrangements are genetically but not 'racially' disastrous. The word 'Race' is plainly used in the sense of 'social class' in a related passage, in which we learn that 'the Race of inferior *Houyhnhnms* brought up to be Servants' are allowed to breed three offspring of each sex, to maintain the supply of 'Domesticks in the Noble Families' (IV. viii. 268). They practise eugenics, on an approved Platonic model, to avoid any 'disagreeable Mixture in the Breed' (even here the logic of colour distinctions is intra-racial rather than inter-racial) and maximize strength and comeliness, but not to swell the numbers of the higher 'races', who are in fact limited to fewer offspring (one of each sex) than the 'inferior Houyhnhnms', to prevent over-population (IV. viii. 268–9).[192]

There is no obvious sign that the Houyhnhnms have 'races' in a sense to which 'racism' would be an applicable concept. If they did, the term 'race' in the relevant modern usage would probably not have been available to Swift anyway, and is certainly linguistically unlikely.[193] The Yahoos are a different species, also enlisted as useful labour, though more in the manner of beasts of burden than of slaves. Every Houyhnhnm of whatever colour is evidently fully indigenous to Houyhnhnmland, and their various colours (corresponding routinely or formulaically to those of horses in the human world) are so to speak a 'local colour': another projection of how it would be in a commonwealth in which the roles of humans and horses were simply transposed. Even hierarchies of colour are reversed, as in human valuations of horses, with white and sorrel below bay and black. You might call it a kind of displaced realism, which often comes with a stinging incremental flourish, as when Gulliver suggests to the Houyhnhnms the option of castrating the Yahoos (which is what humans do to horses) rather than exterminating them (which humans are more inclined to do to each other). 'Aspiring to match out of their own Race' seems just such a flourish, adapting differences of equine pigmentation to the social arrangements of humans: it can hardly mean, in this particular context, anything very different from marrying outside your station, and has more to do with knowing your place than your race.

This is not to suggest that Swift's views on racial difference were especially edifying in modern terms. The idea that crossing social boundaries, in a well-regulated commonwealth, is as outlandish as marrying outside your race is implicit in the allegory, and does not suggest a genial view of either process. One might be tempted to compare it to human caste systems, in which gradations of skin-colour play a role, but the Houyhnhnm demarcations seem so precise and unfraught that they seem to be without the element of quasi-racial revulsion implicit in the real-life models. I suspect that, on the racial as distinct from the social plane, the Houyhnhnm code conforms to unthinking norms more than to outright convictions, as well as not being much preoccupied with race anyway. In a real-life or human world where multi-ethnic societies, and even transcultural travel, were still the exception rather than the rule, the tenuousness of this preoccupation, if it is present in the passage at all, may have as much to do with the improbability of mixed matings as with their undesirability. Such matings, as we saw, were part of the exotica of exploration and conquest, sufficiently remote from domestic or 'metropolitan' experience to seem unthreatening.

No atmosphere of scandal seems to have surrounded the sixteenth-century Spaniards who turned Indian and were able to interpret the local languages for Cortés in Mexico. Interpreters had an integral function in the process of empire, and Spaniards turned Indian after capture were important in this role. Although regret or disapproval might be expressed at the defection, these were not manifestly fraught with preoccupations of 'respectability' or class betrayal. Any perceived scandal would be on religious grounds (apostasy or heresy), or in special cases over some notably shocking act, such as man-eating, to which Spaniards were sometimes driven by starvation. Typically, attempts seem to have been made to reintegrate and use such persons without turning them into pariahs.[194] The situation seems to have been broadly similar in French and other territories, though intermarriage between French and Indians was forbidden on Villegagnon's colony.[195] Nor did scandal, except mainly on grounds of apostasy, seem to attach to the Norman sailors who lived for a time among the Indians of Brazil, any more than for Indian go-betweens themselves. In 'Des cannibales', Montaigne expresses contempt for his Brazilian interpreter with the Indian chiefs at Rouen, but that was because the man was stupid and barely understood Montaigne's thinking, and Montaigne liked to talk to sailors and merchants who had been among Indians and could speak with inwardness about them.[196] Even in the age of Cook, there seems to have been a relaxed attitude to those sailors reported to have 'turned Indian'. The issue seems to have acquired a new charge after the affair of the *Bounty*, when the lure of South Sea paradises was invoked as a libertarian incentive, and undoubtedly tapped a strain of counter-cultural and even revolutionary sentiment.[197]

The idea that the attractions of Tahiti might provoke further shipboard rebellions clearly had an important impact on official attitudes. There is evidence of a considerable missionary effort, after the *Bounty* affair, to present Tahitian mores as depraved rather than paradisal, and to propagate a tarnished view of the romance of defection.[198] The trial of the returned mutineers, and the hanging of three of them in October 1792, their bodies dangling for about an hour while work in the fleet was suspended, seems to have made, according to a report to the Admiralty, 'a great impression upon the minds of all the ships' companies present'. If this was the design, it was insufficient to prevent a more widespread mutiny five years later, when, as Greg Dening says, 'most of these ships' companies mutinied against most of these ships' captains ... at Great Nore', and when thirty-six men were hanged.[199] There had been from the start a tendency, promoted by Bligh himself, but also tapping a public prurience on the subject of imperial erotica, to attribute the *Bounty*'s mutiny to sexual greed rather than shipboard grievances. Bligh's attribution of the revolt to fantasies 'of a more happy life among the Otaheitians ..., which joined to some Female connections has most likely been the leading cause of the whole business', expressed the disreputable, or at least unillusioned, underside of the libertarian island idyll, and defenders of the mutineer Fletcher Christian made a point of playing down his sexuality. It quickly became known 'that Christian and eleven others on the *Bounty* had had the "venereals"', to which would be added some lurid details of racial and sexual violence in Tahiti, and later on Pitcairn island.[200]

The *Bounty* court martial brought to light an example of 'going native' in which the idea of the Tahitian idyll competed sharply with what seems to have been a new or enhanced censoriousness. The seventeen-year-old midshipman Peter Heywood (who was sentenced to death, pardoned thanks to high naval connections, and subsequently had a successful naval career, rising to captain in six years) was said, in some verses by his sister, who actively interested herself in his defence, to have experienced, among the 'most generous Indians' of Tahiti, 'Sure friendship ... and gratitude and love / such as ne'er reigns in European blood'. But he was disparaged by others for turning Indian himself. On the quarterdeck of the *Pandora*, which brought the mutineers back to England, his '"going native" in dress, language, and custom encouraged presumptions of his guilt'.[201]

The concerted revulsion against going native seems increasingly to have been a feature of nineteenth-century colonial cultures. For example, in Australian settlements, any white man escaping to the bush and adopting a native lifestyle might be seen as a rubbing in of disreputable origins and a threat to the standing of a territory seeking to establish respectable credentials. Variations on these anxieties evidently existed in Victorian India, or in the more unstructured settlements of South East Asia, where an expatriate community was jealous of its status as a governing class in an alien culture. The Conradian or Kiplingesque aura of scandalous group-betrayal and its mythologized pariah status derive from such later imperial circumstances, as does the strong opposition to mixed marriages, and the contempt for their product, the half-caste, which J. M. Coetzee has discussed in the novels of the South African novelist Sarah Gertrude Millin.[202] The phenomenon is related to anxieties about miscegenation discussed in the next section of this chapter, whose origins are partly traceable to some precursors of race 'science', and therefore of scientific racism, in the period between Gulliver and the Hottentot Venus. Its Nazi form, to which I return in the next two chapters, came much later and drew (as Coetzee points out) on Millin's fiction, despite the fact that she herself was a Jew, resisted the spread of Nazism into South Africa, and tried to prevent the translation of her own work into German.[203]

Hottentots have a special place in her fiction: 'Maria had a trace of Malay in her Hottentot face', we read in *King of the Bastards*, and more generally, as Coetzee paraphrases *God's Stepchildren*, 'Hottentots, with their "Mongolian" faces', are at the opposite extreme from those aristocratic pure black natives, the Zulus. From occupying a pariah status on the old border between man and ape, they have descended, or ascended, to a fully human status on an even more disreputable border, between races.[204] The badness of being a hybrid, which other writers, like Lawrence in the *Plumed Serpent*, locate in other races in other places, the stereotype of the 'poor white' who mates with the natives, and of the pariah products of such unions, are a far cry from the matings on Tahiti of Cook's or Bougainville's men, or the reported romance of the *Bounty* mutineers. The political or missionary response to the latter phenomenon, the wave of propaganda designed to put a stop to the hijacking of the Admiralty's fleet on the high seas, may have helped to introduce into this topic some of its particular lurid disrepute. As Coetzee suggests, the nineteenth-century obsession with degeneration, in Gobineau as in the Goncourts or Zola, made a more powerful and resonant contribution.[205] That world is no longer that of Gulliver, even if 'going native' may seem to be what sometimes befalls him, though not sexually (he is not, as he informs us, a very sexual animal), in some of the societies he visits. The fact, however, reflects his genial adaptability rather than any depraved instinct.

It is not my purpose here to sentimentalize Swift's views on race. As far as the Houyhnhnms are concerned, their 'racism', which some critics find more distressing than others, is not found in the passage about horses of colour. To the extent that they are 'racist', it is not at the expense of their own kind but of the Yahoos. It is a trans-specific dislike, directed at another species and not another race in one's own, and strictly speaking no more racist than a human's dislike of cats, or for that matter horses. Their anatomical differences from the Yahoos being what they are, an equal and opposite counterpart among humans would have to be called 'equism', and it is unnerving to contemplate the idea of a possible 'humanism' among them. Gulliver approved of this feeling, which entailed much self-abasement on his part, as he approved of their colour-coded class distinctions, in the sense that he approves of everything among the Houyhnhnms. The colour-coding also suggests that Gulliver, like his creator, assumed that hierarchies were a good thing, but it does not tell us anything either way about his views on race. Whatever the relation of this passage to Swift's own political opinions or his psychobiography, Gulliver's aspiration is to be of the Houyhnhnm species, irrespective of any place he might have in their social rankings, and the point about his exclusion is that, unlike all the other peoples or groups in *Gulliver's Travels*, they are neither human nor humanoid. Conversely, Gulliver's feelings about the other peoples, including his own, is that they *are* human, rather than that they belong to any despised group, social *or* racial.

Nevertheless, Gulliver's cross-specific aspirations, his desire for Houyhnhnmhood, though quite distinct from ethnic differentiations within his own or the Houyhnhnm species, are impregnated with metaphorical and other formulations which bring to mind the crossing of racial boundaries among humans. (I use the words cross-specific or trans-specific to refer to a traffic between humans and other species, and cross-racial between humans of different race). A comic subplot in Book IV is Gulliver's assumption of the gait, gesture, voice, and manner of the Houyhnhnms, and when he is back in the human world he takes it as a compliment when people tell him he trots like a horse or sounds as if he is neighing when he speaks (IV. x. 279, xi. 285). This is prefigured by his habit, after leaving Brobdingnag, of expecting people to be giants and of shouting to make himself heard, and a contrary tendency to suppose himself a giant, seeing other Englishmen as Lilliputian pygmies whom he is afraid of trampling, calling 'aloud to have them stand out of the Way', bending down to enter his own house, and so on (II. viii. 143–9). This seems to happen mainly in the wake of visits to societies he admires, even though the post-Brobdingnagian experience is purely a function of size and might be supposed to be 'value free'. If we regard Gulliver's pliable or impressionable habit of falling into the manners and perspectives of these societies as an embryonic form of going native, then his last and most lasting experience of doing so is the relationship he strikes up with the horses in his stable. It is a belated version, like its post-Brobdingnagian analogue, because it occurs after Gulliver returns to England and not in the country which originally provoked it. Gulliver is a slow fellow in this as in other ways.

Even so, the lineaments of a classic breakdown of clan solidarity are discernible despite the fact that the actual breach is of species solidarity. Like so many cases of men turning Indian, he is alienated from his wife and family, preferring, however, not the company of natives, but that of two horses in his stable (IV. xi. 289–90). These provide a kind of alternative society, in defiance of the work's systematic contrary tendency to insist on their otherness as a species. The characteristic double bind this generates is teasingly reinforced by the homonymous relationship of 'Houyhnhnm' to 'human'. Gulliver's new mode of life is a development which Swift subjects to some playful mystification. It is interesting that Gulliver's cousin Sympson, in 'The Publisher to the Reader', makes no mention of this bizarre lifestyle. He reports that Gulliver, 'growing weary of the Concourse of curious People coming to him at his house in *Redriff*' (he had become something of an exotic freakshow in his own right, a paradoxical casualty of the imperial scenario at home as well as abroad), had moved back to his native Nottinghamshire, 'where he now lives retired, yet in good Esteem among his Neighbours' (9).

This omits any hint of Gulliver's misanthropy, as well as of his predilection for the horses. Both these states of mind, however, are manifest from the beginning in Gulliver's own letter *to* Sympson (8), though they would not be known to the first-time reader of the first edition. It is almost as if the bland Sympson were being put up by Swift to do a public relations job, pre-emptively undercut (after 1735) by the letter to Sympson, and (in all editions) by any first reading of the work as a whole. Sympson's words imply that the Nottinghamshire experience is later than that described in Chapter xii of Book IV, which still seems situated at Redriff, and which already represents an element of reacculturation to English ways. Gulliver's own suggestion in the final chapter that a process of adaptation was going on may be consistent with this:

I began last Week to permit my Wife to sit at Dinner with me, at the farthest End of a long Table; and to answer (but with the utmost Brevity) the few Questions I asked her. Yet the Smell of a *Yahoo* continuing very offensive, I always keep my Nose well stopt with Rue, Lavender, or Tobacco-Leaves. And although it be hard for a Man late in Life to remove old Habits; I am not altogether out of Hopes in some Time to suffer a Neighbour *Yahoo* in my Company, without the Apprehension I am yet under of his Teeth or his Claws. (IV. xii. 295–6)

If the passage hints at a future narrative development of the kind Sympson appears in retrospect to have confirmed (but what reader is likely to remember the detail or experience the retrospect?), its effective force is less to soften than to rub in the alienation, a readerly equivalent of those acts of clemency which turn out in various episodes of *Gulliver's Travels* to exceed the rigours of the punishments they purport to palliate. It belongs with those concessions that add to rather than reduce the original sting, like Swift's remark in the letter to Pope of 26 November 1725 that it is not Swift but *vous autres* who 'hate mankind', though he would be no more sorry to have some of them shot than he was was for the kite who stole one of his chickens. The rhetorical manœuvre is one which continually deceives readers, and is one of Swift's most characteristic signatures. The comic elements of Gulliver's post-Houyhnhnm condition will escape no one. But for all the talk of a progressive socialization, the glimpse of a wife kept at the end of a long table, of Gulliver's nose stopped with herbs and tobacco against human smells, and his confessedly irrational fear of being eaten by a neighbour, seem hardly designed to evoke a return to normal life, and the work's closing accents remain outlandish and cantankerous. The authoritative tableau of Gulliver's English resettlement, the one indelibly sketched in his preceding chapter, is that of a truly alternative habitat and mode of life:

During the first Year I could not endure my Wife or Children in my Presence, the very Smell of them was intolerable; much less could I suffer them to eat in the same Room. To this Hour they dare not presume to touch my Bread, or drink out of the same Cup; neither was I ever able to let one of them take me by the Hand. The first Money I laid out was to buy two young Stone-Horses [i.e. stallions, not statues] which I keep in a good Stable. My Horses understand me tolerably well; I converse with them at least four Hours of every Day. They are Strangers to Bridle or Saddle; they live in great Amity with me, and Friendship to each other. (IV. xi. 289–90)

The collapse of English or European habits or modes of life, the abandonment of family, the defiant shacking up in an alien mode, are hallmarks of going native. It is as though Mister Kurtz had transplanted his jungle to the banks of the Thames, always allowing that the Houyhnhnms were a more decorous type of native than Kurtz's African tribesmen, so that the doings are going to be more sedate.

There is no sex, of course. Gulliver is British, unlike the Yahoo female who lusts after him, and whose lust is cross-racial and not cross-specific: the Yahoo 'Females had a natural Propensity to me as one of their own Species'. At least there is no overt sexuality, and for the purposes of the present discussion the stallion-smelling groom may be left to the psychobiographers, as may the fact that earlier, in Houyhnhnmland, the male 'Sorrel Nag (who always loved me)', bid a tender farewell to the departing Gulliver, by repeatedly 'crying out, . . . Take Care of thy self, Gentle *Yahoo*' (IV. xi. 283), an uncharacteristically 'sentimental' tableau, later painted by Sawrey Gilpin. Perhaps someone will even discover that the stallions were groom-smelling, or aroused in Gulliver or his author or his readers sentiments which dared not speak their name even in the absence of humanized olfactory aids. But most readers might agree that cross-specific matings do not fall within the scope of Gulliver's admittedly lukewarm and circumscribed libido in any way of which he, or any potential sexual partners, appear to be aware.

On the other hand, the idea of cross-racial coupling, not only with the Yahoo female but with other humans and humanoids in Brobdingnag and elsewhere, does from time to time proffer mild excitations of an alternative kind, and coexists with at least one comic episode of cross-specific intimacy, forced on a discomfited Gulliver by the young Brobdingnagian monkey. This is part of a teasing overlap between the cross-racial and the cross-specific which characteristically defies, or complicates, or undermines, certain clarities of demarcation on which the work simultaneously insists. It is a form of conceptual slippage very similar in style to the deliberately unstable verbal slippages in the use of terms like 'nature' and 'reason' as the spotlight shifts both between and within the categories of Houyhnhnm, human, and humanoid.[206]

Apes and Angels

Gulliver's Travels is knowingly or unknowingly implicated in the well-known phenomenon whereby the vocabulary of ethnic or racial difference sometimes slips over into trans-specific metaphors, insults, or imputations, as when this or that group are spoken of as animals. These animals were often monkeys, for historic reasons. The resemblances and differences between apes and humans have been part of attempts to define the human from at least as far back as the fifth century BC, when the Carthaginian Hanno discovered a hairy people called gorillas on an island off the West African coast. Vulgar analogies are a commonplace in the portrayal of 'natives' at many different periods, as in the illustration, by Will Robinson, entitled *A few of the natives brandished spears*, to J. Lang's *Story of Captain Cook* (1906).[207] Other animals sometimes take the place of monkeys. And variations exist on simple resemblance, as when persons or groups are spoken of as addicted to unions with other species or as the products of such unions, like that much-sung hero of several cultures, the son of a bitch ('fils de chienne', for example, occurs in Scarron's *Roman Comique* (1651–7), and the Russian *sukin syn* is a common insult).[208] It is interesting to set beside *Gulliver's Travels* a passage by Edward Long (author of a *History of Jamaica*, and the 'father of English racism'), from *Candid Reflections* (1772), in which, in a much cited passage, considerations of social class and sexuality spill over into issues of both race and species:

The lower class of women in *England*, are remarkably fond of the blacks, for reasons too brutal to mention; they would connect themselves with horses and asses, if the laws permitted them. By these ladies they [the blacks] generally have a numerous brood. Thus, in the course of a few generations more, the English blood will become so contaminated with this mixture, and from the chances, the ups and downs of life, this alloy may spread so extensively, as even to reach the middle, and then the higher orders of the people, till the whole nation resembles the *Portuguese* and *Moriscos* in complexion of skin and baseness of mind.

This anticipates the view of nineteenth-century race scientists like John Beddoe, discussed in the next chapter, that the lower orders in England, and the Irish, tend to be 'nigrescent'. A marginal note in the copy of the anti-slavery activist Granville Sharp (1735–1813), now in the Beinecke Library at Yale, remarks that 'The Contamination among the Creols is not unlike what the Author here describes, and therefore, as a *West India* Planter, he has no right to taunt our English Women for loving the Blacks'.[209]

The scenario crudely outlined by Long bears a ghoulish resemblance to the one the Houyhnhnms guard against, partly as a means of keeping the lower orders in their place. Their colour-coded marriage customs are designed to ensure that. The cross-specific idea of connecting himself with horses, like Long's low-class women, is not one that enters Gulliver's head, in any sexual sense, as we saw, but if it did the laws of the Houyhnhnms would undoubtedly prevent it. Trans-specific behaviour in Houyhnhnmland, as when the Yahoos suck the teats of cows (IV. ix.271), is treated as mildly obscene on the rare occasions when we see it at all (not the only or inevitable perspective on such situations, as may be seen from the tender comedy of the she-goat suckling the puppies whose mother was dead in the *Roman Comique*).[210] Gulliver's aspirations to Houyhnhnmhood are simultaneously 'ideal' and impossible, Utopian in the sense of Nowhere, and thus doubly separated from the sexual sphere. But his sexual revulsions are not presented as matters of either class or race. *Gulliver's Travels* differs sharply from the episode in Voltaire's *Candide*, in which the hero, in the South American territory of the Oreillons (*Orejones*), slays two monkeys who he thinks are molesting native women, but who turn out to be their lovers—a cheerful insouciance on nowadays 'sensitive' issues which is followed with some brio by the scene in which Cacambo goes on to encourage the Oreillon menfolk to eat Jesuits.[211]

No suggestion in *Gulliver's Travels* exists to the effect that any 'natives' mate with monkeys, but monkeys seem to think Gulliver is one of their own, and there are some odd scenes of intimacy, closer to suckling than coupling. When Gulliver is taken by the Brobdingnagian monkey, a male, for a baby of its own kind, it is the English Gulliver's humanity, not his race, that is insulted, even as the event is presented as a trans-specific confusion, a mistake pointedly scoring at the human form divine, and of the same order as the minor unnaturalnesses of Yahoos with cows. A parallel episode in which Gulliver holds a three-year-old Yahoo male, just before the episode of the lusting female, is itself preceded by a reminder of monkeys. The preamble to both episodes announces that he had 'Reason to believe, they [the Yahoos] had some Imagination that I was of their own Species, . . . they would approach as near as they durst, and imitate my Actions after the Manner of Monkeys' (I. vii. 265). Monkeys appear here in the role of the imitative beast, as when we say we ape somebody, but the resemblance of the ensuing scene to that of the young Brobding-nagian monkey brings to the foreground the old insulting issue of a generic resemblance between apes and humans, as well as belonging with the web of associations that links Yahoos with savages in general, the Irish in particular, and all natives with monkeys (the old English habit of portraying the Irish as savages was routinely extended, in Victorian caricature, to ascribing simian features to them).[212] The notion of generic resemblance had figured in the Locke–Stillingfleet controversy, which also takes in horses and lies behind some of Swift's play with the idea of defining the nature of man. Resemblance to monkeys was to continue to play a role in a variety of eighteenth-century theories of the human.[213] Monboddo's orang-utan, who copulated with 'negroe girls', was deemed to represent an early stage of humanity, a quasi-evolutionary notion with a considerable prehistory, and one which makes Stepan's remark about the 'novelty' of Darwin's argument 'concerning the descent of man from some ape-like ancestor' seem puzzling.[214]

The issue of sexual transactions, and therefore of a presumptive biological kinship, between humans and apes, is implicated in, though not identical with, the distinction in racial science between the monogenism of those who, like Linnaeus, Buffon, and Blumenbach, thought of the human races as forming a single biological species, and the polygenist view, exemplified in the eighteenth century by the likes of Edward Long and even then regarded as of lower scientific reputability, that the white and non-white races were so different as to constitute separate species with distinct origins.[215] In the words of Léon Poliakov, 'Christianity taught that all men descended from a common ancestor, Adam, through the patriarch Noah and his sons'. The sons, according to Genesis 10, were Shem, Ham, and Japheth, to whom was some-times added a fourth, Jenithon or Manithon, and a tradition developed that Asians were descended from Shem, Africans from Ham, and Europeans from Japheth. The sons of Ham were cursed, it was said with biblical authority, and we are familiar with the special valorizing of those of Japheth, so that the origins of racism are inherent in this tradition. But the myth of origin also pre-supposed total biological identity between the descendants of all three brothers as a species. Science, not always hand in glove with the Old Testament, has historically supported the monogenist hypothesis, even as it found ways of furthering seemingly contrary forms of scientific racism.[216]

The present state of scientific thinking is described thus by a recent commentator:

At the moment, the evidence favours the 'Noah's Ark' school. Genetics, as well as examination of the fossils, points to a recent common origin in Africa. Physical differences between races are superficial, and any human can, in principle, mate with any other to produce viable offspring. 'Noah's Ark' accords with current thinking in zoology, that new species arise in small populations which then spread more widely, competing with similar forms and often replacing them.[217]

Monogenesis, as well as commanding scientific assent, was, in the words of Marshall and Williams, 'a fundamental part of the Christian belief [in a single act of creation from which all men descended], not to be lightly challenged'. In their account, Long himself is described as going only 'halfway towards accepting polygenesis', and Kames, 'who did believe that there were "different species of men as well as of dogs", was deterred by the force of Scripture from taking his arguments very far'.[218] African Negroes were more likely to be thought distinct species than, for example, Amerindians, and seem correspondingly to have been the more frequent focus of polygenetic speculation.[219]

Buffon proposed that the Negro races, whose females he reported to be given to 'compulsive or voluntary intermixture ... with the apes', were of the same species as Europeans and ultimately distinguishable from apes, while Long thought Negroes were a different species within the same genus, and, on sexual evidence, 'very nearly allied' to apes. (Aryans, according to Himmler's later belief, were not descended from apes, unlike the rest of mankind.)[220] Unlike Buffon, Long believed that the orangoutan matched the intellectual capacities of many Negroes and had 'a much nearer resemblance to the Negroe race, than the latter bear to white men'. Long's remarks about women may be contrasted with the old-style gallantry of the South Pacific traveller, Johann Reinhold Forster, whose translation of Bougainville's *Voyage* appeared the same year as Long's *Candid Reflections*, denouncing 'the long exploded opinion, that monkies are of the same species with mankind', on the grounds that this is impossible to square with 'the better half of our species, the fair sex'. 'I cannot think that a man looking up to this inimitable masterpiece, could be tempted to compare it with an ugly, loathsome ouran-outang!', Forster opined optimistically, though this was precisely what Blainville and Cuvier were to do with the Hottentot Venus. Forster himself in any case admitted that if one made 'a sudden transition' from 'the fairest beauty of Europe' to a 'deformed negro', one might be tempted (though incorrectly) 'to think them of a distinct species'.[221] Of the 'deformed negro', in other words, his view was more or less Gulliver's of the Yahoos: 'I observed, in this abominable Animal, a perfect human Figure.'

Both Long and Buffon agreed on the existence of sexual commerce between apes and Blacks, using 'scientific' evidence to some-what different conclusions while effecting some con-vergence of racial sentiment between the monogenism of the one and the polygenism of the other. In Long's case, neither scientific pretension nor the formal context of his *History of Jamaica* pre-vented his language from becoming 'crudely abusive'.[222] His remarks in the more overtly polemical *Candid Reflections*, cited earlier, about lower-class women's willingness to couple with Blacks as analogous to coupling with animals suggest a familiar homology between women, the lower orders, savages, and beasts, presumably also placed (as these things increasingly came to be) on a quasi-scientific footing. The *Encyclopédie* article 'NEGRES BLANCS, (*Hist. nat.*)' reports suggestions that albinos are the off-spring of monstrous unions (*commerce monstrueux*) between great apes and negresses, and finds the theory improbable only because it is said that these white negroes (unlike, for example, mules) are able to reproduce.[223]

One sees in these cases the idiom of scientific or philosophical consideration about the human species slipping into the idiom, and even into the service, of ethnic defamation, just as brutal racism sometimes adopts in reverse a vocabulary of factitious sci-entific precision. The history of how racism acquired scientific pretensions is a familiar one. Although the formal 'scientific' study of race was a nineteenth- and twentieth-century phenomenon,[224] it had its eighteenth-century precursors. In particular, it has been long understood that supposedly value-neutral studies of race by non-racist or anti-racist men of science often reflect deep-seated assumptions about the inferiority of non-white races.[225] By a complementary process, suggestions of scientific discourse readily insinuate themselves into expressions of vulgar racism, and in the half-century preceding the comments of Buffon or Long, the half-century of *Gulliver's Travels* itself, many remarks with an import similar to theirs may be found which have little or no pretension to scientific substance.

Francis Leguat's observation of 1708 that 'An Ape and a Negro-Slave born and brought up out of the knowledge of God, have not less Similitude between them, than an Ass and a Mare' may just about pass for a travel-writer's attempt at ethnography.[226] The same cannot so easily be said of Lady Mary Wortley Montagu's comment ten years later about the tent-dwelling women near Carthage, and their kinship to the Baboons:

> Their posture in siting, the colour of their skin, their lank black Hair falling on each side of their faces, their features and the shape of their Limbs, differ so little from their own country people, the Baboons, tis hard to fancy them a distinct race, and I could not help thinking there had been some ancient alliances between them.

It is of interest that this brutal comment on North African women was made by a sophisticated, widely travelled woman of broad racial sympathies, capable elsewhere of speaking lyrically to the proposition that all humans are 'essentially the same species': 'the little black wood cherry is not nearer akin to the Dukes that are serv'd at Great Tables, than the wild, naked Negro to the fine Figures adorn'd with Coronets and Ribands.'[227] The comment of Leguat, on the other hand, and even the vulgar racism of Long (so preoccupied with the fondness of low-class women for Negroes and animals), often announces itself in general and indeed degenderized terms, so that Long could say of Negroes, in one of many crude slippages from the pretences of scientific speech, that 'their genius (if it can be so called) consists alone in trick and cunning, enabling them, like monkeys and apes, to be thievish and mischievous'.[228]

Sexism and racism clearly come together in such contexts, though this is seldom a matter of simple equations. But both spheres variously involve monkeys, as well as issues of class. When Aphra Behn's Oroonoko protests at a slave-trade in which Blacks '*are bought and sold like Slaves or Monkeys, to be the sport of Women*', a more attenuated sport than crude coupling is doubtless envisaged, one which ascribes quasi-erotic roles to ladies' lapdogs and other pets.[229] Something of the homologizing collapse of distinctions between humans, monkeys, and pets, powered by a trivialized sexuality, is suggested in the famous dégringolade of Pope's *Rape of the Lock*, IV. 120, 'Men, Monkies, Lapdogs, Parrots, perish all'.

Lapdogs had already been equated with husbands in an earlier line (III. 158), but part of the suggestion is that to these ladies lapdogs may be sexier than husbands, as well as more important than humans. Monkeys are analogues of both humans and pets, and the status of pets as in some ways humanoid providers of sexual satisfactions extends *a fortiori* to monkeys. The idea of slaves as similarly 'the sport of Women' is a throwback to the old conceit of the lover enslaved by his mistress, and both have their connection to the erotomanic fantasies of chains and whips of a Boswell, a Jean Paulhan, or a 'Pauline Réage'.

The depiction of both black servants and pets, from Hogarth to Manet and after, has been shown to be fraught with sexual content and closely linked with some portrayals of prostitutes.[230] It is interesting, in this connection, that Lombroso and Ferrero, in a short section on the predilection for animals ('Affetto delle bestie'), report that an excessive love of animals, the accumulation of what is actually described as 'un serraglio' of pets, is a common trait of prostitutes (Mme de Pompadour, the famous mistress of Louis XV, is named as an instance). The authors note that the kindnesses lavished on pets by these women are inappropriate, for the odd reason (inversely symmetrical to Oroonoko's complaint) that an animal is a slave ('un schiavo') for whom such attentions and sacrifices are unwarranted ('per cui non fa bisogna avere riguardi e far sacrifici').[231] Where Behn's 'slave' is reduced to a pet animal, Lombroso's scheme has the pet animal reduced (not enhanced) to a slave. For a benign and affectionate portrayal of the use of lapdogs and pet monkeys by 'savages', one might compare the photographs in Lévi-Strauss's *Saudades do Brasil* discussed earlier. The young woman with the lapdog quite uncensoriously projects harmless sexual comfort, registering a similar perception to those of the satirists, or of Lombroso, with a quite different valuation. No doubt similar things might be said about the pet monkeys, which seem entirely disconnected from the context of exploitative consumerism in which Gilman and Laura Brown tend to discuss the phenomenon of monkey pets, unless the fact that

Lévi-Strauss took the photographs, or that one of the girls gave him her monkey to take back to France, are themselves part of a sexist-imperialist script. South American natives were, incidentally, portrayed with monkey pets from an early date.[232]

Outright couplings are not alleged in this context, any more than in Behn, for all Lombroso's own analogies between prostitutes, primitives, and monkeys. The interaction of sexual and racial slurs even here may seem more complicated than is allowed for in recent discussions. Couplings with animals, an old folkloric theme, are, however, a real-life feature of disturbed relations between men and women, and cases are recorded of women forced by sadistic men into sexual contacts with dogs or other animals. Edward Long was evidently not aware of such things, but a shocking account is given in a recent volume, *Animals and Women: Recent Feminist Explorations*, one of whose themes is that sexism and speciesism are 'interlocking oppressions', calling for a new solidarity between animals and women. The volume, which reveals a good deal of disturbing information, also makes a plea for more interspecific tenderness. The result is an upward revision of the old sexual jokes about lapdogs, and suggests that sympathetic as well as hostile versions are possible, not only of the homologies of natives and women and natives and animals, but of women and animals. The volume, a serious collective statement with elements of lugubriously sentimental fatuity, provided some amusing and not wholly gratuitous commentary in the *TLS*. It is grim to think what Long would have made of it.[233]

The older analogies with apes were themselves a form of homologizing. They oscillated between ethnic slur and generic definition, and *Gulliver's Travels*, which in its way also purports to be a work of philosophical categorization, typically exploits a familiar slippage. But if the usual pattern in such scramblings of categories is to redirect generic observations about missing links or whatever to an ethnic insult about the resemblance of natives to monkeys, *Gulliver's Travels* almost always operates in the reverse direction, with monkey analogies directed not at specific nations (though sometimes by way of them) but at the general character of the human. Instead of allowing ideas of generic resemblance to other species to slide into ethnic slurs, Gulliver typically borrows unflattering ethnographic comparisons to produce a generic slur at the whole human species.

The direction of this slippage is perhaps the less common of the two. We find it also in Juvenal's fifteenth satire, where it otherwise appears revealingly unlike Swift's. The poem is a xenophobic outburst against Egyptians, which begins with their 'monstrous' worship of crocodiles, cats, and 'a sacred long-tailed monkey', moves on to a cannibal atrocity (in what must be one of the earliest accounts of inter-urban gang-warfare), and finally turns into reflections on the degeneracy of human nature and its inferiority to beasts, who do not eat their own kind.[234] The argument shares a Swiftian sense that things are not what they used to be, but not (or not to the same degree) the counteracting Swiftian intimations that the good old days may not have been as good as all that, given the radical depravity of the species. And whereas Juvenal's aggression against Egyptians (like his more diffused cantanker-ousness against miscellaneous foreigners in this poem and else-where) is never really relaxed, so that even the theme of the degeneracy of the times is hitched to the xenophobic bandwagon (and perhaps vice versa), *Gulliver's Travels* at no stage singles out particular races. The Yahoos are identifiable with the Irish, but only partly and subtextually. Swift's use of the imagery and idiom of ethnic defamation is not only generalized to 'all savage Nations' but (as the whole work emphasizes more or less throughout) generically extended to his own European kind. In this context, he is neutral as between races, as well as, at least in principle, between women and men. We need not sentimentalize this. It proceeds less from a tenderness to natives or women than from an animus to humans, rather as a passage about 'harmless People' victimized by imperial conquest in the final chapter exists mainly to bring out the viciousness of the invaders rather than the virtue of the vic-tims. When the Brobdingnagian monkey picks Gulliver up in order to suckle him, natives are not at issue and the joke is at the expense of the human in an impeccably white European (and, as it happens, male) format.

Natives are, on the other hand, at issue with the Yahoos, whose features expressly resemble those of 'all savage Nations', but the effect of a parallel passage about Gulliver and a young male Yahoo is essentially the same: 'I once caught a young Male of three Years old, and endeavoured by all Marks of Tenderness to make it quiet; but the little Imp fell a squalling, and scratching, and biting with such Violence, that I was forced to let it go' (IV. viii. 265). In this the Yahoo brat behaves exactly like the Gorillas discovered by Hanno's men, in the prototype of all man-monkey misprisions. When the Carthaginians captured these 'women with hairy bodies', they 'bit and scratched ... and did not want to follow', and there followed perhaps the earliest recorded removal of natives' body parts to the metropolis: 'So we killed them and flayed them and took the skins to Carthage.' The 'Periplus' does not say the men had sexual designs on the women (though it does not necessarily exclude the idea of a sexual abduction, in some variation of the Sabine story), while the Yahoo female clearly knew she desired Gulliver, so the sexual litmus test applies in a fully specific way in *Gulliver's Travels*, and the brat's behaviour reflects the radical fractiousness of the species. But the parallel of the brat with the Brobdingnagian monkey enforces the insulting likeness of humans to monkeys without neutralizing the even more insulting *identity* of humans with Yahoos. Gulliver dandling the Yahoo brat is comically involved in a further reversal of roles, enacting in his turn the part of the Brobdingnagian monkey, who 'took me up in his right Forefoot, and held me as a Nurse doth a Child she is going to suckle'. As with the Yahoos later on, in phrasings that echo each other, Gulliver had 'good Reason to believe that he took me for a young one of his own Species', and the monkey treats him with tender concern, 'holding me like a Baby in one of his Fore-Paws'. Gulliver 'offered to struggle' (II. v. 122), much as the Yahoo brat does, the latter less decorously and with more success.

It is a curious fact that the monkey playing at suckling Gulliver is a young male mimicking a maternal posture, just as Gulliver himself adopts something of the role of a nurse. It is similarly interesting that Gulliver's 'Protector, the Sorrel Nag' in the episode of the female Yahoo is also male, a protective threesome which, like other elements of *Gulliver's Travels*, doubtless crackles with subtextual beckonings to psychobiography. Swift's psychobiography, like anyone else's, is a *donnée* of his existence, and I do not discount it. But my present concern is with a more or less overt field of implication. On this plane, I assume that neither passage is proposing any principled challenge to established gender categories, nor that notions of same-sex parentage or of homosexual transaction play any very active part, though it would be wrong to exclude the suggestion of a teasing frisson of unnaturalness, a variant, as I have already suggested, of the venial perversity with which the Yahoos suck the teats of the Houyhnhnms' cows. Swift has a penchant for disconcerting jokeynesses of this kind, whose effect is of generalized or indeterminate discomfort. The examples are not grossly accusatory, but they are part of a web of paradoxes about the unnatural character of human nature, which comes packaged with a stinging irony to the effect that civilized humans are even more unnatural than others. A page earlier, at the close of the preceding chapter, describing the similarity between Yahoo women and our own in matters of '*Lewdness*, *Coquetry*, *Censure*, and *Scandal*', Gulliver reports

I expected every Moment, that my Master would accuse the *Yahoos* of those unnatural Appetites in both Sexes, so common among us. But Nature it seems hath not been so expert a Schoolmistress; and these politer Pleasures are entirely the Productions of Art and Reason, on our Side of the Globe. (IV. vii. 264)

It is as though the passages signal a consciousness of the issue of perverse couplings, acting to dispose of it pre-emptively where it might otherwise be thought to have been repressed.

This pre-emptive passage has a bite of its own, beside which trans-specific misprisions like the monkey suckling Gulliver must be assumed to be trivial, perhaps even engaging in the way one of Lévy-Strauss's Brazilian girls plays mother to a small puppy which she carries as a doll.[235] But the 'unnatural Appetites in both Sexes ... on our Side of the Globe' are a serious slur on 'us', cheekily out of line with the fact that, if the Yahoos here represent 'all savage Nations', the literature about Amerindians from the 1490s onwards is full of imputations of sodomy and incest. The local irony is to make 'us' worse than 'them', as in Montaigne, but with an entrapping turn of the screw. Having made the point that the badness of the Yahoos is that they represent humans, and that of humans is that they are like the Yahoos, and having led the reader to assume that despite the resemblances the humans are evidently preferable, Swift then locks the reader in by saying that the things that are supposed to make humans better actually make them worse. This is a characteristic double-bind, exploiting the insulting contradictions inherent in beast analogies, and compounding them by the suggestion both that the beasts are in fact human, and that the more advanced specimen whom we knew to be human is the more depraved.

But when Gulliver dandles the young Yahoo, as when the monkey suckles Gulliver, both players in both episodes being male, one of the effects is to place the episode outside that frame of discourse in which damaging equivalences between beasts, natives, and women are sometimes said to be in play. If the parody of maternal behaviour suggests to some readers some misogynistic eruption, and if we supposed Swift to be at such points aware of imputations, or self-imputations, of misogyny (Gulliver spoke to Sympson of being 'accused ... of abusing the Female Sex', 7), both these passages would stand as conscientious efforts to emancipate the issue of generic discredit from that of gender difference, as the passage about English and Yahoo females rapidly opens out into the remark about 'unnatural Appetites in both Sexes ... on our Side of the Globe'. But an important fact about the two bizarre episodes of male nursing to which Gulliver is subjected in Books II and IV is that they are strongly and protractedly balanced in

Book II by the tender care lavished on Gulliver by the Brobdingnagian girl Glumdalclitch. This represents a benign and loving
version of the nursing motif, the positive feminine counterpart to
the monkey and the Yahoo brat, as in another way she is a virtuous
counterpart to the eleven-year-old Yahoo girl. She saves Gulliver
from choking on 'the filthy Stuff the Monkey had crammed down
my Throat', and he calls her 'my dear little Nurse' (II. v. 123). As a
kindly 'native' protectress of Gulliver in her own country, she is
also a female parallel to the sorrel nag.

Post-colonial Couplings

Suckling is prominent in *Gulliver's Travels*, as indeed breasts are. It
is surprising that Laura Brown, who is much preoccupied with
Swift's treatment of a Brobdingnagian nurse and of the maids of
honour, has little to say about any of these scenes.[236] Some of them
are hard to interpret, but all are difficult to accommodate into a
theory of gross misogyny transcended by good 'anti-colonialist'
credentials. Leaving aside the issue of how good Swift's anti-
colonialist credentials are (the issue does not seem to be a
straightforward one), Brown's argument is that there is an 'implicit
mutuality' between women and slaves in eighteenth-century culture, and that since both categories have oppression in common,
and since Swift was an 'explicit anticolonialist', he can be seen as
an 'early ally' in the liberation struggle. His credentials are complicated by misogyny, but his 'attacks on women occupy the place
of a critique of mercantile capitalist expansion', and the inter-
changeability of woman and native provides grounds for a dialectical critique which 'moves beyond' both misogyny and racism.[237]

The story of the female Yahoo with which this chapter began
occupies an important place in this argument. As we have seen, it
takes place within a very extensive tradition of sexual encounters,
in which the standard account of the native woman offering herself
to the white man is the travel-book prototype. Within European

conventions, as I suggested at the beginning, it is a reversal of accepted courtship roles, since it is men who are supposed to make the passes. The scenario of such native come-ons may be thought to be self-serving, imputing unbridled lust as well as indecorum to savages, and flattering the sexual vanity of the beneficiary, though the idea that such a thing sometimes 'really happened' should not be discounted as the operative impulse for a given narrative.

It is also possible to read the story of the lustful Yahoo in the context of mythologies about human couplings with apes, though most readers would be likely to think of the usual travel-book scenario as the main or effective prototype. Brown's 'political' reading contends that the story reverses traditional accounts of sexual transactions between apes and humans, where it is claimed that the ape is 'invariably' male and the human female. The idea of 'invariability' seems questionable, though this particular fantasy may be the prevailing one. If Hanno's men had sexual designs on the Gorilla women, this formulation stands belied in the proto-type of all such situations. (An English translation, with com-mentary, was included in *Purchas His Pilgrimes* (1625), which Swift owned.) In any event, if the racist equations of Negroes with apes are brought into the picture, in a style of argument Brown practises when she chooses in this chapter, it should not be forgotten that the phenomenon of white men coupling with black women in eighteenth- and nineteenth-century society, including plantation society in the Jamaica of which Edward Long wrote a *History*, was, and was understood to be, far more common than its opposite. This would seem to reflect the white man's overwhelmingly greater access to black women, notwithstanding Long's nightmare about English women mating with Negroes and horses. After cit-ing Long to the effect that orang-utans have 'a Passion for the Negroe women', Brown argues instead that since Yahoos are apes and ape males do the lusting, the female Yahoo acquires a male role, casting Gulliver in that of a woman. But since women and Negroes are close to one another as victims of oppression, he is 'simultaneously placed ... in the position of the Negro'.[238]

As we have seen, white views of non-white races were fraught with a variety of sexual elements, not easily reducible to simple categorizations. They are also intricately bound up with beast analogies, and in the Yahoos of *Gulliver's Travels* the equations between humans, humanoids, savages, and animals are in constant and volatile play. In such a context, Brown's reductive reversals offer a trivializing schematism which collapses the real complexities. Her account seems based on dubious premises, both as to the equivalent status of Negroes and women, and perhaps even as to the 'invariability' of reported behaviour between women and apes. It also bears little relation to the human texture of the story or to the stereotypes of sexual encounter which the episode most closely resembles.

Her suggestion of a 'mutual interaction of gender and race' in the episode of the female Yahoo's craving for Gulliver is right in ways other than she envisages, since both sexes in both human groups are reduced to the same radical and quasi-bestial ugliness. The idea of a special female equivalence with the savage or bestial other, both inhabiting parallel roles in a scenario of imperial degradation, has its points, and her effort is to argue that Swift transcended this scenario as well as acting it out. But the argument that a Swiftian 'critique of racial difference' extends by analogy to a critique of misogyny will not stand up, since there is no critique of racism except one which insults 'civilized' humans by imputing savagery to them, and no critique of misogyny except one which imputes the same shortcomings to men as to women.

The lines I cited earlier from *Cadenus and Vanessa* may reinforce the view of a transcendence of misogyny of the kind some other recent critics have envisaged, in that the lines tend to show the superiority of the Swift-educated Vanessa to the 'brutes' who are her suitors. This implies that if you educate women into states of knowledge and mind which are accessible to men, as Swift frequently advocated, they become equals or quasi-equals. The latter sentiment, in Swift, is subject to some not altogether gracious reservations, but the passage from the poem also implies that men without the same enhancements are equally a fact of existence and equally identified as brutes, like any Yahoo. If women lacked the same educational or social opportunities for improvement as men, this was precisely Swift's complaint. I happen to regard *Cadenus and Vanessa* as an unpleasant poem, because of the complicated bad faith of its embarrassed self-exculpations, but I think that its shortcomings have less to do with difficult feelings about women than with difficult feelings about people, including himself, of which Vanessa was undoubtedly a victim. On what Angela Smallwood calls 'the woman question', Brown's thesis of a transcendence of the analogy of colonial abasement, while designed to do Swift honour, merely misses the point.

For a 'moving beyond' to occur, there must be something to move beyond. That something is identified as a classic misogyny, the brooding over female grotesquerie, and Swift's anti-colonialism enables us to 'move beyond' it, as it moves beyond racism, by means of 'a dialectical critique that provides equal priority to both gender and race'. Thus, on Brown's argument, 'Brodbingnagian gigantism is intimately linked to misogyny. Indeed, the scenes in part 2 that focus on the scale of size are all centered around the female figure.' This statement is in fact baldly (and often immediately) contradicted by Swift's almost automatic habit of balancing female instances with an exact male counterpart. Brown cites the macabre comedy of the Brobdingnagian 'Woman with a Cancer in her Breast, swelled to a monstrous Size, full of Holes', but omits to quote the immediately following example of the gross unsavoury 'Fellow with a Wen on his Neck, larger than five Woolpacks'. On at least two other occasions, to illustrate differences in the 'scale of size', Gulliver invokes the obvious counterexample of himself as perceived by Lilliputians, with 'great Holes in my Skin; ... the Stumps of my Beard ... ten Times stronger than the Bristles of a Boar; and my Complexion made up of several Colours altogether disagreeable' (II. i. 91–2, v. 118–19). Brown cites one of these passages, but still thinks the sting is directed against women, because Gulliver and women are 'interchangeable'.[239]

The effective reality of the situation, however, is that in this context men and women are indeed 'interchangeable', but only in the sense that both are equally Yahoo. The idea that men do not smell in Swift's works, from A Tale of a Tub to Directions to Servants, would surprise most readers. In the Tale, it is 'the Carcass of Humane Nature', not of any woman or man, which 'smelt so strong, I could preserve it no longer'.[240]

Gulliver's report to Sympson about imputations of misogyny in responses to the first edition presents the issue as bound up with that of an attack on 'human Nature': 'I see myself accused of reflecting upon great States-Folk; of degrading human Nature, (for so they have still the Confidence to stile it) and of abusing the Female Sex' (7).[241] This, as I have implied throughout, is not a denial of misogyny, but the diablerie of flaunting something he knows people accuse him of, neither conceding nor denying the imputation but needling those who proffer it. In the present context, the signal is not that Gulliver or Swift is or is not like that, but that misogyny is not what the book is about. The reference to 'degrading human Nature' (or for that matter attacking highly placed politicians) involves a similar flaunting, inviting the reader to take it or leave it, but the whole momentum of the volume enforces the view that the reader is to be vexed by this project and that 'abusing the Female Sex' is subsumed within it and otherwise beside the point.

In the light of such passages, at all events, Brown's assertion that 'the scenes in part 2 that focus on the scale of size are all centered around the female figure' has a certain enormity of its own. Her one-sided emphasis on the female portraiture, a species of critical procedure which makes its points by ignoring contrary evidence, seems to be a staple of recent discussions. It is in exactly this way that Gilman's article, itself one of Brown's sources, describes the picture of the man with the telescope as an 'erotic caricature of the Hottentot Venus' rather than as a satire of the dog-faced or simian white voyeur. The agenda, in each case, and in other similar cases, is to suggest that the animal slur is confined to the female figure.[242]

This selective use of evidence to support currently approved indignations or pieties (or the earlier ones they replace) has recently been anatomized by Marjorie Perloff in a contribution to the volume *Prehistories of the Future*: 'The preferred method is to know what one wants to prove … and then to collect one's supporting exempla, the game being to ignore all "evidence" that might point in a contrary direction.'[243] Extremer versions, described by Sahlins and Vidal-Naquet, are practised by academics who disregard the historical evidence of cannibal practices, offensive to postcolonial sensibilities, on the grounds that they just do not believe it, or, at the other end of the political spectrum, by Holocaust deniers.[244] You would never guess it from Brown's account, but Swift's insistent balancing of male and female examples is evident throughout his work. The almost ostentatious display of even distribution is characteristic of him from as early as the Digression on Madness, where that most celebrated of Swiftian intensities, 'Last Week I saw a Woman *flay'd*, and you will hardly believe, how much it altered her Person for the worse', is immediately followed by a male example: 'Yesterday I ordered the Carcass of a *Beau* to be stript in my Presence; when we were all amazed to find so many unsuspected Faults under one Suit of Cloaths', after which 'I laid out his *Brain*, his *Heart*, and his *Spleen*', only to find 'the Defects encrease upon us in Number and Bulk'.[245] The flayed woman, far from appearing as an image of aggression against women, stands, together with the beau, as part of the validation for the speaker's earlier announcement about 'the Carcass of *Humane Nature*'.

In the episodes of the Yahoo brat and the lusting eleven year old, it is the male who performs the supposedly Hottentot or simian ritual of voiding 'its filthy Excrements of a yellow liquid Substance' all over Gulliver, while the frustrated female merely 'stood gazing and howling' in her disappointment (IV. viii. 266–7). And even independently of the 'filthy Excrements', it is again the male who is described as smelly, not the female in heat, though Swift is fond of attaching smells to sexual desire. Comparable smells are detected in the Portuguese Captain and his crew and in Gulliver himself, as well as Mrs Gulliver and their children of both sexes (IV. xi. 286–90), in a manner closer to the discovery by the author of the *Tale* about the carcase of human nature, than to any targeting of one sex or the other. In a similar spirit, the rank smell of the Brobdingnagian maids of honour is rapidly degenderized, in a manner perversely denied by Brown's decision to consider Gulliver as a woman, when Gulliver notes that a Lilliputian friend had complained to him, after heavy exercise on a warm day,

of a strong Smell about me; although I am as little faulty that way as most of my Sex: But I suppose, his Faculty of Smelling was as nice with regard to me, as mine was to that of this People. Upon this Point, I cannot forbear doing Justice to the Queen my Mistress, and *Glumdalclitch* my Nurse; whose Persons were as sweet as those of any Lady in *England*. (II. v. 119)

A complete reading would have to take in the sarcasm which distinguishes Glumdalclitch and the queen from the maids of honour and any sting which may lurk in the parting phrase about ladies in England, just as it would have to allow for the jokes about relativity of smell as well as size which are built into the arithmetical disproportions between Brobdingnagians, Lilliputians, and Europeans.

The three-year-old Yahoo male is outside the orbit of these, though he shares in the central tendency of the Brobdingnagian examples to generalize, or degenderize, the attack. We meet him only a page earlier than the lustful eleven-year-old female, and he is evidently in his way part of a similar pairing to that of the cancerous breast and the man with a wen, or to the flayed woman and the gutted beau. It may even be that he represents a pre-emptive bid to neutralize any reading of the second episode as anti-female rather than anti-Yahoo. By this I do not, once again, imply any special tenderness to women, only a desire to make clear the full sweep of the animus. It is a case (like that of the Yahoo savages) of assimilating humans to their own ignoble subgroups, which may be consistent with some perceived accesses of surplus intensity in passages about women, or savages. Such things are

difficult to define precisely, and against such passages the deliberate effort to implicate both sexes, and all races, must be given
its due.

The episode, or twin episodes, form a sort of climax in the
unfolding revelation of Gulliver's identity with the Yahoos, providing escalating confirmation of an 'objective' biological sort, as I
suggested, which is apparently independent of Gulliver's jaundiced perception. When Gulliver says just before the incident with
the young male that he had 'Reason to believe, they had some
Imagination that I was of their own Species', he does not mean
that the matter is some tentative perception of theirs but that he
had evidence that they were beginning to realize the true situation, not through any subjective shift of consciousness but on the
basis of anatomical evidence: 'they had some Imagination that I
was of their own Species, which I often assisted myself, by strip-
ping up my Sleeves, and shewing my naked Arms and Breast in
their Sight' (IV. viii. 265).

3 Killing the Poor
An Anglo-Irish Theme?

'I look forward eagerly to their extermination'

In *The Soul of Man Under Socialism*, first published in the *Fortnightly Review* in 1891 some time after he heard Shaw speak in a Fabian debate, Oscar Wilde poured scorn on sentimental do-gooders who 'try to solve the problem of poverty ... by keeping the poor alive'.[1] The phrase has a chilling ring, and may be set beside an utterance by Shaw himself, as late as 1927, in *The Intelligent Woman's Guide to Socialism*: 'I hate the poor and look forward eagerly to their extermination.'[2] It is instructive in turn to read these statements beside a characteristic outburst from an earlier Anglo-Irish spokesman, much admired by Shaw, denouncing the easy conscience-salving dispensation of charity to the poor, the majority of whom are 'fitter to be rooted out of the Face of the Earth, than suffered to levy a vast annual Tax upon the City'. This is Swift, in a late tract, *A Proposal for Giving Badges to the Beggars in all the Parishes of Dublin* (1737), complaining about the cost of maintaining a population of unemployed beggars who have come to the city from country parishes.[3]

The first two meant, you might think, different things from Swift. Wilde's declaration, like all his statements, is made for effect and does not of course mean what it seems to mean. But it contains an element of what it seems to mean, in the context of Wilde's feeling that being 'surrounded by hideous poverty, by hideous ugliness, by hideous starvation', and allowing oneself to 'be strongly moved by all this', prevents a man from 'keep[ing] himself out of reach of the clamorous claims of others' and 'real-is[ing] the perfection of what was in him, to his own incomparable gain, and to the incomparable and lasting gain of the whole world': unless, that is, he already is a Darwin, a Keats, a Renan, or a Flaubert. 'Keeping the poor alive', Wilde explains, 'is not a solu-tion: it is an aggravation of the difficulty' (*SMS* 255–6). Wilde evidently desiderates a solution to the problem of poverty which might, in a manner of speaking, be called final, an aesthetic cleansing if not in the full literal sense an ethnic one. It mingles with a parlour version of social Darwinism ('Humanitarian Sym-pathy wars against Nature, by securing the survival of the failure')[4] which Shaw expressed with greater thoughtfulness as well as force. The congruence with Swift's objections to charity for beggars seems, in such language, to extend to intimations of the Swiftian velleity for seeing them dead.

This is even truer of Shaw's remark about hating the poor and looking forward to their extermination, although it becomes clear in the full context that Shaw is contemplating the disappearance of poverty through improved social arrangements, and that his resentments, like Swift's, extend to other social groups. An exces-sive (or, as Swift might say, 'hyperbolic') vocabulary of punitive exasperation is not hard to reconcile with normal human purposes about disciplining the work-shy or castigating wrongdoers, and should not be identified with genocidal mania. Nevertheless, the language is studiedly death-dealing, a peculiar reversal of a classic equivocation found in much extermination rhetoric, and mimicked in Defoe's *Shortest Way with the Dissenters*, where actual or potential murderous intentions are insinuated in non-mur-derous language. The language of Defoe's speaker, though fraught with deadly menace, tends overtly to affirm less radical solutions, its explicit tenor, for example, sometimes seeming to purport that it is Dissent itself rather than those who practise it which is tar-geted for eradication, and that this does not necessarily imply slaughter. This sinister sweet-reasonableness, with its veiled and deniable intimations of unspeakable purposes, may be detected in Hitler's *Mein Kampf*, no mean evidence of Defoe's understanding of the mentality.

We need not impute Hitlerian propensities to Wilde or Shaw in order to detect, in their upside-down, or inside-out, version of this strategy an eruptive force, a charge of feeling not wholly consistent with the socially generous projects into which these harshly paradoxical sentiments are inserted, even as we recognize that the words do not, as I said, mean what they seem to mean. There was, and indeed is, a culture of *façons de parler* about killing the poor. An extreme example, uncomfortably close to social realities, may be found in Elizabeth Bishop's 'Pink Dog' (1979), an exercise in the 'ghastly' addressed to a beggar with 'hanging teats' in Rio de Janeiro:

> Didn't you know? It's been in all the papers,
> to solve this problem, how they deal with beggars?
> They take and throw them in the tidal rivers.[5]

The life of the poor in Brazilian cities brings this knowing and sarcastic piece of scare-speech into a disconcertingly close proximity with a literal truth. Put another way, it shows typical forms of speech taking unexpected directions, and suggests that when death-language is used of the poor, ideas of enactment are not wholly absent, even though Bishop's poem is expressing facts of the culture rather than any murderous velleities of her own, in particular the fact that people with such velleities exist, and do implement them.

A more benign example, closer in time to Wilde and Shaw, occurs in Ezra Pound's 'The Garden' (1913). A refined lady in Kensington Gardens is 'dying piece-meal of a sort of emotional anaemia', while 'round about there is a rabble Of the filthy, sturdy, unkillable infants of the very poor'. 'Unkillable' may just be a strong way of saying 'the poor are always with us', but strong ways of saying bring out intimations buried in their more commonplace counterparts.[6] 'The filthy, sturdy, unkillable infants' thrust themselves from the languid world-weariness of the poem's emotional habitat. The lady shares with Wilde a disgusted fastidiousness at the sight, but wrought to a high neurasthenic pitch, not to provocative *bons mots* or a passing shot at a social programme. Wanting to be spoken to, yet 'almost afraid that I will commit that indiscretion', she is not one to propose killing, but if the brutal disturbance of the poor is called 'unkillable', the idea of killing them must have arisen and been found wanting.

Hers is a faded society variant of Wilde's aestheticism, aimed at the preservation of a delicate emotional torpor rather than any exalted ideas of beauty. Behind it lies an essentially similar thought that the poor are ugly and inconvenient, and killing them might remove the problem, except that killing too might be ugly, so one doesn't do such things or even say them. So thinking them is what passes for dealing with the problem, and has the merit of its own inaction. She wouldn't mean what she might seem to mean if she uttered the thought, as Wilde plainly doesn't, and Shaw perhaps doesn't, though Shaw's case is complicated by other utterances which, as we shall see, have inescapably literal meanings and some notions of implementation.

Swift's outburst against beggars may also mean less than it seems, but, unlike Wilde's, it does not mean something other. It belongs to an extermination rhetoric which is assumed not to be quite literal but flirts actively with its literal potential, like the phrase 'they ought to be shot'. It is frequent in Swift, and especially evident in this pamphlet, which, unusually for Swift, is signed in his own name and also openly acknowledged on the title-page (*PBB* 129, 140).[7] Half a page earlier, after noting that if all 'sturdy Vagrants' were properly horsewhipped, as the laws clearly prescribed, 'we should in a few Weeks clear the Town of all Mendicants, except those who have a proper Title to our Charity', he adds: 'As for the Aged and Infirm, it would be sufficient to give them nothing, and then they must starve or follow their Brethren' (*PBB* 138).[8] Not quite, in other words, a simple extermination, but hardly its ironic opposite either, though the words may sound close to an irony of *A Modest Proposal* (memorably echoed in *Uncle Tom's Cabin*) about people 'every Day *dying*, and *rotting*, ... as fast as can be reasonably expected'.[9]

The *Proposal for Giving Badges* is not an ironical tract in this sense, and it is nowadays increasingly understood that the *Modest Proposal* itself (unlike Fielding's imitation of it in the *Covent-Garden Journal*,[10] or Stowe's adoption of some of its ironies in *Uncle Tom's Cabin*) is something other than the compassionate protest against injustice that later readers sometimes take it to be. Swift was not incapable of compassion. The outburst against beggars is not his only considered statement on the subject. An extended passage in the uncompleted 'Maxims Controlled in Ireland' touches on the sale of bodies and the death of the poor in quite other accents:

It is another undisputed Maxim in government, that people are the riches of a nation; which is so universally granted, that it will be hardly pardonable to bring it in doubt. And I will grant it to be so far true, even in this island, that, if we had the African custom or privilege, of selling our useless bodies for slaves to foreigners, it would be the most useful branch of our trade, by ridding us of a most unsupportable burthen, and bringing us money in the stead. But, in our present situation, at least five children in six who are born lie a dead weight upon us for the want of employment. And a very skilful computer assured me, that above one half of the souls in this kingdom supported themselves by begging and thievery, whereof two thirds would be able to get their bread in any other country upon earth. Trade is the only incitement to labour: where that fails, the poorer native must either beg, steal, or starve, or be forced to quit his country. This hath made me often wish, for some years past, that instead of discouraging our people from seeking foreign soil, the public would rather pay for transporting all our unnecessary mortals, whether Papists or Protestants, to America, as drawbacks are sometimes allowed for exporting commodities where a nation is over-stocked. I confess myself to be touched with a very sensible pleasure, when I hear of a mortality in any country-parish or village, where the wretches are forced to pay for a filthy cabin and two ridges of potatoes treble the worth, brought up to steal or beg, for want of work, to whom death would be the best thing to be wished for, on account both of themselves and the public.[11]

This touches on many themes that have haunted Irish debates, including emigration and the persistent analogy with slavery. Swift is speaking here with none of the deadpan flippancy of *A Modest Proposal* or the exasperated rage of the *Proposal for Giving Badges*. His accents are those of a heartfelt commiseration for the oppressed. But even when he is speaking in his most eloquently compassionate mode about Irish poverty, the death of the victims is what he looks to, both for their own and the public's good.

The public good was what Wilde and Shaw also claimed to be concerned with. Like Swift, neither of them much liked the poor. All three would probably have concurred with Wilde's description of them as having 'no grace of manner, or charm of speech, or civilization, or culture, or refinement in pleasures, or joy of life', though not all of them would place as high a value on 'charm of speech' or 'refinement in pleasures' (*SMS* 257). All three are on record as wanting to eliminate the poor in some sense. Wilde and Shaw, you might say, sought to do so through socialism rather than extermination. 'Under Socialism', Wilde wrote, as though consciously putting the street-life of *A Modest Proposal* into reverse,

there will be no people living in fetid dens and fetid rage, and bringing up unhealthy, hunger-pinched children in the midst of impossible and absolutely repulsive surroundings ... we shall not have a hundred thousand men out of work, tramping about the streets in a state of disgusting misery, or whining to their neighbours for alms, or crowding round the doors of loathsome shelters to try and secure a hunch of bread and a night's unclean lodging. (*SMS* 256)

It is true as far as it goes that Wilde's or Shaw's solution to the problem of poverty involves removing the condition rather than its victims. It is not, in the grimly modern sense, a 'final solution', a phrase for which 'modest proposal' or 'shortest way' might, with hindsight, be considered to be eighteenth-century counterparts. Allowing for ironic usage in these two counterparts, it would also be partly true to say that the mercantilist tendency, as broadly represented by Swift (or Defoe, Mandeville, or Fielding), and repudiated by Wilde, valued the institution of poverty as a basis of 'material prosperity'. Preserving the poor and keeping them poor were unabashedly considered necessary to an economy and a culture that depended on cheap labour and a supply of servants. Swift's and Mandeville's reservations about charity schools expressed an anxiety that the poor might be educated away from their station and usefulness, an anxiety still active a century later, in Hannah More, for example.[12]

Wilde acknowledged that 'Humanity gains much in material prosperity' from what he calls the 'collective force' of the poor, and one would suppose he was not backward in sampling the benefits, but the argument of his essay is that there are no substitutes for 'grace of manner, or charm of speech', the lack of which was one of his chief complaints against the poor (*SMS* 257). In general, the aspiration of Wilde and Shaw is for radical social change, that of Swift or Mandeville for the preservation or smoother functioning of the status quo, or a notionally improved conception of it. Swift wrote a sermon 'On the Poor Man's Contentment', in which he showed the poor 'that your Condition is really happier than most of you imagine'.[13] Connoisseurs of such sentiments will recall potential analogues, or near-analogues, like Boswell's propositions in *No Abolition of Slavery* about the happiness of slavery for both slaves and lovers (repeated, on an even more firmly erotomanic plane, by Jean Paulhan and Pauline Réage),[14] or Ian Smith's remark, as Premier of pre-Zimbabwe Rhodesia, that 'his' Africans were 'the happiest Africans in the world'.[15] Wilde's ideas about the poor man's contentment and the happiness of slavery is that 'no class is ever really conscious of its own suffering':

They have to be told of it by other people, and they often entirely disbelieve them. What is said by great employers of labour against agitators is unquestionably true. Agitators are a set of interfering, meddling people, who come down to some perfectly contented class of the community, and sow the seeds of discontent amongst them. That is the reason why agitators are so absolutely necessary. Without them, in our incomplete state, there would be no advance towards civilization. Slavery was put down in America, not in consequence of any action on the part of the slaves, or even any express desire on their part that they should be free. It was put down entirely through the grossly illegal conduct of certain agitators in Boston and elsewhere, who were not slaves themselves, nor owners of slaves, nor had anything to do with the question really. It was, undoubtedly, the Abolitionists who set the torch alight, who began the whole thing. And it is curious to note that from the slaves themselves they received, not merely very little assistance, but hardly any sympathy even; and when at the close of the war the slaves found themselves free, found themselves indeed so absolutely free that they were free to starve, many of them bitterly regretted the new state of things. To the thinker, the most tragic fact in the whole of the French Revolution is not that Marie Antoinette was killed for being a queen, but that the starved peasant of the Vendée voluntarily went out to die for the hideous cause of feudalism. (*SMS* 259–60)

Such moments of impassioned political lucidity occur occasionally in Wilde's essay, and may be what prompted some interesting comments by Terry Eagleton about how Wilde sometimes comes closer to Marx's thinking than William Morris does, 'though Morris is a Marxist and Wilde is not'.[16]

The Swiftian position on poverty, then, unlike Wilde's, requires the elimination of neither the condition nor its victims, since removal of the former means renouncing the uses of the latter, though outbursts about rooting out the unproductive subgroups off the face of the earth are part of Swift's rhetoric on the subject. To suggest that he differs from the others as mercantilism differs from socialism is a truism that conceals more than it confirms. Wilde's socialism differed widely from Shaw's in leading mainly to an 'Individualism' of self-realization and a universal cultivation of aesthetic refinement, and the socialism of both probably differed as much from everyone else's as from one another's. Shaw struck a pre-emptive blow against Wilde's doctrine of Individualism in *An Unsocial Socialist* (1884). Shaw was using the term 'individualism' in a variant sense, especially current in the 1880s and 1890s, which denoted the exact antithesis to socialism, Wilde's later usage thus being provocatively contrary.[17] But the kind of socialism Shaw's hero Trefusis is propounding is inimical to all versions of that concept, and Shaw's own aestheticism almost seems like a proleptic riposte to Wilde's. When, in the same conversation, the aesthete Erskine declares as his 'one article of belief . . . that the sole refiner of human nature is fine art', Trefusis replies: 'I believe that the sole refiner of art is human nature. Art rises when men rise, and grovels when men grovel.'[18]

The differences are complicated by the fact that Trefusis's retort is itself Wildeian in style, and *An Unsocial Socialist* often has the air of a novel aspiring in advance to be a Wilde play. Wilde too is affronted by the idea of human grovelling. But Trefusis's words to Erskine are a reminder of decisive differences. These are probably more striking than those which might distinguish, in economic and social doctrine, the mercantilism of Swift from that of Defoe, or Mandeville, or Fielding. But perhaps the most interesting fact is not that differences exist among socialists, or among mercantilists, but that unsettling *resemblances* reveal themselves between, rather than within, the two groups. The chief of these is the likeness of Wilde's shocking suggestion that it is wrong to 'keep the poor alive', and of Shaw's utterances on the same point, to Swift's expression of death-dealing velleity. Nor should the hard streak of Mandevillian thinking in Shaw's play be overlooked: the insistence that the public benefits of social 'salvation' derive from private vices of 'murder, envy, greed, stubbornness, rage and terrorism, rather than from public spirit, reasonableness, humanity, generosity, tenderness, delicacy, pity and kindness' (*MBP* 50), for example, or Barbara's descant on the profitability of Bodger's Whisky and Undershaft's gunpowder, which endows hospitals, builds churches, and paves streets (*MB* 182–3). A Mandevillian streak appears very early in Shaw's thinking. Louis Crompton comments on the lecture 'Our Lost Honesty' (22 May 1884) that 'not since Mandeville has economic logic cavorted so gaily'.[19]

'The Worst of our crimes is poverty'

Another perhaps unexpected distinction is that a hard-line mercantilist like Swift is more inclined to admit a limited application of charity to deserving cases, whereas both Wilde and Shaw express an absolute repudiation of it. On this Wilde is again vividly eloquent:

The proper aim is to try and reconstruct society on such a basis that poverty will be impossible. And the altruistic virtues have really prevented the carrying out of this aim. Just as the worst slave-owners were those who were kind to their slaves, and so prevented the horror of the system being realised by those who suffered from it, and understood by those who contemplated it, so, in the present state of things in England, the people who do most harm are the people who try to do most good; and at last we have had the spectacle of men who have really studied the problem and know the life— educated men who live in the East-end—coming forward and imploring the community to restrain its altruistic impulses of charity, benevolence, and the like. They do so on the ground that such charity degrades and demoralizes. They are perfectly right. Charity creates a multitude of sins. (SMS 256)

Shaw said similar things (appealing incidentally to Swift's King of Brobdingnag for authority), in the Fabian lecture 'Socialism and Human Nature' (1890), which Wilde may have been influenced by when he wrote of the social necessity of restraining 'altruistic impulses of charity, benevolence, and the like' (SMS 256).[20] Shaw professed a huge admiration for Swift, and reverted frequently to the King of Brobdingnag in particular.[21] He claimed, for example, that Butler's *Erewhon* was 'the only rival to *Gulliver's Travels* in English Literature', and that *Gulliver's Travels* was one of his favourite books since he 'was two months old or so'.[22]

Swift himself was insistent, both in his sermons and the *Proposal for Giving Badges*, on the bad influence of charity and the dangers of its being misdirected to, or intercepted by, the undeserving. He thought charity schools would have the effect of corrupting the servant population, and the sermon in which he makes this point contains an obsessive prefiguration of the comic nightmare of the *Directions to Servants*. He thought not more than one in twenty (a recurrent 'statistic'), or one in a hundred, beggars deserved charity, on the grounds that the rest were themselves to blame for their poverty.[23] It was not open to him, as a clergyman sometimes called upon to give sermons on charity, to be quite as flippantly dismissive as Wilde was of those 'who are always chattering about one's duty to one's neighbour'.[24] But even at the pulpit Swift showed a degree of guardedness over the scriptural injunction. In 'Doing Good: A Sermon', he begins by reminding his congregation that 'We are, indeed, commanded to love our Neighbour as ourselves, but not as well as ourselves', and when he comes to the practical business of advocating 'doing good', his interest is not in personal charities but in loving 'our neighbour in his public capacity', insisting that everyone, however weak or mean, may be useful to his country, though the sermon also warns against a corresponding power in each to do harm.[25] It is a home-style version of the Houyhnhnm ethic. And when, in the last paragraph of the sermon on the 'Causes of the Wretched Condition of Ireland', it crosses his mind that he might seek to persuade his congregation to charity, the thought is briskly despatched: 'I might here, if the Time would permit, offer many Arguments to persuade to Works of Charity; but you hear them so often from the Pulpit, that I am willing to hope you may not now want them. Besides, my present Design was only to shew where your Alms would be best bestowed.'[26]

Nevertheless he did advocate and enact a discriminating form of charity to individuals, and praised Stella for practising this.[27] One would suppose Swift to have stopped short of the spirit of Wilde's assertion that 'the worst slave-owners were those who were kind to their slaves' (SMS 256), a remark which brings to mind a comment by Flaubert about Uncle Tom's Cabin, deploring the novel's do-gooding sentimentality, in which it was the aesthete's rather than the moralist's view which proposed (in this case for fictional portrayal) an unflinching realism without softness.[28]

Here Shaw, who is a phrase-maker too, but largely free of the aestheticizing frivolity to which Wilde's argument eventually tends, is instructive. For him too poverty is a danger to society, and the remedy excludes the principle of keeping the poor alive at all costs:

the greatest of our evils, and the worst of our crimes is poverty, and . . . our first duty, to which every other consideration should be sacrificed, is not to be poor. (*MBP* 23)

This affirmation in the Preface (June 1906) to *Major Barbara* is consistent with the mood of the play itself. The hero Undershaft, a multi-millionaire armaments manufacturer, partly modelled on Alfred Nobel, makes this clear. He embodies Shaw's paradoxical thinking about military force and its potential for shaping society to Shaw's idea of a genuine socialism, much as Nobel, who patented dynamite in 1867 and endowed the Nobel Peace Prize in 1901, claimed that his 'factories may end war sooner than your peace congresses'.[29] Undershaft actually goes one better, arguing, on Mandevillian lines, that the more destructive the war, the better (*MB* 89–90). And the play's concern with poverty develops an analogy, not unworthy of Margaret Thatcher, between the military efficacy of deterrent force against foreign enemies, and a parallel treatment of the unproductive or acquiescent poor, expressly defined as an enemy within:

UNDERSHAFT. I hate poverty and slavery worse than any other crimes whatsoever. And let me tell you this. Poverty and slavery have stood up for centuries to your sermons and speeches and leading articles: they will not stand up to my machine guns. Dont preach at them: dont reason with them. Kill them.
BARBARA. Killing. Is that your remedy for everything?
UNDERSHAFT. It is the final test of conviction, the only lever strong enough to overturn a social system, the only way of saying Must. (*MB* 174)

Shaw's endorsement of Undershaft, and the congruences between the Preface and Undershaft's speeches, have something of that 'hardly concealed admiration . . . for the ruthless millionaire operator' which, according to Martin Esslin, Shaw shared with Brecht.[30] But Pierpont Mauler, who is Undershaft's counterpart and derivative in Brecht's *Saint Joan of the Stockyards*, is manipulative and cheaply sentimental. His good deeds are done to benefit his business, like Undershaft's, but his conception of self-interest is a mean and small-minded one, not part of a thoughtful system which is backed by the author's Preface. Undershaft's system is capable of winning over his recalcitrant daughter Barbara, whereas Joan, Barbara's Brechtian counterpart, dies deeply disillusioned with her supposed benefactor. The issue of the rich exploitative industrialist was a matter of unresolved ambivalence for Shaw. Trefusis's long diatribe in *An Unsocial Socialist* against his father, a self-made Manchester tycoon presented in a much worse light than Undershaft, is repudiated in the Appendix, which consists of a backtracking 'Letter to the Author from Mr. Sidney Trefusis'. There Shaw makes Trefusis apologize for this portrayal, saying not only that the father's activities, like Undershaft's, benefited society in various ways, but also that 'Industrial kingship, the only real kingship of our century, was his by divine right of his turn for business'. He bids the author to 'respect the crown whose revenues I inherit', which the author, who after all wrote both Trefusis's scripts, plainly did.[31]

That poverty is 'criminal', as the Preface states, is in Shaw's perspective an 'irresistible natural truth which we all abhor and repudiate':

Security, the chief pretence of civilization, cannot exist where the worst of dangers, the danger of poverty, hangs over everyone's head, and where the alleged protection of our persons from violence is only an accidental result of the existence of a police force whose real business is to force the poor man to see his children starve whilst idle people overfeed pet dogs with the money that might feed and clothe them. (*MBP* 23)

We may note in passing the classic sarcasm against the rich, analogous to Swift's comment, after urging pedestrians like himself not to give money to street beggars, that 'as to Persons in Coaches and Chairs, they bear but little of the Persecution we suffer, and are willing to leave it intirely upon us' (*PBB* 135). But Shaw's analysis of the notion of leaving the poor to their poverty, praising them for being 'poor but honest', and the rest, leads to something which does not carry necessary implications of not letting them die:

Now what does this Let Him Be Poor mean? It means let him be weak. Let him be ignorant. Let him become a nucleus of disease. Let him be a standing exhibition and example of ugliness and dirt. Let him have rickety children. Let him be cheap, and drag his fellows down to his own price by selling himself to do their work. Let his habitations turn our cities into poisonous congeries of slums. Let his daughters infect our young men with the diseases of the streets, and his sons revenge him by turning the nation's manhood into scrofula, cowardice, cruelty, hypocrisy, political imbecility, and all the other fruits of oppression and malnutrition. Let the undeserving become still less deserving; and let the deserving lay up for himself, not treasures in heaven, but horrors in hell upon earth. This being so, is it really wise to let him be poor? Would he not do ten times less harm as a prosperous burglar, incendiary, ravisher or murderer, to the utmost limits of humanity's comparatively negligible impulses in these directions? Suppose we were to abolish all penalties for such activities, and decide that poverty is the one thing we will not tolerate — that every adult with less than, say, £365 a year, shall be painlessly but inexorably killed, and every hungry half naked child forcibly fattened and clothed, would not that be an enormous improvement on our existing system, which has already destroyed so many civilizations, and is visibly destroying ours in the same way? (*MBP* 25–6)

There are, as in Wilde, distorted or inverted shadows of *A Modest Proposal* here, the portrait of depraved mores, the idea of the 'hungry half naked child forcibly fattened', the perhaps self-consciously anachronistic vocabulary of deserving and undeserving poor: that fattening the child is for purposes of life-saving rather than a cannibal commerce is balanced by the allusion to painless but inexorable killing, which is probably more literally intended than any of Swift's utterances on the subject. This is amplified in a later passage, after Shaw first introduces an updated version of the mercantilist distinction between the 'deserving' and the 'undeserving' poor. Shaw actually used the specific vocabulary, as in the passage just quoted, though he began, on the previous page, by putting 'the undeserving' in quotation-marks, probably more a sign of self-consciousness—not disavowal—in invoking an older and partially discredited cast of thought than a value-neutral quotation (*MBP* 25). In a Fabian essay of 1896, revised in 1901, Shaw had used quotation-marks around 'The Deserving Poor', as if to signal scepticism about the category itself, in a context which argues that 'it is economically impossible to be kind to beggars'.[32]

The Preface to *Major Barbara* affirms the first of Shaw's preconditions for saving society from 'soul atrophy':

that the daily ceremony of dividing the wealth of the country among its inhabitants shall be so conducted that no crumb shall ... go to any able-bodied adults who are not producing by their personal exertions not only a full equivalent for what they take, but a surplus sufficient to provide for their superannuation and pay back the debt due for their nurture. (*MBP* 60)

Here too we may detect echoes of the *Modest Proposal* and the *Proposal for Giving Badges*, with their implicit insistence on the notion that the poor have nothing to contribute but their labour. With only minor differences of emphasis, Shaw's 'able-bodied adults', whose withholding of 'personal exertions' makes them unproductive, are the exact equivalent of Swift's 'sturdy Beggars', except that the older term 'sturdy', applied to beggars or vagrants or vagabonds, had the double connotation of 'able-bodied and apt to be violent', and combined ideas of culpable idleness and a propensity to violent crime.[33] The phrase had legal force, and naturally combined ideas of culpable idleness with the suggestion or menace of physical violence or a propensity to crime. Legislative concern with the regulation and punishment of sturdy beggars goes back at least as far as Henry VIII, and under Elizabeth I 'An Acte for punyshment of Rogues, Vagabonds and Sturdy Beggars', which is said to mark the origin of the transportation system, became law in 1597. It stipulated that obdurate idlers 'shall ... be banyshed out of this Realme and ... shall be conveied to such parts beyond the Seas as shalbe ... assigned by the Privie Counsell'. A banished rogue returning to England would be executed.[34]

It is Shaw's second precondition, however, which canvasses lethal action, though it seems at first to diverge from Swift in so far as it attacks the criminal code and the practice of imprisoning malefactors (*MBP* 25–6, 60–1). But it leads in fact to a more literal and considered proposal for extermination than either Swift's cannibal fiction or his rhetorical outbursts about rooting beggars out from the face of the earth. Shaw actually found the latter rhetoric distasteful. A few pages earlier, he had denounced those who talk about driving malefactors 'off the face of the earth' while insisting that 'we are a civilized and merciful people', though Shaw may have been more repelled by the hypocrisy of the claim than by the primary sentiment (*MBP* 54). The phrasings might almost be a deliberate mimicry of the Modest Proposer's unctuous tones, and are hostile like Swift's mimicries. But Shaw does not repudiate the Swiftian impulse towards radical riddances which lies explosively beneath the surface of the Proposer's blandness, and if anything seems to suggest outdoing Swift in sheer literal follow-through. Like Wilde, Shaw opposed punitive sanctions against the poor, not out of sympathy for the poor but from an antipathy to the idea of punishment and a rational preference for functional solutions.[35] His attack on legal retributions is also a plea for a sanitized elimination of wilfully unproductive adults. The argument parallels exactly his view on the treatment of criminals, in *Imprisonment* (1922), which attacks every form of punitive incarceration but insists on society's 'right of self-defense, extending to the destruction or restraint of lawbreakers', so long as it is uncoupled from any 'right to revenge or punish'. He affirms the painless killing of social incurables to be an acceptable option, and makes clear that when punishment disappears, as he predicts it will, 'it does not follow that lethal treatment of extreme cases will be barred'.[36]

The same pattern of thinking seems to extend from the unproductive poor and from unreformed malefactors to instigators of Irish rebellion. In the pamphlet *How to Settle the Irish Question* (1917), writing as 'an Irishman, of the Protestant landlord variety', Shaw derides Sinn Fein's 'dangerous . . . arming and drilling of young countrymen so stupendously ignorant of the magnitude and resources of the Great Powers' that they do not suspect 'that England or any other Western European Power, except, perhaps, the principality of Monaco, could wipe them off the face of the earth from the water or the air without setting foot on Irish soil'.[37] He seems in this case to have overcome his distaste for the biblical phrase, and the idea of the European Powers wiping the Yahoos of Sinn Fein 'off the face of the earth' comes over with some of the gloating satisfaction Gulliver expresses at the thought of the Houyhnhnms repelling an invasion from the Yahoos of the same European powers (IV. xii. 293).

In the face of Sinn Fein's antics, Shaw derides the pusillanimity of the English authorities: 'Dublin Castle says: "This is intolerable. Let us provoke them to fight and then annihilate them". It provokes them accordingly, and finds that it has not the heart to finish the program.'[38] He was to return to the theme in the Preface to *Saint Joan*, a play fraught with Irish meanings and subtexts. Shaw expressed considerable sympathy for Joan's inquisitors on the grounds that 'society is founded on intolerance', and that 'we must persecute, even to the death', those who threaten its foundations, while making sure to 'be very careful what we persecute' and to retain 'a well informed sense of the value of originality, individuality, and eccentricity'.[39]

That a recognition of the practical need to kill remained part of Shaw's considered philosophy, and extended to large-scale exterminations despite vast practical and moral difficulties, is borne out by this extended statement from *Everybody's Political What's What*:

The powers of life and death necessary to civilized States find their widest exercise in the institution called War, through which a whole nation, or an alliance of nations, constitutes itself an international inquisition, and, if it decides that some other nation or alliance is unfit to live, proceeds to exterminate it. Such a decision is necessarily reciprocal, as the sentenced parties can hardly be expected to agree with the verdict, and their only way to escape execution is to exterminate the exterminators. And the powers of life and death must begin at home on both sides, because, as the armies, if they had any sense, would run away or fraternize instead of slaughtering one another at appalling risks to themselves, soldiers must be shot at dawn by their own comrades if they do not fight, kill, blow-up, burn and destroy: in short, behave like homicidal madmen.

All this extermination, though faultless logically, is finally impossible. Not only would it cost too much to carry it out to its bitter end, but its human agents, the soldiers and citizens, could not bear it: it would break down as it did in Germany in 1918. Besides, to exterminate a nation, you do not waste time killing its men, who can be reproduced by its women. You kill its women. Obvious as this is, no exterminator has ever dared to propose it as the object of a war. Even Adolf Hitler, whose anti-Semite phobia out-does Joshua's anti-Canaanite phobia or the reciprocal rage of the Crusaders and Saracens, stops short of a general order to kill all the Jewish women and not bother about the men.

But the extreme cases settle nothing except the boundaries within which our choice must be made. Though we can neither exterminate hostile nations nor allow them to invade and subjugate us, we not only can but must exterminate individuals, and slaughter our enemies sufficiently to give us reasonable hopes of defeating them and imposing our own terms on them, wisely or unwisely.[40]

The heady rationality of this has its minor slippages. The Nazis did experiment with the sterilization of women, a matter noted below, though his general statement of this point appears to have broad historical validity. The clear-eyed no-nonsense exhilaration of the passage as a whole (written during the Second World War) is pure Shaw; and, as in *Saint Joan*, the thinking is sobered by cautions about the responsible exercise of conscience. 'Our best consciences are still far more humane than our criminal and military codes; and the gap between them can be closed only by giving our best consciences command of the situation.'[41]

Such passages inject an unmistakable literalness into Shaw's thinking about the necessity or desirability of killing to achieve social or political ends. They underlie, with appropriate reservations, his own and Undershaft's ideas for dealing with the unproductive poor. In the Preface to *Major Barbara*, Shaw argues in particular that we do not imprison dogs 'But if a dog delights to bark and bite, it goes to the lethal chamber'. We should similarly treat 'men who bark and bite and steal' (*MBP* 60–1).[42] Undershaft's version, as we saw, was quite brutal: 'Kill them.' It should not be confused with the callow parody of it by the play's Lomax: 'Ive been through the Woolwich Arsenal; and it gives you a ripping feeling of security, you know, to think of the lot of beggars we could kill if it came to fighting' (*MB* 153).

But Undershaft is seriously proud of the family motto carved on the wall of his headquarters: 'NOTHING IS EVER DONE IN THIS WORLD UNTIL MEN ARE PREPARED TO KILL ONE ANOTHER IF IT IS NOT DONE.' Shaw endorses this in the Preface when he dismisses 'public sentiment against killing which is propagated and endowed by people who would otherwise be killed themselves' (*MBP* 27), and he speaks approvingly of Undershaft's 'sense that he is only the instrument of a Will or Life Force which uses him for purposes wider than his own' (*MBP* 31).

In a Postscript to *Major Barbara* itself in 1933 Shaw added: 'Until we have a general vital hatred of poverty, and a determination to "liquidate" the underfed either by feeding them or killing them, we shall not tackle the poverty question seriously' (*MBP* 63). Although the alternative of 'feeding them' is implicit in Undershaft's enlightened industrial methods (*MB* 172), the play's emphases are often on the shocking obverse. Shaw's Preface, denouncing lesser judicial sanctions, says of the poor that, rather than put them in jail,

It would be far more sensible to put up with their vices, as we put up with their illnesses, until they give more trouble than they are worth, at which point we should, with many apologies and expressions of sympathy, and some generosity in complying with their last wishes, place them in the lethal chamber and get rid of them. Under no circumstances should they be allowed to expiate their misdeeds by a manufactured penalty, to subscribe to a charity, or to compensate the victims. If there is to be no punishment, there can be no forgiveness. We shall never have real moral responsibility until everyone knows that his deeds are irrevocable, and that his life depends on his usefulness. (*MBP* 61)

The analysis goes on to suggest that if Cain had been 'allowed to pay off his score [in prison], he might possibly have killed Adam and Eve for the mere sake of a second luxurious reconciliation with God afterwards' (*MBP* 62). Shaw's notions of a non-punitive euthanasia for the unproductive poor differ diametrically from those of the Benthamite Panopticon, in which a commercially productive imprisonment is upheld as the preferred and rational alternative to capital punishment. The idea originated with Jeremy Bentham's brother Samuel, an employee of the Russian Prince Potemkin, who applied it in his 'model factory to discipline indolent and dishonest Russian workers' in the last quarter of the eighteenth century (Jeremy's *Panopticon Letters* were printed in 1791).[43]

But Shaw did embrace, in a non-punitive or non-carceral context, Beatrice Webb's Minority Report (1909) of the Royal Commission on Poor Law, which Shaw thought might 'make as great a difference in sociology and political science as Darwin's "Origin of Species" did in philosophy and natural history' (Webb had been appointed to the Commission five days before the first night of *Major Barbara* on 28 November 1905). Holroyd describes the report as 'somewhere between Bentham and Beveridge', a blueprint for the Welfare State with traces of the Benthamite conception of the workhouse as a means of '"grind[ing] rogues into honest men"'.[44] 'Beatrice was haunted by this problem of the able unemployed . . . For those who lacked capacity she recommended compulsory training; and for those who lacked will, disciplinary supervision and treatment that came close to a penal labour colony.' She later criticized Beveridge's proposals for 'unconditional unemployment doles' as soft.[45]

Shaw's remarks on compelling the poor to work, in the discussion sarcastically entitled 'The Deserving Poor' in *Socialism for Millionaires*, are similarly hard-line, with an acerbity comparable to Swift's on the same subject: 'It is possible to treat them humanely, which means that they can be enslaved, brought under discipline, and forced to perform a minimum of work as gently as the nature of the process and their own intense objection to it permit; but there is no satisfaction for the compassionate instincts to be got out of that.'[46] Both Shaw (*MBP* 26-7) and Undershaft (*MB* 171-2) endorse a more benign capitalist version with an emphasis on good working conditions: 'Only fools fear crime: we all fear poverty. Pah! [*turning to Barbara*] you talk of your half-saved ruffian in West Ham: you accuse me of dragging his soul back to perdition. Well, bring him to me here; and I will drag his soul back again to salvation for you. Not by words and dreams; but by thirtyeight shillings a week, a sound house in a handsome street, and a permanent job' (*MB* 172). Taking up in the Preface the issue of the minimum wage and the old age pension, Shaw promotes a scheme of lifetime security based on the opportunity and duty to work: 'give every man enough to live well on, so as to guarantee the community against the possibility of a case of the malignant disease of poverty, and then (necessarily)...see that he earned it' (*MBP* 26–7).

Dreams of the Beggar as Nobleman

Swift differs from Shaw and Wilde, and both of them from one another, over various aspects of social policy, including the means of regulating crime. Swift would not have abolished imprisonment 'or whatever legal Punishment may be thought proper and effectual' (*PBB* 132–3) but increased the salaries of law-enforcers (like some modern governments), though the actual use of the death penalty even for small felonies in Swift's or Fielding's time would doubtless have exceeded what Shaw would think proper, even had his project of killing the poor been thought of as punitive. And Swift's indignation at paupers who 'are not afraid to steal, nor ashamed to beg, and yet are too proud to be seen with a Badge' (*PBB* 134) is in sharp contrast with Undershaft's 'I had rather be a thief than a pauper' (*MB* 174) or Wilde's affirmation that beggary and stealing are preferable to poverty:

Man should not be ready to show that he can live like a badly fed animal...and should either steal or go on the rates, which is considered by many to be a form of stealing. As for begging, it is safer to beg than to take, but it is finer to take than to beg. (*SMS* 258–9)

Wilde's aestheticization of this issue, which should in turn be distinguished from Shaw's version of similar sentiments, is a throwback to a politically unfocused form of late romanticism, exemplified in a prose poem of Baudelaire, 'Assommons les pauvres' (1865: 'Let's brain the poor'). In this poem, which was found unpublishable by the *Revue nationale* in 1865, the poet remembers an angry reading, during 1848, of fashionable books telling the poor that it was their happiness to be slaves, and that they were really unthroned kings. On his way to a *cabaret* for a drink, he is approached by an old beggar whom he beats up because of his presumed abjection. But when the old man turns round, and, with miraculous energy, gives the poet two black eyes and breaks four of his teeth, the poet rewards him for asserting his spirit, while claiming credit for restoring the old man's pride and vitality. The poem's mood, oscillating between compassion and contempt, expresses an aesthetic connoisseurship which views fineness of character rather than deprivation as grounds for remedy or reward.[47]

The conception of human dignity and freedom which holds that a beggar's pride and fighting spirit are better reasons for feeding him than his hunger would not have impressed Swift, who took a deflating and distinctly unBaudelarian view of beggarly 'dignity'. Wilde's version might be described as Baudelarian in a late decorative phase. The 'fineness' of stealing, the exaltation of crime as preferable to poverty, which Wilde affirms, is elaborately bound up with a broader set of ideas assimilating the criminal to art which we find in 'The Decay of Lying', 'Pen Pencil and Poison' ('There is no essential incongruity between crime and culture'), and 'The Critic as Artist', as well as in the *Soul of Man under Socialism*. He described sin as an 'intensified assertion of individualism', and Individualism was what was going to make the world beautiful under socialism. Commenting on Thomas Wainewright the poisoner, Wilde notes among what Ellmann calls his interesting tastes his 'curious love of green, which in individuals is always the sign of a noble artistic temperament, and in nations is said to denote a laxity, if not decadence of morals'.[48]

This nudging intimation of Irishry, of national greenery, is a shade more oblique than Seamus Heaney's declaration that his 'passport's green', as one would expect.[49] But it is very much in line with the Irish spin he was giving to his relations with Shaw in the early 1890s: 'we are both Celtic, and I like to think that we are friends', maestros 'of the great Celtic school', collusive operators (as Wilde seems to see it) in the enterprise of clearing the 'intellectual fog' of England.[50] Some corroboration from Shaw exists, to the effect that anonymous reviews by either author were often attributed to the other (a confusion which extended also to William Archer, excluding reviews 'of distinctly Irish quality'), and that Shaw sometimes defended Wilde by drawing attention to Irish characteristics which might have been misunderstood by his critics.[51] The relations between Wilde and Shaw were respectful and wary, a remarkable record of personal and intellectual generosity laced with mild malice and mutually imitative admiration. One of Shaw's finest personal traits is his loyalty to Wilde and to Wilde's memory in his time of trouble and after his death. Holroyd perhaps understates the degree of mutual regard, and perhaps overstates Shaw's sense of a collaborative Irishry: 'They were compatriots rather than friends and, within the intellectual fogs of England, they were bright comrades-in-arms against a common enemy.'[52] In any event, it seems that from one Anglo-Irishman to the other it was not easy to avoid the idea of an Irish rogue or beggar beneath the skin. In an extraordinary outburst to Alfred Douglas on 18 April 1938, Shaw spoke of Wilde's shameless sponging, and his lying and ingratitude to Frank Harris, Robert Ross, Douglas himself, and others:

Let me again remind you that I am an Irishman. I know that there is no beggar on earth as shameless as an Irish beggar. I have seen them beg when they are perfectly well off—beg from poor people. And I know that flexibility which enables them to charm you to your face, and tear you to pieces the moment your back is turned.[53]

This might be taken as an unconscious riposte to the national greenery of 'Pen Pencil and Poison'. The outburst has Swiftian parallels, both as to 'shamelessness' and on the notion that 'there is not a more undeserving vicious Race of human Kind than the Bulk of those who are reduced to Beggary, even in this beggarly Country' (*PBB* 135). Perhaps the most interesting feature of both passages is the suggestion of an association or near-equivalence between beggary and Irishness, at least to the extent that the latter is taken as the superlative or quintessential condition of the former. Indeed, at the level of national political behaviour, Shaw declared in 1916: 'We are the champion mendicants of the world', accepting money from America 'without shame, and without perceptible gratitude.' Responding two years later to an Irish judge who wanted to send 'shoes and stockings' for Irish children, Shaw again said: 'Ireland is perfectly well able to feed and clothe her children if she chooses. It is a mistake to suppose that she is poor; she is only an incorrigible beggar', adding that, with nations as with men, 'charity is only a poisoned dressing on a malignant sore.'[54] Shaw's use of 'beggar' to bring out Wilde's disreputable Irishness reads like a variation on the use of 'nigger' among American Blacks, insulting or mock-insulting in its ironic appropriation of the white oppressor's term,[55] except that Anglo-Irishmen like Shaw, Wilde, and Swift nursed a dual affiliation, to both oppressor and oppressed, and were self-consciously poised between the two roles. It seems evident in any case that a degree of quasi-synonymity existed between 'beggar' and 'Irish', at least in satirical contexts. An American cartoon *c.*1843 shows a well-fed O'Connell being addressed as 'you jolly old Beggar' while he clutches a large box of Repeal campaign money.[56]

As to Wilde's preference of stealing to poverty, poverty being not so readily reducible to the aesthetic mode, Shaw might accept the preference while not wholly assenting to the aestheticizing gloss. In the Preface to *Major Barbara*, he says: 'Would [a poor man]

1. Long breasted women cooking human limbs. T. de Bry, *Americae Tertia Pars*, 1592

2. Abyssinian 'matron', late 19th century (see pl. 9)

Americen Americus retexit, & AMERICA. Semel vocauit inde semper excitam.

Ioan: Stradanus invent.

Theodor Galle fecit.

3. Vespucci 'Discovering' America, by Theodor Galle, after Stradanus, late 16th century

4. John Webber, *Poedua* (1777)

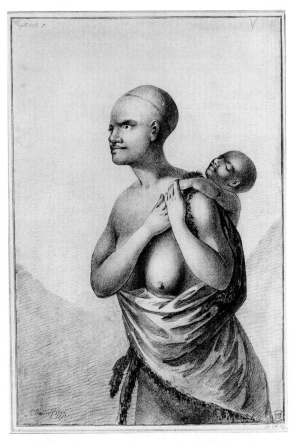

5. John Webber, *A Woman of New Holland* (1777)

6. Albert Eckhout, *Tupi Woman with Child* (1641)

7. Albert Eckhout, *Tarairiu Woman* (1641)

8. Hans Baldung Grien, *The Ages of Man and Death*, 16th century, Prado, Madrid

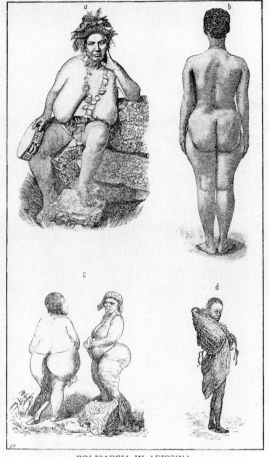

POLISARCIA IN ABISSINA.
CUSCINETTO POSTERIORE IN AFRICANE.

a) Ballerina o prostituta Abissina (Ploss) (tipo di polisarcia africana). — *b)* Ottentotta con cuscinetto posteriore (Ploss). — c¹) Donna Bongo (Schweinfarth). — c²) Donna Koranna con cuscinetto posteriore e ipertrofia delle natiche e delle coscie (Ploss). — *d)* Donna selvaggia che porta un bambino sul dorso, come in tutti i popoli primitivi (Ploss).

9. *Polisarcia in Abissina* (c.1893) (see pl. 2)

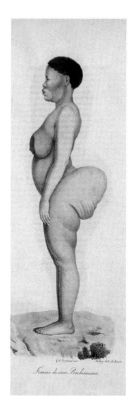

Femme de race Bushemann

10. Jacques Christophe Werner,
Profile of Sartje Baartman
(1824, based on Huet, 1815)

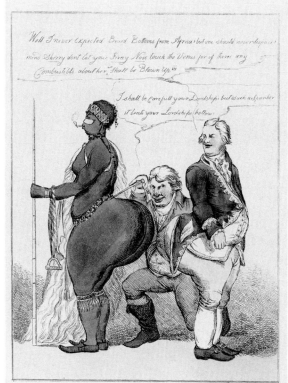

Well I never expected Broad Bottoms from Africa: but one should never dispair,
mind Sherry dont let your Firey Nose touch the Venus for if theres any
Combustibles about her, I shall be Blown up!!!

I shall be carefull your Lordship: but such a Spanker
it beats your Lordships hollow

11. William Heath, *A Pair
of Broad Bottoms* (1810)

A PAIR of BROAD BOTTOMS

12. George Cruikshank, *The Examination, of a Young Surgeon* (1811)

13. Richard Newton, *The Full Moon in Eclipse* (1797)

14. *The Hottentot Venus (Die Hottentottenvenus)*, early 19th century

15. Thomas Rowlandson, *The Exhibition 'Stare' Case*
(*c.*1811)

16. John Webber, *Habit of a Young Woman of Otaheite, Bringing a Present* (1777)

17. French Dress (1770s)

18. *A Modern Venus*: (1) Print (1786); (2) Sketch, by Miss Hoare (1785); (3) Sketch, by Countess of Upper Ossory (1785)

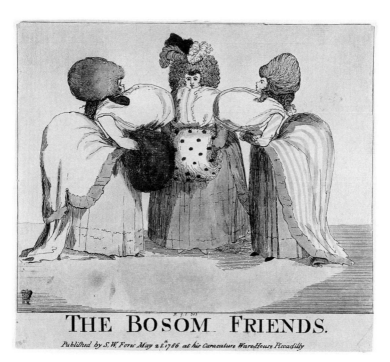

THE BOSOM FRIENDS.

Published by S. W. Fores May 28. 1786 at his Caracature WareHouse Piccadilly

19. George Towneley Stubbs, *The Bosom Friends* (1786)

THE INCONVENIENCE OF DRESS

Rage for Dress — Bewitching passion!
Who'd not starve to lead the Fashion?
Starve! where's the Beaux so very dull,
To think they'll starve with frops so full?

Published 19th May 1786, by S. W. Fores, at the Caricature Warehouse, No. 3 Piccadilly.

20. George Towneley Stubbs, *The Inconvenience of Dress* (1786)

not do ten times less harm as a prosperous burglar, incendiary, ravisher or murderer . . . ? Suppose we were to abolish all penalties for such activities, and decide that poverty is the one thing we will not tolerate' (*MBP* 25–6). These words from the Preface are developed by Undershaft: 'I had rather be a thief than a pauper. I had rather be a murderer than a slave. I dont want to be either; but if you force the alternative on me, then, by Heaven, I'll choose the braver and more moral one' (*MB* 174). In 'Socialism and Human Nature', a few months before Wilde's essay, Shaw had written: 'The man who hates servitude with starvation, but can tolerate it with eighteen shillings a week, will never be free.'[57] But he stops just short, though decisively so, of Wilde's flourish about its being 'finer to steal': for Shaw, a phrase like 'splendidly criminal', and the glamorizing antics that went with it, were 'as intolerable and as immoral' as references to the 'poor but honest' or 'the respectable poor' (*MBP* 23). Shaw might almost be targeting a Wildeian use of 'splendid', as in 'the very violence of a revolution may make the public grand and splendid for a moment' (*SMS* 276), though perhaps he (and certainly Undershaft) would have agreed with Wilde's statement that 'one cannot possibly admire' the 'virtuous poor' (*SMS* 259). For Swift, of course, Wilde's 'go[ing] on the rates' was precisely what the *Proposal for Giving Badges* was designed to avert, while stealing, far from being 'finer', made the beggary worse.

As a trio of Anglo-Irish writers, Swift, Wilde, and Shaw had at least this in common, that they did not share an attitude to beggary which their compatriot Yeats ascribed to his great Anglo-Irish exemplars, and specifically to Swift himself. Beggary had a special place, as the complement to nobility, in Yeats's anti-mercantile dream of the noble and the beggarman.[58] In 'The Seven Sages' (1931), Yeats salutes four great cultural ancestors of the Ascendancy, 'Goldsmith and Burke, Swift and the Bishop of Cloyne', who are said to have hated Whiggery,

> A levelling, rancorous, rational sort of mind
> That never looked out of the eye of a saint
> Or out of drunkard's eye.

A curious beggar's pastoral, or idyll of destitution ('Roads full of beggars, cattle in the fields'), closes with Swift, Berkeley, Goldsmith, and Burke, carrying on rather improbably:

> They walked the roads
> Mimicking what they heard, as children mimic;
> They understood that wisdom comes of beggary.

I think Swift might *not* have understood this. As Declan Kiberd has said, 'though Goldsmith, Swift,...and Berkeley were all recruited by Yeats...for his pantheon of ascendancy intellects, they were each of them impeccable representatives of the Irish Protestant middle class: hard-working men who lived by the pen and who felt, if anything, a very unYeatsian contempt for the idleness and mendacity of the Irish ascendancy.'[59] Swift would certainly have extended this contempt, with increments, to the beggars, and Wilde and Shaw might have thought Yeats's utterance as not among the stronger bonds between them.

Their differences from one another are as nothing beside their difference from Yeats's poem, and it is interesting to see in all three how closely and naturally the ideas of poverty and criminality interpenetrate; how, even where, as in the two later writers, 'criminality' is in one way or another accepted as preferable to the degradations of indigence, and *a fortiori* in Swift, where it is not, the notion, or at least the vocabulary, of exterminating the poor, or at least of not keeping them alive (equivocation and slippage are almost inescapable in this mode of thinking), slides into the discourse. In this, their cast of thought is not as unconnected as one might suppose from the view variously propounded by Sade or by Malthus, that poverty, famine, disease, and death interact, valuably and instrumentally, to contain population growth, restore nature's equilibrium, and the rest. In Sade, if not in Malthus, the thinking turns to philosophically grounded defences of infanticide and mass-extermination, though the Sadeian instances occur mainly in fictional dialogues and are partially protected, as Swift's ironic fables are partially protected, from suggestions of literal follow-through or directly advocated enactment.

Malthus was popularly represented as advocating infanticide himself. One example, noted by the Webbs and others, was a spoof called *Marcus on Populousness*, 'written in the form of a report from a Poor Law commissioner, that pressed the case for infanticide as a solution to overpopulation and made plausible the rumoured arrival of an educational inspector in South Wales in 1839 whose brief was to prepare a census of children for extinction'.[60] That this was a gross travesty of Malthusian thought hardly needs saying. Ironically, Ireland came to be widely thought of as the classic 'Malthusian country', despite the fact that the *Essay on the Principle of Population* (1798), as Malthus self-critically acknowledged, dealt perfunctorily with that country. Those of his writings and public statements which did concern Ireland, moreover, were warmly sympathetic to the Irish on civil rights issues and severely critical of English rule, insisting that the removal of injustices took precedence over economic considerations.[61]

Beggars and Hottentots, or Exterminate all the Brutes

Sade and Malthus speak as relatively amoral analysts of social forces, whereas Swift and Shaw, from opposite perspectives, and with whatever discount of literalism such rhetoric calls for, are affirming the retributive or functional appropriateness of executions. They come over as notional advocates, in some sense, of mass-slaughter. The phenomenon transcends ideological differences, just as Kurtz's 'Exterminate all the brutes!' in *Heart of Darkness* emanates not from a hardened racist, but from a putative proponent of enlightened and liberal views on empire and race.[62] The resemblance is not fortuitous, since the two spheres are connected by the pathologies of domination, metropolitan or imperial, and by a familiar equation of class and race which saw the domestic mob and inferior races as similar, and as

constituting a similar combination of useful labour and barbar-
izing menace.

Equations of class and race have sometimes received 'scientific'
support from practitioners of race science. John Beddoe, author of
The Races of Britain (1885), devised an elaborate 'index of nigrescence' which placed the light-skinned Anglo-Teutonic races at the
top and Negroes and other dark peoples at the bottom. Beddoe
thought the Irish were 'Africanoid', darker than the people of east
and central England, and that the darker-skinned in England were
'largely the offspring of the proletariat'. Beddoe claimed that the
aborigines of the British Isles had traces of 'negro' ancestry.[63] But
this 'scientific' thinking was superimposed on a constant English
folklore about racial difference. The '*wild Irish*' were assumed and
expected to look different and outlandish, and Swift remarked on
how 'upon the Arrival of an *Irish-man* to a Country Town, I have
known Crouds coming about him, and wondering to see him look
so much better than themselves'. The sting in that ending is not
quite what it seems, since Swift is in fact distinguishing his own
settler class, affronted by undiscriminating English prejudice, from
the wild Irish themselves, who, he insists, are not significantly
representative of Irish society, and outlandish (unlike himself) in
their own country of birth.[64]

It goes without saying that the analogies between the foreign
and domestic mob, the indigene and the indigent, which underlie
the speech habits I am describing, are as lacking in inwardness of
understanding as the individual typecasting of either group. The
experience of poverty and a sympathy for alien cultures are outside
the purview of the rhetoric. That begging, as Henry Reynolds said
in relation to Australian Aborigines, might be a natural response
from people who shared without question and who believed that
reciprocity was the greatest social good, who thought they were
owed a debt for their appropriated land, and who had no mar-
ketable skills,[65] are not perceptions that play much part in
the death-dealing speech modes of social aggression or defamation, though not always beyond the range of the speaker. That

there is a gap between speaker and speech in such cases has doubtless saved some lives. The opposite has usually happened when the gap closed.

The use of colonies to absorb idle as well as seditious elements of the population was well established in both ancient Rome and Renaissance Europe.[66] The vices attributed to these groups were frequently those also attributed to the natives of overseas territories. J. M. Coetzee has pointed out in a remarkable discussion how, in South Africa, from the seventeenth century onwards, 'the idleness of the Hottentots is denounced in much the same spirit as the idleness of beggars and wastrels is denounced in Europe', commenting that 'the force of the righteous condemnation that the Discourse of the Cape brings to bear on the Hottentot comes from the accumulated weight of two centuries of denunciation of idleness, from the pulpit and the judicial bench, in Europe'.[67] Coetzee also offers a concentrated digest of the Hottentot stereotype, taken from the same travel-writers to whom Swift went for many elements of the Yahoos, whom in a collateral twist he identified with the Irish. Coetzee's summary, reporting 'that the Hottentots are ugly, that they never wash but on the contrary smear themselves with animal fat, that their food is unclean, that their meat is barely cooked...that male and female mix indiscriminately, that their speech is not like that of human beings', might almost have been lifted from *Gulliver's Travels*, whose Hottentots (an acknowledged source) turn into Irish (a recognized feature of Swift's fiction).[68]

It is not only in Swift that the equation of Hottentots and beggars, or of beggars and Irish, merged or coexisted with that of Hottentots and Irish. Sidney and Beatrice Webb wrote from Dublin on 29 July 1892, a few days after their marriage: 'The people are charming but we detest them, as we should the Hottentots—for their very virtue. Home Rule is an absolute necessity [*the sentence was completed by Beatrice*]—in order to depopulate the country of this detestable race!' Beatrice then adds a postscript saying 'We are very very happy—far too happy to be reasonable' (the editor of the Webbs' *Letters*, Norman MacKenzie, reports that 'Beatrice's interpolations into this letter reveal an unusual lightheartedness').[69]

Versions of Kurtz's 'Exterminate all the brutes!' were common among English writers in the sixteenth and seventeenth centuries, and Swift was, with subtle (and not so subtle) individual variations, writing within the same tradition. It has more than once been noted that the *Modest Proposal*'s fantasy of making, out of the skins of the cannibalized babies of the Irish poor, 'admirable *Gloves for Ladies*, and *Summer Boots for fine Gentlemen*' (*MP* 112), looks forward to what was sometimes done in or near the Nazi camps.[70] The Nazis were not available to Swift for comparison, as they are to us. What is invoked in *A Modest Proposal* are not the practices of a modern state, but an analogue associated with older barbarians, imputed ancestors of both the Irish and Amerindians, the Scythians, who also (in Herodotus) manufactured useful objects from human parts.[71] It is in one of their common guises among English authors, as cannibal savages, that the Irish are seen making clothes of human skin, and the *Proposal for Giving Badges* strongly reinforces the perception of alert readers that the compassion for poor beggars in *A Modest Proposal* is only a mock-compassion, deriding the accents of liberal do-gooders quite as much as Wilde or Shaw did, though with a different agenda.

Swift is not, of course, advocating this. The conceit belongs to a sphere of cruel play which André Breton described as black humour and which is more fully discussed in the next chapter: an unmoralized surreal eruptiveness which transcends or exceeds, in a sphere of unfettered ludic aggression, the borders of satiric or hortatory discourse.[72] It is a grotesque version of the notion of finding a 'usefulness' for the poor. It is not, contrary to a conventional misapprehension nowadays more or less discredited by compelling historical evidence, an attack on what the governing oppressor does to the foreign or domestic inferior (the Irish, in this case, are both), but a gruesome gloss on what the Irish are presumed to do to themselves.

The Nazi version is a hideous real-life activation of the clothes-making scenario from the other end of the telescope: it is the oppressor, not the oppressed, who thus industrializes the by-product of extermination. The activity is removed from the cottage industry of the primitive poor to the factories and laboratories of a modern European nation-state.[73] The Irish, like the Jews in Germany, were an 'inferior race' within European borders, 'at home'. They were foreigners in their own land, Ireland being both outlandish, an island in the Virginian sea,[74] and adjacent to England. It was, notionally if not actually, a metropolitan kingdom in its own right, ruled, according to a constitutional doctrine enunciated in William Molyneux's *The Case of Ireland* (1698), and which Swift forlornly defended, independently by the same king.[75] It has been called an 'internal colony'.[76]

Borges and others have seen the insider–outsider status of both Jews and Irish as a source of creativity, attributing the contribution of both groups to Western, including English, culture not to any racial characteristics—many 'illustrious Irishmen (Shaw, Berkeley, Swift) were the descendants of Englishmen' and had 'no Celtic blood'—but to their sense of cultural distinctness.[77] That the situation was not uniformly a blessing, especially for those who did have 'Celtic blood', or for Jews, will also be evident. The particular combination of perceived racial otherness and economic or social deprivation made itself variously felt at the hands of ruling groups. But the Jews are not, in the principal stereotype, represented as 'poor'. That there were poor Jews in ghettos might fuel some Nazi propaganda about germs, infection, and disease, but the real grievance against them was that, unlike the Irish, they were *not* poor, that they had rejected or escaped from the proper sphere of the useful inferior, the deserving or productive poor, and risen, through social change and cultural integration or accomplishment, to positions assumed to be the prerogative of the master race.

In the Webbs' *Industrial Democracy*, Jews were faulted both because 'their wage-earning class is permanently the poorest in all

Europe' and because 'individual Jews are the wealthiest men of their respective countries'. Thus, while the Anglo-Saxon skilled artisan 'will not work below a customary minimum Standard of Life', and 'the African negro...will work...for indefinitely low wages, but cannot be induced to work at all once their primitive wants are satisfied', the Jew 'will accept the lowest terms rather than remain out of employment' (thus depressing the Standard of Life). On the other hand, according to the Webbs, as the Jew 'rises in the world new wants stimulate him to increased intensity of effort, and no amount of income causes him to slacken his indefatigable activity'. Thus the hard-working Jewish immigrant 'might be (besides increasing the overcrowding of the slums) a constant influence for degradation', by contrast with the sort of immigrants who, 'like the Huguenots, introduced a higher Standard of Life'. But when the Jews become rich, 'there is also', as the Webbs judiciously conclude, 'the obscure question of the intermixture of races to be considered', which may be why rich Jews, unlike rich Huguenots, come over, 'obscurely', as not a good thing.[78] Several decades later, however, Beatrice Webb disapproved of 'the Nazi government [and] its outrageous persecution of the Jews'.[79]

Niall Ferguson has suggested, in his history of the Rothschilds, that this illustrious family is the product of a situation in which, 'at a time when most fields of economic activity were closed to them, Jews had little alternative but to concentrate on commerce and finance'.[80] In a more specialized variant of this explanation (whose consequences are glanced at in *Major Barbara*), the stereotype of the 'rich' Jew was itself a result of the early Church's prohibition of usury to Christians, a convenient way of simultaneously securing banking services for the economy and creating an outsider-scapegoat for any consequent (or non-consequent) economic imbalances or hardships. The Undershafts are said to have operated a benign and modernized version of such scapegoating. In a passage inserted in the screen version, in what might seem an impish piece of timing (1940), Undershaft says: 'It is part of the tradition that they should take a partner with a Jewish name. It suggests financial ability; and he gets all the blame when our profits are considered exorbitant', though Undershaft recognizes that it is the name, not the reality, that does it.[81] In the play itself, Undershaft tells his future son-in-law Cusins, who is to become an executive of the firm, that his own Jewish partner, Lazarus, 'is a gentle romantic Jew who cares for nothing but string quartets and stalls at fashionable theatres', but who 'will be blamed for your rapacity in money matters, poor fellow' (MB 167).

Ironically, something not unlike this happened at Shaw's own hands in the 'Author's Note' for the London production of 5 March 1929, surveying the First World War from the vantage point of later financial turmoils:

When the war came Undershaft and Lazarus did not do so well as was expected of them, because Lazarus had obtained too much control; and after a frightful slaughter of our young men through insufficient munitions the Government had to organize the business in national factories, and to send public officials to teach Lazarus how to conduct as much of it as was left to him. (MB 199)

The exact resonances of this are obscure to me, but when recovery comes, the focus returns to Undershaft and to an updated reaffirmation of his methods: 'Undershaft, however, survived the wreck. His policy of high wages and ruthless scrapping of obsolete methods proved more lucrative than sweating and doing what was done last time. His well-paid employees became his best customers. He emerged in fiction as Clissold and in fact as John Ford' (MB 200). Whatever the circumstances, Lazarus got the blame and Undershaft the credit, even (it would seem) from the author.

Lazarus, in his shadowy and unrealized way, nevertheless remains a not unfriendly conception of the rich Jew, and his putative 'real-life' fate, though evidently a harsher version than that presupposed by Undershaft's words in the play, is relatively benign. In the vicious reality of Nazi Europe, as doubtless in more attenuated scenarios of modern life, the effects are not so benign.

Once banking is permitted to everyone, the rich Jew loses his usefulness, and belongs to that deviant obverse of the undeserving poor, the undeserving rich, his culpability compounded by the impertinence of wealth, an aggravated version of not knowing his proper place. For the Nazis, who actually implemented the Shavian velleities about beggars and other unproductive groups, the Jew's perceived concentration on financial rather than productive processes reinforced his status as not useful and thus 'undeserving'. Immanuel Kant gave voice to this view when, for example, he spoke of the Jews as 'a nation composed merely of merchants, that is to say of unproductive members of society', and the idea reappears with some harping in Hitler's *Mein Kampf*.[82] Sartre spoke of Jews being blamed for engaging in 'unproductive trades' ('métiers improductifs'), having historically been forbidden access to other occupations.[83] This reproach surfaced in (relatively infrequent) expressions of anti-semitism in Ireland itself, in the nineteenth and twentieth centuries.[84] A fringe-Marxist version of this reasoning was used in the 1960s and 1970s as a 'materialist' explanation of the Nazis' destruction of the Jews: 'not as *Jews* but as *rejects from the process of production*, useless for production.'[85]

This image readily acquires a shadowy companion fantasy of sexual barrenness, as Michael Rogin, reviewing David Mamet's novel *The Old Religion* (1997), remarked about the Leo Frank case, in some ways the Dreyfus case of the American South, in which an innocent Jewish factory manager in Marietta, Georgia, was framed and lynched in 1915 for the unconsummated rape and sexual murder, actually committed by Jim Conley, a black sweeper, of a thirteen-year-old white employee:

Jews such as Frank were vulnerable standing for the forces of Northern capital invited into the defeated Confederacy by proponents of the New South. Combining non-productive financial conspiracy with unnatural, unreproductive sexuality, the Jew of anti-semitic fantasy enticed young girls from their farm homes to the factory, there to fall prey to perverted Jewish lust. The absence of an intact hymen without any evidence of rape suggested the unthinkable, that the move from country to city had liberated a sexually active Southern white girl. The notion of Jewish perversion could now be invoked to lay that ugly suggestion to rest, as a stereotypical black sexual assault could not. Innocent black men were lynched for real or imaginary defiance, but Conley's tale of assisting a Jewish pervert was just what prosecutor and jury wanted to hear.[86]

Conley the black sweeper 'claimed that Frank had ordered him to remove the girl's body from the main floor to the basement . . . and to write the notes implicating Newt Lee, the black nightwatchman who found the corpse'. In this scenario, the Jew becomes the sexual counterpart or mirror opposite of the black man, whose sexual stereotype was one of excessive potency rather than barrenness. (The accusations against Frank were that he had 'ungovernable sexual tastes but, unlike [the Blacks], was incapable of satisfying them [.] That he, the Jew, was the same ravening lecher as the black, but his "performance", unlike that of the black in the Southern fiction, was pathetic'.)[87] The mutations of ethnic hatred are doubtless no more predictable than anything else, and I do not know enough about Nazi attitudes to Blacks to know whether (at the time, for example, of the 1936 Olympics) similar antitheses were in latent or overt circulation.

The Anglo-Irish situation did not, at least within what used to be the British Isles, have the built-in complication of a third race, though I have argued elsewhere that there is often, in another sense, a triadic rather than a simple binary pattern to our conceptions of the 'other'. This typically takes the form of an us and two thems, Caribs and gentle Arawaks, a good as well as a bad savage, like Crusoe's Friday among the cannibals, or the good Jew, 'our' Jew, of the anti-Semites, or the good German of some war novels, like Vercors's *Silence de la mer* (where the German, von Ebrennac, does not have a German name, and is of Huguenot stock, and where it is suggested that the 'goodness' of such Germans is in any case inevitably tainted).[88] In the American South of David Mamet's novel, where (as not in Ireland or Germany) there is a substantial presence of a more radically 'other' race, the Jew acquires an in-between status akin to, but subtly different from, that of the conventional 'good' other like Crusoe's Friday. The victim of a false conviction and a lynching is thought of as the Kike, the Nigger 'who should have *known* better, having been granted the almost-more-than-provisional status of a White Man'. In Harriet Beecher Stowe's South, the Irish were also evidently regarded, like Mamet's Jew, as precariously poised between the two main races, their whiteness a not altogether securely held acquisition.[89] Irish readers were among those who complained that Stowe's novel favoured the Blacks at the expense of the poor whites, and a piece appeared in the *Irish American*, entitled 'Mrs. Stowe in Cork', which defended 'the case of "Father Pat" against that of Uncle Tom'.[90] The ambiguous solidarities and complex tensions between Blacks, Irish, and 'native' whites are widely reflected in the lore of blackface minstrelsy in America, in which the Irish had an exceptionally prominent role, and which became part of the subject-matter of *Punch* cartoons in England.[91] 'Strong tendencies existed in antebellum America to consign the Irish, if not to the black race, then to an intermediate race located socially between black and white'.[92]

The range of Irish stereotypes on Irish soil can accommodate the blackface or half-alien stereotype, but does not naturally accommodate a Negro or Jewish *tertium quid*. There are small numbers of Irish Blacks and especially Irish Jews, but they do not figure prominently in the Anglo-Irish equation, despite some perceptions of English encouragement of Jews, in Cromwell's time and later, as a counterweight or else as a supplement to the Catholic population, and although Irish fellow-feeling for Jews as a persecuted race was frequently expressed. In 1829, O'Connell (who later in the Commons voted for the unsuccessful Bill to remove Jewish disabilities) wrote to Isaac Goldsmid, leader of the Jewish emancipation movement in Britain: 'Ireland has claims on your ancient race, as it is the only Christian Country that I know of unsullied by any act of persecution against the Jews.'[93] The claim has been repeated many times in the nineteenth and twentieth centuries, despite occasional localized flare-ups, and expressions of anti-Semitism by individuals or small extremist groups.[94] But the Jewish population in Ireland has always been very small, and the two facts were tendentiously brought together by Mr Deasy in *Ulysses* who boasted that Ireland 'has the honour of being the only country which never persecuted the jews ... do you know why? ... Because she never let them in', whereas, in his view 'Old England is dying' because it is 'in the hands of the jews'.[95]

Mr Deasy gives the story an unwarranted spin, but the population statistics (341 Jews in what is now the Irish Republic in 1861, 230 in 1871, 3,907 in 1946, and declining thereafter to 1,581 in 1991), confirms the remark of Chief Rabbi Immanuel Jakobovits, in a book published in 1967, that the ratio of Jews to non-Jews was 'perhaps the lowest in any English-speaking country'.[96] It also suggests that the Jewish presence, despite some distinguished contributions to Irish national life, and despite the spectacular fact of Leopold Bloom himself, was a relatively marginal one in the Irish cultural consciousness, compared with that of other countries in Europe or America, except perhaps in the exacerbated atmosphere of the 1930s and 1940s.

The African presence was even smaller.[97] It seems likely that the now modish self-image of the Irish as the 'niggers' of Europe (Roddy Doyle's phrase,[98] but an old idea, probably going back to the original Amerindian parallel as well as to English habits of describing the Irish as 'white negroes', which go back at least as far as 1700)[99] suggests a comparable sense of not having any 'niggers' of their own. The Negro analogy seems to have taken over (though never completely) from the Amerindian as Africans came to replace Indians, in European imaginations, as the principal exemplars of cannibalism and savagery.[100] Both equations have existed for centuries, but 'niggers' came to be used in the nineteenth and twentieth centuries, as 'Indians' previously, for all non-European groups, including Indians (of both India and America) and the Esquimaux of Greenland (the word 'nigger' is first recorded in 1786 in a poem by Robert Burns, while Negro and Black go back to 1555 and 1625 respectively).[101] Needless to say, these equations do not stand up to empirical observation, but they are potent in the vocabularies of old oppressors and new ideologues. In all the toing and froing of these transferred nomenclatures, however, real Africans or Indians (as distinct from the self-conscious awareness of imputed analogy) were hardly a significant part of the social fabric of Ireland itself.

Some fellow-feeling existed in Ireland for the plight of Africans, as for Jews, and was comparably ambivalent. Frederick Douglass noted as far back as 10 May 1853:

The Irish, who at home, readily sympathize with the oppressed everywhere, are instantly taught when they step upon our soil to hate and despise the Negro ... Sir, the Irish-American will one day find out his mistake.[102]

The idea of the Irish as a victim of the same kind of oppression as Blacks was not merely a matter of Irish or Negro self-perception. A moving caricature of 1866 by Daumier shows John Bull, presumably representing Edward John Eyre, the draconian Governor of Jamaica, standing over two desolate figures, one of whom, a Jamaican, whispers 'Patience' to the other, an Irishman.[103] But as Douglass perceived, the process by which Irishmen merged into white America often involved a renunciation or disavowal of solidarity with the American Negro, a story fully expounded in Noel Ignatiev's *How the Irish Became White*. In Fintan O'Toole's words, 'once in America ... the Irish cease to be the Indians and become the cowboys', a phenomenon fraught with ambivalent reconfigurations of allegiance. Ignatiev says that 'in becoming white the Irish ceased to be Green'.[104]

The process described by Ignatiev and O'Toole was a gradual one, and perspectives existed which saw both Blacks and Irish as comparable pariah groups, equally deserving of extermination. An Englishman, Edward Augustus Freeman, writing from New Haven, Connecticut, in 1881, said:

This would be a grand land if only every Irishman would kill a negro, and be hanged for it. I find this sentiment generally approved—sometimes with the qualification that they want Irish and negroes for servants, not being able to get any other. This looks like the ancient human weakness of craving for a subject race.[105]

The remark anticipates Nazi controversies between exterminators and 'economists', and, as the author, a historian, understands, taps into an old dilemma, for those contemplating mass-killings, which is discussed in the next chapter. A feature of this utterance is the 'plague on both their houses' symmetry of the animus. Such flourishes of rhetorical fantasy are not infrequent in the literature of group hatred. Southey denounced the Irish in 1798 as a 'half-christened herd', comparable to the British soldiery, so that 'one may be easily reconciled to the slaughter of either or both'. Céline entertained Wagnerian fantasies in which Hitler and Stalin might exterminate each other, but really wanted Hitler to wipe out the Russians, taking in all the Jews, Ukrainians, Rumanians, and Czechs as he did so.[106]

Freeman's letter, almost thirty years after Douglass's remark about the Irish in America, shows that Irish ambitions of white status were slow to realize themselves, though the pretensions which went with them made their appearance quite soon. One of the perils of being a *tertium quid* in racial equations is that there will always be people like Freeman, who are impatient of fine distinctions, and whose reductiveness does not discriminate among lesser breeds. But Douglass was undoubtedly right in his view that the Irishman in America became like the English in Ireland, whereas at home his self-perception was of pariah status, and identified with subject races, including the 'brutes' whom Kurtz had delirious fantasies of exterminating, and the 'niggers' of Conrad's other African story, 'An Outpost of Progress', who were the objects of a more lucid longing to the same effect.[107] As late as 1891, a retired member of the Indian Civil Service in County Mayo told Horace Plunkett he 'could not bear to treat the Irish like white men' and Plunkett himself described some inhabitants of Mayo as 'little removed from savages'.[108]

The citizen in *Ulysses*, whose nationalism provoked him to reverse Swift's formula by calling the English rather than the Irish 'unfortunate yahoos', was by the same token given to saying they were 'not European', which is also a way of standing the phrase about the 'niggers of Europe' in *The Commitments* on its head.[109] Such *tu quoques* are a staple of ethnic self-consciousness, but in the Anglo-Irish relationship the jokerie is inevitably complicated by the fact the Irishmen, like it or not, had white skins. Charles Kingsley, unjokingly observing the 'human chimpanzees' of that 'horrible country', found the sight much more 'dreadful' than if they had been black, 'but their skins, except where tanned by exposure, are as white as ours'.[110]

The situation seems to have undergone subtle and sometimes unexpected modifications after the founding of the Irish Free State. Shaw reports, and himself exhibits, some bizarre variations, when he notes in 1923 'that whereas my Irish nationality was formerly a valuable asset to me in England, I am now expected to apologize for it by men with wooly heads or number six noses' (he had recently been invited to serve on the Irish Senate and 'replied that I would consider it if the seat of the Irish Government was transferred to London').[111] But for all the dizzying complexities of racial nuance that exist between English and Irish, the current self-image of the Irish as 'niggers', while plainly not unconnected with English rule and British outlooks, is in some of its variants (including Roddy Doyle's) an ironic and playful self-consciousness. It seems safely uncoupled from any active pressures in the Anglo-Irish relationship, an appropriation or extension, for mainly domestic consumption, of a largely American association of blackface minstrelsy with Irish performers, audiences, and comic types, and of a wide range of black-and-white-minstrel-show jokes linking Irish and Blacks (a variation is the special place held by Jews in Black American popular music recently explored by Jeffrey Melnick).[112] In a not unrelated way Leopold Bloom's status as an insider-outsider is less a matter of English perception than of social forces internal to Irish society itself.

Bloom is himself, of course, sexually unproductive, and the fact is inseparable from his Jewishness. The main sexual component of

English fantasies about the Irish, traditionally poor and not rich, is that they are all too productive, a family-producing variant of the potent Negro, given to multiple breeding on an almost animal scale, as the *Modest Proposal* and many other writings are at pains to suggest, and hence an especially suitable case for the more lethal exercises in population control. There is a tendency to say such things about other groups which are political rather than numerical minorities. The received view among Balkan Slavs is said to be that Albanians are Muslims and 'breed like rats', which prompted a British academic observer to reflect recently on 'the danger if thousands of Catholics suddenly found themselves forced to flee from the Republic to Belfast'. Sir Charles Dilke, in the 1860s, thought the Chinese as well as the Celts were racially inferior 'prolific breeders' competing for supremacy with the Anglo-Saxon races.[113]

A thoughtful Anglo-Irish commentator in 1798, William Parnell (1777–1821), suggested a correlation with political oppression: 'If you examine different nations you will find that the people breed in exact proportion to the tyranny of the Government.' He instanced as a contrary case the Dutch, whose pride in liberty and industry made them see poverty as a 'disgrace' and discouraged 'imprudent marriages', and he claimed to have persuaded his friend Malthus that he was 'wrong in supposing that population can only be checked by vice and misery and that no country can be without a class of poor'.[114]

But 'the rich get rich and the poor get children', as the song says, and stereotypes continue unabated, fuelled by the usual ethnic, sectarian, and economic forces.[115] In an old joke, the Irish father of fifteen children who is summoned to the Vatican for a pontifical commendation, and bemusedly makes it known that he is Protestant, is then indignantly told by the Holy Father that in that case he must be an oversexed monster. Papists are prolific breeders, but that does not, in the discourse of Ireland, make them productive in any approved sense. If people are the riches of a nation, as the old mercantilist axiom proposed, the Ireland of Swift's imagination was in this and other ways like no other country, whose 'singular fate' it was to be in defiance of all normal laws.[116] 'As this is the only Christian Country where People contrary to the old Maxim, are the Poverty and not the Riches of the Nation; so, the Blessing of Increase and Multiply is by us converted into a Curse' (*PBB* 135). One of the ways in which it defeated the expected benefits of populousness was that Irish 'productivity' merely multiplied the numbers of unproductive poor: beggars, thieves, and, of course, more breeders of beggars and thieves.

Badging, Branding, and Castration

Swift's *Proposal for Giving Badges to the Beggars in all the Parishes of Dublin* has an obvious resemblance to the Nazi insistence on Jews' wearing an identifying yellow star.[117] (Other marks existed for other groups, including pink triangles for homosexuals.)[118] The regulation was in some cases relaxed for Jewesses married to Aryans, provided they had been sterilized, an idea which, had it appeared in a satirical or Utopian fantasy, might have given Swift some wrily complicit notions about how beggarly breeders might be rewarded (or punished).[119] The resemblance, in the crucial sense that Swift was no Nazi, is obviously superficial, but it is also a resemblance. This is not to propose equivalences but to recognize a relationship. A matter of interest is the way some extravagant real-life horrors have imitated the fictions of Swift and other writers, not only in their circumstantial aspects, but, if in grossly distorted ways, in the apparent tendency of their thought. Swift's extermination fantasies and velleities, like the one expressed about beggars in the *Proposal for Giving Badges*, may not have been literal, but they were punitive.

That *Proposal*, moreover, was not a fiction. It belonged to the world of practical action. Nor were the badges a solitary fancy of Swift's own. At the time of the *Proposal*, they were already notionally in place, partly in execution of an earlier recommendation by Swift. The idea was to identify the parish from which the beggars came, which was the institution legally responsible for supporting them when they could not support themselves. Beggars were unproductive, by definition, and since, in Swift's view, most of them were able-bodied and capable of employment, they fell into the category which mercantilist thinking, and Shaw's, described as 'undeserving' (*PBB* 135; *MBP* 25). When they came to Dublin from the country, they became what American immigration authorities reprovingly call a public charge, that worst of foreign menaces in a modern economy (Swift repeatedly uses the word 'Charge' in this sense—*PBB* 134, 138, 139), and what Wilde meant by going on the rates.

An ingenious twist to this line of thought occurs in Ian McEwan's *The Child in Time* (1987), set in a near-future of post-Thatcherite blight, in which beggars are licensed, and wear badges, for which they have to 'qualify', thus 'aiming for a leaner, fitter public charity sector', saving rather than spending on 'social security payments', and introducing large numbers 'to the pitfalls and strenuous satisfactions of self-sufficiency long familiar to the business community in this country'. The practice is highly regulated. Not only must the badges be worn 'correctly', but the beggars may not work in pairs, must be continuously on the move, are confined to 'authorised thoroughfares', must not 'pester the public', are 'not allowed in stations' or anywhere near Parliament or Whitehall.[120] We have moved a long way, in this curious dystopia, blending Thatcherite laissez-faire and dirigisme with such comprehensive exactitude, from Swift's somehow simpler severities about badging beggars. I have a chilling suspicion that Swift might not have disapproved of some aspects of this, whatever his views about a 'Government programme' whose 'success' was fostered by private charities to beggars,[121] though his ultimate insistence would undoubtedly have been on extracting productivity, not mere self-sufficiency or the raising of money from nothing. He would have felt the same contempt for these beggars as for the millionaire yuppies of currency dealing and the stock exchange. From his restricted perspective, resisting a plan to allocate funds for a poorhouse in Dublin, Swift was advocating the compulsory and visible wearing of badges, so that 'Foreign' (this too is a habitual term) beggars could be identified and returned to the parish which had responsibility for their support (*PBB* 132–3).

He has, he says, been advocating 'for some Years past' (the nagging accents of the Modest Proposer and behind him of Lemuel Gulliver are detectable, but we should not on that account infer any significant attenuation of Swiftian commitment in this case, only perhaps an incidental impish jokerie)

a very plain Proposal, I mean, that of badging the Original Poor of every Parish, who begged in the Streets; that, the said Beggars should be confined to their own Parishes; that, they should wear their Badges well sown upon one of their Shoulders, always visible, on Pain of being whipt and turned out of Town; ... I never heard more than one Objection against this expedient ... The Objection was this: What shall we do with the Foreign Beggars? Must they be left to starve? I answered, No; but they must be driven or whipt out of Town ... until they reach their own Homes. By the Laws of *England* still in Force, and I presume by those of *Ireland*, every Parish is bound to maintain its own Poor. (*PBB* 132–3)

The accents, expressly evoking harsh Henrician and Elizabethan legislation, nevertheless seem a shade less hard-line than Shaw's Preface to *Major Barbara*.

Swift was not alone in contemplating the idea, as we have seen. Badges were actually already in use, if not within the full and focused terms of Swift's project, as a result of poorly implemented administrative action already addressed in an earlier, unpublished memorandum by Swift, 'Upon Giving Badges to the Poor', which is dated 26 September 1726, close to the publication of *Gulliver's Travels*. In it he reports that 'several Lord Mayors did apply themselves to the Lord Archbishop of Dublin, that his Grace would direct his clergy, and the church-wardens of the said city, to appoint badges of brass, copper, or pewter, to be worn by the poor of the several parishes'. They were 'to be marked with the initial letters of the name of each church, and numbered 1, 2, 3, & c. and to be well sewed and fastened on the right and left shoulder of the outward garment of each of the said poor'. The Archbishop gave appropriate directions to the clergy, but the results were ineffectual, most beggars refusing to display their badges, hence Swift's recommendation (in 1726) 'That his Grace the Lord Archbishop would please to call the clergy of the city together, and renew his directions and exhortations to them'.[122] In the published *Proposal* of 1737, he said he was too much of 'a Desponder in my Nature' (*PBB* 140) to think his advocacy was to much purpose, venting a literal version of the mock-despair we associate with the fictive *Modest Proposal* of 1729. In fact, it may have been partly as a result of the *Proposal for Giving Badges* that, as the *Dublin Gazette* reported on 8–11 October 1737, a Lord Mayor's proclamation was issued requiring the arrest of all beggars 'except those badged by the several Parishes'.[123]

The reluctance of beggars to follow these orders, which Swift complained of both in 1726 and in 1737, had to do, as he reported in both places, with an attitude he found offensive:

They are too lazy to work; they are not afraid to steal, nor ashamed to beg, and yet are too proud to be seen with a Badge, as many of them have confessed to me, and not a few in very injurious Terms, particularly the Females. They all look upon such an Obligation as a high Indignity done to their Office. (*PBB* 134)[124]

One is reminded of the Newgate scene in Fielding's *Amelia*, where an otherwise unknown 'very pretty Girl' with 'great Innocence in her Countenance' passes by the hero Booth and discharges 'a Volley of Words, every one of which was too indecent to be repeated'.[125] The surprise is eruptive, as in Swift. But whereas Fielding seems to register pain or shock at the inexplicability of a world that no longer makes sense, Swift's trick in the *Proposal for Giving Badges* is to suggest that the sight of beggars or whores coming out in 'injurious Terms' is merely habitual, and shocking only because the insolence of beggary is 'absurd' (*PBB* 135).

At the beginning of *The Child in Time*, the main character Stephen Lewis gives a five pound note, an unusually large gift, to a girl beggar, duly badged, who 'rolled it tight into her fist and said,

"Fuck you, mister"'. The situation is fraught with pain: Stephen is grieving for his own kidnapped daughter, of whom the beggar momentarily reminded him. The girl despises him as a 'rich creep'. Near the end of the novel, he sees the same badged girl, apparently dossed down in a railway station, and gives her his coat, but she turns out to be dead.[126] The surprise is also eruptive, close to Swift and to Fielding in its brevity and its fabular form, its structural expectation of an explanatory pay-off, but radically unlike both, and especially Swift, in the personalized intimacy of its pathos.

Swift, closer in other places to a later literature of cruelty and black humour, is here playing a straight bat. The bafflement, if any, is a moralist's rhetoric about pride, about uppity beggars, and female at that. Swift's wording will add fuel to the myth of Swiftian misogyny, but it includes something of Fielding's surprise, so to speak, at seeing women doing it at all, as well as, and perhaps at the expense of, the ostensible suggestion that the women are the worst. But the main point is that Swift was affronted by such arrogance, and refers to it in the two pieces on badges and in the sermon on the 'Causes of the Wretched Condition of Ireland' (yet another repository of his notions about beggars, badges, the undeserving poor who beg out of idleness and a refusal to work, their bad marriage-customs, and the rest).[127] Wilde and Shaw would both have understood the pride of these beggars as indeed responding to a 'high Indignity', an affront to their humanity. For Swift, it was such an 'absurd Insolence' that 'for several Years past, I have not disposed of one single Farthing to a Street Beggar', though his grounds are not those of Wilde's or Shaw's view of charity itself as degrading.

At all events, you might say, this is quite different from yellow stars and *l'univers concentrationnaire*. The 'Foreign' beggars are foreign in a local sense, a legal and economic category rather than an ethnic one, even when, to the possible confusion of modern readers, the noun 'foreigners' is used of them in both 1726 and 1737.[128] The emphasis is on caste and behaviour rather than race, quite apart from Swift's real though perhaps also grudging concessions to the obligations of charity. But though in this context foreign is a quasi-legal or technical concept, there is a larger sense in which, whatever their parish, the beggars belong to the tribe of savage Irish, descended from Scythians and on a par with Indians of the New World. In the *Proposal for Giving Badges*, as in *A Modest Proposal* eight years earlier, xenophobic outbursts occur which tap into traditional English characterizations of the Irish, viewed as literally on a par with Amerindian cannibals. Like all savages, they are improvident and sexually profligate, taking on their trulls and breeding offspring without 'any Prospect of supporting their *honourable State* but by Service, or Labour, or Thievery' (the italics are Swift's, referring sarcastically to marriages where they occur), or postponing marriage (in a parallel flourish of italics): 'Nay, their *Happiness* is often deferred until they find Credit to borrow, or cunning to steal a Shilling to pay their Popish Priest, or infamous Couple-Beggar' (*PBB* 136; Wilde, by an amusing contrast, thought the abolition of marriage would be one of the happy consequences of the abolition of poverty under Individualism—*SMS* 265).

Swift's portrayals of Irish vagrants, their trulls, their priests, their loose sexual and domestic arrangements, were given a compassionate spin in the famous poem by Oscar Wilde's mother, 'The Famine Year', a sort of *Modest Proposal* turned inside out. Owen Dudley Edwards speaks of its 'starving children left with dead mothers' and of the poem's 'kind ... construction' on the subject of 'vagrant and nomadic fathers' and 'their desertion of wives and children'.[129] (Wilde's father, the surgeon Sir William Wilde, is still regarded by economic historians and others as the best medical and statistical analyst of the Great Famine, so that this event came to Wilde's consciousness from both parents, though views might differ as to its effect on him).[130] It was Swift's rather than 'Speranza' Wilde's view of the Irish poor which might be called the prevailing one, going back to Camden and others, Camden being especially pointed about the morals of the priests whom Swift called couple-beggars, who, Camden says, 'have converted the Temples into Stews' and whose 'whores follow them wherever they go'.[131]

'Couple-Beggar' is familiar *Proposal*-speak, though the phrase was in common use for disreputable priests who performed irregular marriages.[132] It conforms, unsettlingly, with the dehumanizing jargon and xenophobic phrasing of *A Modest Proposal*, and the priests, like other savages, belong to that world where humans are objects, beasts (of burden as well as, and simultaneously, of the wild), and cannibals (against the run of another topos, discussed in Chapter 1, which alleges that only humans eat their own kind). My point is not that Swift would have exterminated them, but that in Ireland in 1729 or 1737 Popish was as much an ethnic as a religious category, and almost invariably pointed to those 'savage old Irish' whom English writers talked of exterminating. Moreover, only ten years before *A Modest Proposal* and seven before *Gulliver's Travels*, a statute was mooted for castrating them. The Irish House of Commons passed a Bill in 1719 requiring that unregistered Irish priests be punished by branding on the cheek 'with a large P to be made with a red-hot iron', a completer and more corporal method of giving badges to the beggars, if you like.[133]

Branding and badging, indeed, have an old association, the objective of both, in such contexts, being simultaneously to identify and humiliate. An intermediate point on this scale might be the inscription of written words or other physically non-wounding marks on people's bodies. In the suburb of North Charleston, South Carolina, in 1996, a teacher, described as given to 'innovative' methods of instruction, wrote the words '"Where are my glasses!" in bold, blue letters' on the cheeks of a five-year-old girl. The child's lawyer 'initially compared the incident to the Ku Klux Klan's branding of blacks in the past', but later backtracked, apparently not because he thought the analogy was intrinsically inaccurate or silly, but because he believed no racism was involved in this particular case. A secondary dispute, as to whether the ink was 'permanent' or 'water soluble', indicates that many gradations exist on the scale between badging and branding.[134]

In the case of the Irish priests, the Irish Privy Council identified yet another point on the scale when they forwarded the branding proposal to England with a recommendation to replace branding by castration. The signatories included Viscount Midleton, later Swift's ally on Wood's halfpence, to whom the unpublished *Letter to Lord Chancellor Middleton* (the 'sixth' Drapier's letter) is addressed.[135] The English Privy Council supported branding. (Poyning's Law, which Swift resented as giving English authorities control over Irish legislation, was for once, as Oliver Ferguson notes, put to humane use).[136] The Bill was then thrown out by the Irish House of Lords, as Lecky reports, not for humanitarian reasons but because they objected 'to a retrospective clause' concerning certain Papist leases.[137] The Irish Parliament in fact went on to pass even more draconian legislation against priests, but this 'was not returned from England, and...never revived'.[138] Lecky observes that it is 'a memorable fact in the moral history of Europe that as late as 1719 this penalty [branding] was seriously proposed by the responsible Government of Ireland', and adds 'that a law imposing it upon Jesuits was actually in force in Sweden in the beginning of the century'. A paper advocating this Swedish example, on the grounds that Sweden 'hath never been infested with Popish clergy or plots', was circulated in England in 1700.[139]

There is no evidence that Swift supported either branding or castration, but seven years later, and eleven years before the *Proposal for Giving Badges*, in the safety of a Utopian fiction, meaning no-place as well as good place, he did allow a similar plan to be entertained. The Yahoos of *Gulliver's Travels*, an allegory of the savage Irish, are the subject of a periodic debate in the Houyhnhnm assembly, in which 'The Question to be debated was, Whether the *Yahoos* should be exterminated from the Face of the Earth', precisely the words Swift himself applied to the beggars in the *Proposal for Giving Badges*. Swift, remembering perhaps the Bill of 1719, made Gulliver tell his master how humans castrate horses, which put the Houyhnhnm in mind of a more humane expedient which 'would in an Age put an End to the whole Species without destroying Life' (IV. ix. 271–3).[140] Here, too, an unsettling Nazi parallelism rears its head, in the fact that both castration and sterilization were widely used in Nazi 'medicine', and sterilization was debated at the Wannsee conference in 1942 at least as thoroughly as at the Houyhnhnm Assembly, with full attention to administrative factors as well as the 'biological realities'.[141]

'The old sow that eats her farrow': The Beggarly Kingdom from Spenser to Joyce

Swift's phrase about putting 'an End to the whole Species without destroying Life' belongs to a series of ironies, more fully discussed in the next chapter, purporting that some notionally lesser atrocity is a sign of lenity, the more obvious and harsher alternative being conceded as perhaps 'a little bordering upon Cruelty', or seeming to (*MP* 113). But it also taps into a rhetoric for dealing with the Irish question which has one of its clearest prototypes in Spenser's opinion that the Irish do not need to be put to the sword since alternatives exist for achieving the same result without force. The speaker Irenius in *A View of the Present State of Ireland* has notions for exterminating the Irish which have the double advantage of precluding formal slaughter and being capable of quick execution:

The ende will I assure me be verye shorte and muche soner than Cane be in so great a troble (as it semethe) hoped for, Allthoughe theare should none of them fall by the sworde nor be slaine by the soldiour, yeat thus beinge kepte from manuraunce and their Cattle from Comminge abroade by this harde restrainte they woulde quicklye Consume themselues and devour one another

Spenser is adapting a current myth of the Irish as cannibals, like American Indians, which provides one of the not always recognized ironies of *A Modest Proposal* and the basis of a famous phrase by Joyce's Stephen Dedalus. Spenser's application of it is generically akin to Gulliver's castration proposal, and permits a similar and wholly straight-faced show of humanity:

The profe whearof I sawe sufficientlye ensampled in Those late warrs of mounster, for notwithstandinge that the same was a moste ritche and plentifull Countrye full of Corne and Cattell that ye would haue thoughte they Coulde haue been able to stande longe yeat ere one yeare and a haulfe they weare broughte to soe wonderfull wretchednes as that anie stonie harte would have rewed the same ... sure in all that warr theare perished not manie by the sworde but all by the extreamitye of famine which they themselves had wroughte[142]

One recognizes also in this passage Swift's familiar theme of the Irish as unable to act in their own self-interest, though from a somewhat different perspective, and Swift concedes that his beggars must not actually 'be left to starve' (*PBB* 133).

Critics differ as to whether Spenser was offering 'a terrible proposal, uttered with cold deliberateness' or a neutral or even compassionate view. 'Anie stonie harte would have rewed the same' may suggest the latter, but one authority writes that Spenser, 'far from ruing it, proposed later on to repeat the performance in the north, as the most convenient way of disposing of Hugh O'Neill's adherents', and R. F. Foster has described 'the scorched-earth policy in Munster after the Desmond wars', with its systematic exploitation of famine, as 'Spenser's preferred form of warfare'.[143] If Spenser was the author of the notorious 'A breife note of Ireland', his advocacy of 'great force' and 'spedie finishing' in Ireland's subjugation expressly adds that 'Great force must be the instrument but famine must be the meane for till Ireland be famished it can not be subdued'.[144]

The *Brief Note* has many views in common with the somewhat milder *View*, but whether Spenser wrote it or not, its notions about 'rooting out' the Irish, give or take the odd hesitation or attenuation, represent a distinct strand in the English discourse of Ireland: 'should the Irish haue ben quite rooted out? That were to bloudie a course: and yet there continuall rebelliouse deedes deserue little better.'[145] Its spirit is detectable in many of Swift's explosive utterances, and is variously echoed in later writers including Southey and Carlyle. The latter thought the Irish, unless they acquired an English outlook, would become extinct, like American Indians. In his essay on 'The Repeal of the Union' (1848), Carlyle specifies, in an update of Spenser's sentiments, as well as a preview of Shaw's, that 'if no beneficent hand will chain [the Irishman] into wholesome *slavery*, and, with whip on back ... get some work out of him—Nature herself ... has no resource but to exterminate him'.[146] Wilde and Shaw undoubtedly belong, at some distance and with variations, in this tradition.

It is easy to misrepresent Carlyle. He had compassion for Ireland, hardly 'governed and guided in a "wise and loving" manner' of the kind Las Casas desired for the Indians and Gulliver in a muddled moment thought the British were good at. He wrote in *Chartism* (1839) of the long centuries of cruel injustice, 'fifteen generations of wrong-doing', which have degraded the national character and reduced Ireland to a demoralized beggary. The theme of Irish beggary is as insistent in Carlyle as in Swift, with vivid vignettes of the stereotype appearing in the pages of *Chartism* and in the correspondence. He stresses its pathos (more than Swift does), as well as its economic sterility. Like Swift and Shaw, Carlyle sees productive labour as the only solution, though he is more insistent on England's obligation to 'manage' the Irish into it, 'redressing' the Irish population on a national scale if she is herself to escape being dragged down.[147]

The discussion in *Chartism* almost ten years before the article on the 'Repeal of the Union', is, for all its compassion and good sense, equally strongly caught up in the rhetoric about killing the Irish poor. 'The time has come when the Irish population must either be improved a little, or exterminated.' As in the passage from 'The Repeal of the Union', Carlyle's remark, like several of Shaw's, lies somewhere between constatation and exasperated velleity. Literalness is its most elusive feature, though there is literalism of a sort. Irish people are starving and an immediate necessity is to save lives, but this recognition does not altogether neutralize the

accents of punitive velleity. The pathos of beggary is acknowledged, but seen as contaminated by 'squalor and unreason, ...
falsity and drunken violence', 'sunk ... to squalid apehood', in a
way unthinkable in the Saxon poor. Even here, the harangues of
the strident hardliner are not disarmed by their own hyperbole.[148]

These tones reappear in 'The Nigger Question' (1849), originally
entitled 'Occasional Discourse on the Negro Question', where the
idleness of emancipated West Indian plantation workers has produced 'a *Black Ireland*' in the Caribbean. 'Our own white or sallow
Ireland, sluttishly starving from age to age on its act-of-parliament
"freedom", ... hitherto the flower of mismanagement among the
nations', now yields the palm to the West Indies.[149] These too are
described as a catastrophic case of 'idleness', where the governing
power's 'mismanagement' has been compounded by the feeble
sloth of the human material. The Irish gain small credit for coming
second worst in this context, becoming a classic mid-point in the
triadic arrangement into which, as I have argued, such attitudes
tend to fall. 'Our own white or sallow Ireland' belongs in the
category of '*our* Jew' in Mamet's novel, the Nigger with 'the
almost-more-than-provisional status of a White Man', who
'should have *known* better' than revert to type, and was lynched for
it.[150] Carlyle, at all events, was an admirer of Governor Eyre. On 11
April 1866, the exact day when Daumier's caricature of Eyre, in
'Irlande et Jamaïque', appeared in *Le Charivari*, Carlyle opined in a
letter to his wife that if Eyre had 'shot the Whole Nigger population, and flung them into the sea' not much harm would have
been done.[151]

The 'Occasional Discourse' is ascribed to a Dr M'Quirk, and its
overheated brassiness, a parody of an evangelical address, is a
camped up version of one of Carlyle's usual styles. Its excess is
hardly of a kind to disengage the author from its content, though
it allows the slight opening for stunned disbelief that sometimes
passes for decent attire when the enormity of the naked truth risks
appearing unhinged, or at least unsocial. In the correspondence
with his wife, like that of Philip Larkin with his friends, similar

eruptions were coded into contexts of personal understanding which are not easy for outsiders to recover, but might also claim something of the sanitizing effect of invisible quotation marks. The remark about shooting the Niggers is preceded by a conspiratorial '(*privately very!*)', no great softening but a sign of unease. Carlyle, like Swift, was a master of such exaggerative indirection, though Swift would have shrunk from the species of cantankerous buffoonery which Carlyle adapted into his own volcanic metamorphosis of Shandean self-inflation. He did not, of course, 'not mean' any of it, and his treatment of the 'nigger question' provoked an outrage he expected and did not disrelish.[152]

Spenser's application of slaughter to the Irish problem is grounded in the fact that the victims are rebels. This is also true, in an attenuated or residual form, in Carlyle's remarks about both Irish and West Indians, to the extent that demands had been made which in his view called for tough responses. But many post-Spenserian utterances use a similar idiom in contexts free of rebellion, and Spenser's and Carlyle's remarks about the Irish way of starvation reflect a chronic identification of the Irish with the somehow wilfully poor, poverty acquiring increments of culpability by that association. Spenser's language might be said to reflect an early stage in the evolving image of the Irish, from outlandish savage to domestic poor, which came eventually to dissolve the potent and customary analogy between the two groups, the one becoming 'socialized' and partially incorporated into the other. Poverty and famine are a major feature of Irish history and of the cultural consciousness of commentators on Ireland. The Webbs describe the widespread perception of an intimate association, at the time of the Whately Commission, between Irish poverty and the 'plague of mendicancy' which taxed the generosity of the poor Irish peasantry, as well as putting 'the English Counties to heavy costs' for the repatriation of Irish vagrants.[153] In the nineteenth century, as we are told in a recent book by Lynn Hollen Lees, the Irish in England were regarded with exacerbated resentment because of their poverty and the strain to which this put the English welfare services.[154] The complaint echoes Swift's about the beggars of Dublin.

In a recent discussion of the Great Irish Famine, Colm Tóibín cautioned against the facile analogies between that catastrophe and the Nazi Holocaust which have inserted themselves into the vocabulary of post-colonial self-righteousness.[155] His account of differences, both in the sphere of factual circumstance and on the scale of criminal enormity, is compelling. Cormac Ó Gráda's 'post-revisionist interpretation . . . also keeps its distance from the wilder populist interpretations' of the Famine, while claiming to be 'closer to the traditional story': 'Food availability *was* a problem; *nobody* wanted the extirpation of the Irish as a race.'[156] The gap between such observations, in the cold light of economic and social history, and the long tradition of death-dealing imprecations, places the latter in a different and more problematic light. It may be pertinent that the Hitler who masterminded a genocidal Holocaust was, in matters of public verbal expression, more guarded than many of the English advocates of rooting the Irish, or the poor, from the face of the earth. Confronting an unwelcome analogy is not the same as asserting the similarities it implies. I am not equating Swift with Nazis but exploring a larger configuration which there is no good reason to ignore merely because the Nazi version went monstrously out of hand. There is no more resemblance between Hitler and Swift, for example, than there is between the behaviour of ethnic cleansers in Eastern Europe and that of a teenager colloquially inviting another to 'drop dead'. But the language of both inhabits widely separated points on what is nevertheless the same spectrum of notional impulses.

The 'Whole' People

This is true even of formulations which boast the most impeccably righteous credentials. Gulliver's language about exterminating from the face of the earth, like that of the *Brief Note of Ireland* or the

Shortest Way with the Dissenters, is of course the language of Genesis 6: 7 in the Authorized Version: 'I will destroy man whom I have created from the face of the earth', and the Book of Genesis, like *Gulliver's Travels*, is in the business of suggesting not that God, or the Houyhnhnms, are genocidal maniacs, but that mankind, or the Yahoos, deserve the punishment. At the same time there is an unsettling overlap between the idiom of punitive righteousness and that of ethnic opprobrium, which will be explored more fully in the next chapter. The universal denunciations of the Old Testament are often thought to have their origins in regional disasters and ethno-specific animosities, just as local visitations of divine wrath, as in the cities of the plain, tend in a reverse direction to shade into accounts of humankind.

The Yahoos, as everyone knows, are not simply Irish brutes. They stand more prominently not as members of an individual race but as representatives of the human species in its most radical and degraded form. The fact that humanoids are also expressly represented as having the characteristics of 'all savage Nations', and in particular those specifically attributed to the Irish, is a characteristic double-bind. It reflects a deep Swiftian tendency to identify mankind as a whole with its own despised subgroups, using the idiom of racism less against particular ethnic groups than at the species as a whole, whereas I suspect that hardened ethnic aggressors will more typically use the idioms of a generalized misanthropy against individual groups.

Another uncompleted work, 'Considerations about Maintaining the Poor', gives an especially precise sense of how each group's depravity is implicated in that of all others. Like 'Upon Giving Badges', this was later published by Deane Swift, and like 'Upon Giving' and the published proposals, modest and otherwise, 'Considerations' is preoccupied with beggars, especially of the 'foreign' variety, with their laziness, profligacy, improvident marital arrangements, and the rest:

The prodigious number of beggars throughout this kingdom, in proportion to so small a number of people, is owing to many reasons: To the laziness of the natives; the want of work to employ them; the enormous rents paid by cottagers for their miserable cabbins and potatoe-plots; their early marriages, without the least prospect of establishment, the ruin of agriculture, whereby such vast numbers are hindered from providing their own bread, and have no money to purchase it; the mortal damp upon all kinds of trade, and many other circumstances too tedious or invidious to mention.[157]

There is nothing here that we do not read in better-known works, but it comes over with an unusual summarizing thoroughness, comparable only, perhaps, to that of the sermon on the 'Causes of the Wretched Condition of Ireland'. And although the beggar problem is described as the 'single point ... of greatest importance', what also comes through with peculiar concentration is the sense that others are contributing to the natives' predicament. The beggars lose none of their squalor, and any sympathy for them is severely circumscribed. But the sense that unemployment, exploitative landlords, a ruinous agriculture, 'the mortal damp upon all kinds of trade', are massive contributors to the problem is vividly stated.

The force of this has less to do with exculpating the beggars than with inculpating others. The landlords, many of whom, as we know from *A Modest Proposal*, spend the revenue of their lands in England, contributing to the ruin of their estates as well as pauperizing their tenants with unaffordable rents, are a particular case in point. The merchants get an exceptionally particularized dressing-down in 'Considerations', not only for 'knavery': 'I do not remember to have met with a more ignorant and wrong-thinking race of people in the first rudiments of trade; which, however, was not so much owing to their want of capacity, as to the crazy constitution of this kingdom, where pedlars are better qualified to thrive than the wisest merchants.'[158] As with the beggars, the merchants are caught up in the larger disarray, and Swift's disavowal of their 'want of capacity' is again not so much an exculpation of them as a still wider *in*culpation. The exposure of the commercially and nationally self-destructive effects of their shoddy manufactures, their short-sightedly dishonest trading, and their venality, a theme which runs through the Irish tracts and is highlighted in the 'other Expedients' passage in *A Modest Proposal*, is, despite its striking specificity, immediately absorbed, as in *A Modest Proposal*, within an all-enveloping reflection on 'the crazy constitution of this kingdom'.

This is a principal tendency of Swift's Irish writings, and even a work with the narrowly specialized focus of the *Proposal for Giving Badges* has moments in which the beggar problem is glimpsed as the exacerbated and defining feature of a comprehensively 'singular' state, the essence and epitome of a 'beggarly Country' (*PBB* 135). The subtextual force of such outbursts extends the scope of the attack to the entire population, implicating the ruling groups in a predicament ostensibly reserved for the poor. In Irvin Ehrenpreis's words, the tract places the beggars, the immediate or ostensible target, within 'the general category of Irish people bringing down on their own heads the misfortunes that oppress them'.[159] But it is *A Modest Proposal* which gives the most fully orchestrated sense of an inclusive self-consuming national catastrophe. The Irish beggars, with all the thieving, idleness, and profligacy they share with their real-life counterparts of the *Proposal for Giving Badges* and the cannibalism with which they return to an imputed tribal type, become at the same time, in the fullness of the cannibal allegory, part of a general condition which implicates the other Irish classes, the merchants and bankers and Members of Parliament and fashionable women, with a sweep comparable to the extended outburst by Shaw whose key sentence about the poor is cited at the beginning of this chapter: 'I hate the poor and look forward eagerly to their extermination. I pity the rich a little, but am equally bent on their extermination. The working classes, the business classes, the professional classes, the propertied classes, the ruling classes, are each more odious than the other: they have no right to live.'[160]

Shaw's explicit concerns extend beyond Ireland, but his death-dealing persiflage, and its extension from beggarly targets to the whole of society, have their own way of reaching back to Swift. It is a more reductive way, delocalized and discursive, abstracted from the fictive solidities of Swift's cannibal Ireland. Shaw's way of derealizing the dispensing of deserved exterminations is to make clear that no one will have to carry them out: 'I should despair if I did not know that they will all die presently, and that there is no need on earth why they should be replaced by people like themselves.' It reads like a social planner's version, sanitized and good-natured, of Spenser's feeling that you do not actually need to put the Irish to the sword since they can be got rid of by starving or eating each other.

Swift also derealizes the literal impact of his proposal, making clear, as Shaw also did, and as Spenser did not feel any impulse to do, that it was not literal. But Swift's way was to gain Shaw's effect by using Spenser's example, relying on its outlandishness to uncouple him from any suggestion of literal commitment. Where Shaw seems to rely on social progress to perform his 'exterminations' for him, Swift's version expresses no genial optimism. But it protects the *Proposal* from its full literal horror through an insulting exploitation of the traditional cannibal slur, enunciated metaphorically rather than (as in Spenser) literally. Swift, like Montaigne, shrank from the literal implications of his cannibal discourse when it came too close to home, as we saw in Chapter 1. But he had no difficulty, under cover of a 'cruel' fictive fantasy, in reapplying it to the entire *dramatis personae* of the *Modest Proposal*, landlords and merchants as well as beggars. These attacks on multiple social groups are both extended and derealized by being merged into what is in effect an 'impossible' attack on the whole Yahoo race, whom, like Pound's unkillable infants of the very poor, nobody can exterminate, except in the mind, or in the Book of Genesis. But within the guardedness of such aggressive fabulations, he presented the moral depravity and political turpitude of these widely inclusive groups as a mercantile update of that cannibal reversion which Stephen Dedalus's description of Ireland as 'the old sow that eats her farrow' was to evoke in more rural terms.[161]

The Irish poor who embrace a scheme of selling their babies for food are no more literally cannibal than the real-life exploiters who are the targeted consumers of the new meat-product. There is an ironic reversal in the fact that the 'cannibal' natives are envisaged as starting a business enterprise while the prosperous ruling groups revert to behaviour they traditionally ascribe to those natives. But this amusing paradox is safely abstracted to the realm of metaphor. For all the harping on the cannibal formula, there is no suggestion even of an episode like that of the meat-factory worker in Upton Sinclair's *The Jungle* (1906), who falls into a boiling vat and is changed into lard, a story which reappears, in a mode of black humour rather than social protest, in Thomas Harris's *Hannibal* (1999).[162] Sinclair's novel came out in time to be referred to repeatedly in the Preface to *Major Barbara* (June 1906, *MBP* 36, 38, 52) and was a model for Brecht's *Saint Joan of the Stockyards* (1929–31), a play with close links to Shaw's *Major Barbara* as well as *Saint Joan* (1923).[163] It is said to have led to a tightening of food regulations in America and a temporary drop in the sale of meat, but its interest in the present context is that it allowed a literally cannibal happening to support a theme of industrial exploitation, as Tolstoy's *Resurrection* (1899), a few years before, had juxtaposed tragic cases of famine cannibalism with the deadly oppressions of the Tsarist government bureaucracy.[164] It is said that 'it was from the Chicago stockyards that the Nazis learned how to process bodies'.[165]

Swift, as we have seen, kept information about real-life Irish famine cases carefully under wraps, and his flirtation with literal imputation is in the end confined to a jokey intimation of the old mythologizing slur. His contribution is to extend the scope of this beyond the 'savage old Irish' to whom it is usually applied, associating the ruling Anglo-Irish element with its own despised subgroup. This may be seen as a more radical version of the satirical tactic, common in Augustan satirists, including also Pope and Fielding, of attacking the moral turpitudes of high persons as low-class: here they become, so to speak, 'low-race'. Within the fiction, the actively anthropophagous practices, which provide the main metaphor of politically and economically suicidal behaviour, is the work of the various politically dominant Anglo-Irish groups. The *Modest Proposal*, as is now widely recognized, is more directed against Irish self-destruction than against English exploitation, though Swift's attitude to the English is the traditional distrust of the *colon* for his compatriots from the *métropole*. The English appear briefly at the end as not only unlikely to be disobliged by the Proposer's cannibal scheme but willing '*to eat up our whole Nation without [Salt]*' (*MP* 117). The cannibal reversion thus ultimately encompasses not only the rich as well as the poor, but the imperial power as well as the colonial subjects, native or not. Swift, like other *colons*, whether in eighteenth-century Ireland or twentieth-century Kenya or Algeria, disliked the metropolitan masters not for their treatment of the native subjects but for an alleged betrayal of the *colons* themselves.

In this perspective, they merge all the more readily in the universal turpitude. In the *Proposal for Giving Badges*, where we are back mainly to Irish beggars rather than the Anglo-Irish establishment, the latter nevertheless remain at their usual occupation of destroying themselves by ignoring Swift's advice, while the English appear in the role of exporters of beggars, 'sent over Gratis, and Duty-free' in order 'to advance the *English* Protestant Interest among us' (*PBB* 136). As a preamble to these sarcasms, Swift announces that 'I profess to mean real *English* Beggars in the literal Meaning of the Word, as it is usually understood by Protestants', itself a sarcasm, betraying an unusually explicit sensitiveness of the issue of literalness, with something of the point-scoring style of Eucharistic debates. (One may recall the Protestant Léry's mocking phrase, 'manger reellement (comme on parle)').[166] For these beggars, who have the same vices as their Irish counterparts and whose home parishes are even further away, he was 'so ignorant' as to advocate a stepped-up version of the same treatment: they should be imprisoned for a month, whipped twice a day, fed with bran and water and put to hard labour, and then returned to England 'as cheap as they came'. Alternatively, since one Englishman is said to be worth twelve Irishmen, we should send a dozen Irish beggars to England for every English beggar in Ireland (*PBB* 136–7).

The tendency of Swiftian satire to spread like grapeshot to all neighbouring groups amounts cumulatively to a calculated form of universalism, for which the Yahoos of *Gulliver's Travels* provided an allegorically more complete prototype. We need not sentimentalize Swift's views of beggars or savages, in order to understand that they are really part of a larger anatomy of the human creature. It has recently been the fashion to align Swift's supposed misogyny with his attitude to the same disadvantaged groups, and it is one of the curiosities of the *Proposal for Giving Badges* that women beggars sometimes seem to come in for special opprobrium, for example the women who used bad language when they refused badges.

Or so it might be represented. I do not know the exact resonance of this observation, or its social any more than its psychobiographical source. But the passage, discussed earlier, is not, as these things go, a particularly striking example of Swiftian shock tactics. The strongest charge in the passage has to do with the 'absurd Insolence' of beggars being too proud to wear badges, not the fact that these are more likely to be women or that the women use injurious terms. There is nothing here of the almost surreal betrayal of expectation, the sense of unexplainable or gratuitous outrage, of the comparable passage from Fielding's *Amelia*. The latter is one of several vignettes, from Fielding's early periodical writing in the *Champion* to his last novel and his pamphlets on poverty and crime, in which a stark reversal of normal expectation accompanies the portrayal of beautiful women, in the later works usually in circumstances of penury and degradation.[167] The effect in each case is to register the pained sense of the inexplicability of things. You might think this recipe more Swift's than Fielding's, but it is harshly played off against the typical Fielding air of command, and perhaps Fielding was more radically pained at beautiful women in outlandish situations or more willing to be surprised that women behaved like men.

A Flayed Woman, and Brother Footman going to be Hanged

Even in this difference from Fielding, it seems misplaced to emphasize a misogynistic targeting. There is a passage where a whore appears, in Swift, not Fielding, in a set piece with a startling pay-off, which has also been seen as a case of gendered aggression. It concerns the prostitute in the Digression on Madness, carted and whipped in public, who nearly forty years earlier became the heroine of Swift's most famous sentence: 'Last Week I saw a Woman *flay'd*, and you will hardly believe, how much it altered her Person for the worse.'[168] The passage has provoked some bizarre interpretations, imputing a misogynistic brutality, or else a compassion for 'not very advantaged groups in Augustan England'.[169] The first is at least partly disposed of by the male example of deceptive appearance which immediately follows, that of the beau whose carcase is dissected to reveal that he looks less attractive with his innards exposed,[170] much as apparent degradations of the female form divine in *Gulliver's Travels* tend to be balanced by adjacent male counterparts. For all the passing references to trulls, or to dehumanized 'Females' travelling with the primary beggar thief, the predominant *dramatis personae* of the Irish tracts and sermons are male, and there are perhaps more male offenders than whores. The second interpretation does not sound plausible as to 'compassion', in the light of Swift's other known pronouncements about whores and beaux, or as to disadvantaged groups, since beaux (and probably whores) are not likely to have been thought by Swift to belong to these, and since Swift is not conspicuously soft on such groups anyway. Both examples are more accurately read as eruptive sarcasms against disreputable types, no kinder than the outbursts against the beggarly profligates of the Irish tracts. Like these, though more strikingly, they exhibit an unmistakable slide into universalism, since if whores and beaux look worse when flayed or dissected, so would anyone else, including Gulliver, the Portuguese captain, Arbuthnot, Stella, and Swift himself: one of the points of the Digression on Madness is that it takes a fool like the speaker to require such violent evidence to discover the obvious. By the same token, however, a satirical overplus occurs which identifies the whole of humanity with whores and beaux: an irrational but potentially guilt-inducing intimation which is one of Swift's signatures, to which I drew attention in an earlier book.[171]

The countering of female by male examples, turning the issue into a human rather than a specifically female one, has the effect of defusing a potentially misogynistic intensity. Certainly Swift was conscious of imputations of misogyny, and may thus have sought to parry or disavow them. It is a fact that women were sometimes grouped by analogy with other disadvantaged groups, including those subject to ethnic defamation. The Irish, like the American Blacks of Gunnar Myrdal's *American Dilemma*, were repeatedly compared to the 'dependent and subordinate groups' in the ethnically dominant population, 'namely women and children'. The stereotype of the 'savage' as a child, or childlike, is especially familiar in both Irish and Negro contexts, and the Irish also came within the purview of descriptions of Celtic races as soft and feminine, implying charm and incapacity for government.[172] Swift provides interesting testimony, which does not self-evidently implicate him in such correlations, when he speaks in 1709 and again in 1724, of '*Irish Papists*; who are as inconsiderable, in Point of Power, as the Women and Children'.[173] He has been accused of 'easy callousness', but he is in such contexts writing factually, to describe the lack of power, or even legal status, of the native Irish and not their intrinsic character, and to argue that Anglican fears of a Papist menace were exaggerated or unfounded.[174] The example is nevertheless interesting as evidence of the assimilation of depressed categories, ethnic and other, to one another.

The passage about the whore is famous for another Swiftian speciality, the deadpan understatement of 'altered her Person for the worse'. It is a manner elaborated throughout the *Modest Proposal*, and which led André Breton to confer on Swift the title of 'véritable initiateur' of *humour noir*, an insight whose wider implications are considered in the next chapter.[175] The sentence from the *Tale* has an eruptive force that has much to do with its extreme brevity, as well as with the casualness of its treatment of a violent scene, the sudden and surreal gratuitousness of its punitive cruelty, its precisely calibrated note of apparent insouciance.

The offhandedness, the surreal acceptance of the shocking, including transportation and hanging, as well as flaying, reappear in the *Directions to Servants*, a work of many years which Swift intended to publish soon after the *Proposal for Giving Badges*, and which was actually published a few weeks after his death at the end of 1745.[176] Suggested excuses for a servant to offer their angry employers in the event of lateness include 'taking leave of a dear Cousin who is to be hanged next *Saturday*'. It sounds outlandish, but was obviously more usual then than now.[177] It might serve not only as an excuse but as a real event for which an excuse might be needed. Thus the Footman is advised:

When you step but a few Doors off to tattle with a Wench, or take a running Pot of Ale, or to see a Brother Footman going to be hanged, leave the Street Door open, that you may not be forced to knock, and your Master discover you are gone out; for a Quarter of an Hour's Time can do his Service no Injury.[178]

What is here casually presupposed, is that the Footman might really, and typically, need to absent himself for a friend's hanging, and only for a quarter of an hour, as much a part of daily routine as tattling with a wench or taking a pot of ale, which heightens the force of the other passage, where a cousin's hanging is proposed as a plausible reason for being late when it happens not to be true.

The apparent levity of this kind of thing is presumably what led Breton to include the *Directions* as his opening text in the *Anthologie de l'humour noir*, though these examples are not among his extracts, calling Swift the inventor of 'la plaisanterie féroce et funèbre': his second text is *A Modest Proposal*, and his next author is Sade, whose projects for infanticide and wholesale slaughter were written as straight, more or less unironic, versions of Swift's cannibal scheme.[179] If Swift's own idea, in the *Directions* and the *Modest Proposal*, as well as in the *Proposal for Giving Badges*, has to do with the depravity of servants, or beggars, Breton's interest begins at the point where 'l'intention satirique, moralisatrice' is exceeded, or transcended, in a mode of ludic 'cruelty'. I shall be considering in the next chapter some aspects of the aesthetics of black humour, and of the senses in which the satiric or moralistic may be thought to be a negation of it or an *influence dégradante* on its functioning.[180] What I wish to stress here are the element of shock that is generated by the casualness, the flip taking-for-granted of the deadly, and the treatment of capital punishment not as something to be reacted to as justified or otherwise, but as quotidian fact unflappably taken on board. Levity is not the only condition for such surreal effects, such suddennesses of revelation, in eighteenth-century treatments of 'not very advantaged groups' such as whores and beggars: Fielding, as we have seen, is vivid testimony to that.

The examples from Fielding I have cited do not concern capital punishment. Passages which do, concerning the hanging of Jonathan Wild, for example, and the fact that he was born to be hanged (and the joke that perhaps Tom Jones was also born to be hanged), belong to a different category. They revolve around 'ideal' situations of poetic justice, punishment for the wicked in romance resolutions, and to a semi-punning play with the proverb that he that was born to be hanged shall never be drowned.[181] For all the compassion shown in the novels for the misfortunes of the virtuous driven by poverty to crime, Fielding was, as a social thinker and pamphleteer, outside the realm of fiction, with its special opportunities for taking the full human view in relative freedom from the reality principle, an unbending exponent of the difference between the productive and the impotent poor, and an advocate for the capital punishment of felons convicted of stealing, as he phrased it, 'a few Shillings'. Even the *Enquiry into the Causes of the Late Increase of Robbers* (1751), contemporaneous with *Amelia*, from which this is taken, does not propose 'the Life of a Man and a few Shillings to be of an equal Consideration', and may dwell on the pathos of a family about to be bereaved by his hanging. But the social utility of sacrificing 'one Man...to the Preservation of Thousands' is the paramount issue, and 'of what Man? Why, of one who being too lazy to get his Bread by Labour,...declares War against the Properties, and often against the Persons of his Fellow Subjects...'[182] This is not far removed from Swift, or an unsarcastic variant of Swift. A difference may be that Fielding speaks of killing one to save thousands, whereas Swift speaks of exterminating the whole tribe. Here, too, the reality principle asserts itself over fiction and rhetoric: we know Fielding meant it literally, and who knows what Swift meant literally, ever.

They Ought to be Shot: The 'desperate Experiment' of Figures of Speech

In raising the question of whether killing the poor was an Anglo-Irish theme, I do not mean to suggest that it is, or could be, exclusively Anglo-Irish. Indeed, one of my concerns is to explore a certain universality in this type of thinking, both in its application to the poor (as, for example, in Baudelaire's two prose poems) and in its relation to broader themes and fantasies. Death-dealing utterances about the poor occur in a continuum which stretches from divine announcements of annihilating the species, through outright declarations or projects of specific genocidal intent, to mere *façons de parler* about how this or that group 'ought to be shot'. They include anarchist and other revolutionary projects of large-scale destruction in order to rebuild (Oscar Wilde's first play, *Vera; or the Nihilists* (1883), set in Tsarist Russia, is concerned with these, as well as with the tyrants' reciprocal counter-threat); the aesthetic ideal of removing poverty by removing the poor, because poverty is ugly, or inhibits genius (which Shaw and Wilde both entertained in one form or another); and the alternative and more extreme aestheticism of 'cruel' play in a pure state (*à l'état pur*), which André Breton identified in *A Modest Proposal* and Sade, and called *humour noir*.[183]

This 'aesthetic' dimension has an elusive but uncomfortable historical relation with Fascism, sometimes referred to as an aestheticization of politics. Breton is hardly to be accused of Hitlerian sympathies, though Artaud, like Céline and Genet, had an intermittently expressed admiration for Hitler. Céline, for whom the extermination of Jews and others were in one sense a species of mental theatre, with elements of ballet, also said after the war that Hitler's crimes 'were the result of bad taste', and spoke to Milton Hindus of his poor taste and skill in painting.[184] (We may recall Ezra Pound's reported post-war dismissal of his own anti-Semitism as a stupid suburban prejudice).[185] But death-dealing utterances have ethnic rather than aesthetic priorities, even in such contexts. Their scope is wide and includes every form of ethnic cleansing and every murderous expression of neurasthenic group-hatred; children's curses, and social idioms like 'drop dead', as well as the fulminations of Céline and the deadly public reticences, on this subject, of Hitler; and ironic fantasies like Defoe's *Shortest Way With the Dissenters* and Swift's *Modest Proposal*, which do not mean what they say but are sometimes mistakenly taken to do so.

It is part of any proper enquiry to consider the status of such utterances, both as to literal intent and as to practical follow-through and enactment; to register the relationship between Hitlerian reticences and his actual operations, and between the unreticent imprecations of Céline and whatever outlets for his sentiments might have presented themselves to him in Nazi-occupied France (Céline wrote to his judges that the Jews 'should put up a statue of me for all the harm I didn't do them, but which I could have done'!);[186] and to ask why so many were taken in by the irony of the *Shortest Way*, and relatively few by those of *A Modest Proposal*, bearing also in mind, with the hindsight of history, that these titles are potential counterparts to our own century's 'final solution'. That both authors used the phrases with ironic self-disengagement must be registered alongside the fact that Defoe was taken straight, and the even starker fact that Swift's utterances in the *Proposal for Giving Badges* were delivered straight.

It is one of the ironies of history that, in recent years, Protestant extremists in Northern Ireland, a group Swift would have detested even more than he despised the Irish natives, seem to have taken to applying the threat of 'final solutions', 'incinerators', and the rest, to the Catholic minority, an extension to its most perverse modern logic of an ancient English discourse which Swift had a share in perpetuating. Swift, and doubtless Defoe, would have been disconcerted to find themselves in such company. Instances of the thuggish reductiveness of the Loyalist spokesmen are reported in Liz Curtis's *Nothing but the Same Old Story*, an informative book which is also reductively polemical in its opposite sympathies, and seems to express triumphalist approval for an English politician's alleged assertion of 'a parallel between British treatment of the Irish and Nazi treatment of the Jews'.[187]

Discriminations are called for between such language and that of the earlier writers, not only because of huge differences of implication and register, but also because of an inescapable continuity and the unresolved indeterminacies which surround it. In the various utterances of Defoe or Swift, however 'ironic', there is an interplay between 'meaning it', not meaning it, and not *not* meaning it. This needs recognition, if only because, as Defoe discovered to his cost, and as Swift warned about the irresponsible bandying of death-dealing talk in the *Sentiments of a Church-of-England Man*:

I suppose it is presumed, the common People understand *Raillery*, or at least *Rhetorick*; and will not take *Hyperboles* in too literal a Sense; which, however, in some Junctures might prove a desperate Experiment.[188]

The comment also has applications, though of a cruder kind, to the spokesmen cited by Liz Curtis.

A dialogue in Ian McEwan's *Enduring Love* (1997) raises the issue in a different form. Jean Logan says of the woman whom she suspects of being her late husband's lover, 'if she comes near this house ... I'll kill her'. Her son tells the narrator Joe Rose:

'It's completely wrong to kill people' ... I said to the boy, 'It's just a way of speaking. It's what you say when you really don't like someone.'
    'If it's wrong to do it,' the boy said. 'It's wrong to say you're going to do it.'[189]

The baldness of the boy's response 'naïvely' ignores the working distinctions we take for granted between *façons de parler* on the one hand and practical intentions and their implementation on the other. But like Swift's warning it also draws attention to the lines of connection between them, and if the study of human expression has responsibilities to exercise in this context, there is an obligation to understand these connections.

The evidence of history is that 'in some Junctures' it has indeed proved 'a desperate Experiment'. Swift's warning about 'the common People' taking '*Hyperboles* in too literal a Sense' is perhaps his most vivid and revealing acknowledgement of the perils of literalism in the slippery world of verbal obliquity which was his own natural element as a writer. The dispensing of death-dealing utterances is a great deal more frequent than their implementation. The controlled rhetorical slippages I have been discussing, and to which Swift partly alludes, are part of an imperfect system of constraints on radical violence, as well as species of invitation to it. It seems likely that some of history's great genocidal outbursts have been unplanned results of outlooks and ways of speaking whose murderous content was not generally or widely intended or taken at face value.

There seems in particular always to have been a need, or a perceived need, to generate hatred for an underclass, often allegedly or actually foreign, in order to justify its dispossession or the exploitation of its members as contributors to the economy and as political scapegoats, like the Undershafts' token Jew. Immanuel Wallerstein has recently expressed some pertinent thoughts about the outbursts of ethnic resentment against foreign immigrants in the affluent West, and the emergence of political parties of the extreme right with policies of active hostility towards them. He points out that the elimination of the despised group by expulsion or slaughter would, if implemented, deprive affluent capitalist economies of one of the engines of their affluence. In this context, he advances the view that 'while almost everyone in the pan-European world had been openly and happily racist and anti-semitic before 1945, hardly anyone had intended it to lead where it did'. The Final Solution, on this view, 'missed the entire point of racism within the capitalist world-economy'. It was an illogical swerve: 'what the French would call a *dérapage*—a blunder, a skid, a loss of control. Or perhaps it was the genie getting out of the bottle.'[190]

The wording captures exactly the Swiftian apprehension of 'a desperate Experiment', and also his understanding that the danger came from inner forces all too readily released. Wallerstein suggests that such things have been going on since the time of Las Casas and that the Final Solution is only the most bureaucratically complete manifestation of the syndrome.[191] It is not evident that such phenomena are confined to the capitalist phase of history, or that they did not exist long before Las Casas. But the tension between considerations of economic advantage and the counter-productive urge to exterminate remained active, and indeed erupted into peculiar prominence, within the Nazi programme even as it was being implemented, a subject taken up in the next chapter. Swift had a wry understanding of that too. The economic constraint, like the social, which tends to ensure the deliteralization of extermination threats, sometimes, as Swift understood, simply breaks down.

The putative victims of the contemplated final solution in Book IV are the Yahoos, who in a sense stand not for a specific ethnic group, but for the entire human race and, as I shall be arguing, seem to appear in Houyhnhnm eyes much as humanity appeared to God when he decided to destroy it 'from the face of the earth' in a great Flood. The design, though presented as entirely justified, is not actually implemented. The Yahoos are also an underclass, or the representatives of all underclasses, foreign and domestic, 'all savage Nations' and the Irish in particular. Part of the argument of this discussion has been that the Irish combined the roles of foreign savage and domestic mob, with beggary or poverty as a defining feature, and the dereliction of the duty of productive labour as a driving force of denunciations against them.[192]

In the case of the Irish and the poor in English and Anglo-Irish imaginations, my contention has been that the two categories became semantically linked, as in an older time the categories of Irish and savage or Indian were semantically linked, as a result of earlier English discourses which ultimately derive from European accounts of Amerindians. The Old Testament's way of merging the language of universal castigation with that of specific slaughters fed variously into the discourse of Ireland, lending incidentally to the vocabulary of extermination, of destroying from the face of the earth, a coloration of righteousness. In Swift's case, this takes the form of identifying humankind itself with its own despised subgroups, represented in his work, and especially in the Yahoos of *Gulliver's Travels*, separately and in combination, by primitive savages, the Irish, and (as some think) women. The latter form an especially contested issue, sometimes reductively misunderstood, though Swift's female beggars in *A Modest Proposal* and elsewhere suggest that they do have an awkward place in this equation.

The flavour of Wilde's writings and Shaw's is undoubtedly different. The thought and language of both are in their various ways implicated in the more international vocabularies of socialism and aestheticism. But their formulations also tap into an old Anglo-Irish discourse, the discourse of Spenser and Camden, at least to the extent of a visible derivation from Swift. Neither Wilde nor Shaw, any more than Swift, would endorse the crude brutalities of that discourse in its most starkly literal mode. They are not among those who, in the words of Wilde (reviewing Froude), 'will welcome with delight the idea of solving the Irish question by doing away with the Irish people'.[193] But such writings sound not wholly unlike Shaw's or even Wilde's own ideas of solving the poverty question, whose language owes much of its character to the type of spokesman Wilde is repudiating, as well as to the teasing equivalences of Irish and poor.

In both Wilde and Shaw, moreover, as in Swift's Yahoos, the issue, whether literally or fictively conceived, is 'killing' the poor, the Irish, or 'all savage Nations', not letting them die, or (its euphemistic obverse) eat cake. In the case of the poor, it is 'killing' them not because they are a revolutionary menace in the sphere of political action, but because they are poor, for what they are rather than what they do. Since the issue for both Shaw and Wilde was not punitive, the stark logic, to the admittedly problematic extent that they 'mean' what they say, suggests that killing the poor resembles the way you might kill, or contemplate killing, a racial group, the Irish, savages, and ultimately, for Swift, humanity at large: except, of course (the evasions and slippages are of the essence), that what 'they' are, at least intermittently, is said to be partly defined by what they do, or don't do, and except (again) that in this Anglo-Irish context, the Irish are and are not a racial group, are both 'ourselves' and 'other', and that Wilde and Shaw are not specifically speaking about Irish poor, though the old language about these rubs off on what they say.

4   God, Gulliver, and Genocide

Yahoos, Helots, and Extermination

Towards the end of *Gulliver's Travels* the Houyhnhnm Grand
Assembly holds a debate, reverted to every four years, on the only
subject that ever comes up before it. The Houyhnhnms have no
word for opinion or for lying, because there is only one truth (IV.
viii. 270, 267; iv. 240). So there is never anything to debate, except
the single recurrent question, 'Whether the *Yahoos* should be
exterminated from the Face of the Earth' (IV. ix. 271). For some
reason, they have never settled this matter, though they once
thinned out the Yahoo population, which threatened 'to over-run
and infest the whole Nation'. They 'inclosed the whole Herd', and
killed all the older Yahoos, keeping only 'two young Ones in a
Kennel' for the use of each Houyhnhnm.

Enclosing the whole herd, killing elders who cannot work,
keeping those who can (or some of them, or for a time), even the
divided purposes, as between total extermination or exploitation
of labour, have distressing resonances in our time, of which Swift
cannot have been aware. The resemblances do not, any more than
those considered in the last chapter, make the Houyhnhnms, or
Gulliver, or Swift into proto-Nazi exterminators, but they raise a
host of questions about the relations of imaginative activity to
real-life events. Swift's satire includes more than one extermin-
ation-fantasy, and these are usually presented as punitive in a primary way, rather than as self-deriding. That is to say, they seem to
attack the targeted victims rather than the would-be exterminator.

This is true even of the *Modest Proposal*. The speaker and his project are outlandish, but the main satiric charge is against a people whose conduct has reduced them to the single option of a reversion to barbarism, which is suggested to be their natural state anyway. This does not imply that Swift thinks his Irish are literally cannibal (as we saw in Chapter 1, he was if anything concerned to keep real-life cases out of view), or that he would literally approve the activity his Proposer puts forward. But the note is one of 'serves them right', not of compassion for the victims of a genocidal oppressor.[1] If it is the case that Swift endorsed the Houyhnhnm plans to exterminate the Yahoos, and if these bear uncanny resemblances to what the Nazis did to the Jews, the fact has to be explained in the context of his known loathing, evident throughout *Gulliver's Travels*, for mass-slaughter and genocidal atrocities.

The Houyhnhnm debate about the Yahoos takes place in a fictional Nowhere, with Irish and other applications, but insulated from some 'real-life' implications in a way that even *A Modest Proposal*, as a tract for the times concerned with specific political and economic issues (notably those listed in the 'other Expedients' passage),[2] cannot be, for all its ghoulish fantasy. The difference, which should not be overstated, will be an object of intermittent attention in this chapter, and has an obvious bearing on how we interpret Swift's sweeping punitive gestures. It was George Orwell, in 1946, who was perhaps the first to suggest that the Yahoos 'occupy rather the same place in their community as the Jews in Nazi Germany', though he did not have much to say about the extermination project itself.[3] A question is whether the Houyhnhnms' contemplated exercise in ethnic cleansing or population control is an issue of 'biology', like Nazi plans for the Jews, or of crime and punishment, killing people, or a people or humanoid species, for something they do rather than for what they are, and whether that activity is itself separable from ethnic cleansing or population control. The same question might be asked of *A Modest Proposal*, where an extermination project consists of thinning out a subgroup of the population, in order to find an application for Ireland of the mercantilist commonplace that people are the riches of a nation. This is the ostensible point, but its real subtext is punitive inculpation, somewhere between 'serves you right', 'I told you so', and 'this is what you're really like'.

In the No-place or Utopia of *Gulliver's Travels* there is a freer hand to invent the enactment, or proposed enactment, of what a punitive rhetoric, of the sort that exclaims 'they ought to be shot', literally says but the 'real author' doesn't literally mean. The Houyhnhnm Assembly's recurrent inaction may have the effect of further enforcing the idea that the rhetoric isn't 'for real', and we are never told that the project is executed anyway. A tactical silence is explicitly maintained about the outcome of the debate, a characteristic Swiftian tease sustaining an already considerable readerly discomfort.[4] But Gulliver and the Houyhnhnms are certain that this is what the Yahoos deserve, and the book is not in the business of giving us the solace of an opposite or competing view. There happen to be, as I shall argue, some uncannily detailed correspondences, beyond the mere extermination debate, between what may happen in the discourse and actions of a genocidal atrocity in the real world, and the macabre jokeries of *Gulliver's Travels* and *A Modest Proposal*. They may suggest Swift's intuitive sense of the depths of a potential human depravity, as well as an ability to entertain these in himself at a level of 'cruel' play. They also remind us of the disturbing resemblances between our fictions and *façons de parler* on the one hand, and the language and performance of historical cruelties on the other.

But these relationships are hardly simple, and this creates problems for critics who look for direct correspondences between what the Houyhnhnm Assembly proposes and a supposed 'meaning' of the Fourth Book. Either Swift endorses this and is a Nazi monster, which nobody really believes, or he must repudiate it, in which case the Houyhnhnms are assumed to carry some of the genocidal discredit, and the Assembly debate becomes evidence of their proto-Hitlerian instincts. Recent post-colonial studies have emphasized either a 'racism' on Swift's part, which endorses the 'racial' slurs in Book IV, or a Swiftian castigation of the Houyhnhnms' genocidal proposal and 'the violent colonial programme' of which it is a part.[5] The second view is generally the product of what used to be called a 'soft' interpretation of Book IV, which holds that Gulliver's high estimation of the Houyhnhnms is as misguided as his view that the Yahoos represent humankind, and that the true representatives of a decent humanity are the King of Brobdingnag and the Portuguese sea-captain Don Pedro de Mendez.[6] According to this thinking, Gulliver's vision is distorted, and the institutions and behaviour of the Houyhnhnms are held to belie their own and Gulliver's opinion of them as *the Perfection of Nature* (IV. iii. 235). These include the perceived despotic character of their social organization, their harsh treatment of inferior races (indeed their evident belief that there are such things), their presiding over what has been described as a slave state with Yahoos in the role of slaves, and the genocidal inclinations implied by the debate in the Grand Assembly.[7] Connoisseurs of police-state analogies will wish to add that Gulliver's Houyhnhnm Master is told he must not harbour a Yahoo in his house, so that Gulliver must be enslaved like other Yahoos or expelled from the country (IV. x. 279).[8]

To this it seems appropriate to repeat that the ideal society of the Houyhnhnms approximates to those of Plato and More,[9] and also that Yahoos are not in relation to the Houyhnhnms an alternative race but another species, as rats or cats or, for example, horses belong to other species in the human world. Strictly, a Houyhnhnm plan to exterminate the Yahoos most closely resembles some hygienic undertaking to exterminate a farmyard pest, except of course that in the reader's perspective the Yahoos resemble humans.[10] In the terms of the story the extermination is trans-specific, and designed to get rid of a population of beasts. According to some present-day thinking, which holds that 'speciesism' is comparable to racism, this would not lessen the culpability of the Houyhnhnms. The idea (explored most recently in J. M. Coetzee's *The Lives of Animals*, 1999) of a possible equivalence between the way humans treat animals and the Nazi treatment of the Jews exists on a wavelength almost certainly outside Swift's range or that of his presumed readers.[11] But there is a sense in which the Yahoos are portrayed as 'our' representatives, and the Houyhnhnms consider carrying out against them what seems to us, and may have seemed to Swift, one of the versions of the human slaughter of rejected human groups. The impression is doubtless planted for a reader's discomfort. It is consistent with a large network of small effects of its kind, and more a matter between Swift and his readers than a characterization of the Houyhnhnms.

At the same time, the Yahoos seem to occupy in Houyhnhnm society a role analogous to that of the Helots in Sparta.[12] In particular, it has been suggested that the massacre of the Helots by the Spartan *krupteia*, a secret police, may have been Swift's inspiration for this project.[13] The resemblance is limited by the fact that the Spartan exercise was selective, not total. But the previous Houyhnhnm massacre of the Yahoos, though fuelled by ideas of total riddance, or final solution, had in fact been selective too. Swift had a sympathy for Spartan disciplines and solutions, as did the two inventors of ideal commonwealths whom he most admired, Plato and More, though these are not on record as admiring the treatment of the Helots.[14] Plato notes that 'probably the most vexed problem in all Hellas is the problem of the Helot-system of the Lacedaemonians, which some maintain to be good, others bad', concluding that in a well-run slavery system it is preferable 'not to allow the slaves . . . to be all of the same nation, but, so far as possible, to have them of different races—and . . . to accord them proper treatment.'[15]

The 'elimination' of the Helots is shrouded in reticence. The account by Thucydides is in veiled and (in the words of Vidal-Naquet) 'partially encoded language'. The Spartans themselves apparently 'kept their secret rather well'. The Helots and other despised groups hated their rulers, and Xenophon says that an informer reported that 'whenever among these classes any mention was made of Spartiatae, no one was able to conceal the fact that he would be glad to eat them raw'.[16] The expression recalls what Hecuba said about Achilles in the *Iliad* and what Amerindian warriors were reported to say to one another in sixteenth-century accounts: expressions of impressive ferocity, easily represented as savagery from the 'civilized' perspective of ruling groups invoking the menace of barbarism, who kept their own slaughtering activities under wraps.[17] Plutarch, though an admirer of the Spartan constitution, said the *krupteia* carried out repeated smaller slaughters, thought the institution 'abominable', and hoped or believed it was post-Lycurgan. Since, over the centuries, the idea of Sparta developed into a species of Utopian model, it is perhaps not surprising that the treatment of the Helots was usually passed over in silence by writers in the Utopian tradition.[18]

Swift's position seems to have been subtly different. He was not only, like the others, drawn to aspects of the Spartan constitution and the disciplined rigour of its civil and moral conventions,[19] but nourished a particularized distaste for the Helots, whom he is likely to have identified with the savage Irish (quite apart from the latter's connection to the Yahoos): the identification of the Irish with the Helots was an obvious one, and later became current in European and English thought.[20] Gulliver reports that in Glubbdubdrib 'a *Helot* of *Agesilaus* made us a dish of *Spartan* Broth, but I was not able to get down a second *Spoonful*' (III. viii. 198), a passage which finds an echo in Swift's accounts of the repellent diet of the Irish poor, somewhat as the Houyhnhnms' debate about destroying the Yahoos from the face of the earth echoes the sentiments of English writers about the Irish. Swift was writing within the imaginative freedom of a fictional plot set in a Nusquama or Utopian Nowhere. This made it possible for him, as it was not for Plato or Plutarch, to signal a subtextual complicity, or fictive 'secret sharing', with velleities of punitive mass-killing, of the 'serves them right' or 'they ought to be shot' kind.

Swift made very clear what his own relation to such remarks was. In the famous letter to Pope of 26 November 1725 about *Gulliver's Travels*, he says he is 'no more angry' with mankind, or with '—[probably Walpole]', than he 'was with the Kite that last week flew away with one of my Chickins and yet I was pleas'd when one of my Servants Shot him two days later'. The non-humanity of the bird acts here as an enabling 'fiction' for the expression of a death-dealing sentiment about humans, sufficiently establishing that it isn't 'for real', but in its way near enough. The words express with unusual explicitness the mixture of meaning it, not meaning it, and not *not* meaning it, which was a theme of the last chapter. The remark comes soon after the exclamation 'Drown the World, I am not content with despising it, but I would anger it if I could with safety', words which (I shall suggest) evoke the Deluge, probably intentionally, and add to the sense that the 'ought to be shot' reflections extend beyond individuals, named or unnamed, to the species as a whole.[21] It can be said more generally, without any implication of murderous impulses, that Swift was temperamentally drawn, in a notional or imaginative sense, to the simplifying resolutions of mass-extermination. This is especially evident in the rhetorical outbursts in which he liked, in his own name, to denounce beggars, bankers, and other groups as fit to be exterminated from the face of the earth. In general, these outbursts declare their reasons: the case against beggars, for example, is that they will not work for a living and are a charge on the city.

The main accounts of the Helots' massacre suggest a political agenda to get rid of a potentially subversive underclass. The Helots were an early example of the convergence, or combination, of two despised groups, the lower orders and foreign immigrants.[22] There was a sense in which they were killed, at least in part, for what they were, not for what they did. It seems to be thus with the whole race of Yahoos, though of course what they are entails many bad doings on their part. Their evil is absolute, even if part of our sense of it is derived from an accumulation of specified turpitudes (greed, lechery, and so forth), so that even good men, like the Portuguese captain, turn out to be Yahoos. Those of the bush, with whom the Houyhnhnms are concerned (they would presumably not exterminate the Portuguese captain, any more than they contemplate exterminating Gulliver himself),

were the most filthy, noisome, and deformed Animal which Nature ever produced,... the most restive and indocible, mischievous and malicious...

This is a description of group-character, not a list of actual transgressions. When this particular passage goes on to exemplify, the worst that we learn of them in the report of the Assembly debate (which might be expected to give the strongest available arguments for killing them) is that 'they would privately suck the Teats of the *Houyhnhnms* Cows', behaviour which suggests a touch of trans-specific unnaturalness rather than radical evil (they do not slaughter cattle, like the Irish Houghers, who may be one of the models for the Yahoos).[23] Even as the passage continues, freakishness and nuisance, as much as any serious malignancy of either action or purpose, seem to remain the dominant note: they would also 'kill and devour their [the Houyhnhnms'] Cats, trample down their Oats and Grass... and commit a Thousand other Extravagancies' (IV. ix. 271). These petty predations of animal survival hardly constitute a major indictment, whatever the work tells us, in a larger sense, about human depravity. In fact, they never do anything quite as bad as their human counterparts. For example, they 'had their Females in common', but are free of the 'politer Pleasures' practised 'on our Side of the Globe' (IV. vii. 263–4); and their aggressions cannot compete with human wars, which the Houyhnhnms find incredible even on anatomical grounds (IV. v. 247). It is as though, for all their repulsiveness, and its way of rubbing off on ourselves, there is a disproportion in their contemplated punishment which suggests that their depravity is less in their doings than in the fact of their being humanoid, meaning approximately human.

The Yahoos are a multiple phenomenon in the allegory of Book IV. They are, in one sense, the Houyhnhnms' Helots, a pariah group who, like all such, are readily seen also as beasts. They embody characteristics, as we are specifically told, of 'all savage

Nations', including especially the Amerindian and other primitive peoples whom travel writers reported on, and the savage old Irish of whom Swift often spoke in the tones of earlier English writers, who did not distinguish them from other savages. They simultaneously appear as humanoids, not fully human, and as the lowest common denominator of all humanity, whose radical and instinctual depravity is shared, if we believe Gulliver, by himself, Mrs Gulliver, the children, the Portuguese captain and the rest. These, at all events, have to be tested by a Yahoo yardstick. In a work sparse in signposted religious preoccupations and scriptural allusion, the Yahoos are given, in the Assembly debate, origins which any British reader would identify as a scriptural evocation of primordial humanity, anthropologized in a down-beat way, but clearly recognizable. Immediately after we learn of their habit of sucking the teats of the Houyhnhnms' cows and related 'Extravagancies', we read that an advocate of extermination in the Assembly

took notice of a general Tradition, that *Yahoos* had not been always in their Country: But, that many Ages ago, two of these Brutes appeared together upon a Mountain; whether produced by the Heat of the Sun upon corrupted Mud and Slime, or from the Ooze and Froth of the Sea, was never known.

This impudently deadpan piece of primordial anthropology is a secularized version of the Genesis story of Adam and Eve, with the mountain setting presumably taken from the 'steep savage Hill', the 'shaggy . . . Mountain' on which Eden is placed in *Paradise Lost* (IV. 172, 224–6).[24] These first ancestors increased, and multiplied, and 'engendered, and their Brood in a short time grew so numerous as to over-run and infest the whole Nation'. But they could not be aborigines, the speaker continues, or 'they would have long since been rooted out' (IV. ix. 271–2).

Gulliver's Master Houyhnhnm, who is on the other side, pro-posing a less hardline method for dealing with the Yahoo ques-tion, agreed with his opponent's biblically coloured historical account, adding

that the two *Yahoos* said to be first seen among them, had been driven thither over the Sea; that...being forsaken by their Companions, they retired to the Mountains, and degenerating by Degrees, became in Process of Time, much more savage than those of their own Species in the Country from whence these two Originals came. (IV. ix. 272)

Gulliver is on this account a less degenerated Yahoo from the country of ultimate origin. The scenario of an imported primal couple carries rough and ready associations of a degraded Adam and Eve.[25] In its most guilt-inducing form, this playful fabulation makes of our ultimate ancestors an English or a British couple, floating the idea, or tease, of a primordial nastiness closer than expected to the reader's home. A passage in the first edition, subsequently deleted from the final chapter, which originally followed Gulliver's opinion that no European had ever visited Houyhnhnmland, or any of the places he had visited, before him (IV. xii. 295), adds:

unless a Dispute may arise about the two *Yahoos*, said to have been seen many Ages ago on a Mountain in *Houyhnhnmland*, from whence the Opinion is, that the Race of those Brutes hath descended; and these, for any thing I know, may have been *English*, which indeed I was apt to suspect from the Lineaments of their Posterity's Countenances, although very much defaced. But, how far that will go to make out a Title, I leave to the Learned in Colony-Law.[26]

This passage was omitted from the Faulkner edition of 1735, and the reasons for this omission have exercised interpreters. One reason which has been adduced is that the mention of primordial English Yahoos may have seemed inconsistent with Gulliver's praise, in the previous paragraph, of 'the *British* Nation' (IV. xii. 294) as superior to others in probity and efficiency in founding and administering colonies.[27] As an 'explanation', this seems neither true nor false but largely irrelevant, assuming the deletion was Swift's rather than his publisher's. The 'inconsistency' is no more than that which exists between the praise of British colonialism and the attack on the European variety in the preceding paragraph, especially since Gulliver now believes all Yahoos to be vicious and no longer shows any disposition to favour his own people. The coy formula of British is best, which Swift might not necessarily disavow in certain cases, is here placed under sarcastic scrutiny. The explanation underestimates the mercurial opportunism of Swift's irony, his habitual and manipulative disregard of 'consistency' in the service of a local aggression or sarcasm, his penchant for deadpan mystification. One might equally argue that the idea of aboriginal English Yahoos appears to conflict, subtextually, with the identification of Yahoos with the Irish, unless Swift is here, with an unusually specific pointedness, conflating the English, or 'the *British* Nation', with the Irish and 'all savage Nations' (IV. ii. 230), a characteristic style of wholesale inculpation. It is my view that Swift would not knowingly abstain from such an effect, so that the later omission of the passage is unlikely to have been for this reason either. The reasons for removal seem not to be recoverable. It is possible that Swift's publisher removed it because of a perception of the potential 'inconsistency' which has indeed ended up exercising the interpreters anyway.[28] In any event, it is the original *inclusion* of the passage which is of real interest, and since the question of resemblances is expressly referred to in the first edition as a matter of 'Dispute', it would appear that some sort of insulting tease was part of Swift's agenda.

Gulliver and Biblical Survivors

The more lenient treatment which the Master Houyhnhnm proposes for the Yahoos, in contradistinction to extermination, is something to which I shall return. For the present I wish to note two things. First, that I do not believe Swift is suggesting that Adam and Eve were English, but that they were, like the rest of us, common Yahoos, or perhaps, more clearly, that all Yahoos, again like the rest of us, are descended from them. That a further

escalation of guilt-inducing insinuation, which identifies the
Yahoos with specifically English nastiness, is not a reinterpreta-
tion of the Book of Genesis, but a playful and disorientating tease,
rubbing in the point that all of 'us' are included in the indictment.
The puzzle is designed to induce panic rather than allegorical
exegesis, if you like, thus contravening Gulliver's own sober
announcement to the gentle reader at the beginning of this
chapter that his 'principal Design was to inform, and not to amuse
thee' (IV. xii. 291), but confirming the spirit of Swift's own
declaration to Pope on 29 September 1725 that his objective was to
vex the world rather than divert it.[29]

The second point about the evocation of a sleazy primordial
ancestry is that it appears to be part of a whole network of parallels
to the Old Testament, and most specifically to the Book of Genesis,
in Gulliver's closing chapters, and in Swift's correspondence about
Gulliver's Travels at the time. It reinforces, if the matter needs
reinforcement, the sense that the Houyhnhnm debate about
exterminating the Yahoos from the face of the earth is an echo of
Genesis 6: 7, where God speaks, in the King James version, of
destroying 'man whom I have created from the face of the earth'.[30]
The allusion is to the impending release of the Deluge, an allusion
also present in a famous passage in Swift's next letter to Pope, of 26
November 1725, which contains his 'Drown the World' outburst.
The Noah story seems to be clearly in Swift's mind at this time, as
is that of Lot, its quasi-analogue, including God's declaration in
Genesis 18: 32 that if there were as few as ten righteous men in
Sodom God would spare the city. Swift was highly conscious of
this biblical passage, which he quoted two years earlier in the
sermon 'Doing Good': God 'Promised Abraham to save Sodom, if
only ten righteous men could be found in it'. Remembering it
again in the first of the two letters about *Gulliver's Travels*, he told
Pope 'O, if the World had but a dozen Arbuthnetts in it I would
burn my Travells'.[31] The parallels between the two great destructions of Genesis, the Deluge and the destruction of Sodom,
including the parallels between Noah and Lot (and even their

wives), are commonplaces of the literature of divine retribution, and juxtaposed as such in the New Testament (2 Peter 2: 5–8).[32]

Gulliver is Swift's Noah or Lot, who would probably have survived the Houyhnhnm final solution. The work's handful of examples of good humans, or good Yahoos, like Glumdalclitch, or the King of Brobdingnag, or Lord Munodi, or that evidently unforgettable hero of soft-school interpreters, the Portuguese captain, also have a claim to rank as righteous exceptions, evidently not amounting to a dozen, or even ten, either in *Gulliver's Travels* or in life. If the Yahoos are both the Irish and humankind (including the Anglo-Irish as well as the English at some layer of consciousness), an Irish application may be found in some seventeenth-century writers about Ireland: Stephen Jerome (1624), who said 'God hath his Lot in Sodom, his Noah among the worldings... but alas these godly ones are thin sown' in Ireland, and R. Olmstead (1630), who adds that the saved there are 'very rare, scarce one of a family, or ten of a tribe'.[33]

The relationship of *Gulliver's Travels* to the Book of Genesis is not that of a scriptural allegory (like Dryden's *Absalom and Achitophel*), still less a doctrinal or theological one. I concur with the generally accepted view that any specifically Christian, or Judeo-Christian, dimension is neither affirmed nor questioned, but merely submerged or even neutralized in the broader anatomy of humankind on which *Gulliver's Travels* is engaged.[34] On the other hand, Swift clearly had an enhanced awareness of this Old Testament book at the time.[35] It provided a classic model of situations in which guilt is comprehensive and to some extent unspecific (early readers of the Bible were uncertain of the nature of the 'wickedness' said in Genesis 6: 5 to have caused the Flood), and in which the virtue of the righteous themselves comes over as uncertain or tainted.[36]

It is true that localized readings of the Flood story have existed in competition, or conflation, with the sense of a universal catastrophe, just as the idea of exterminating Yahoos as representative of the human species coexists with an English rhetoric about exterminating the Irish. There seems, on such topics, usually to be a dialogue, or oscillation, between the universal and the local. Noah's curse against Ham's son Canaan (which I discuss below) is sometimes seen as referring to the subjugation of Canaanites, and ultimately led to much wider racial mythologies about the sons of Ham. Canaan was in turn invoked in English claims of righteous conquest of the Irish: Cromwell told his troops embarking at Bristol that they were Israelites about to extirpate the idolatrous people of Canaan.[37] The destruction of Sodom and Gomorrah concerns two cities, though Lot's daughters think the whole world has been destroyed, as in the Flood, but when, like Noah's sons, they try to replenish the earth, they produce two tainted races rather than a rebirth of humanity as a whole. These are part of a traffic between the universal and local which is germane to *Gulliver's Travels*, but the starting-point of the analogy between Noah's Flood and the idea of exterminating the Yahoos is a targeting of the whole species rather than particular groups. The project of destroying mankind from the face of the earth, however, comes over in the Genesis account of Noah's Flood not as a matter of racially motivated ethnic cleansing but of divine retribution, and the implication, as I have suggested, is not that God, or the Houyhnhnms, are genocidal maniacs, but that mankind deserves this treatment.[38]

In the freedoms of a Utopian fiction (Utopia meaning more No-place, More's Nusquama, than good place), no special exceptions are contemplated, and any exceptions that may none the less be inferred, like Gulliver himself, a Noah figure who belongs to the 'real' world outside, or such other 'righteous' exceptions from that world whom one might imagine straying into Houyhnhnmland, also indicate that they are themselves Yahoo. No group within the Yahoo race is being singled out as being distinct from others by the Houyhnhnms, and least of all by some rival Yahoo group considering itself of superior race. The Houyhnhnms themselves have class distinctions based on colour, and they are, and know themselves to be, superior to the Yahoos, much as God is to humans, or humans to beasts. They belong to another species rather than a different race, and 'racism' among the Houyhnhnms does not therefore arise.[39]

Nevertheless, the extermination fantasy exists, with a clear punitive dimension, and one which, as I have been arguing, is to some extent distinct from any idea of specifiable misdeeds. The Yahoos are being punished more for what they are than for what they do, for a radical and perverse anti-naturalness that is the hallmark of their nature. We should notice the curiously absolute and global character of the punitive project. Exceptions are allowed, but they have an exceptional character, even as exceptions. It is not only that they are non-existent, like the ten righteous men or the twelve Arbuthnots, or else radically insufficient to make a difference, like the less than twelve Arbuthnots—in real life perhaps the three or four surviving Scriblerians, or the handful of good persons in the story itself. These cases are in their way substantial. But they serve mainly as a satirist's concession, without which the indictment might be dismissed as excessive, and they act more as enabling agents for the total inculpation than as truly functional exceptions. These so-called exceptions, moreover, are themselves reinterpreted into the absolute trap by a recognition, especially pointed in the case of the Portuguese captain, that being a good Yahoo does not stop you being a Yahoo.[40]

The same perception may be extended to Mrs Gulliver and the children, surely innocent victims of Gulliver's somewhat deranged undeception about humanity after his sojourn among the Houyhnhnms. 'The long suffering Mrs Gulliver' has been called a 'highly underestimated heroine', but I think she is a shadowy figure, not given a role in the narrative designed to encourage readers to take notice of her. In some ways she resembles the wives of Noah and Lot, whom Genesis treats perfunctorily. Unlike Mrs Gulliver, the two biblical wives have no names of their own in Genesis, which gives them a curious mixture of unimportance and of generic or exemplary status. (Both women acquired a variety of names in post-biblical tradition).[41] The fate of Mrs Lot in particular, famously transformed into a pillar of salt (19: 26), is highlighted as an exemplary punishment, though our sense of her personal identity is almost nil. Noah's wife, who became quite a character in later literary and popular tradition, is in Genesis a similarly shadowy and recessive figure, and the fact that she has no name has little of that spectacular and mythologized anonymity which attaches, for example, to such other unnamed figures as Kurtz's two women in Conrad's *Heart of Darkness*,[42] another work preoccupied with ideas of large-scale extermination.

But she remains, as Noah's wife, a mother of the human race, while Mrs Gulliver, who does have a name, is exemplary only of human ordinariness, not even of a generalized womanhood or wifehood. She is the mother of no one but her own children, and commits no dramatic transgression, like Mrs Lot. The Gulliver children also have names, in this case like Noah's sons, but without the status of the latter as progenitors of nations, a status shared, in a less honorific and less inclusive sense, by Lot's daughters, who in turn, like their mother and unlike Noah's sons, are unnamed (doubtless a reflection of the biblical conception of the relative importance of women and men).[43] Gulliver's children, like their mother, exist as embodiments of ordinariness, insignificant except as projections of Gulliver's quotidian typicality, and later as the innocent victims of his antisocial antics as a confirmed misanthrope.

If the latter behaviour is itself, as everyone knows, comically excessive, that too is to be viewed in a special way: partly as a disengagement, of course, showing that Swift knows that things have gone over the top, but also as a concessive manœuvre, without which the onslaught loses credibility, so that it too, paradoxically, becomes an enabling and reinforcing element. Though Swift is uncoupled from what I have elsewhere called 'the taint of excess' he attaches to Gulliver's behaviour, the inculpating reinforcement is intensified and exacerbated by the reader's radical uncertainty as to what, and how much, is to be discounted, remembering always that the volume offers us, in those final pages, no alternative perspective to that of Gulliver.[44]

The hypothetical righteous men of Genesis and Swift's twelve Arbuthnots have a prototype in the persons of Mr and Mrs Noah, actually rather than hypothetically spared in the great destruction from the face of the earth mentioned by Genesis, evoked in the language of the Houyhnhnm Assembly, and alluded to in Swift's apocalyptic jokeyness about 'drowning' the world. They clarify the status of such 'exceptions' in a further way, proving that they are irrelevant *either* to a total inculpation *or* to a total chastisement. Neither Noah, nor that 'second Noah', Lot (the two are more than once juxtaposed in Scripture),[45] was enough in practice to prevent the respective catastrophes they survived, any more than the single Arbuthnot, or his fictional counterpart the Portuguese captain, can do much in practice to abate the guilt of merely being human. Some commentators hold that the ten just men of Abraham's bargain with God are the smallest number to constitute a group or administrative unit, so that Noah, Lot, and company can only be saved as individuals.[46] In this regard the just men cannot be considered as prototypes of Gulliver or the Portuguese captain, though Noah and Lot can, but they are direct analogues to the twelve Arbuthnots, the minimum sufficient for Swift to burn the castigation of mankind he asserted *Gulliver's Travels* to be.

On the question of survivors, it seems useful to register incidentally that it is a structural precondition of myths or fables of universal destruction that there should be at least one, or, in fictions of a 'realist' orientation, two: an unusually visible example of how the formal necessities of narrative play a major role in shaping or determining the fabular content. The story would not exist if the Houyhnhnms had carried out their *earlier* extermination of the Yahoos to the full. And this may also be why, though having no notion of 'how a Point could be disputable', wherein they 'agreed entirely with the Sentiments of *Socrates*, as *Plato* delivers them', the Houyhnhnms regularly debate the extermination of the Yahoos but can apparently never agree on effecting it (IV. viii. 267–8).[47] This is not because they waver in their Socratic assumption that true Reason is not 'a Point problematical as with us...but strikes you with immediate Conviction', but that the strict logic of the extermination project would have led them to carry it out long ago, with the consequence that the Yahoos would not exist to be written about. The repeated deferment of any decision is a key feature in the continuing enforcement of the idea of deserved punishment, without dispelling it by an actual 'final solution' or courting the readerly instinct to discount or reject such action as extreme. Similarly, the deferred method of castration, suggested to the Houyhnhnms by Gulliver, and itself not clearly stated to have been carried out, offers a further reprieve, and helps additionally to bridge the gap between the fable's sense of the Yahoos' fitness for total extermination, and the fact that if you exterminated them they would be no longer available for the punishment the fable exists to say they deserve.

The pattern of survival in twos provides an obvious mechanism for ensuring this continued availability. We see it in the story of Noah, and when it breaks down in that of Lot, the situation has to be adjusted by somewhat extreme procedures. In the first Yahoo holocaust, Swift made sure the Yahoos were preserved not only in twos, but in multiple twos, a pair for each Houyhnhnm. Swift seems to have nursed an instinctive and teasing awareness of such questions, to the extent of creating, in the Yahoo primal couple, who are introduced in the Assembly debate and who go on to a chequered textual history in the final chapter, an inversion of the pattern. Expelled from their land of origin, abandoned 'by their Companions' in exile (IV. ix. 272), they are 'alternative' survivors, one step out of phase with the correct regenerative rhythms. They were targeted for elimination rather than, like Noah, righteously preserved from it, and they engender a race fit for destruction instead of being charged with restarting the species after it had already been punitively destroyed. Their quasi-biblical trappings give them representative or mythologized status, a perverse variation on the stories of Noah and Lot which reduces the scope of positive valuation by a further turn of the screw.

If Noah had not been spared, moreover, there would be no humankind for the Book of Genesis to be addressed to or even narrated or composed by, just as *Gulliver's Travels* would have no effective existence if the Houyhnhnms had carried out their project and also extended it to Gulliver himself, and the rest of the Yahoo species, including (if that were technically possible) its human subgroup. (Some such awareness that the fate of the narrative itself depends on less than total implementation must, one assumes, always have played a role, however subtextual, in myths of universal destruction, and may be observed in a more sophisticated or self-conscious form in modern biblical commentary).[48] The demands of both narratives are, in practice, that there should be a survivor to tell or at least witness, and an audience to hear, the fable; and also that there deserves to be such an audience, a satirical concession to the reality principle, and to ordinary human sentiment. This does not exactly abate the force of the punitive velleity, though it casts doubt on the integrity of the fabular import, raising questions (as tradition often has) about the extent and purity of Noah's or Lot's righteousness, for example, or in a more self-consciously plotted way, about the nature and extent of Gulliver's differences from other Yahoos.

Gulliver is proposed as an exception to the scheme for eliminating the Yahoo race, in the Master Houyhnhnm's speech in the Assembly. He knew of a good Yahoo, 'of a whiter Colour, less hairy, and with shorter Claws', who spoke in a language of his own 'and had thoroughly learned theirs', who came from a country where 'the *Yahoos* acted as the governing, rational Animal, and held the *Houyhnhnms* in Servitude', who had 'all the Qualities of a *Yahoo*, only a little more civilized by some Tincture of Reason', though 'as far inferior to the *Houyhnhnm* Race' as the Yahoos of their country were to him (IV. ix. 272). As a result of this eloquent plea, Gulliver is accorded a sort of honorary Noah status, 'from whence I date all the succeeding Misfortunes of my Life'. The hardline Houyhnhnm Assembly *exhorts* Gulliver's Master (their exhortations are, in more senses than one, our commands) 'either to employ me like the rest of my Species [i.e. as a slave or beast of burden], or command [not, in Gulliver's case, exhort] me to swim back to the Place from whence I came' (IV. x. 279).

Another formula is evident here, familiar in works which have extermination as their text or subtext, from the *Shortest Way with the Dissenters* to *Mein Kampf*, where an alternative course of action to extermination is proposed, partly as an obligatory gesture establishing the proposer's humanity, when it is not a masked language for the extermination itself. Expulsion is perhaps more usual than castration, though the Houyhnhnms and the Nazis contemplated both. Much consideration was given by the Nazis to the expulsion of the Jews to an American or African colony, eventually converging on the idea of Madagascar, a land to be made available by the conquered French, and the destination, as it happens, of Gulliver's mutinous crew when they take control of his ship before his arrival in Houyhnhnmland (IV. i. 222, xi. 283–4). This might be taken to be a Nazi version of commanding Gulliver 'to swim back to the Place from whence I came', or perhaps *in*version, since the Madagascar plan was designed to prevent a return to Palestine.[49] More pertinently, Gulliver's Houyhnhnm friends demand for him the special treatment of assisted passage, or at least safe-conduct, accorded to some special Jews.[50]

'With the Skins of *Yahoos*, well stitched together'

Gulliver's transition from Houyhnhnmland to the tribal terrors of New Holland and its possibly poisoned missiles may or may not have been comparable with the travails of refugees among the aborigines of the Swiss border, or the guardians of that country's banks. Gulliver is allowed to return by boat, a boat of his own making, like Noah's, who was *God*'s special Jew, another clear (if paradoxical) recognition that all Yahoos are Yahoos. Quite soon Gulliver, who has already made bird springes of Yahoo hair, and shoes of Yahoo skin, is building his ark, or boat, 'with the Skins of *Yahoos*, well stitched together' (IV. x. 277, 281). This further ghoulish prefiguration of some Nazi manufactures is brought into relief by the remark of an SS *Unterscharführer* at the Belzec camp that the stored sacks of inmates' hair were 'to make something special for the submarines, to seal them and so on'.[51] Gulliver made a sail 'likewise composed of the Skins of the same Animal; but I made use of the youngest I could get, the older being too tough and thick' (IV. x. 281). This remark additionally anticipates the preference for younger infants to older ones in *A Modest Proposal*, as well as that work's own flirtation with the manufacture from human skin of 'admirable *Gloves for Ladies*, and *Summer Boots for fine Gentlemen*', a practice, noted in the previous chapter, which Swift himself associated with those ancestors of the Irish Yahoos, the Scythians. But even in cadence it has something in common with an SS directive of 1942, as translated by Robert Harris, decreeing that female hair 'will be used as thread to make socks for U-boat crews and felt stockings for the railways'.[52]

The issue of making objects from human parts offers some insights into the relationship between obscene cruelties and playful exercises of imaginative freedom: the radical differences as well as the hard fact of resemblance. The theme belongs to the history of barbaric acts, to the writings describing or condemning these, and to a range of imaginative fascinations, in life and letters, in facts that read like fictions and in fictions pretending to be, or triggered by, facts. The 'industrial exploitation of corpses',[53] the use of human hair or skin or fat for manufacturing clothes, soap, and other products, is frequently asserted, but for whatever reason is one of the less precisely documented aspects of the Holocaust. It may be that as an activity secondary to mass-killing and the enforcement of slave labour, it had in itself no legal status as a crime against humanity, so that the search or publication of evidence has been less extensive. This appears to have given special encouragement to Holocaust deniers. Responsible scholars are largely agreed that there was no soap manufacture on an industrial scale, but some evidence of experimental production in Danzig seems to have survived, and the *Encyclopaedia Judaica* reproduces two photographs of 'A German soap factory near Danzig' showing a box or tub full of human remains and some crude manufacturing equipment.[54]

The use of rumours or threats of such manufactures in propaganda about an enemy, or as a means of frightening victims, is an old one. The fears arise naturally in contexts of war, invasion, and slave-traffic. Angolan slaves in the seventeenth century were terrified that the Spaniards would either eat them or make them into oil or gunpowder.[55] The rumours about soap manufacture appear to have originated in British propaganda in the First World War. The Nazis 'resuscitated' this rumour and Jews are said to have been taunted by Nazi guards with threats of being turned into soap. Vercors recalls such things from 1914, and how resistant he became to such rumours, but speaks of authenticated discoveries of medical experiments, and of lampshades and bookbindings made of human skin in the Vosges at the end of the Second World War.[56]

There seems in general to be enough evidence to authenticate some quasi-industrial practices, but perhaps not enough, or not visible enough, to have generated a significant body of fully documented description. This has helped to precipitate a buzz of mythologizing, to which the topic may be exceptionally hospitable. There are times, however, when direct testimony seems compelling, even as the story reads like an extravagant fiction. The younger Martin Bormann, Hitler's godchild and son of Hitler's close associate, has more than once reported an autobiographical anecdote in which, aged fourteen and at the time an ardent Nazi, he went to tea with his mother and sister at the residence of Himmler and his mistress Hedwig Potthast near Berchtesgaden. Bormann Jr. told Gitta Sereny around 1990 that after chocolates and cake the children were taken to see an interesting collection in

Himmler's special retreat in the attic:

'When she opened the door and we flocked in, we didn't understand what the objects in that room were—until she explained, quite scientifically, you know,' Martin said, his voice now toneless. 'It was tables and chairs made of parts of human bodies. There was a chair . . . the seat was a human pelvis, the legs human legs—on human feet. And then she picked up a copy of *Mein Kampf* from a pile of them—all I could think of was that my father had told me not to bother to read it as it had been outdated by events. [Speer had told me that Hitler had said exactly the same thing to him]. She showed us the cover—made of human skin, she said—and explained that the Dachau prisoners who produced it used the *Rückenhaut*, the skin of the back, to make it.'

The children fled, terrified, and their mother did not altogether manage to calm them by saying their father had been sent a copy of the book by Himmler and had refused to have it in the house.[57]

Inga Clendinnen also heard Bormann repeat the story on television. She says, 'it is so extravagant as to test credulity', but 'at fourteen Martin was not quite a child; he has made the story public; there were other witnesses'. While 'it would be more comfortable not to believe', she takes the view (rightly, I think) that 'we must (a sensible scepticism found the rumours of death camps incredible, too)'.[58] A year or so later, separated from his parents after the war, the young Bormann saw newspaper photographs of concentration camps. He told Sereny that people said these 'had to be fakes, but I knew it was all true . . . After what I had seen in that attic I had no doubts at all, ever'.[59] Such enormities, however strongly attested by factual testimony, carry their own presumption of fiction, beyond the scope of the more routine interplays of the factual and fabulous discussed in Neil Rennie's book on travel narratives, *Far-Fetched Facts*. Some Nazis assumed this would carry an immunity from conviction, in both senses of the term. Heinrich Lohse, the Nazi commissioner for Ostland, was convinced that any exposure of such grisly realities would be dismissed as Allied propaganda, 'since those who hear or read it would not be willing to believe it!'. Primo Levi reports an

SS militiaman who boasted, on these grounds, that 'we will be the ones to dictate the history of the Lagers'.[60]

Presumably not every Nazi shared Himmler's taste for trophies or his lover's gauche vulgarity and prurience. If Potthast's account was not true, then the need to invent it invites enquiry. It is not the only reported example. Rumours of the 'utilization of bodies for commercial purposes' spread from Germany to the Vatican and the United States in 1942, and Himmler, concerned in any case to keep the primary genocidal activity secret, was also necessarily anxious to stifle this secondary publicity, and ordered that all bodies of Jews be buried or burnt, and all misuses of bodies reported to him.[61] There are persistent accounts, many of them associated with Karl Koch, commandant of Buchenwald, and his wife Ilse, the 'bitch of Buchenwald', of collections of objects made of tattooed skins, sometimes of live victims. Many were said to have been made from dead bodies in the camp's pathology department by SS Captain Müller, and hundreds of tanned skins were sent to Berlin on the orders of Dr Lolling, chief medical officer for concentration camps. Others were displayed to SS visitors as 'special treasures' in the pathology department. Lampshades and handbags were said to have been made for the Kochs and some families of SS officers. (A witness in the *Buchenwald Report* says Ilse Koch was as proud of her handbag 'as a South Sea island woman would have been about her cannibal trophies', and Lolling is said to have used American army reports of headshrinking techniques among 'cannibals of the South Sea islands' for experiments in shrinking skulls to the size of a fist.[62] Whatever the exact truth of the imputed events, these reports suggest a close link, in the perception of both victims and perhaps perpetrators, between the practices of cannibal 'savages' and the scientific experiments of an advanced industrial state. Such a link, in its own way, is germane to the satirical formula of *A Modest Proposal*).

Stripped of the horrors of enactment, such episodes belong to the tradition of imaginative play which Breton called black humour. It is valued by him on the principle by which Artaud defended the theatre of 'cruelty', as a freedom to entertain the unspeakable in a form of interior replay ('interior' rather than 'illusory', in the language of Artaud's own distinction).[63] The second author, following Swift, in Breton's *Anthologie*, is Sade, mainly represented by a scene from the *Histoire de Juliette* (c.1801), which is a remarkable anticipation of the one described by Bormann Jr. It takes place in the castle in the Apennines of the monstrous Minski, a cannibal ogre of Homeric appetites and advanced Sadeian tastes in collateral gratification. This castle includes a Gothic chamber of horrors where the seats were human bones and skulls, though a detail which might have grated on Frau Potthast's domestic susceptibilities is that one could hear the cries of live victims from the dungeon below. Other parts of the castle were furnished with the bodies of live women, artistically contorted to serve as chairs and tables, on which hot food was placed (Breton omits additional details of obscene extravagance), and as chandeliers hanging from the ceiling. There was also a lamp whose rays shone through the eyes and jaws of twenty-four skulls.[64] This doubtless outdid commandant Koch's ' "artistic" table lamp made ... of human bones stretched over with human skin'.[65] Sade was prevented, by the limitations of prolonged incarceration as well as by psychological constitution, from enacting most of his fantasies, and his case thus provided a perfect laboratory for the project, later formulated by Artaud and Breton, of liberating the imagination for the unthinkable without releasing the fantasies into practice. Sade's constraints did not encumber Himmler's functionaries, but Frau Potthast would presumably have had no difficulty with Minski's bland statement that though his practices were often fatal for the victims, the stock of victims was always easy to replenish.[66] Like the Nazis, Minski kept his project totally secret, though he considered that he had nothing to fear.

Freedoms were available to Sade in the realm of fantasy from which the tender sensibilities of Nazi mountain retreats desired to be protected. It was in the realm of practical application that Sade was outdone. What is remarkable is the degree of similarity of detail between historical reality and the wildest imaginings, and the extent to which each draws on the other. Swift and Sade gave imaginative or imaginary expression to what was reported by historians and ethnographers from Herodotus onwards. They sometimes outdid their bookish or documentary sources in the completeness of fantastic re-enactment, only to be matched and themselves outdone in the historical reality of the Nazi enterprise. What that enterprise, in turn, may have owed to bookish sources, and what it merely took from common motions of the human mind, is not a question which can be answered, though it insists on being asked. Sade's project, as Breton interpreted it, and Swift's too in Breton's account, was to give these motions their head, while remaining clear of reductive implementation.

Sade's episode, and even Breton's anthologizing of it (in 1939), go back, like the Swiftian analogues, before the extermination camps of the Second World War. Breton's point, I take it, is not that such doings invite approval, or that one should not repudiate them when they occur. This is evident from the fact that he takes pains to play down Sade's real-life scandals, and to emphasize his acts of altruistic courage during the Revolution.[67] It was possible for an associate of Breton to see Sade as 'preparing the nihilism of the Nazi slaughter houses', as Raymond Queneau did. But Breton continued to insist on a free exercise of imagination, in which unspeakable doings can be contemplated without the interposition of moral or satirical judgements. It is the perceived opening up of this territory by Sade which hugely impressed the young Flaubert, and which made Apollinaire (as cited approvingly by Breton) call him the freest spirit who ever lived.[68] This encompasses even the doctrinaire elements, Minski's principled defence of his cannibalism and debaucheries, and the project of satisfying an inexhaustible range of desires (the whole universe seemed not vast enough for that).[69]

If Sade was the spectacular liberator, it is Swift, in Breton's scheme, who, as we have seen, was the true begetter, the *véritable initiateur*, of black humour. This will seem hard to reconcile with

Breton's feeling that black humour only flourishes where the 'degrading influence' of satirical or moralistic intentions is not felt. Puzzlement is not abated when the earliest anticipations in painting (where he says humour came later than in literature, or *poésie*), are said to be found in Hogarth and Goya.[70] Breton's theorizing is unsystematic, but one would hardly suppose him to have missed the 'intention satirique, moralisatrice' in these artists, or in Swift. There may be some sense (to which I shall return) in which the satirical or moral intention can be seen to have been side-stepped or transcended by Swift rather than eliminated, in conformity with Breton's conception of going beyond good and evil. In Sade, the problem arises less starkly, except that the discourse of immoralism in his work has many of the features of a doctrinaire morality, and one is not always sure where Breton located the humour.[71]

But the Minski episode, however Sade saw it, seems to be offered by Breton as a full-blown example of the 'plaisanterie féroce et funèbre' of which he honoured Swift as the master.[72] It is curious that the brief reference to the manufacture of gloves and boots in *A Modest Proposal* is part of a section Breton deleted in the abridgement of Swift's pamphlet he anthologized. This may have been inadvertent, or he may have thought that particular topic more than adequately represented in the ensuing Sadeian extract. It is also possible that he perceived more of the undue influence of satire or moralizing in this section of the *Modest Proposal* than in others, especially since Swift presents this idea as a pointedly nasty programmatic refinement of a sinister project, whereas Sade's presentation of Minski is lugubriously unmoored from ideas of right and wrong. Breton also left out the closing pages of Swift's pamphlet, which include his positive prescription of serious and practical 'other Expedients' for Ireland.[73]

Gulliver's use of Yahoo skins for his boat and sails offers an alternative model (Breton gives no extracts from *Gulliver's Travels*). Despite an unsettlingly close likeness to the Nazis' use of human hair in their own naval manufactures, these are not among the book's darker moments, though a jokey frisson of discomfort is undoubtedly on Swift's agenda. There is no pressing suggestion that this is regarded as a monstrous thing to do. In this sense, Gulliver's handicraft differs somewhat from the example of *A Modest Proposal*, where the cheeky shockingness is presented as the outlandish fantasy of a once sensible social thinker, crazed with exasperation at his people's self-destructiveness. An implied moral that the Irish are nothing but savages, and have reduced the Proposer to acknowledging that he must settle for their cannibal ways, contains the kind of focused sarcasm which is absent from the Gulliverian episodes, and which might have precipitated Breton's excision of the passage from his anthology, if that was more than inadvertent. No such critique is involved in Gulliver's 'cannibal' manufactures. The shock, such as it is, is attenuated by the exigencies of survival, and by the fictional local colour which sees the Yahoos as lower animals, even as their human status is being relentlessly intimated. But Gulliver's sense that the Yahoos do belong to his species makes the passage gratuitously disconcerting, in a characteristic Swiftian mode. That it carries for once no particular charge of disapproval, instead of coexisting with, or overspilling, such disapproval, places it fully within Breton's idea of an unmoralized play of 'cruel' fantasy, and it would probably have found a more comfortable home in the *Anthologie* than the later passage Breton cut out.

Had Swift written after the Holocaust, he might not have included such passages, and in a sense it is because the Nazis had not yet happened that he had some freedom to write in this way. Had he somehow written with the knowledge, the passages would have a different meaning, which would have to be judged by the nature of his apprehension and mastery of the implications. Nazi practices have not wholly precluded, and may in some cases even have activated, subsequent fictional exploitations of similar manufacturing fantasies. When they occur in the universe of Hannibal Lecter, for example, we do not suppose Thomas Harris's novels to be defending Holocaust industries. Unlike Gulliver, Lecter and the other psychopaths among whom he acts as a presiding deity are presented as very evil, but no reader of the Hannibal stories would see them mainly as admonitions against, any more than as encouragements of, their cannibal and cannibal-related atrocities. They are offered as more or less playful disturbances of our healthy sensibilities, in the credible expectation that the experience will be found entertaining by non-psychopathic readers. They conform in this sense to Breton's recipe for black humour, which would exclude any element of exhortation for or against.

Lecter himself is an aficionado of fun.[74] He has wit and a fiercely economical playfulness, and his atrocities are a combination of extravagant ingenuity and demonic precision, as of slapstick gone murderous. The psychopathic protagonist of the *Silence of the Lambs* (1988), whose name is Jame Gumb (the 's' in James was accidentally left out of his birth certificate, and he 'gets livid' if people pronounce it) is several steps ahead of those of Swift's *Tale* or *Modest Proposal*. He actually flays women, and makes garments out of their skin. He uses the name Mr Hide, Inc., Leather Goods as the convenience address for the delivery of live moth pupae which he employs as accessories in his highly specialized killings.[75] If Harris was remembering Swift, that too would be part of the joke. Gumb's doings are extravagantly evil, but the fiendish playfulness is an essential ingredient. It is even arguable, in this case, that any Nazi association contributes to the permitted frisson of outrage, on condition, or to the extent, that we do not suspect the author to be harbouring unacceptable sympathies.

Lecter remains wicked as Gulliver is not, which suggests that the issue and role of satirical or moral judgements are more complex than is allowed in Breton's definition. The *Modest Proposal*, which Breton sees as a founding text, offers an especially testing challenge since the Proposer, while not personally psychopathic in Lecter's way, is the spokesman for a systematic project of mass-infanticide, behind which, furthermore, is his author's own satirical commentary on the political and economic predicament of Ireland. The Proposer's thoughts about producing luxury goods from the skins of Irish babies do not emanate from a Gulliverian

No-place in which such deeds are mere fictional trimmings. There is a 'historical' fact behind his allusion, more distant than the Nazis are to us and less enormous in its dimensions, which nevertheless purports to have a present application and may even cast a retrospective light on Gulliver's accounts. Swift is remembering accounts in Herodotus and Strabo of Scythian tribes which manufactured napkins and garments from human scalps, weapon-covers from skin and fingernails, and drinking cups from skulls and skin, so that some pre-Nazi atrocities are in the subtext.[76] Swift is clearly playing on common ideas of the Irish not only as cannibals but also as descended from the Scythians.[77] To the extent that the Yahoos represent the Irish too, this association would also rub off on them, though the Yahoos are not the perpetrators but the victims of the shocking manufacture. The Proposer's vision is plainly held up for disapproval, of himself as well as of the despicable customs he describes his people as disposed to practise, a fact which, as I suggested, may possibly be connected with Breton's omission of the passage in the abridged version given in his *Anthologie*. Breton plainly was not deterred by the atrocity of the idea, since he includes the much fuller example from Sade.

The Proposer's scheme is presented as wicked in a way that Gulliver's actions are not, though both have something of the same shock value, and, in spite of Breton's excision, the Proposer's suggestion is not without its own deadpan jokerie, the kind of thing Breton praised as Swift's 'plaisanterie féroce et funèbre'. Swift is not, either here or elsewhere, adrift from the moral or satirical project, but overspills it. The principal tendency of the satire would clearly be against any Nazi-style activities, except that we detect the familiar residual implication of 'it's only what they deserve' in his treatment of his fellow Irish. Swift's writings also take on the issue of inhumane scientific or 'medical' experiments on human bodies, a topic, among Nazi projects, closely related to the manufacture of luxury goods from human body parts, and much more fully documented.[78] Swift's treatments of this theme are in the research projects of the Academy of Lagado (III. v–vi.

179–92), and to a lesser extent the Academy of Modern Bedlam in *A Tale of a Tub*.[79] These contain satire on medical and other scientists, and, in Lagado especially, on politics and indeed on totalitarian practices. The 'intention satirique, moralisatrice' is evident. The researchers' activities are for the most part neither good medicine nor, with some exceptions, radically evil. They display instead a perverse extravagance of mind (analogous in some ways to the venial unnaturalnesses of the Yahoos in sucking 'the Teats of the *Houyhnhnms* Cows'), a free exercise in human fatuity, which might be said, within limits, to be displayed in the mode of partially unmoralized imaginative freedom postulated by Breton. But Swift is also saying these experiments are at best idiotic and at worst obscene and unacceptable. He is, in such cases, attacking the perpetrators in ways which do not operate in the episode of Gulliver manufacturing sails, and which operate differently from the analogue in *A Modest Proposal*, where the note struck has a certain element of 'serves them right', cheekily punitive.

There is a relatively subdued association between Lagadan experiments and political tyranny, and we read about the Academy soon after we have been introduced to the menace of mass-destruction posed by the Flying Island to the people who live below (III. iii. 167–72), an allegory of English tyranny over the Irish. But the Academy's experiments have nothing of the 'central role in genocidal projects' which Lifton speaks of in the Nazi experiments, and they are in any case deemed culpable, whether of folly or depravity or both.[80] There is no doubt of Swift's view of the global hatreds of genocidal exterminators, whom in his whole being he would undoubtedly have despised and rejected, if the outbursts against the slaughters of war and conquest in *Gulliver's Travels* are anything to go by.[81]

Swift knew nothing of the Nazis, and would have hated the cruelty they represented. Some of his most eloquent writing is devoted to denouncing mass-killings and the terrorizing of 'harmless People'. We cannot imagine him entering programmatically into such projects. But he had an awareness of the nature of the underlying sentiments, and indulged them, in the verbal sphere, against detested groups, including the European exterminators of the last chapter of *Gulliver's Travels*. Nothing better illustrates his self-implication in the satirical anatomy of the human psyche to which his major writings are devoted. He shared in some of the vast aggressions, as we all do, and showed it, as many don't.

He not only understood the phenomenon, but had an uncannily playful sense of some of its forms. The energies of genocidal hatred applied in the Hitlerian treatment of the Jews are in some respects pre-enacted, in a biblically sanctioned, righteously punitive context, against a sinful mankind, in a text which provided Swift with a model for his own treatment of this theme. Nazi officials did not often speak openly of genocidal intent, but when Himmler declared the necessity of making the Jews disappear from the earth ('dieses Volk von der Erde verschwinden zu lassen') he is likely to have been self-rightously conscious of the Old Testament phrasing, presumably in Luther's version.[82] At all events that phrasing hovers over his statement, as it is part of the force of the words of the Houyhnhnm Assembly. The rest of the story we know. Gulliver sets off, arrives in New Holland, or Australia, his first stop in the world of which we have maps, and is there attacked by the first humans he sees, a group of savages 'round a Fire', and is wounded ('I shall carry the Mark to my Grave') by an arrow which he 'apprehended . . . might be poisoned' (IV. xi. 284).

The Reprieve of Castration and other Leniencies

Speaking of exceptions in the Houyhnhnm Assembly, and morally defeated on the subject of Gulliver, since the case of the Yahoos admits no exceptions, the Master Houyhnhnm nevertheless also proposes his other, more specialized alternative to wholesale extermination. This suggestion is itself suggested by Gulliver's information of what men do to horses in the human world, one of those many symmetrical inversions of the man–horse relationship: humans castrate horses in order to make them tame, and the Master Houyhnhnm thinks that 'this Invention might be practiced among the younger *Yahoos* here, ... rendering them tractable and fitter for Use'.[83] Lest you think this might be a diversionary tactic, designed to spare the race, however, he takes care to point out to his colleagues that this 'would in an Age put an End to the whole Species without destroying Life', while evidently benefiting from their labour, though not necessarily in camps, in the interim. 'Inclos[ing] the whole Herd' had, in the previous Yahoo riddance, been for killing only (IV. ix. 271). To maintain the supply of servants from their own lower orders, the Houyhnhnms employ the opposite method of allowing these 'inferior *Houyhnhnms*' a higher quota of offspring than their betters, a clear sign of differentiation between their own species and what are, to them, literally brutes (IV. viii. 268).

The passage quite faithfully reflects a recurrent feature of the ethos of group-extermination, since the despised other is often a source of useful labour as well as a candidate for killing. The Helots of Sparta were needed for menial tasks and for war service. Sparta, which Hitler thought of as the first *völkisch* state, was variously admired by the Nazis and sometimes associated with them.[84] It is of interest that in the administration of the Final Solution, a 'tension' existed between the 'economists', who wanted to use Jewish labour, and the 'exterminators', headed by Himmler. This was partly resolved, at Auschwitz, Majdanek, and other camps, by employing Jews to service neighbouring factories as well as the death-machine itself.[85] A proclaimed objective was 'extermination through work' ('Vernichtung durch Arbeit').[86]

Castration and sterilization were actively important elements in the Nazis' eugenics programme and featured prominently in their projects of racial purification. The programme included women as well as men, contrary (at least in part) to the spirit of Shaw's comment that 'even Adolf Hitler, whose anti-Semite phobia outdoes Joshua's anti-Canaanite phobia or the reciprocal rage of the

Crusaders and Saracens, stops short of a general order to kill all the Jewish women and not bother about the men'.[87] On the other hand, the main targets in most such schemes (including the Houyhnhnms') seem to have been male, as the frequent specific emphasis on castration makes clear. The Shavian scheme of arresting births is indeed slowed down, but the targeting of men for slaughter rather than castration usually has the short-term objective of limiting the aggressive or productive strength of the enemy. If the enemy no longer poses danger, however, and can support the economy of the ruling group, castration offers a good balance between ultimate elimination and present exploitation of labour (plus, in the Houyhnhnms' case, rendering the labour force more tractable). Women were killed in huge numbers by the Nazis, along with the men, but in the particular context, singling out the women for sterilization becomes a less pressing option, except for the simple purpose of 'purifying' the species. The Nazis had this in mind, as we know, but their motives were evidently neither simple nor wholly consistent, and one sees that this seemed irrational to Shaw's tidy mind.

Sterilization was debated at the Wannsee Conference in January 1942 much as castration was in the Houyhnhnm Assembly, and castration was expressly proposed in a Reich Secret Document of 23 June 1942 by SS Oberführer Viktor Brack as a way of preserving a workforce for a time while ultimately 'produc[ing] the same results' as extermination, precisely Gulliver's argument in his briefing for the Houyhnhnm Assembly. Like other advocates, Brack also shared the Modest Proposer's concern for cheapness and efficacy. (Similar considerations are said to have governed attempts to control the slave population in the West Indies in Swift's time, since slave children, far from adding to productivity, were a liability for the first twelve years or so, and it was cheaper to import slaves than foster their production *in situ*).[88] Gulliver also reported that Yahoos were not 'fit for Service' until the age of twelve (IV. ix. 273), and on the basis of this coincidence, the idea that West Indian slave-owners used 'the same method of population control' as Gulliver recommended is tendentiously implied in a recent post-colonial critique, which seems to misrepresent its own sources.[89] There seems no evidence of any such policy, though cases of punitive castration are on record in the West Indies. Sir Hans Sloane reported the use of 'Gelding' in 1688 for crimes of a 'lesser nature' than slave-rebellion, which was itself punishable by live burning. In the aftermath of a slave conspiracy in Barbados in 1692, a woman named Alice Walker was paid for castrating forty-two rebellious slaves, and four deaths following castration are reported in another document.[90] In his Nuremberg defence, Oberführer Brack claimed to be trying to stall the final solution, in itself a passable *ex post facto* version of Gulliver's idea that his own castration scheme 'would in an Age put an End to the whole Species without destroying Life' (IV. ix. 273).[91]

Swift had no notion of such activities, but since Gulliver unwittingly (and indeed uncensoriously) captures the mindset, it is evident that Swift did so intuitively, just as (in a more obviously condemnatory mode) he displayed, in Orwell's phrase, 'an extraordinarily clear prevision of the spy-haunted "police State"'.[92] The example offers a glimpse of Swift's extraordinarily sensitive insight into what the 'modern' world might one day throw up: both the good (like some of the later books he parodied in advance) and the bad, neither of which he liked, while being unable to avoid an element of inward participation in either. Even Gulliver's playful notion that castration of the Yahoos would be less cruel than outright extermination was echoed in the thinking of Nazi opinion-formers, as in the report of the propaganda division in occupied Lublin in 1942 that sterilization was considered by Jews as a 'more humane' method leading to the same result.[93] It was arguably because Swift could not know of Nazi horrors that he was able to indulge in the notional 'cruelty' of such a scenario, in something like the spirit attributed to him in Breton's account of black humour.[94] The main force, or overt irony, of the castration proposal is that it is presented as more humane than outright extermination. The concessive flourish bears a characteristic

Swiftian mark. It belongs with those complacent discountings or disavowals of cruelty we meet with most famously in *A Modest Proposal*, where the speaker, after listing the substantive arguments against cannibalizing older children (the males' flesh is 'tough and lean' and ill-tasting, and the females are more useful as breeders), remarks 'that some scrupulous People might be apt to censure such a Practice (although indeed very unjustly) as a little bordering upon Cruelty; which, I confess, hath always been with me the strongest Objection against any Project, how well soever intended'.[95]

There are several Gulliverian instances of objections to cruelty, as when Gulliver is being arraigned for putting out the palace fire in Lilliput with his urine (I. v. 56), in a Rabelaisian re-enactment of the Deluge, copying the scene in which Gargantua drowns 260,418 persons, not counting women and children, by urinating on Paris from the towers of Notre-Dame, a passage which, together with its Gulliverian derivative, aroused the interest of Freud.[96] In the Lilliputian debates on the impeachment of Gulliver, the Emperor 'gave many Marks of his great *Lenity*' while his ministers urge 'the most painful and ignominious Death', which includes setting fire to Gulliver's house at night and getting twenty thousand men to shoot him 'with poisoned Arrows' (I. vii. 69, a menacing theme which returns, as we saw, in the New Holland episode in IV. xi. 284). Reldresal the Emperor's principal private secretary suggested the alternative castigation, itself related, in Freudian teaching, to castration, of sparing Gulliver's life and putting out both his eyes, a lenity which would (he thought, incorrectly) be universally applauded, and a course of action which, if found insufficient, could be supplemented by a slow starvation, which would allow Gulliver to die, like the castrated Yahoos, 'without destroying Life', while keeping his 'bodily Strength' and remaining 'useful to his Majesty' (I. vii. 70–2).[97]

Another Gulliverian prefiguration is the King of Luggnagg's 'great Lenity to his Subjects' (III. ix. 203). That king was approached by crawling on one's belly and licking the dust before his footstool. Since Gulliver was a stranger, care was taken to clean the floor, but sometimes it was left deliberately dusty for punitive purposes, 'And I have seen a great Lord with his Mouth so crammed, that when he had crept to the proper Distance from the Throne, he was not able to speak a Word. Neither is there any Remedy, because it is capital for those who receive an Audience to spit or wipe their Mouths in his Majesty's Presence' (III. x. 204–5). The great orchestration of royal lenity follows:

There is indeed another Custom, which I cannot altogether approve of. When a King hath a Mind to put any of his Nobles to Death in a gentle indulgent Manner; he commands to have the Floor strowed with a certain brown Powder, of a deadly Composition, which being licked up infallibly kills him in twenty-four Hours. But in Justice to this Prince's great Clemency, and the Care he hath of his Subjects Lives, (wherein it were much to be wished that the Monarchs of *Europe* would imitate him) it must be mentioned for his Honour, that strict Orders are given to have the infected Parts of the Floor well washed after every such Execution; which if his Domesticks neglect, they are in Danger of incurring his Royal Displeasure. I my self heard him give Directions, that one of his Pages should be whipt, whose Turn it was to give Notice about washing the Floor after an Execution, but maliciously had omitted it; by which Neglect a young Lord of great Hopes coming to an Audience, was unfortunately poisoned, although the King at that Time had no Design against his Life. But this good Prince was so gracious, as to forgive the Page his Whipping, upon Promise that he would do so no more, without special Orders. (III. ix. 205)

The sarcasms here are widely diffused, not only against purported leniencies which are not, but also against actual leniencies improperly applied, both functioning as additional twists of the sarcastic knife. The treatment of persons out of favour is not lenient but vicious, and the forgiveness of the careless page is clearly misplaced. The play of ironic qualifiers in the final sentences is particularly resourceful, applying incremental stings to secondary motives and suggesting a comprehensive diffusion of disreputable motive and muddled laxity: 'a young Lord of great Hopes... unfortunately poisoned, although the King *at that Time* had no Design against his Life' (italics added), the page's negligence nevertheless condoned, 'upon Promise that he would do so no more, without special Orders'. These are the staple lenities of *Gulliver's Travels*, and Gulliver himself, in relation to them, adopts the lax censoriousness, the moralistic gesturing without teeth, of the Modest Proposer: all this is nothing more than 'another Custom, which I cannot altogether approve of', a friendly mock-evocation of Montaigne's relativist neutrality, taken back as an afterthought, after recording much else without blame.

The complacent leniencies of the Lilliputian and the Luggnaggian courts, which not even Gulliver wholly approves of, are different from Gulliver's own tame refusals of acquiescence, his poised and worldly stance of standing up for a certain moderation in cruelty. The irony at his expense at that point is similar to Swift's sarcasm, in the *Sentiments of a Church-of-England Man*, against the political extremists whose species of moderation towards their opponents is designed to make us 'erect Gibbets in every Parish, and hang them out of the Way', one of a handful of extermination velleities from which Swift is dissociated with unusual clarity.[98] The Modest Proposer's disavowal of cruelty parodies the meddlesome sanctimoniousness of the interfering do-gooder, rather than the substantive import of his discourse, which is a punitive rubbing-in of Swiftian inculpations of the Irish, cannibalistically self-destructive and by tradition regarded as actual cannibals. Indeed, his measured retreat from the idea of slaughtering adolescents, whose meat is tough, as 'a little bordering upon Cruelty', is qualified in the next paragraph by the reflection that if 'the same Use were made of several plump young girls in this Town', who waste their substance on 'foreign Fineries' to the detriment of the Irish economy, 'the Kingdom would not be the worse'.

The Master Houyhnhnm's castration proposal is of a different character. The Swiftian sarcasms that variously attach to the other declarations against cruelty do not in the same way apply to him. In his case, the sting attaches not to the speaker or holder of the 'moderate' outlook, but wholly to the victims of the supposed moderation. The value of his proposal is not so much its leniency, as its clean and tactical phasing-in of a punishment whose essential character or justice is not questioned, and which the Houyhnhnm Master himself regards as no less inevitable or absolute than the Assembly members who demand an immediate extermination: *his* moderation, doubtless coloured by affection for Gulliver, consists only of a sanitized and limited deferment, avoiding conclusive violence, and cashing in on Yahoo labour besides.

Castrating the Yahoos, as we saw, is in one sense merely what humans do to horses, and a logical exchange of roles in a land where the governing creature is equine. But it has another resonance, less immediate, but nevertheless connected, or potentially connected, with *Gulliver's Travels* by that nexus of associations which variously link the Yahoos with the savage old Irish, those loose beggarly hordes and their disreputable priests, who haunt the pages of *A Modest Proposal* (1729) and *A Proposal for Giving Badges to the Beggars in all the Parishes of Dublin* (1737). The latter work's argument, direct rather than oblique, is that beggars should be compelled to wear badges indicating their parishes of origin and if caught outside these in Dublin should be whipped back to their own parish, which alone has responsibility for their upkeep. Swift's line on beggars, as we saw in the preceding chapter, is that they are usually sturdy, idle, and immoral vagrants, roaming the country with their trulls and brood of bastards, with the exception of those who happen to have been married by their equally disreputable Romish priest or couple-beggar. That this is part of an old English discourse, going back to Spenser and others, has already been noted. But it is apposite to recall in the present context that Swift thought of these people, in something like the way the Houyhnhnms thought of Yahoos and God of Noah's fellow men, as 'fitter to be rooted out off the Face of the Earth, than suffered to levy a vast annual Tax upon the City' (XIII. 139).

The biblical phrasing, as we have seen, has become idiomatic, and we should not suppose it to be meant literally, though it is also not *not* meant. A serious programmatic tract written in Swift's own name does not enjoy the verbal freedoms of a Utopian fiction, and the formulation is not, as in Houyhnhnmland, absolute. Even the syntax is comparative and relational, 'fitter to be rooted out ... than suffered to levy a vast annual Tax', extermination being not an actual programme but a hypothetical improvement on existing conditions. But it is clearly an option not considered inappropriate to sturdy vagrants and the couple-beggars. Some years before, in 1719, the Irish House of Commons passed a Bill proposing that unregistered Irish priests be punished by branding on the cheek with a large 'P', which the Irish Privy Council improved on by suggesting castration, though the scheme, discussed more fully in the previous chapter, was eventually abandoned. There is no reason to suppose Swift would have supported this literally, but we know his opinion of Popish priests, and, as I suggested, he was perhaps remembering the Bill of 1719 when he made the Master Houyhnhnm propose castration, as a more humane expedient which would put an end to the Yahoos 'without destroying Life'.[99]

It is interesting that immediately after this proposal in the Houyhnhnm Assembly, the narrative is interrupted, and Gulliver will not be told what sentence is to be passed in respect of himself until the next chapter, though he tells us in narrative hindsight that he dates 'all the succeeding Misfortunes' of his life from that event (IV. ix. 273). Instead, the discourse shifts to one of those ethnographic accounts of the Houyhnhnms, beginning 'The Houyhnhnms have no Letters', and taking in their healthy way of life, and astronomical skills; their oral poetry, celebrating friendship, benevolence, victory in races, and other bodily exercises; their longevity and civilized way of death; their lack of a word for evil (IV. ix. 273–5), just as elsewhere we know they have no word for lying or for opinion, because there is only one truth. It is one of the places which links them particularly closely to traditions of social organization associated variously with Plato's *Republic*, the constitution of Sparta, More's *Utopia*, and the Utopian elements in Montaigne's account of the Tupinamba, in the famous essay 'Des cannibales' (I. xxxi), which is among other things an eclectic amalgam of the others. It is a view of mine, argued in Chapter 1, that the link with Montaigne's essay is particularly strong.

There is, in that essay, a brief and shocking account of how these Indians treat their priests, when they prove to be false prophets: 'if things turn out otherwise than he has predicted, he is cut into a thousand pieces . . . For this reason, the prophet who has once been mistaken is never seen again': ('s'il leur advient autrement qu'il ne leur a predit, il est haché en mille pieces . . . A cette cause, celuy qui s'est une fois mesconté, on ne le void plus'). Montaigne explains that since divination is a gift of God, abuse of it should be punished as an imposture. He cites the Scythians, who placed their erring soothsayers on ox-carts full of heather, and set fire to them.[100] Montaigne is deadpan in the narrative, but sympathetic rather than horrified, twice endorsing the idea that imposture in sacred matters is particularly punishable. This is all the more remarkable in view of the fact that his account is much more brutally graphic than that of Thevet, his probable source.[101] It is noticeable that he is not here affronted at the idea of the live burning in the way that he becomes within a page or two when he speaks of live burnings in the French religious wars, so much more barbaric than the cannibals. In this, he resembles the kind of post-colonial rectitude which is quick to condemn bad practices by his own society, but to think of those by alien, and preferably 'minority', groups, as 'culturally' determined and therefore to be defended, as wife-beating might be, or female circumcision, provided the perpetrators have a sufficient alterity factor. (Swift, incidentally, deplored wife-beating even among the tribal Irish, but as far as I know did not have a view on the other matter).[102] This comparison may be unjust. Montaigne on live burnings is a separate, complicated matter, too large to enter into here. But I suggest that his imagination accommodates the idea of summary, punitive violence in a way Swift found congenial, and that both had a flat take-it-or-leave-it notation for such things.

The cannibal priests and Scythian soothsayers were chastised for imposture. The Irish priests too were considered disreputable.

They were Romish, encouraged beggars in their dissolute ways, and were, moreover, viewed, with some factual basis, as a subversive group by the Anglo-Irish establishment and by the *colons*, to whom Swift belonged and whom he also often disliked, though he shared their dislike of native mob and English masters alike. The cannibals of *A Modest Proposal* are studiously identified, in a variety of ways, with all groups, though the old slur of English writers, which went back to the Greeks and to the Scythian connection, was directed only at the indigenous or bog Irish. That the slur was made to spread, identifying all-comers with their own despised subgroups, is something that *Gulliver's Travels* had especially taught Swift to do, on an even more comprehensive scale: the Yahoos are Irish, Amerindians, Hottentots, 'all savage Nations', and everyone else, including especially you and me. The denunciation implied in *A Modest Proposal* has helped to make that phrase, along with 'shortest way', into an eighteenth-century equivalent of final solution, as I suggested in the previous chapter.

But *A Modest Proposal*, which seems to replay a whole series of biblical prophecies, in which God announces to the Jewish people that unless they mend their ways they will be punished by being turned into cannibals eating their own children (punishment *by*, it may be noticed, and not *for*, cannibalism),[103] is also, like the Book of Genesis, comprehensively insistent about reasons for punishment: the wholesale failure of the Irish to manage their trade, their economy, their marriage customs, their whole social morality, and particularly their relations with the English in such a way as to avoid their avoidable ills. In Genesis, it is a comprehensive depravity in mankind, not specified in detail, indeed left vague, but presumably or ostensibly specifiable in principle.

In the final chapter of *Gulliver's Travels*, on the other hand, the punishability is of a subtly different order. There is a vast accumulation of specified depravities and follies, among humans and among Yahoos, throughout the four Books. But there is, over and above that, a dimension of non-specifiable incrimination in the mere fact of belonging to the species. The distinctive feature of

Swift as a satirist is his interest in a whole area of non-specific punishability. The Yahoos embody this over and above anything they do. The impression is reinforced by the allegorical schematism in Book IV, but it is not merely a matter of formal schematism. We do not get the same sense of an absolute and non-specific inculpation in the equally (if not more) schematic pairing of Books I and II. It is partly that the character of the two schematisms is different, that of Books I and II being designed to bring out relativities of perspective, while the pairing of Yahoos and Houyhnhnms posits a confrontation of stark and immutable absolutes, whose definitional status includes and transcends particular validations or exceptions.

Ten Righteous Men: Abraham Haggles with God

Yahoos remain Yahoos whether they thieve or not, or whether or not they act aggressively or lecherously or with acquisitive greed. And it would be the same if a Yahoo were found who was kind, considerate, and selfless, as the Portuguese captain turns out to be. By that stage of the story, one might not be far wrong in thinking that if there were ten of him, as there were not in Sodom, or twelve of him, like the non-existent twelve Arbuthnots, the case would not be altered. It is not that there are not enough of him, but that he is what he is, even if, as some think, the Judaic quorum of ten adult males was at issue in the biblical versions. You could say that the work had gone too far by the time he appears, and that the remark about Arbuthnot in the letter (of 29 September 1725), written after most of the *Travels* were written but before they were published, was in any case more concerned to praise Arbuthnot to their mutual friend Pope than to be a serious commentary on the fiction. The remark's significance for us, moreover, is not in its application of a biblical parallel, but in the additional confirmation it offers of the presence of the Book of Genesis, and especially of its passages of collective punishment, in Swift's thinking about his story.

The Portuguese captain in some ways occupies the position of Lot, though there are differences. In the Genesis story there were originally to have been fifty just men. Abraham asked God whether he thought it right to kill everyone, even the righteous. God relents for the sake of the putative fifty, a total which then drops, at Abraham's prompting, to forty-five, and then forty, and then thirty and twenty and finally ten (18: 23–32). Abraham does not press him further, but the ritually repetitive rhythms of this high-toned haggling elicit from the Almighty all the genial pliancies of a divine bazaar, and induce a feeling that if he had gone on to five and two and finally one, God would have gone on agreeing, subject to the quorum theory, not universally accepted as applicable here. The Midrashic view that Abraham could not go below ten, because eight—Noah, his three sons, and their wives—had not been enough to prevent the Flood, is not explicit in either of the Old Testament stories. (Noah is called 'the eighth *person*' in the King James version of 2 Peter 2: 5, meaning he was preserved with seven others). And an alternative view was that Noah's family, and ultimately mankind, were 'only saved for Noah's merit', so that in some circumstances one righteous man might have done, if Lot was counted such).[104] And if God had agreed to one, and counted Lot, the story of Sodom and Gomorrah would not have been written, always bearing in mind, however, that the haggling scene is considered to be a later insertion.[105]

Lot survives, like Noah. He does so not in an ark, but by moving to another town, Zoar, and later to a cave in the mountain, while Sodom and Gomorrah are destroyed by fire and brimstone rather than a Deluge, on the principle, doubtless, that those who are born to be burnt shall never be drowned. Lot remains righteous, but preserves thereafter an existence unwittingly touched with pollution. His wife, first of all, had disobeyed the instruction not to look back, and been turned into the famous pillar of salt. And then his two daughters, lacking the company of men, and under pretext, or with the objective, of continuing the race, get their father drunk so they may lie with him (19: 1–38).[106] Thus incestuously and furtively fertilized, they inaugurate the tainted races of, respectively, the Moabites and Ammonites, who, according to Deuteronomy 23: 3, 'shall ... not enter into the congregation of the LORD for ever'.[107]

Here too there are parallels with Noah. This is not the first time that the drunkenness of an Old Testament elder has come to be seen as a trigger for momentous racial exclusions. The story of Noah's curse on the sons of Ham has its origin in an episode in Genesis 9: 20–7 in which the drunk Noah is seen naked by his son Ham.[108] Ham told his brothers Shem and Japheth who, going backwards so as not to see, covered their father's nakedness, while Ham's punishment for what his father realized he 'had done unto him' was a curse on Ham's son Canaan. (What Ham 'did' is unclear, if it is not that he just saw his father naked: in Steven L. McKenzie's words, 'castration, sexual assault, and incest' have all been suggested, but the Book of Genesis is not as explicit on this as it was to be in the later case of Lot).[109]

It has been said that Noah cursed his grandson Canaan rather than Canaan's father Ham so that the story might serve to discredit the Canaanites and legitimate their subjection by Israel and the Philistines. This is part of the story's local dimension. At the same time, Noah's three sons, Shem, Ham, and Japheth, according to early exegetic tradition, represent the progenitors of the nations, whose roll call is given in the next chapter (10: 1 ff.), though an alternative view insists on a more limited Palestinian significance. Ham's progeny is ill-omened from the start. Noah began by consigning his grandson Canaan to slavery (9: 25–7), a fact which doubtless helped to shore up the nowadays better-known, and more recent, tradition whereby the passage is 'used to support another kind of racism', interpreting the 'curse on Ham' to be 'black (Negroid) skin color', an interpretation first occurring in the Talmud.[110] It brought with it in due course all the familiar equations between Ham, Negroes, apes, and chimpanzees, which are likewise those of the Yahoo stereotype, including bestiality and slave status, and the teasing interpenetration of universal and ethno-specific defamation.[111]

It is ironic that the first recorded use of the word 'nigger', by Robert Burns, is one which retells this story:

> How graceless *Ham* leugh at his Dad,
> Which made *Canaan* a niger.

Conrad's friend R. B. Cunninghame Graham's essay 'Niggers' scorchingly travesties Genesis as an allegory of the evolution of empires, culminating in the British: 'Jahve created all things, especially the world in which we live, which is really the centre of the universe, in the same way as England is the centre of the planet':

> The Ethiopian cannot change his skin, and therefore we are ready to possess his land and to uproot him for the general welfare of mankind, smiting his hip and thigh, as the Jews did the Canaanites . . . Niggers who have no cannons have no rights.[112]

The specific evolution of the Negro connection seems to derive from the fact that another of Ham's sons, Cush (10: 6), is identified with 'Ethiopia' or 'Nubia', though in Amos 9: 7–8 God speaks of the Cushites as like the children of Israel, 'an example of God's universal concern', according to Steven L. McKenzie. But the passage seems to mean mainly that the children of Israel are as bad as the Cushites.[113] Subsequent extensions have included Amerindians, whom Léry, for example, thought of as descended from Ham, but whose humanity was affirmed by this Noachite ancestry;[114] and the Irish (who were already Canaanites in Cromwell's eyes). The common analogies between Africans and Irish led predictably to theories by race scientists, including John Beddoe, affirming an 'Africanoid' ancestry for Ireland. The idea has more recently undergone an honorific reversal, claiming African, and specifically Cushite, origins, partly on the basis of an extension of the biblical account and the fact that 'there is even a town in Ireland called Cush'.[115]

Amos's difficult book is concerned with Israel's transgressions, said to be as bad or worse than those of other nations, including those of the Ammonites and the Moabites. The idea of universal castigation for universal depravity is internalized as divine punishment for the sins of the Jewish people. It is ironic, in the light of Himmler's invocation of Old Testament phraseology in announcing the need to annihilate the Jews from the earth, that an ultra-Orthodox former chief rabbi of Israel, Ovadiah Yosef, recently caused outrage by claiming that the Nazi Holocaust was a deserved punishment for past sins.[116] An alternative or inverse pattern, equally familiar in the Old Testament, is the visiting of destruction on the enemies of Israel: 'I will be an enemy unto thine enemies' (Exodus 23: 22). This is one of the potent subplots of the book of Amos, and powerfully implicit in the readings of the stories of Noah and Lot in which a curse on the Canaanites, and a sense of the tainted nature of Moabites and Ammonites, accompany the regenerative aftermath of God's punitive destruction. The phrases 'from the face of the earth' and 'from the earth' are evidently idiomatic, but they have intensive force, usually implying finality, or a universal or extensive sweep, or both, and in punitive contexts inevitably recalling the universal punishment of Genesis 6: 7. That is the first punitive use of the words in the Old Testament portending a mass-destruction. In these punitive contexts, the phrasing follows the general run of divine affirmations, often narrowing, with some blurring of categories, to include all the wicked, or the Jewish people, or (most often) the enemies of the Jewish people, whom God exterminates or helps the Jews to exterminate when he is not doing or threatening to do it to the Jews themselves.[117]

In the book of Joshua, which celebrates the conquest of Canaan (which Cromwell saw as a prototype of his subjugation of the Irish) and the redistribution of its cities among the tribes of Israel, God directs Joshua to the appropriation of the promised land, beginning with Jericho (Joshua 1–6). Divine destruction is firmly directed at the enemies of Israel, though even that develops in a context in which the sins of Jews narrowly escape the retributions visited on them in the Genesis stories of Noah and Lot. When Joshua tells the Lord that 'the Canaanites and all the inhabitants of the land shall . . . cut off our name from the earth', he is referring to the consequences of a theft by Achan son of Zerah at the siege of Jericho, a violation for which the Israelites face extreme punishment in both reputation and life. God tells Joshua that 'Israel hath sinned' and that he won't 'be with you any more, except ye destroy the accursed from among you' (7: 9–12). The Lord is appeased by the stoning and burning of Achan and his family in Achor, to this day known as the Valley of Devastation (7: 24–6), and the sequence of divinely ordained destructions, ritually modelled on that of Jericho, is resumed. Joshua proceeds to city after city, 'utterly' destroying 'all the inhabitants', making each 'an heap for ever, *even* a desolation unto this day' (8: 26, 28). Thus it was with Ai, and with Makkedah, which he 'smote ... with the edge of the sword', and whose king 'he utterly destroyed ... and all the souls that *were* therein; he let none remain: and he did to the king of Makkedah as he did unto the king of Jericho' (10: 28–9). Then likewise at Libnah and Lachish (10: 30–2), and Hazor and other places (11: 10–23). The full list, in summary from, occupies a whole chapter (12: 1–24). The Lord prescribed a similar fate for the Amalekites (1 Samuel 15: 3) and laid out a detailed scenario for obliterating Tyre (Ezekiel 26: 1–21). It is easy to see how a people might claim divine authority for destroying enemies and even enshrine this in its Scriptures, but the ultimate model for the claim of righteousness, and sometimes the specific vocabulary, are to be found in Genesis 6: 7, where human sinfulness is the occasion and no question arises of including or excluding any other tribe or race.

The passage in the Book of Amos about the Ethiopians is followed by another divine extermination outburst, which (like that concerning Noah's Flood) comes over both as not quite complete and as regenerative:

Behold, the eyes of the Lord GOD *are* upon the sinful kingdom, and I will destroy it from off the face of the earth; saving that I will not utterly destroy the house of Jacob, saith the LORD. (Amos 9: 8)

This selective genocide will be succeeded by yet another regeneration, not forgetting the planting of vineyards and drinking of 'the wine thereof'. The words remind us of the biblical importance of wine and vineyards, which is not unrelated to the story of Noah himself.[118] The passage is from Amos 9: 14, at the end of a book whose punitive catalogue had already included God's over-throwing of Sodom and Gomorrah (4: 11).[119] Humanity keeps bouncing back, and apparently asking for more. If that had not been so, there would be no Book of Genesis, or it would have no readers.

The episode brings home the closeness of ideas of guilt and of genocidal punishment, but also the curious lack of demarcation between genocide as the slaying of ethnic groups and that of the whole human race, an indeterminacy of a type Swift often put to use, insinuating that the whole species is reducible to its most ignoble subspecies. In the repetitive relationship between the stories of Noah and Lot, as they have come down to us through all the transformations of the text, the essential distinction between destruction of the species and destruction of particular cities appears to have been formally preserved, though the history of their composition and their subsequent interpretation suggests that both stories oscillate to some degree in the direction of each other. The later history of the Flood story, in particular, suggests a continuing uncertainty as to whether it could be accepted as a universal event. Speculations about its historical basis were often concerned to identify specific locations, on an understandable assumption that universalist myths tend to develop from specific conditions on localized sites. It was at one time a pagan conten-tion, distressing to Christians, that Noah's Flood was a local affair. But this contention was not exclusive to pagans, and was taken up, in the Renaissance, by 'scientific' or rationalist explanations also tending against universalism.[120] The most recent explanation, resulting from geological and oceanographic researches by scien-tists from the United States and Eastern Europe, proposes a huge flooding of the Black Sea some 7,600 years ago. This created a human diaspora in the Middle East, Europe, and Asia whose folk memory embraces the closely related Mesopotamian, Hebrew, and Greek flood stories as well as more widely dispersed analogues or variants surviving into the present century.[121] Flood myths are recorded in various parts of the world, including 'all ancient nations' and the New World of the Americas, a fact which in itself seemed to support the idea of a universal Flood. But individual stories, like that of Deucalion, combine their universal claim with a localized, in this case Greek, setting.[122]

It seems to be part of the early histories of peoples to think of themselves and their readily visible neighbours as constituting the whole human race. This may or may not be a natural reflection of 'primitive' perspectives, especially at times or in conditions where the visibility of the world outside was constrained by the absence of technologies we have increasingly taken for granted (distant travel, print, radio, television). But it seems likely that outright ignorance in this sphere, though nowadays rare, readily shades into forms of ethnocentrism in which the existence or humanity of aliens is 'ignored' in the more usual English sense of that verb. The fact is not unrelated to the old impulse of treating ethnic others as sub- or non-human, as well as to the inverse, and more specialized or sophisticated, formula of identifying humankind itself with the despised subgroups of one's choice. It is also part of the same blurring of categories, a programmed confusion on the twin subjects of generic human kinship and ethnic differentiation, that for example all non-Europeans are more or less identical, with characteristics (nakedness, flat noses, thick lips) 'common to all savage Nations', or that the Yahoos are Irish savages, equivalent to Indians or Blacks, and also, in some radical sense, ourselves.

The old equation of Indians and Irish continued into the nineteenth century. From this it is a short step to the post-colonial appropriation of damaging labels in an honorific sense, to Irishmen calling themselves the 'niggers of Europe', or to an Irish President addressing famine-stricken Somalis as the Irish of Africa, and to the same distinguished person later defending her tenure of a United Nations office which Third World leaders did not wish to confer on a European by insisting on her 'Irishness'.[123]

Such reversals precede post-colonialism, and in some of their twentieth-century forms were partly triggered or made self-conscious by Sartrean doctrines about the defensive or defiant assumption by pariah groups (Jews, Blacks, homosexuals) of pariah identities conferred on them by their oppressors.[124] Behind these and related mythologies of the 'white Negro' stand descriptions of the Irish at least as far back as 1700, Chamfort's declaration that 'Les pauvres sont les nègres de l'Europe', Dostoevsky's description of the London poor as 'white Negroes', and especially Rimbaud's famous 'Je suis une bête, un nègre ... J'entre au vrai royaume des enfants de Cham', which is of interest in the present context not only for its activation of Noachite genealogy in reversal of a racial slur, but because of a reapplication of the racial formula to himself in his revalued role as a pariah who, in the Conradian phrase (from *Lord Jim*), is 'one of us'.[125]

Such self-alignments with despised subgroups are reversals, or rather resublimations, of what Swift did in contempt, or even self-contempt. They have the same universalizing sweep as the hanging breasts of Elizabeth Bishop's poem, discussed in Chapter 2, and something of the same tendency to rewrite the Yahoo version in a mode that embraces rather than deplores the analogy. The Yahoos as 'savages' also represent the Irish as domestic mob, and other domestic groups: beggars, whores, servants, and ultimately all of 'us', including Swift himself. It is apposite that the Rimbaud who asserted his honorary negritude, and whom Verlaine post-humously called 'nègre blanc', had written a page or two earlier of his European connectedness, 'j'ai vécu partout. Pas une famille d'Europe que je ne connaisse', rather as it is said of Conrad's Kurtz, the white man gone native, that 'all Europe contributed to the making of Kurtz'. That Rimbaud ended up, like Kurtz, as a merchant in Africa, with something of Kurtz's outlook and trading instincts, is an irony not to be overlooked.[126]

To return to Lot. His story is a replay of Noah's Flood, and exhibits, in reverse form, a similar interplay of the universal and local, in which humankind as a whole seems implicated in the crimes and the punitive extermination of particular groups. Comparing the Deluge and the destruction of Sodom, Westermann writes: 'Annihilation by water corresponds to annihilation by fire; local features, however, are in evidence in the latter. The inhabitants of a city might well experience its destruction as the destruction of the world.'[127] The crimes of Sodom, which are not specified in Genesis, though they were usually interpreted to include unnatural lust and violation of hospitality codes, rub off on the whole species independently of specific doings. In other books of the Old and New Testaments the punishment of Sodom is always destruction of the city, but the nature of the crimes varies widely.[128] 'As in the primal event (Genesis 4: 2–16 and the reason for the Flood, Genesis 6: 5–11) the concern is about wrong which affects the whole of mankind and threatens the worldwide human community.'[129] Ideas of sexual misconduct usually attach themselves to momentous archetypes of undisclosed sinfulness, including humanity's 'wickedness' before the Flood and the secret shame of Ham's visit to Noah, as well as in the case of Sodom.[130] The example of the *Tale*'s flayed woman, the whore who is all of us, is Swift's micro-version of this. An atmosphere of enhanced and sinister taint thus attaches to the curse of generalized culpability, without being allowed to settle into a particular imputation whose effect might be to delimit guilt or make it deniable.

The combination of universalizing and despecifying reinforces the sense that punishment is being visited on whole groups, irrespective of their doings. The process marks a seemingly ultimate term of the universalizing pattern. But both episodes in Genesis have regenerative extensions, in which stories of particular families turn into origins of peoples or tribes, so that the daughters of Lot think themselves called to repopulate the world, and their sons 'become the progenitors of two tribes', just as the three sons of Noah spread their progeny over 'the whole earth' (Genesis 9: 18–19, 10: 1–32).[131] There is no regenerative extension in *Gulliver's Travels*. In one sense, there is no need for one. Humankind is in place in the world outside Houyhnhnmland, and is not under threat within the story, though Gulliver entertains entranced imaginings of a total rout of Europeans in any war with the Houyhnhnms, as well as noting the risks of our trying to conquer Brobdingnag or living with a flying island over our heads (IV. xii. 293). It would be one of the sarcastic assumptions of Swift's discourse that this is at best a mixed blessing, since the point of the Houyhnhnm Assembly's deliberations is that humankind deserves extermination. But it also removes any narrative pressure to get the species restarted, and circumvents any risk of inserting any celebrative note into the process. This would have posed a serious rhetorical inconvenience for Swift, as of course it does not for the author of Genesis, though if Swift had had to invent the restarting he would doubtless have found a downbeat way of dealing with the event.

The exegetic tradition on Lot is extensive. He is, as Michael D. Coogan and others say, 'a less than heroic figure', but surely not ignoble, and he enjoys the favour of Abraham.[132] His protection of the divine emissaries who are his guests, and the offer of his daughters to the men of Sodom to deflect their inhospitable as well as vicious lust for those emissaries, were usually represented as a supreme devotion to right. The offer of the daughters is distressing to later readers. Robert Alter, most recently, calls it shocking, 'one of the most scandalous' utterances 'by any character in ancient literature', and sees Lot's subsequent unwitting incest with his daughters as a just retribution ('measure-for-measure justice', evidently a sexual variant of the Thyestean feast). On this much debated element Westermann is surely right to say that it 'is aimed at preventing something worse in accordance with that age's way of understanding, and one should neither explain it away...nor condemn it by our standards'.[133] In later texts, 'Lot is recalled as a righteous man, whose goodness saved him from Sodom's punishment', and compared to Noah in this regard (2 Peter 2: 5–8).[134] Lot, the good man, trying to do right in fraught circumstances, muddles through, comes out of it reasonably well, except that his wife and daughters act sinfully, like Eve, and implicate him in their sinfulness, not only by mere association, but through an incest of which he is unaware because he is drunk.[135]

None of this happens to Don Pedro de Mendez, because, in Swift's system, all that is needed is that he should be Yahoo. This is another way of describing the definitional activity of Book IV as absolute in its inculpations. The attribution of guilt in abstraction from specific doings has theological support in the doctrine of original sin, and it is possible that Swift drew on this at some level of consciousness. Original sin is not an Old Testament concept, though sometimes read into the Old Testament by Christian commentators.[136] *Gulliver's Travels* offers a kind of secularized counterpart, abstracted from theological concern, but not from Old Testament associations. Swift was notoriously indifferent, even as a priest, to theological niceties, and *Gulliver's Travels* is not a theological book in any significant way. But he held unquestioningly to received doctrine. The playing down of original sin by some contemporary thinkers, whom his cousin and biographer Deane Swift described as 'these mighty softeners; these kind pretenders to benevolence; these hollow charity-mongers', affronted him, and Book IV has been persuasively seen as a response to the complacencies of this climate of thought.[137] Even without this reactive impulse, it is easy to see how the doctrine appealed to him as a poetic resource, enabling or reinforcing the mechanisms of inculpating entrapment on which his satire thrives.

I will close by instancing in summary form the satirical mechanisms through which, in the micro-context of individual sentences, images, or episodes, the targeting of despised subgroups, women, the Irish, or primitive savages, for example, is subjected to comparable transformations. It is not just that Swift almost invariably widens his memorable examples to include their symmetrical opposites, the gutted beau as well as the flayed woman in the *Tale of a Tub*, male Brobdingnagian monsters as well as the large-chancred females, non-primitive humans as well as bush Yahoos, and finally, in Book IV and many of the Irish tracts, the English and Anglo-Irish as well as the savage bog Irish, all of whom, in *A Modest Proposal*, come under the umbrella of the cannibal attribution. These are the more schematic ways in which Swift typically identifies the insults of misogyny and racism as applicable to everyone, characteristically giving this as the most stinging way of conducting his offensive against the species, including its representative the reader.

As I suggested in the previous chapter, the procedure is similar to that by which Augustan satirists attacked the vices of high persons (including arrogant pride of rank) as low-class, except that here a complacent humanity (whose vices include racial oppression and ethnic cleansings) is being shamed into the recognition that it is low-race. The trick of taking a group rejected by your culture, like the Hottentots or Irish, and saying that they represent nothing more than our basic humanity, may not be altogether attractive. Nor is Swift seeking to endear himself through it. But it is not the usual style of ethno-specific slurs, which are more likely to attribute common human turpitudes, or apply an idiom of basic human degradation, to individual groups, than the other way round, though such things are always to some extent a two-way traffic. When Swift appears to do this himself, as with the whore whose appearance is altered for the worse by flaying, or the beau for whom dissection does the same thing, he is saying of them only what is true of everyone else. But some readers are bound to perceive as the distinctive Swiftian effect the gratuitous suggestion that humans are assimilable to whores, this form of the equation carrying a special charge. This quality of diffused aggression needs restating. It is a Swiftian signature, not always adequately recognized. I like to think we understand it better if we acknowledge the extent to which it rests on what seems to be a deep impulse, in the languages of castigation and defamation, to subject the distinction between the species and individual groups to an infinite series of tactical and wounding confusions, of which the various resonances of biblical inculpation and massacre are an allegory and a prototype, and of which *Gulliver's Travels* is a replay.

NOTES

Chapter 1. Indians and Irish from Montaigne to Swift

1. For fuller discussion of this passage, and some of the matters raised in these opening pages, see Claude Rawson, *Order from Confusion Sprung* (1985; rptd. London and Atlantic Highlands, NJ, 1992), 73 ff., and 'Savages Noble and Ignoble', in Jonathan Lamb, Robert P. Maccubbin, and David F. Morrill (eds.), *The South Pacific in the Eighteenth Century: Narratives and Myths, Eighteenth-Century Life*, NS 18/3 (Nov. 1994), 172 ff. I use the form 'Cortez', instead of the correct Cortés, in all contexts concerned with Swift's, and Montaigne's, references to him, which are in this form.

2. Bartolomé de Las Casas, *Brevísima Relación de la Destruición de las Indias*, ed. André Saint-Lu (Madrid, 1982), 65–75; *A Short Account of the Destruction of the Indies*, trans. Nigel Griffin (London, 1992), 3–13. This is the most easily available English version, but readers should be warned that the translation is somewhat free, and suffers from an element of sanitizing modernization. Griffin translates Las Casas's *Indias* (Indies) as Antilles and *indios* (Indians) as '"Amerindians", "natives", and "local people"', on the surprising grounds that it would be 'anachronistic' to preserve Las Casas's forms (p. xliii). The volume has an introduction by Anthony Pagden.

3. On this theme, see especially Chapter 4, *passim*. The biblical locution, as applied, with slight variations, to various large-scale massacres, first appears in Genesis 6: 7, in God's announcement of the Deluge. It reappears in a key section of *Gulliver's Travels* (IV. ix. 271), and elsewhere in Swift's writings, in the words of the King James version. Las Casas's Spanish reads, 'estirpar y raer de la haz de la tierra' (74), *raer* meaning to erase or wipe out, which is the literal sense of the original Hebrew and the Greek Septuagint. It corresponds to the Vulgate's 'Delebo [from *deleo*, delete] ... hominem ... a facie terrae', whose alternative emphasis or connotation appears in the King James version: 'I will destroy man ... from the face of the earth.' Las Casas's wording was evidently an idiomatic echo of the Vulgate. The Church discouraged vernacular translations. The first printed versions of the Old Testament in Spanish were non-Catholic, and appeared after the *Brevísima Relación*, in 1553 (from a Jewish press in Ferrara) and 1569 (a complete Protestant Bible, from Basel), though there were several manuscript translations of the Hebrew Masoretic text in the fourteenth and fifteenth centuries. See Erroll F. Rhodes, in *Oxford Companion to the Bible*, ed. Bruce M. Metzger and Michael D. Coogan (Oxford, 1993), 758, 767–8 s.v. Translations). The first complete Catholic Bible published in Spain was translated from the Vulgate by Felipe Scio de San Miguel (1793), and uses the language

Las Casas had used in his non-biblical context: 'Raeré ... de la haz de la tierra al hombre' (cited from edition of 1823, p. 5). For recurrences of this idiom in the Old Testament, and in the secular literature of extermination, see Chapter 4, pp. 301–4 and *passim*, and n. 117.

4. See 'Note on Editions', *Short Account*, p. xlii.

5. See *A Catalogue of Books, The Library of the Late Rev. Dr. Swift... To be Sold by Auction* (Dublin, 1745), No. 261, 'Purchas, his Pilgrims, in 5 vol. [London] 1625'. The *Catalogue* is reprinted in facsimile in Harold Williams, *Dean Swift's Library* (Cambridge, 1932).

6. Montaigne, *Essais*, ed. Pierre Villey, rev. V.-L. Saulnier (Paris, 1988), iii. 909, 910–11; *Complete Essays*, trans. Donald M. Frame (Stanford, Calif, 1965), 694, 695. Future references to the French and English texts will take the form: iii. 909, 910–11 (694, 695).

7. See Frank Lestringant, *Le Huguenot et le sauvage* (2nd edn., Paris, 1999), 254 and n. 69. Three French editions (1579, and two in 1582) are known to have appeared before Book III of the *Essais* appeared in the edition of 1588 (ibid. 126 n.158, 321); for the likelihood of Montaigne's reading Las Casas, see Juan Durán Luzio, 'Las Casas y Montaigne: Escritura y lectura del Nuevo Mundo', *Montaigne Studies*, 1 (1989), 88–106, and *Bartolomé de Las Casas ante la conquista de América* (Heredia, Costa Rica, 1999), 1999, 223–85.

8. Bartolomé de Las Casas, *Historia de las Indias*, volume i, ed. Miguel Angel Medina *et al.*, in *Obras Completas* (Madrid, 1994), iii. 338 (Prologue, section 4); my translation differs in some details from that of Andrée Collard, *History of the Indies* (New York, 1971), 4, an abridged version of the work.

9. See Pagden, introduction to *Short Account*, trans. Griffin, pp. xiv–xvi; Tzvetan Todorov, *La Conquête de l'Amérique: la question de l'autre* (1982; Paris, 1991), 216–17; for a more rounded account of Las Casas's developing views, see Rolena Adorno, 'The Intellectual Life of Bartolomé de las Casas', Andrew W. Mellon Lecture, Tulane University, New Orleans, 1992.

10. On Montaigne, see below, pp. 34–5.

11. When Gulliver sets out on his fourth voyage, it is with orders to 'trade with the *Indians* in the *South-Sea*' (IV. i. 222; also i. 224 and ii. 228), a generic term for most non-European races; see Rawson, 'Savages Noble and Ignoble', 178–80; for poisoned projectiles in classical authors, and in Erasmus and Swift, see Claude Rawson, *Satire and Sentiment 1660–1830* (corrected edn., New Haven and London, 2000), 65–6.

12. Sir Walter Ralegh, *The Discoverie of the Large, Rich and Bewtiful Empyre of Guiana* (1596), 59–60, ed. Neil L. Whitehead (Manchester, 1997), 170–1, and introduction, 56 n. 17. References to the edition of 1596, whose pagination is supplied by Whitehead, and to Whitehead's own pagination, will henceforth appear in the form: 59–60 (170–1); Edward Gibbon, *History of the Decline and Fall of the Roman Empire*, chs. 18, 42, ed. David Womersley, 3 vols. (London, 1994), i. 656 and n. 39, ii. 692. Gibbon also cites Ovid, *Ex Ponto*, IV. vii. 11–12.

13. Ralegh, *Discoverie of Guiana*, 52, 100–1 (165, 199); on Hakluyt and Conrad, see Rawson, *Order from Confusion Sprung*, 74, 101 nn. 10–11; Gibbon, *History*, 'General Observations', ii. 516 n. 15; Charles Darwin, *The Voyage of the Beagle*, ed. Leonard Engel (New York, 1962), 502; on the patriotic utterances in

Hakluyt, Purchas, and Lionel Wafer and Swift's possible uses of them, see Arthur Sherbo, 'Swift and Travel Literature', *Modern Language Studies*, 9 (1979), 117–8, 120–1. An entry for 21 Dec. 1774 in *The Resolution Journal of Johann Reinhold Forster, 1772–1775*, ed. Michael E. Hoare, 4 vols. (London, 1982), iii. 438–9, reads like an unironic version of Gulliver's rhapsodic speech; foreign (French and American) praise of the political virtues and moral character of British officers abroad had some circulation in the nineteenth century, see Lionel Trilling, *Sincerity and Authenticity* (Cambridge, Mass., 1973), 110, 112.

14. *Essais*, i. 209 (155). The habit of referring to French, or European, customs as barbaric, or more barbaric than those of 'barbarians', was widespread. French examples include Etienne Jodelle's 'A. M. Thevet. Ode', prefixed to André Thevet, *Singularités de la France antarctique* (1557), cited by Lestringant, *Le Huguenot et le sauvage*, 30, and see Lestringant's edition of the *Singularitiés*, *Le Brésil d'André Thevet* (Paris, 1997), 312–13 (hereafter *Singularités*); Jean de Léry, *Histoire d'un voyage fait en la terre du Brésil* (facsimile of 2nd edn., 1580), ed. Jean-Claude Morisot (Geneva, 1975), 228–30, 342, 433 nn. (hereafter *Voyage*), trans. Janet Whatley as *History of a Voyage to the Land of Brazil* (Berkeley, 1990), 131–3, 198 (references to the English translation will appear in parentheses after those to the original text); Agrippa d'Aubigné, *Les Tragiques* (1616), I. 191, in *Œuvres*, ed. Henri Weber *et al.* (Paris, 1969), 25.

15. *Essais*, i. 210 (156).

16. *Les Tragiques*, V. 1282, I. 495–562, V. 1371 ff., in *Œuvres*, 32–4, 181, 183, 913–14, 1038, 1041. In addition to the Pléiade commentary, see *Les Tragiques*, ed. A Garnier and J. Plattard (Paris, 1932), III. 200, I. 73–8, III. 209; Josephus, *Jewish War*, VI. 201–19. A diary of the siege of Paris in 1590 looked back to the siege of Sancerre as being (in the same phrase as Montaigne's about the atrocities of the religious wars) 'de fresche memoire', cited in Géralde Nakam, *Au Lendemain de la Saint-Barthélemy* (Paris, 1975), 131.

17. Léry, *Voyage*, 228–30, 229 (131–2, 132); see also Natalie Zemon Davis, *Society and Culture in Early Modern France* (Stanford, Calif., 1975), 324 n. 100; and Anthony Pagden, *The Fall of Natural Man* (Cambridge, 1982), 84. On the likelihood that Montaigne read Léry's *Voyage*, see Morisot's introduction, p. xxiv; also, for example, Bernard Weinberg, 'Montaigne's Readings for *Des Cannibales*', in George Bernard Daniel Jr. (ed.), *Renaissance and other Studies in Honor of William Leon Wiley* (Chapel Hill, NC, 1968), 261–79; Nakam, *Au Lendemain de la Saint-Barthélemy*, pp. xi, 128; *Les Essais de Montaigne: miroir et procès de leur temps* (Paris, 1984), 335 ff.

18. Nakam, *Au lendemain de la Saint-Barthélemy*, 130–9. The second part of this volume, 175 ff., consists of an edition of Léry's *Histoire mémorable*. All page references to the latter are from this edition. Léry also wrote a *Sommaire discours de la famine* in Aug. 1573, which is a first version of chapter x of the *Histoire mémorable* (see Lestringant, *Le Huguenot et le sauvage*, 51 and n., 78–9). Léry reverted to the siege of Sancerre in *Voyage*, 367 ff. (211 ff.).

19. *Histoire mémorable*, 279–80; sieges of Samaria (2 Kings 6: 25–9), Numantia (133 BC; Appian, *Roman History*, VI. xv. 96–7) and Jerusalem (see Nakam, *Au Lendemain de la Saint-Barthélemy*, 27, 98, 131, 136–8, 164–70, for the importance of successive sieges of Jerusalem, especially that by Titus in AD 70, and of Josephus's *Jewish War*; see also Léry's *Voyage*, 363–4).

20. *Histoire mémorable*, 279–90, and cf. Léry's *Voyage*, 363 ff. (209 ff.), *Les Tragiques*, I.
311 ff., 483 ff., *Œuvres*, 28–34. A prototype of such descriptions, familiar to Léry
and d'Aubigné as well as to Flaubert (probably at the time of *Salammbô*,
and certainly later), is in *Jewish War*, VI. 193–200, immediately preceding the
episode of the cannibal mother at the siege of Jerusalem referred to on p. 25 and
n. 19. See also pp. 72 ff.

21. *Histoire mémorable*, 290–1; my translation, as in other quotations from this
work. For Old Testament warnings see Leviticus 26: 14 ff. esp. 29 (cf. also 16);
Deuteronomy 28: 53–7.

22. *Histoire mémorable*, 291; for the references to Sancerre in the Brazilian context,
see *Voyage*, 367–9 (211–12), where Léry is, however, comparing an experience of
starvation on the return journey to France with the famine of Sancerre, rather
than invoking Amerindian practices; on 'unheard of' atrocities, *Voyage*, 229
(132), and in Las Casas and Montaigne, see Rawson, *Satire and Sentiment 1660–
1830*, 36–7; and see below, n. 38.

23. *Histoire mémorable*, 293.

24. *Histoire mémorable*, 293; Swift, *A Modest Proposal*, in *Prose Works*, ed. Herbert
Davis *et al.* (Oxford, 1939–74), xii. 113 (hereafter *Works*).

25. *Histoire mémorable*, 294; see ibid., n. 15 for a source of Léry's account from
Paradin, *Annales de Bourgogne* (1566).

26. *Histoire mémorable*, 294–5; cf. *Voyage*, 217 ff. (125 ff.). See the commentary in
Whatley's translation, 244–5 nn. 6, 8, and her 'Food and the Limits of Civility:
The Testimony of Jean de Léry', *Sixteenth Century Journal*, 15 (1984), 397 n.10. For
a modern anthropologist's account of the role of women in these rituals, see
Isabelle Combès, *La Tragédie cannibale chez les anciens Tupi-Guarani* (Paris, 1992),
42, 56–7, 101–2, 155, 193 ff., 207 ff. Léry added an excursus on Brazilian women
and European witches in the third edition (1585) of the *Voyage*: on this strand in
his thought, see Michel de Certeau, *L'Ecriture de l'histoire* (Paris, 1975), 243 ff.,
Lestringant, *Le Huguenot et le sauvage*, 50, 53–4 and nn., and Stephen Greenblatt,
Marvelous Possessions: The Wonder of the New World (Chicago, 1991), 15 ff.

27. *Histoire mémorable*, 291–5; Fynes Moryson, *An Itinerary* (1617; Glasgow, 1908),
iii. 282 (discussed in the latter part of this chapter); Edmund Burke, citing 'M.
de Lally Tollendal's Second Letter to a Friend', *Reflections on the Revolution in
France* (1790), in *Writings and Speeches of Edmund Burke, viii. The French Revolution 1790–1794*, ed. L. G. Mitchell (Oxford, 1989), 124 n.

28. *Iliad*, XXIV. 212–14, XXII. 345–8; on Greeks and cannibalism, see Herodotus,
III. xxxviii, and *Essais*, i. 116 (115); Claude Rawson, 'Narrative and the Pro-
scribed Act: Homer, Euripides and the Literature of Cannibalism', in Joseph P.
Strelka (ed.), *Literary Theory and Criticism: Festschrift in Honor of René Wellek*
(New York, 1984), ii. 1164–9 and 1181–3 nn. For predatory females and related
interactions between cannibal and sexual discourses, see Claude Rawson,
'Cannibalism and Fiction, Part II: Love and Eating in Fielding, Mailer, Genet,
and Wittig', *Genre*, 11 (1978), 227–313.

29. Euripides, *Hecuba*, ll.1265–73, and references in 'Narrative and the Proscribed
Act', 1183 n. 49. For dogs and wolves, see pp. 1164 ff., 'Cannibalism and Fiction,
Part II', 310–13 ('Appendix A: Wolves and the Cannibal Theme'), and below,
nn. 23, 92–6. For some examples from seventeenth-century French texts,

including two which represent female cannibalism with dog and wolf imagery, see Frank Lestringant, 'Rage, fureur, folie cannibales: Le Scythe et le Brésilien', in Jean Céard (ed.), *La Folie et le corps* (Paris, 1984), 59 ff. For other connections between dogs and cannibalism, see also Lestringant, *Cannibals: The Discovery and Representation of the Cannibal from Columbus to Jules Verne*, trans. Rosemary Morris (Cambridge, 1997), 15–22, and below, n. 36.

30. Thevet, *Singularités*, 243–4; for a convenient summary of classical Amazon legends, and their revival in the literature of New World discovery and of other imperial explorations, see Hermann Heinrich Ploss, Max Bartels, *et al. Woman: An Historical, Gynaecological and Anthropological Compendium* (1885–1927), trans. Eric John Dingwall, 3 vols. (London, 1935), i. 464–74.

31. *Histoire mémorable*, 294–5.

32. *Essais*, i. 209 (207–8).

33. Rawson, 'Narrative and the Proscribed Act', 1167. See also Gilbert Murray, *The Rise of the Greek Epic* (4th edn., rpt. Oxford, 1967), 120 ff. (on expurgations), and Jasper Griffin, *Homer on Life and Death* (Oxford, 1980), 20–1.

34. Cited in 'Narrative and the Proscribed Act', 1164, from Hans Staden, *The True History of his Captivity* (1557), trans. and ed. Malcolm Letts (London, 1928), 152; for a parallel example from Thevet, see Frank Lestringant, 'Le Cannibale et ses paradoxes', *Mentalities/Mentalités*, 1/2 (1983), 7. Staden's account is a standard text. For a sceptical view of his testimony (as of all reports of cannibal customs), see W. Arens, *The Man-Eating Myth* (Oxford, 1980), 22 ff.

35. *Iliad*, XXII. 345 ff.; Rawson 'Narrative and the Proscribed Act', 1164 ff. On analogies with the New World, see pp. 1162–3; J. M. Levine, 'Ancients and Moderns Reconsidered', *Eighteenth-Century Studies*, 15 (1981), 83.

36. On dogs, wolves, and cannibalism, see also nn. 126–31 below, and David Gordon White, *Myths of the Dog-Man* (Chicago, 1991), *passim*; Arens, *Man-Eating Myth*, 141; on 'vicarious cannibalism' in the Homeric passage, see James M. Redfield, *Nature and Culture in the Iliad* (Chicago, 1975), 192–9, esp. 198–9; on cannibal etymologies, see Frank Lestringant, 'Le Nom des "Cannibales" de Christophe Colomb à Michel de Montaigne', *Bulletin de la société des amis de Montaigne*, 17–18 (Jan.–June 1984), 51–74, esp. 53, and Lestringant, *Cannibals*, 15–22, 36–40. On the quasi-human status of dogs, and human/canine homologies and interactions, see Claude Lévi-Strauss, 'La Femme au chien', *Histoire de lynx* (Paris, 1991), 207–24, esp. 213.

37. Las Casas, *Short Account*, 26, 32, 40, 60, 67, 73–4, 113, 120, 125; Theodore de Bry, *Americae Pars Qvarta* (Frankfurt, 1594), plate xxii, reproduced in Peter Hulme, *Colonial Encounters: Europe and the Native Caribbean 1492–1797* (London and New York, 1986), 113; Thevet, *Singularités*, 170–1. On the possibility of Montaigne's knowledge of Las Casas's short work, see above, n. 7. In another mood, in 'De la coustume' (I. xxiii), Montaigne listed without comment various burial customs, instancing (from Plutarch, *Moralia*, 499D) societies where 'la plus desirable sepulture est d'estre mangé des chiens, ailleurs des oiseaux': *Essais*, i. 113 (81) and commentary iii. 1237 n. (81). The immediately preceding sentence is a casual listing of a cannibal burial custom.

38. *Essais*, ii. 430–2, 700, iii. 912–13 (314–16, 530, 696–7). See also 'Défence de Sénèque et de Plutarque' (II.xxxii), ii. 724–5 (547–8). On the change in 'man's

view of virtue and vice' which, in Montaigne's perception, had been brought about by the French wars of religion, see Margaret M. McGowan, *Montaigne's Deceits* (London, 1974), 106. The idea of an appalling novelty of torture, of something 'horrible et inouy', also occurs in Montaigne's account of Spanish atrocities on Indians in 'Des coches', *Essais*, iii. 912 (696), and may derive from Las Casas, whose rhetoric is insistent on the point, e.g. *Brevísima Relación*, 73, 83, 85, 104, 106, 143; *Short Account*, 11, 23, 25, 48, 51, 96; the English translation is loose and almost invariably underplays this emphasis on novelty in Las Casas, sometimes obliterating it altogether, as when the Spanish 'más nuevas maneras de tormentos' (*Brevísima Relación*, 88) is rendered as 'more ingenious...torments' (*Short Account*, 25); on the theme of novelty, see also Rawson, *Satire and Sentiment 1660–1830*, 36–7.

39. *Essais*, iii. 791 (600); for an explanation of the three layers of text, A (mainly 1580), B (1588), C (post–1588 additions, mostly deriving from Montaigne's manuscript notes in his own copy of 1588, known as the *exemplaire de Bordeaux*, which became the basis for the posthumous edition of 1595), see the introductory material in *Essais*, i, pp. xv, lxxv, and R. A. Sayce, *The Essays of Montaigne: A Critical Exploration* (London, 1972), pp. ix, 8–24 ('The Text of the Essays').

40. See the Villey-Saulnier headnote, iii. 789–90, and Sayce, *Essays of Montaigne*, 252–58.

41. See Montaigne, *Journal de Voyage*, ed. François Rigolot (Paris, 1992), 13–46 *passim*; and discussion in Claude Rawson, 'Noble Observer', *Yale Review*, 82/1 (Jan. 1994), 113, 119–21.

42. Lestringant, *Le Huguenot et le sauvage*, 152, citing Gilbert Chinard, *L'Exotisme américain dans la littérature française au XVIe siècle* (Paris, 1911), 201–2; *The Essays of Michel de Montaigne*, trans. and ed. M. A. Screech (London, 1991), 892 n. 4; *Journal de Voyage*, 3; Madeleine Lazard, *Michel de Montaigne* (Paris, 1992), 213–14, offers heated speculation on the missing pages, but the copy of Beuther is very defective, with many missing pages, including several for August and October, and there seem to be no entries at all for 1572 anyway (*Le Livre de Raison de Montaigne*, ed. Jean Marchand (Paris, 1948), 65, 339). But the suggestion of deliberate excision, whether right or wrong, has a haunting force.

43. *Essais*, ii. 430 (314).

44. *Essais*, iii. 911–13 (696–7). The closing words of III.vi, *Essais*, iii. 915 (699), describing the brutal striking down of the Peruvian king by a mounted Spaniard, who 'l'avalla par terre', may contain a subtextual or perhaps deliberate pun on *avaler*, to swallow, in line with the impish use of 'guerres intestines' and 'se sont entremangez' two pages earlier.

45. *Essais*, iii. 913 n. 5.

46. Léry, *Voyage*, e.g. 218 ff. 223 ff. (126 ff., 128 ff.); for 'canaille', rabble, 226 (131), see also Thevet, *Singularités*, 125, 141, 232–3.

47. *Essais*, i. 209 (155); Diogenes Laertius, *Lives of Eminent Philosophers*, VII. vii. 188 (Chrysippus, 188); Sextus Empiricus, *Outlines of Pyrrhonism*, III. 247–9; Juvenal, XV. 93 ff.

48. Caesar, *De Bello Gallico*, VII. lvii–lviii.

49. For quotations from Leviticus and Deuteronomy, see above, n. 21; for *A Modest Proposal*'s biblical antecedents, see below, Chapter 4, p. 297, n. 103.

50. Léry, *Histoire mémorable*, 290 ff.; *Voyage*, 229–30 (132–3).
51. *Essais*, i.157 (116). The preceding sentence alludes playfully to the 'cannibals' of Brazil, as though to enforce the connection of this passage to the preoccupations of 'Des cannibales'.
52. Montaigne used *canaille* twice in the essays, in both cases of 'low' people in a social and moral sense, once in reference to the cruelties of an armed 'canaille de vulgaire' and once of flatterers: II. xxvii, III. xiii, in *Essais*, ii. 694, iii. 1078 (524, 825). He does not seem to have used it of any racial group.
53. Léry, *Voyage*, 229 (132).
54. 'Au lecteur' ('To the Reader'), *Essais*, i. 3 (2); François Rigolot, personal letter, 5 Jan. 1993.
55. Léry, *Voyage*, 228–9 (132). Léry also speaks figuratively, in the same paragraph, of usurers sucking the blood and marrow of widows and orphans, calling them 'plus cruels que les sauvages', but in a context in which the literal imputation is unmistakable (228).
56. Léry, *Voyage*, 342 (198, translation modified), 228–9 (132). Léry's information on Old World atrocities was further expanded in later editions; see Whatley, *History of a Voyage*, 246 n.14, and Morisot, in *Voyage*, 433.
57. *Essais*, i. 201 (149).
58. *Essais*, iii. 912, 908–9 (696–7, 693).
59. Rawson, 'Gulliver, Marlow and the Flat-Nosed People: Colonial Oppression and Race in Satire and Fiction', in *Order from Confusion Sprung*, 86–92.
60. See Rawson, 'Narrative and the Proscribed Act', 1169–70; 'Savages Noble and Ignoble', 180–8. The issue, in Polybius as in Homer, is partly revealed in language, the allies and mercenaries being distinguished by non-language, animal-like noises, or a wild multilingual chaos. For an important recent discussion of the linguistic factor in cultural defamation, with mainly sixteenth-century examples, see Stephen Greenblatt, *Learning to Curse* (New York and London, 1990), 16–39; also Todorov, *Conquête*, 42–3, 99–101.
61. Flaubert to Ernest Feydeau, 17 Aug. 1861 and 29 Nov. 1859, *Correspondance*, ed. Jean Bruneau (Paris, 1973–), iii. 170, 59; Swift to Pope, 29 Sept. 1725, *Correspondence*, ed. Harold Williams (Oxford, 1963–5), iii. 102.
62. On Montaigne as 'a favourite of Swift' (*Complete Poems*, ed. Pat Rogers (London, 1983), 661 n. 372), see pp. 69–70, nn. 110–13. For Flaubert's closeness to Montaigne, Margaret Collins Weitz, 'Flaubert et Montaigne: Parallèles', in Charles Carlut (ed.), *Essais sur Flaubert: En l'honneur du professeur Don Demorest* (Paris, 1979), 79–96, esp. 92–3 (on Flaubert's admiration for authors of the French sixteeenth century, principally Rabelais and Montaigne).
63. *Essais*, iii. 913 (697–8).
64. But see, on this question, Preserved Smith, *A Short History of Christian Theophagy* (Chicago and London, 1922), Preface, 7: 'The idea of the god sacrificed to himself, that his flesh might be eaten by worshippers thus assured of partaking of his divinity, arose at the dawn of religion, was revived by the mystic cults of the Greeks, and from them was borrowed by Paul and implanted, along with the myth of the dying and rising Savior God, deep in the soil of the early church.' Smith's whole book is a witty and erudite exploration of the connection between the Eucharistic rite and the sacrificial practices of pagan tribal

cults. For various Amerindian analogues to the Eucharist, mostly taken from Frazer's *Golden Bough*, see 27–9.

65. Sigmund Freud, *Totem and Taboo* (1913), IV, and *Moses and Monotheism* (1939), III. i (D), *Standard Edition of the Complete Psychological Works*, trans. and ed. James Strachey *et al.* (London, 1975), xiii. 154–5 and 155 n. 1, and xxiii. 84. Frazer is frequently invoked by Freud, as well as by Preserved Smith (see previous note). Among his many identifications of the Eucharistic rite with tribal practices in various parts of the world, see *Golden Bough*, V. x, *Spirits of the Corn and of the Wild* (London, 1963), ii. 48–108 ('Eating the God').

66. *Essais*, i. 113, 116 (81, 84). See iii. 1237 for the source in López de Gómara. According to Reay Tannahill, *Flesh and Blood: A History of the Cannibal Complex* (London, 1975), 7, a custom similarly described in 'De la coustume' survives in the twentieth century in Eastern Peru. Ancient father-eating practices from central Asia and Ireland, reported by Herodotus and Strabo, are also cited by Tannahill (7, 192 nn.).

67. *Essays of Michael Lord of Montaigne*, trans. John Florio (London and New York, 1923), i. 105; *Essays*, trans. Screech, 122; *Essais*, i. 108, 114 (77, 82).

68. For some sixteenth-century predecessors, including Las Casas, who questioned the notion of an absolute 'barbarity', see J. H. Elliott, *The Old World and the New 1492–1650* (Cambridge, 1996), 46, 49–50, and Todorov, *Conquête*, 239–40, who thinks Las Casas the first 'modern' to do so, but cites Strabo and St Paul as precursors. For a discussion of Montaigne's perspectives on barbarity, see Edwin M. Duval, 'Lessons of the New World: Design and Meaning in Montaigne's "Des Cannibales" and "Des Coches"', *Yale French Studies*, 64 (1983), 95–112.

69. See headnote, *Essais*, i. 108; on Montaigne's oscillations between an absolute standard and relativist perspectives, and his disposition in favour of the retention of cultural habits, see also Claude Lévi-Strauss, 'En relisant Montaigne', *Histoire de lynx*, 277–97, esp. 280–81, 288–9.

70. *Essais*, ii. 581 (438). Tannahill, *Flesh and Blood*, 7, reports that 'a nineteenth-century Mayoruna cannibal remarked to a European visitor: "When you die would you not rather be eaten by your own kinsmen than by maggots?"'

71. On the manufacture of objects from human skin or parts, see below n. 157 and Chapters 3–4; for Swift's flayed woman, see *Tale of a Tub*, IX, in *Works*, i. 109.

72. *Gulliver's Travels*, IV. xii. 293–5); 'Des coches', *Essais*, iii. 908–14 (693–9).

73. Among the significant treatments are: Nakam, *Les Essais de Montaigne*, 344; Luzio, 'Las Casas y Montaigne', 93 ff., 102, and *Las Casas ante la conquista*, 238 ff., 267 ff.; and David Quint, *Montaigne and the Quality of Mercy: Ethical and Political Themes in the Essais* (Princeton, 1998), 96–101.

74. Swift, *Works*, xii.10. For the special character of this winter blossoming in Swift, by comparison with examples of a more obviously festive nature in Pope and in Christopher Smart, see Claude Rawson, *Henry Fielding and the Augustan Ideal Under Stress* (1972; rptd Atlantic Highlands, NJ, and London, 1991), 50–1, and *Order from Confusion Sprung*, 375.

75. *Essais*, i. 206-7 (153). This passage, in Florio's translation, is the source of Gonzalo's speech in the *Tempest*, I. ii.154 ff.

76. The classicizing of the Amerindian, from the earliest travellers onwards, is too commonplace to need documenting, but one of the most extended and most

passionate attempts to view Indian cultures as similar to those of other ancient civilizations and as superior in some respects is found in Las Casas, *Apologetic History*, an offshoot of his *History of the Indies* which remained unpublished in his lifetime: see Henry Raup Wagner with Helen Rand Parish, *The Life and Writings of Bartolomé de las Casas* (Albuquerque, N. Mex., 1967), 200–4, 287–9. For an excellent history of the Greek concept of the barbarian, see Edith Hall, *Inventing the Barbarian* (Oxford, 1989).

77. *Essais*, i. 202, 213 (150, 158).

78. cf. Léry, *Voyage*, 306 (177); for other references, see Morisot's commentary, 439 n. 306; Weinberg, 'Montaigne's Readings for *Des Cannibales*', 277–8; and Greenblatt, *Learning to Curse* 19, 34 n. 14. For a survival of the notion that Indian and Greek verse-forms have things in common, see Helen Addison Howard, *American Indian Poetry* (Boston, 1979), 29–30; and for Robert Frost's table-turning dislike of Amy Lowell's suggestion that an Indian Chief made Greek mourning noises, because of Frost's ambition to establish an independent native American classicism, see Tom Paulin, *Minotaur: Poetry and the Nation State* (London, 1992), 180–1. More's Utopians have a particular affinity for the Greek language and literature, perhaps because of some ancient racial connection: *Complete Works of St. Thomas More, iv*, ed. Edward Surtz, S. J., and J. H. Hexter (New Haven and London, 1979), 181; *Utopia* (1516) had strong New World associations (*Utopia*, ed. cit., p. xxxi and *passim*; and see Arthur J. Slavin, 'The American Principle from More to Locke', in Fredi Chiappelli (ed.), *First Images of America* (Berkeley and London, 1976), i. 139 ff., on the importance of Amerindians in *Utopia*, and of *Utopia* in Montaigne). But the Utopians' interest in, and closeness to, Greek seems also and probably mainly to belong to an English Humanist agenda rather than to any attempt to mythologize Amerindians (ed. cit., 467, 465–9). More's advocacy of the learning of Greek may be paralleled by the special esteem of Greek in France, exemplified by Henri Estienne's view in 1579 that the highest compliment he can make for the French language is that it equals Greek, which provides a particular indication of the strength of Montaigne's almost exactly contemporaneous compliment: see McGowan, *Montaigne's Deceits*, 113–14, 186 n. 22. For more general comparisons between Indians and Greeks by Fontenelle and Lafitau, see Timothy Webb (ed.), *English Romantic Hellenism 1700–1824* (Manchester and New York, 1982), 14–15.

79. *Critical Remarks on Capt. Gulliver's Travels. By Doctor Bantley* (1735), 28, reprinted in facsimile in the first volume of *Gulliveriana, VI: Critiques of Gulliver's Travels and Allusions Thereto*, ed. Jeanne K. Welcher and George E. Bush, Jr. (Delmar, NY, 1976), 3 vols. On the question of authorship, see the editors' introduction, i. pp. xl–xliii; the *Remarks* have been attributed to Arbuthnot, and are included among 'Doubtful Works' in *The Life and Works of John Arbuthnot*, ed. G. A. Aitken (Oxford, 1892), 491–506.

80. The idiom was well established: see *Julius Caesar*, I. ii. 284; and R. W. Dent, *Shakespeare's Proverbial Language: An Index* (Berkeley, 1981), G439.

81. *Essais*, i. 206 (153).

82. See Elizabeth Rawson, *The Spartan Tradition in European Thought* (Oxford, 1969), 62–5 and *passim* for the influence of the Spartan constitution on Plato's

Republic and other works; 171 ff., on More's *Utopia*; and 183–4 on Montaigne. For the influence of Sparta on ideas about Indians, from Las Casas and Montaigne to Lafitau's *Moeurs des sauvages américains* (1724, close in time to *Gulliver's Travels*), see 87, 177–84, 222, and index, s.v. Indians (of America); and for a specific analogy, Léry, *Voyage*, 196 (113). On the influence of Sparta and of Plato on *Utopia*, see *Utopia*, pp. clvi ff. Plato is one of the most frequently cited authors in Montaigne's *Essais*, and Plato's influence on Swift has been widely discussed; on Sparta in Swift's work, see Ian Higgins, 'Swift and Sparta: The Nostalgia of *Gulliver's Travels*', *Modern Language Review*, 78 (1983), 513–31. The best discussions of the relation of *Gulliver's Travels* to the intellectual atmosphere of Plato and More are by Jenny Mezciems, notably 'The Unity of Swift's "Voyage to Laputa": Structure as Meaning in Utopian Fiction', *Modern Language Review*, 72 (1977), 1–21, and 'Utopia and "the Thing which is not": More, Swift, and other Lying Idealists', *University of Toronto Quarterly*, 52 (1982), 40–62. For other studies, and further discussion, see also Chapter 4.

83. For the various items corresponding to Montaigne's paragraph in *Gulliver's Travels*, see IV. ii. 230 (no clothes), IV. iii. 235 and IV. ix. 273–4 (no letters), and the general accounts of the Houyhnhnms at IV. iv. 240 ff., IV. viii. 267–70, IV. ix. 273–5, IV. x. 276 (*Essais*, i. 210 (156)). On the Houyhnhnms' contempt for false needs, see IV. vii. 259, and for the relation of Houyhnhnm virtues and customs to those of Sparta and of Plato's good society, see the commentary on these chapters in *Gulliver's Travels*, ed. Paul Turner (Oxford, 1988), 365 ff.

84. On Amerindian plain food, see *Essais*, i. 207 (153).

85. *Essais*, ii. 491 (362). For the tranquil longevity of the Tupinamba see later in the same essay, ii. 541 (404): 'les Canibales, qui jouissent l'heur d'une longue vie, tranquille et paisible sans les preceptes d'Aristote.'

86. See Thevet, *Singularités*, 122, 171, and *passim*; Frank Lestringant, 'Calvinistes et cannibales: Les écrits protestants sur le Brésil français (1555–1560)', *Société de l'histoire du protestantisme français: Bulletin*, 126 (1980), 15; Greenblatt, *Learning to Curse*, 23; for earlier sixteenth-century views as to whether or not Indians had laws and the other attributes of civilized society, see Elliott, *The Old World and the New*, 26, 45, 49.

87. *A Proposal for the Universal Use of Irish Manufacture*, *Works*, ix. 21. In the *Letter to the Archbishop of Dublin, Concerning the Weavers* (1729), *Works*, i. 65, the same implicit Yahoo parallel, in a characteristic manoeuvre, is extended to a depraved settler population, brought into a startling equivalence with the 'Natives': 'I cannot reflect on the singular condition of this Country, different from all others upon the face of the Earth, without some Emotion, and without often examining as I pass the streets whether those animals which come in my way with two legs and human faces, clad, and erect, be of the same species with what I have seen very like them in England, as to the outward Shape, but differing in their notions, natures, and intellectualls more than any two kinds of Brutes in a forest, which any men of common prudence would immediately discover, by persuading them to define what they mean by, Law, Liberty, Property, Courage, Reason, Loyalty or Religion.'

88. *Gulliver's Travels*, ed. Turner, 370 n. 12; on Swift's regard for Socrates, see below, Chapter 4, pp. 259 ff., 272–3 and nn. 9, 47; Montaigne, *Essais*, i. 212–13 (158);

Plato, *Republic*, V. 457C–458B. For responses to Plato by De Quincey and others, see *Republic*, ed. and trans. Paul Shorey, Loeb Classical Library, 2 vols. (London, 1930), i. 452–3 n. and introduction, i, p. xxxiv.

89. Plato on education of women, and on educating children away from the family, *Republic*, V. 451 C–E, 460 B–D; Plutarch, *Lycurgus*, xvi–xvii. Compare the educational arrangements in the old Utopian Lilliput (I. vi. 60–3).

90. *Essais*, i. 207 (153).

91. *Essais*, i. 210 (156).

92. *Essais*, i. 208 (154).

93. *Letter of Amerigo Vespucci Concerning the Islands Newly Discovered on his Four Voyages* (*c*.1505), in *Letters from a New World: Amerigo Vespucci's Discovery of America*, ed. Luciano Formisano, trans. David Jacobson (New York, 1992), 61.

94. Thevet, *Singularités*, 132 ff.; Léry, *Voyage*, 108; cf. also Whatley, *History of a Voyage*, Introduction, pp. xxv, xxxiii; Greenblatt, *Learning to Curse*, 77 n. 6; Todorov, *Conquête*, 192; Lestringant, *Le Huguenot et le sauvage*, 58; Claude Lévi-Strauss, *Tristes Tropiques* (Paris, 1955), 82; in *Histoire de lynx*, 293–4, Lévi-Strauss says the god Viracocha told the eighth Inca (end of fourteenth and early fifteenth centuries) that his empire and religion would be destroyed by unknown bearded men. To some eighteenth-century writers, including Cornelius de Pauw and William Robertson, the beardlessness of Amerindians was a sign of unmanly weakness; see P. J. Marshall and Glyndwr Williams, *The Great Map of Mankind: Perceptions of New Worlds in the Age of Enlightenment* (Cambridge, Mass., 1982), 219.

95. Inga Clendinnen, *Aztecs: An Interpretation* (1991; Cambridge, 1995), 267–73 and 357–8 nn., esp. 267, 271; see also the fuller account in her '"Fierce and Unnatural Cruelty": Cortés and the Conquest of Mexico', *Representations*, 33 (1991), 65–100, and the commentary in Hernán Cortés, *Letters from Mexico*, ed. and trans. Anthony Pagden, introd. J. H. Elliott (New Haven, 1986).

96. *Aztecs*, 269, 271; for an episode where a decisive impact of Cortés leading ten horsemen on a large array of Mexicans is claimed, see *Letters from Mexico*, 21–2, and 455 nn. 28–9. See also Robert Moorman Denhardt, 'The Equine Strategy of Cortés', *Hispanic American Historical Review*, 18 (1938), 550–5. Ironically, Machiavelli wrote in 1513 that the Spanish were themselves vulnerable to cavalry (*Prince*, ch. xxvi).

97. *Essais*, iii. 909 (694); on Columbus, see Antonello Gerbi, *Nature in the New World: From Christopher Columbus to Gonzalo Fernández de Oviedo*, trans. Jeremy Moyle (Pittsburgh, 1985), 14. Gunpowder and its effects on the natives play a relatively understated part in the para-Vespuccian *Letter* to Soderini, *Letters from a New World*, 95–6, 83. On its 'para-Vespuccian' state, see p. xxxv. For modern accounts, see J. H. Elliott, 'The Spanish Conquest and Settlement of América', in *Cambridge History of Latin America*, i. *Colonial Latin America*, ed. Leslie Bethell (Cambridge, 1984), 149–206; Hugh Thomas, *The Conquest of Mexico* (London, 1993), esp. ch. 12 ('The Advantage of Having Horse and Cannon'), 158–74. See also Todorov, *Conquête*, 71–82, esp. 81.

98. See Gananath Obeyesekere, *The Apotheosis of Captain Cook: European Myth-making in the Pacific* (2nd edn., Princeton, 1997), 172, 289 nn. 55–6, citing Sheldon Dibble, *A History of the Sandwich Islands* (1843; Honolulu, 1909), 22–4.

For a case in which Cook's gun was used but did not fire, see Obeyesekere, 13. Obeyesekere's account of 'European mythmaking' has been severely challenged by Marshall Sahlins, *How 'Natives' Think: About Captain Cook, For Example* (Chicago, 1995).

99. Louis-Antoine de Bougainville, *Voyage autour du monde*, ed. Jacques Proust (Paris, 1982), 68–9; *A Voyage Round the World*, trans. John Reinhold Forster (1772), 24–5.

100. *Bougainville et ses compagnons autour du monde 1766–1769: Journaux de navigation*, ed. E. Taillemitte, 2 vols. (Paris, 1977), ii. 20–1, 63–4; on Fesche, and on the problematic authorship of his journal, see i. 74, 125–8.

101. Ibid. i. 316 and n. 4, 324, ii. 80–1 and n. 1.

102. *The Diario of Christopher Columbus's First Voyage to America, 1492–1493, Abstracted by Las Casas*, trans. Oliver Dunn and James E. Kelley, Jr. (Norman, Okla., 1989), 67, 287, 301.

103. Captain John Smith, *The Generall Historie of Virginia, New-England and the Summer Isles* (1624), 60, cited *OED*, s.v. Rocket, sb.3, 1, which also cites passages from Gulliver's standby, Sturmy's *Mariner's Magazine* (1669), on the manufacture of rockets. On Cook see J. C. Beaglehole, *The Life of Captain James Cook* (London, 1974), 187, 199–200, 205, 347, 358, 382, 396–7, 402 ff., 535, 541, 638.

104. *Robinson Crusoe*, ed. J. Donald Crowley (Oxford, 1983), 25, 53, 203, 211–2, 231–7.

105. Cited from the Journal of Surgeon John White in John Cobley, *Sydney Cove, 1788* (London, 1962), 30; see Robert Hughes, *The Fatal Shore* (New York, 1988), 15, 612 n. 23. For another episode involving Surgeon White, see Hughes, *Fatal Shore*, 85–6.

106. A few years earlier, describing the Roman '*pilum*, a ponderous javelin', Gibbon was exercised by similar issues and comparable, though not identical, discriminations: 'This instrument was indeed much inferior to our modern firearms; since it was exhausted by a single discharge, at the distance of only ten or twelve paces. Yet when it was launched by a firm and skilful hand, there was not … any shield or corslet that could sustain the impetuosity of its weight', *History*, ch. 1, I. 42).

107. Hughes, *Fatal Shore*, 94, 53–5, 276. Joseph Conrad, *Youth, Heart of Darkness, the End of the Tether* (1902; London, 1956), 62, 110, 134, 128–30.

108. I have discussed this more fully in *Satire and Sentiment 1660–1830*, 34 ff.

109. For Montaigne on gunpowder, see *Satire and Sentiment*, 53–4 and nn., esp. n. 72.

110. Irvin Ehrenpreis, *Swift: The Man, his Works, and the Age* (London, 1962–83), i. 179, iii. 53; also i. 126, 192, 199, iii. 77, 126.

111. *Poems*, ii. 698.

112. Pope owned a French text of Montaigne (1652) and Charles Cotton's translation (3 vols., 1685–93), the latter of which, now at Yale, has some thirty annotations in his hand, including the words 'Alter Ego' against Montaigne's account of his education. Pope also wrote at the end: 'This is (in my Opinion) the very best Book for Information of Manners, that has been writ. This Author says nothing but what every one feels att the Heart. Whoever deny it, are not more Wise than Montaigne, but less honest.' There are marginalia

referring to 'the Cruelty of ye Spaniards' and other matters in 'Des Coches' (see
Maynard Mack, *Collected in Himself* (Newark, Del. 1982), 318–19, 426–31).

113. *Correspondence*, i. 40–1 (ed. David Woolley, i. 149) and n., iii. 373, i. 415, iii. 348;
Works, xii. 246; *The Intelligencer*, ed. James Woolley (Oxford, 1992), 19, citing
a letter from Orrery to Thomas Southerne, 17 Jan. 1736, *The Orrery Papers*,
ed. Emily, Countess of Cork and Orrery (London, 1903), i. 144. For Swift's copy
or copies, see *Correspondence*, i. 40–1 n. (ed. David Woolley, i. 152 n. 2); and
item 21 in the *Catalogue of Books, the Library of the Late Rev. Dr. Swift* (Dublin,
1745), reproduced in facsimile in Harold Williams, *Dean Swift's Library* (Cambridge, 1932), and Williams, 66 n.; William F. Le Fanu, *A Catalogue of Books
Belonging to Dr. Jonathan Swift…(Aug. 19, 1715)* (Cambridge, 1988), 24, 64.

114. See Sir Charles Firth, 'The Political Significance of *Gulliver's Travels*' (1919), in
his *Essays Historical & Literary* (Oxford, 1968), 210–41, esp. 227 ff.; Donald T.
Torchiana, 'Jonathan Swift, the Irish, and the Yahoos: The Case Reconsidered', *Philological Quarterly*, 54 (1975), 195–212.

115. *Intelligencer*, 25, 197.

116. *Intelligencer*, 198.

117. Moryson, *Itinerary*, iii. 283.

118. For other such passages, see *Gulliver's Travels*, ed. Turner, 364 n. 31.

119. Thevet, *Singularités*, 129, 122–5; *Histoire mémorable*, see p. 26; *Intelligencer*, 211.

120. D'Aubigné, *Les Tragiques*, I. 311 ff.; *Œuvres*, 28; my translation.

121. *Histoire mémorable*, 290–5, see pp. 26–30, 77–8; for a comment to the same
effect by another writer about a cannibal tragedy in Florida in 1564, see
Morisot in *Voyage*, p. 441 n. 372/7. On Léry's own starvation crisis on the
return journey from Brazil, experienced before Sancerre but written up later,
with memories of Sancerre, its own sequence of disgusting foods (parrot, rats,
mice), its recognition of the dehumanizing force of hunger, and the threat of
cannibalism, see *Voyage*, 363–72 (210–14); Pagden, *Fall of Natural Man*, 177.

122. Piers Paul Read, *Alive: The Story of the Andes Survivors* (London, 1975), 277–8,
307–8.

123. Pagden, *Fall of Natural Man*, 87–8, 167.

124. See the essays by Firth and Torchiana, n. 114 above. Perceptions of resemblance go back to the eighteenth century: see Robert Mahony, *Jonathan Swift:
The Irish Identity* (New Haven and London, 1995), 59 (182 n. 48), 77 (185 n. 45),
135–6 (Firth); 144 (194 n. 14); see also Edward D. Snyder, 'The Wild Irish: A
Study of some English Satires against the Irish, Scots, and Welsh', *Modern
Philology*, 17 (1920), 718 n. 2 (example of 1771). For a particularly unpleasant
example from *Punch*, 18 Mar. 1862, see R. F. Foster, *Paddy & Mr. Punch: Connections in Irish and English History* (London, 1995), 184.

125. See Rawson, *Order from Confusion Sprung*, 131, 142–3 nn. 21–4; see also Thomas
Sheridan in *Intelligencer*, No. 6, p. 86.

126. See the Appendix on 'Wolves and the Cannibal Theme', in Rawson, 'Cannibalism and Fiction, Part II', 310–13; 'Narrative and the Proscribed Act', 1179;
Homer, *Iliad*, I. 231; Plato, *Republic*, VIII. 565D–566A; More, *Utopia*, ed. cit., 52,
and commentary, 306–7; Erasmus, *Education of a Christian Prince*, trans.
L. K. Born (New York, 1987), 170; d'Aubigné, *Les Tragiques*, I. 197 ff., 617 ff., III.
187 ff. etc., in *Œuvres*, 28, 35, 95–6 and nn., 909, 911, 914–15, 965.

127. Las Casas, *Short Account*, 11, 15, 46, 60, 96, 101, 121, 124; Léry on Protestants, *Histoire mémorable*, 195. For an inverse analogy in which it is Europeans who eat mutton and Indians who eat humans, see Thevet, *Singularités*, 232: 'Cette canaille mange ordinairement chair humaine comme nous ferions du mouton...' For the proverbial enmity of wolves and sheep, see R. P. Eckels, *Greek Wolf-Lore* (Philadelphia, 1937), 24 (the volume may also be consulted for some imagined anthropophagic elements in lycanthropic myths and in some versions of the story of Lycaon, 33, 46–7, 52, 55–6).

128. Lestringant, 'Rage, fureur, folie cannibales', 59 ff., 63 ff.

129. *Les Tragiques*, i. 325–6; *Œuvres*, 28.

130. Léry, *Voyage*, 46, 229; *Histoire mémorable*, 295.

131. Juvenal, XV. 159 ff.

132. Erasmus, *Adages*, IV. i. 1, in Margaret M. Phillips, *The Adages of Erasmus* (Cambridge, 1964), 316; Boileau, *Satires*, VIII. 153–4.

133. Early Christians were frequently accused of cannibalism, of Thyestean feasts and 'horrid rites', in relation to suspected Eucharistic practices: see J.-P. Waltzing, 'Le Crime rituel reproché aux chrétiens du IIe siècle', *Académie Royale de Belgique: Bulletins de la classe des lettres*, 5/11 (1925), 205–39, esp. 211 ff., 216 ff., 227 ff.; W. H. C. Frend, *Martyrdom and Persecution in the Early Church* (Oxford, 1965), 7, 10, 12, 25 ff., 257, and *passim*; Elaine Pagels, *The Gnostic Gospels* (Harmondsworth, 1982), 94, 100. The narrative of the martyrs of Vienne and Lyons in Gaul, including the charges against them of 'Thyestean banquets and Oedipal incest', and the story of Attalus's defiant counter-charge, is given in Eusebius, *History of the Church*, V. i, trans. C. A. Williamson (Harmondsworth, 1965), 193–203, esp. 195, 202. For an extended account of the imputation of Christian cannibalism followed by a retort in kind, see Tertullian, *Apologeticus*, II, VII–IX. Tertullian's sarcastic fantasy has been suggested as a source for Swift's *Modest Proposal* by Donald C. Baker, *Classical Journal*, 52 (1957), 219–20, and J. W. Johnson, *Modern Language Notes*, 73 (1958), 561–3. The *Octavius* of Minucius Felix, a work of Christian apologetics of the early third century derived from Tertullian's *Apologeticus* (AD 197), repeats the accusations of Thyestean banquets and other obscene rituals through an anti-Christian spokesman called Caecilius (VIII–IX), and rebuts them in the voice of the eponymous hero Octavius (XVI–XXXVIII, esp. XXVIII ff.) The *Octavius* is included in the Loeb edition of Tertullian's *Apology and De Spectaculis* (Cambridge, Mass. and London, 1931, rptd. 1984/5).

134. Thevet, *Singularités*, 122–3, 171, 222. Indians and cannibals were not only called beasts but, as Las Casas repeatedly remarked, used as beasts of burden by the Spaniards (*Short Account*, 24–5).

135. For some telling examples from French Protestant polemics, see Lestringant, *Le Huguenot et le sauvage*, 153–4.

136. *Works*, xii. 110–11.

137. On Scythians, Herodotus, IV. lxiv. lxx; Strabo, VII. iii. 6–7; Pliny, VI. xx. 53, VII. ii. 9 ff.; on Scythians and Irish cannibals, Diodorus Siculus, V. xxxii. 3; Strabo, IV. v. 4; Jerome, *Adversus Jovinianum*, II. vii (on Scots; in J.-P. Migne, *Patrologiae Cursus Completus*, xxiii (Paris, 1845), col. 296); see also Rawson, *Order from Confusion Sprung*, 131–2, 142–3 nn. 22 ff. Andrew Hadfield, 'Briton

and Scythian: Tudor Representations of Irish Origins', *Irish Historical Studies*, 28 (1993), 390–408, and *Edmund Spenser's Irish Experience* (Oxford, 1997), 66, 101–8; Robert Mahony, 'The Irish Colonial Experience and Swift's Rhetorics of Perception in the 1720s', *Eighteenth-Century Life*, 22 (1998), 63–75, esp. 64 ff.; for Las Casas on the Irish, see Elliott, *The Old World and the New*, 34.

138. See Lestringant, *Cannibals*, 24–5, 61 (and for an opposite view which uncoupled Indians and Scythians, 86, 90, 99, 212 n. 36).

139. Pagden, *Fall of Natural Man*, 193, 195; Lestringant, 'Rage, fureur, folie cannibales', 55. Thevet compared Scythians and Amerindians in *Singularités*, 163; cf. also 141–2 and (on Scythians and Amazons), 241–2. For theories of Amerindians in the Noachite genealogy, sometimes linked with Scythians, see Don Cameron Allen, *The Legend of Noah* (Urbana, Ill., 1949), 113–37, esp. 121 ff.

140. *Essais*, i. 208–9 (154–5). The account of the Scythian false prophets is discussed in Chapter 4.

141. *Essais*, i. 293 (213); Swift, *Works*, XII. 178; for Swift on the Irish, the Scythians, and the Tartars as eaters of the blood of cattle, see *Works*, xii. 19, and Sheridan in *Intelligencer*, No. 6, 86 and 91 n. 8; also Rawson, *Order from Confusion Sprung*, 131.

142. On the Irish reputation for extreme savagery, and for cannibalism, among English writers (Camden and Spenser as well as Moryson), see *Order from Confusion Sprung*, 130 ff., and 141 n. 13, 142–3 nn.; Snyder, 'Wild Irish', 687–725; Hadfield, *Edmund Spenser's Irish Experience*, 28, 36, 66–7, 69, 101–2, 105, 136–7, 142, 177–81.

143. Sir John Temple, *The Irish Rebellion* (1646), 8. The wording is common, and doubtless not in all cases conscious of paradox; e.g. Marco Polo on the mountain people of Ferlec in Northern Sumatra, who 'live like beasts. For I assure you that they eat human flesh' (*Travels*, trans. Ronald Latham (London, 1958), 253).

144. See the commentary in *Gulliver's Travels*, ed. Turner, 363; *Order from Confusion Sprung*, 68, 101 n. 2; R. W. Frantz, 'Swift's Yahoos and the Voyagers', *Modern Philology*, 29 (1931), 49–57 (parallels with monkeys as well as savages); Torchiana, 'Jonathan Swift, the Irish, and the Yahoos', 201; for other references, see 210 n. 15.

145. Howard Mumford Jones, *O Strange New World. American Culture: The Formative Years* (London, 1965), 167–79, 417–19 nn.; Nicholas Canny, *The Elizabethan Conquest of Ireland* (Hassocks, 1976), 133, 160–3; 'Identity Formation in Ireland: The Emergence of the Anglo-Irish', in Nicholas Canny and Anthony Pagden (eds.), *Colonial Identity in the Atlantic World, 1500–1800* (Princeton, 1987), 200; Richard Slotkin, *Regeneration through Violence* (Middletown, Conn., 1973) 41–2; William Christie MacLeod, 'Celt and Indian: Britain's Old World Frontier in Relation to the New', *The American Indian Frontier* (New York, 1928), 159–71, reprinted in Paul Bohannan and Fred Plog (eds.), *Beyond the Frontier* (New York, 1967), 25–41; Swift, *Works*, xii. 109. On Irish (and English) slaves and servants in the West Indies, see also Robert H. Schomburgk, *History of Barbados* (1848; London, 1971), 144, 284, 299; Vincent T. Harlow, *History of Barbados 1625–1685* (1926; New York, 1969), 189, 295, 299, 306, 308–9; on Sheridan's *Pizarro*, Fintan O'Toole, *A Traitor's Kiss: The Life of Richard Brinsley Sheridan, 1751–1816* (New York, 1998), 350–4.

146. Canny, *Elizabethan Conquest of Ireland*, 163; Karl S. Bottigheimer, 'Kingdom and Colony: Ireland in the Westward Enterprise 1536–1660', in K. R. Andrews, N. P. Canny, and P. E. H. Hair (eds.), *The Westward Enterprise: English Activities in Ireland, the Atlantic, and America 1480–1650* (Liverpool, 1978), 55; Moryson, *Itinerary*, iv. 185.

147. Neil Rennie, *Far-Fetched Facts: The Literature of Travel and the Idea of the South Seas* (Oxford, 1965), 165.

148. *Intelligencer*, 212; *Works*, xii. 176. For the Roman practice, Woolley cites Tacitus' British work, *Agricola*, XXXV.

149. See the sermon on 'Causes of the Wretched Condition of Ireland', *Works*, ix. 209, and the letter to Charles Wogan, July—2 Aug. 1732, *Correspondence*, iv. 51.

150. *Works*, ix. 20–2, x. 103, 64; Edward Said, *The World, the Text, and the Critic* (London, 1984), 86.

151. *Works*, x. 104.

152. *Works*, xii. 111, *Correspondence*, v. 58 (Swift to Pope, June 1737); for these views of Irish domestic and sexual mores, see Oliver W. Ferguson, *Jonathan Swift and Ireland* (Urbana, Ill., 1962), 174, and Rawson, *Order from Confusion Sprung*, 121–44.

153. *Intelligencer*, 211–12; *Works*, xii. 176, i. 172, 179, xii. 116.

154. John Locke, *An Essay Concerning Human Understanding*, II. xvi. 6; for the use in the late seventeenth century of the 'Topinamboux' as types of the savage, see *Tale of a Tub*, ed. A. C. Guthkelch and D. Nichol Smith (2nd edn., Oxford, 1973), 263 n., citing Charles Perrault and Swift's patron Sir William Temple. On the iconographic manifestations of Tupinambization, see William Sturtevant, 'First Visual Images of Native America', in Chiappelli (ed.), *First Images of America*, i. 417–54; and 'La Tupinambisation des Indiens d'Amérique des Nord', in Gilles Thérien (ed.), *Les Figures de l'Indien* (Montreal, 1988), 293–303.

155. Bougainville's Journal, 6 Apr. 1768, ed. Taillemitte, i. 316.

156. *Works*, xii. 111. Léry reports on cannibal cookery in the *Histoire mémorable*, 295, from Brazilian experience, as well as in the *Voyage*, 135, 218–19 (79, 126–7).

157. *Gulliver's Travels*, IV. iii, x. 236, 281, *Modest Proposal*, *Works*, xii. 112; Herodotus, IV. ixiv, ixv; Strabo, VII. iii. 6–7; Thevet, *Singularités*, 172; Léry, *Voyage*, 221 (128: Tupis make flutes and fifes from human limbs, and necklaces from teeth); for other references, see *Order from Confusion Sprung*, 143 n. 25. This is more fully discussed in Chapters 3 and 4.

158. Sheridan, *Intelligencer*, 198.

159. e.g. *Modest Proposal*, *Works*, xii. 114, 116; *A Proposal for the Universal Use of Irish Manufacture* (1720), *Works*, ix. 13–22.

160. *Intelligencer*, 199–200.

161. *Intelligencer*, 201–2 nn.; Moryson, *Itinerary*, iii. 282.

162. *Intelligencer*, 201 n.

163. *Modest Proposal*, *Works*, xii. 109, 110, 115.

164. Las Casas, *Short Account*, 74.

165. Sheridan himself gave voice to the accents of the resentful *colon* in *Intelligencer*, No. 6, 86–7; on the disappointment of both Swift and Sheridan with Ireland, and their desire to leave it, see Woolley's introduction, p. 20. For an interesting perspective on analogies between settlers in Ireland and North

African *colons*, see P. F. Sheeran, 'Colonists and Colonized: Some Aspects of Anglo-Irish Literature from Swift to Joyce', *Yearbook of English Studies*, 13 (1983), 97–115.

166. *Modest Proposal*, *Works*, xii. 111; Ferguson, *Jonathan Swift and Ireland*, 174; Rawson, *Order from Confusion Sprung*, 125, 141 nn. 11–13.

167. *A Proposal for Giving Badges to the Beggars* (1737), *Works*, xiii. 139; on beggars, see David Nokes, 'Swift and the Beggars', *Essays in Criticism*, 26 (1976), 218–35, and Rawson, *Order from Confusion Sprung*, 125 ff.

168. *Tale of a Tub*, III, VII, *Works*, i.60–1, 94; for Scythians and modern dissenting religions, see *Mechanical Operation of the Spirit*, *Works*, i.175 ff.

169. Swift to Archbishop King, 29 Mar. 1712, *Correspondence*, i. 293; see John Gay, *The Mohocks* (1712); the play, which was not performed, contains a character called Cannibal; the name for these marauding bands derives from a visit to London of four Mohawk chiefs in 1710; see John Gay, *Dramatic Works*, ed. John Fuller (Oxford, 1983), i. 77–100, 405–11; also Gay's poem, *Trivia* (1716), III. 321–34; and Ehrenpreis, *Swift*, ii. 536, 556, 558; for Defoe on London Mohocks and their Mohawk originals, see Marshall and Williams, *Great Map of Mankind*, 196; on the Houghers, see Swift, *Journal to Stella*, 26 Mar. 1712, ed. Harold Williams (Oxford, 1948) ii. 525; W. E. H. Lecky, *A History of Ireland in the Eighteenth Century*, new edn., 5 vols. (London, 1892), i. 361–7; James William Kelly, 'A Contemporary Source for the *Yahoos* in *Gulliver's Travels*', *Notes and Queries*, 243 (Mar. 1998), 68–70.

170. *Modest Proposal*, *Works*, xii. 111.

171. *Modest Proposal*, *Works*, xii. 117. Archbishop William King used the phrase about eating 'without Salt' in a memorandum on Irish taxes in 1721. He was speaking of the kind of Englishman who is hospitably entertained in Ireland and returns home 'full of the plenty ... of Ireland', who does not consider that 'for the Good Dinner he met there, three hundred Neighbours or tennants Dined on a potatoe without Salt', cited in *Intelligencer*, ed. Woolley, 228. The passage has a bearing on Swift's *Short View of the State of Ireland* (*Intelligencer*, No. 15), as well as *A Modest Proposal* (see 182 n. 63 and 227 headnote).

172. *Modest Proposal*, *Works*, xii. 109, 113. The belief that Amerindian women were not cannibalized by enemies in order that they might be used as breeders occurs in Peter Martyr, *De Orbe Novo*, I. i, trans. F. A. MacNutt (New York and London, 1912), i. 63, cited in Frank Lestringant, 'Le Nom des "Cannibales"', 57. Peter Martyr is speaking of Carib Indians, whose practice differed from the Tupinamba as described by Thevet, *Singularités*, 161. The practice among Amerindian cannibals of keeping women as breeders is also recorded by Sebastian Münster, in the French translation owned by Montaigne, *Cosmographie universelle* (Basel, 1568), 1322 (Montaigne's copy is at Bibliothèque Nationale, Rés. Fol. Z Payen 494; I owe this information to François Rigolot; for Thevet's copy of Münster's book, see Lestringant, *Le Huguenot et le sauvage*, 328). See Combès, *Tragédie cannibale*, 57–8.

173. Spenser, *View of the Present State of Ireland*, in *Prose Works* (Variorum Edition), ed. Rudolf Gottfried (Baltimore, 1949), 158, and annotation 382; James Joyce, *Portrait of the Artist as a Young Man* (New York, 1978), 203. This is more fully discussed in Chapter 3.

174. See Arens, *Man-Eating Myth*, 84–5, 140, 142 ff.; cf. Herman Melville, *Typee*, ch. iv, in *Typee, Omoo, Mardi*, ed. G. Thomas Tanselle (New York, 1982), 35 ff.: 'It was quite amusing, too, to see with what earnestness they disclaimed all cannibal propensities on their own part, while they denounced their enemies— the Typees—as inveterate gormandizers of human flesh; but this is a peculiarity to which I shall hereafter have occasion to allude.' The name Typee, which signifies a 'lover of human flesh', is said to denote both a 'peculiar ferocity' and a 'special stigma' (35).

175. For Lévi-Strauss's interest in Léry, whose book he described as the 'bréviaire de l'ethnologue', see *Tristes Tropiques*, 89 ff.

Chapter 2. The Savage with Hanging Breasts Gulliver, Female Y*ahoos*, and 'Racism'

1. Another suggested reversal, in this case of customary accounts of sexual transactions between apes and humans, where the ape is 'invariably' male and the human is female, is discussed at the end of this chapter.

2. See James Kelly, '"A Most Inhuman and Barbarous Piece of Villainy": An Exploration of the Crime of Rape in Eighteenth-Century Ireland', *Eighteenth-Century Ireland*, 10 (1995), 78–107, and Paul-Gabriel Boucé, 'The Rape of Gulliver Reconsidered', *Swift Studies*, 11 (1996), 98–114, esp. 99, 111.

3. See Boucé, 'Rape of Gulliver', 111; on West Indian slaves, see Chapter 4, p. 289.

4. *Gulliver's Travels*, ed. Paul Turner (Oxford, 1988), 371 n. 7.

5. "On Stella's Birth-day' (1719), ll. 5–6, *Poems*, ed. Harold Williams (2nd edn., Oxford, 1958), ii. 721; 'On the Death of Mrs. Johnson' (1728), *Prose Works*, ed. Herbert Davis *et al.* (Oxford, 1939–74), v. 227.

6. *Poems*, i. 193, 195; *Gulliver's Travels*, ed. Turner, 371 n. 1, and, more fully, Boucé, 'Rape of Gulliver', 108–9.

7. *Cadenus and Vanessa*, ll. 343–5, 39–40, *Poems*, ii. 697, 687. Swift's poems include other examples of beaux and especially Irish politicians, described as, or in the role of, monkeys, e.g. *Poems*, iii. 782, 788, 832. For Swift's views on the education of women, and his qualified notions of educational equality in *Gulliver's Travels*, see I. vi. 60–3 and IV. viii. 268–9. More generally, see Claude Rawson, 'Rage and Raillery and Swift: The Case of *Cadenus and Vanessa*', in Donald C. Mell (ed.), *Pope, Swift, and Women Writers*, (2nd ptg., Newark, Del., 1998), 179–91, and 'Swift, les femmes et l'éducation des femmes', in Guyonne Leduc (ed.), *L'Education des femmes en Europe et en Amérique du Nord de la Renaissance à 1848* (Paris, 1997), 245–65.

8. Esther Vanhomrigh to Swift, June 1722, *Correspondence*, ed. Harold Williams (Oxford, 1963–5) ii. 428–9.

9. Williams in *Correspondence*, ii. 428 n. 6; Donald T. Torchiana, 'Jonathan Swift, the Irish, and the Yahoos', *Philological Quarterly*, 54(1975), 205.

10. On the 'natural impulse of desire' between apparently dissimilar animals 'of the same species' see Edward Long, *The History of Jamaica*, 3 vols. (1774), ii. 364. On the related criterion of interfertility in the determination of biological

species, as later formulated by Buffon and the British physician John Hunter, see Nancy Stepan, *The Idea of Race in Science: Great Britain 1800–1960* (London, 1982), 33. The idea was, however, an old one.

11. Joseph Conrad, *Youth, Heart of Darkness, The End of the Tether* (1902; London, 1956), 118. The Assembly debate about the Yahoos is discussed in Chapters 3 and 4.

12. Conrad, *Youth, Heart of Darkness*, 97; 'John Esquemeling' (Alexandre Olivier Exquemelin), *The Buccaneers of America* (1678; English trans., 1684), III. vii, ed. William Swan Stallybrass (London, 1923), 230.

13. Buffon, *Of Carnivorous Animals*, 'The Nomenclature of Apes', in *Natural History*, English trans., 10 vols. (London, 1797), ix. 136–7; the extended treatment of apes and monkeys (ix. 107–263) in Buffon's discussion of carnivorous animals runs to many chapters and is recurrently preoccupied with physical resemblance to humans, while insisting on a clear distinguishability not mainly based on physical features.

14. Peter Heylyn, *Cosmographie* (1652), II. iv. 138, Richard Ligon, *A True and Exact History of the Island of Barbados* (1657), 51; Vincent le Blanc, *The World Surveyed* (1660), 180, variously cited in *Gulliver's Travels*, ed. Turner, 363 n. 15; Dirk Friedrich Passmann, *'Full of Improbable Lies': Gulliver's Travels und die Reiseliteratur vor 1726* (Frankfurt, 1987), 191–2, 431 nn. 21–5; Frantz, 'Swift's Yahoos and the Voyagers', 54–5; also Woodes Rogers, *A Cruising Voyage Round the World* (1712, 2nd edn. corrected, 1726), 63. Swift owned a copy of le Blanc, see *Catalogue of Books ... (1715)*, ed. William F. Le Fanu (Cambridge, 1988), 22.

15. Buffon, 'Nomenclature of Apes', ix. 136–7; Hermann Heinrich Ploss, Max Bartels, *et al.*, *Woman: An Historical, Gynaecological and Anthropological Compendium* (1885–1927), trans. Eric John Dingwall, 3 vols. (London, 1935), i. 335 (for convenience, I refer throughout to this work as Ploss, or the Ploss compendium, though H.H. Ploss himself, its orginal author, died in 1885, soon after the appearance of the first edition, and had no part in the work's many subsequent additions); R.W. Frantz, 'Swift's Yahoos and the Voyagers', *Modern Philology*, 29(1931), 53; *The English Traveller and the Movement of Ideas 1660–1732* (Lincoln, Neb., 1934), 104; for important discussions of the mythologized image of Hottentots, see Ezio Bassani and Letizia Tedeschi, 'The Image of the Hottentot in the Seventeenth and Eighteenth Centuries: An Iconographic Investigation', *Journal of the History of Collections*, 2 (1990), 157–86; Andreas Mielke, *Laokoon und die Hottentotten, oder Über die Grenzen von Reisebeschreibung und Satire* (Baden-Baden, 1993), 225 ff., and 'Contextualizing the "Hottentot Venus"', *Acta Germanica*, 25 (1997), 151–69; Linda E. Merians, 'What They Are, Who We Are: Representations of the "Hottentot" in Eighteenth-Century Britain', *Eighteenth-Century Life*, 17 (1993), 14–39, esp. 20–1, 33–6, and '"Hottentot": The Emergence of an Early Modern Racist Epithet', *Shakespeare Studies*, 26 (1998), 123–44; Gérard Badou, *L'Énigme de la Vénus hottentote* (Paris, 2000). On the connections between Hottentots and *Gulliver's Travels*, see pp. 109–11 and n. 41; for Gulliver's Australian geography, see Glyndwr Williams and Alan Frost (eds.), *Terra Australis to Australia* (Melbourne, 1988), 137–8.

16. Sir Thomas Herbert, *A Relation of Some Yeares Travels* (1638), 16–17 (Swift's copy of the first edition (1634), is now at Harvard; for his annotations, see *Works*, v,

pp. xxxii and n. 2, 243); John Nieuhoff, *Voyages and Travels in to Brasil and the East-Indies* (?1669), in *A Collection of Voyages and Travels*, 4 vols. (1704), ii. 188; Nathaniel Crouch, *English Acquisitions in Guinea & East-India*, by R.B. (?1686; 1700), 109; Francis Leguat, *New Voyage to the East-Indies* (1708, 232; cited in A. H. MacKinnon, 'The Augustan Intellectual and the Ignoble Savage: Houyhnhnm Versus Hottentot', *Costerus*, 63 (1987), 61); Daniel Beeckman, *A Voyage to and from the Island of Borneo* (1718), in John Pinkerton, *A General Collection of Voyages*, 17 vols. (1808–14), XI. 152–3.

17. Lorna Schiebinger, *Nature's Body: Gender in the Making of Modern Science* (Boston, 1993), 91–2, 161, and 239 nn.; see p. 92 for an early drawing (1551) of what was taken to be an anthropoid ape, with breasts resembling the savage stereotype, and the anomalous addition of a long tail.

18. William Cornelis Schouten, *The Relation of a Wonderfull Voyage Made by W. C. Schouten of Horne* (1619; London, 1966), 57, cited (with other examples) in Bernadette Bucher, *Icon and Conquest: A Structural Analysis of De Bry's Great Voyages*, trans. Basia Miller Gulati (Chicago, 1981), 135–6 and *passim*, and Passmann, '*Full of Improbable Lies*', 191–2, 431 nn. 21–5; William Lithgow, *The Totall Discourse of the Rare Adventures & Painefull Peregrinations of long Nineteene Yeares Travayles* (1632; Glasgow, 1906); J. R. Forster, *Resolution Journal*, ed. Michael E. Hoare, 4 vols. (London, 1982), iii. 546 (30 June 1774); Jules-Sébas-tien-César Dumont d'Urville, *Voyage de la corvette l' Astrolabe*, 5 vols. 1830–3, (describing a voyage of 1826–9), v. 164. See his *Atlas historique*, ii, plates 153, 167, etc., for various examples of hanging breasts. For the folklore of breasts and money bags, see p.107 and n. 35.

19. (pl. 1) Bucher, *Icon and Conquest*, plates 4, 5, 8a, 10, 11, 12, 18, 19, 21; for mainly seventeenth-century Hottentot examples of hanging breasts, and the standard portrayal of the primitive woman carrying a child, separately or together, in a variety of standard stylizations, see Bassani and Tedeschi, 'Image of the Hottentot', 160, 168, 170, 172, 178–81 (figs. 2, 8, 10, 12, 21–4); Guy Tachard, *A Relation of the Voyage to Siam* (1686; English trans. 1688), introd. B. J. Terwiel (Bangkok, 1999), 58, 61, plates 5 and 6, Hottentot and Namaqua examples; Mary Louise Pratt, *Imperial Eyes: Travel Writing and Transculturation* (London, 1992), 46. For unusual examples of grotesquerie almost matching the verbal accounts, and captured by photography, in Hottentot and other South African and Abyssinian women, see pl. 2, and Ploss, Bartels, *et al.*, *Woman*, i. 303, 435; ii. 418; iii. 181 and esp. 343–4, figs. 271, 362, 647, 863, 951, 952.

20. Thomas Watling, *A Groupe on the North Shore of Port Jackson*, c.1794, in the Museum of Natural History, London, in Bernard Smith, *European Vision and the South Pacific* (2nd edn., Melbourne, 1989), 185, plate 124; Augustus Earle, *Natives of New South Wales*, c.1830, in Robert Hughes, *The Fatal Shore* (New York, 1988), between 450–1. For some examples from the *National Geographic*, see 152/1 (July 1977), 135, 143 ('Fertility Rites and Sorcery in a New Guinea Village', by Gillian Gillison, photographs by David Gillison); 163/1 (Jan. 1983), 69, 73 ('What Future for the Wayana Indians?' by Carole Devilliers); 164/2 (Aug. 1983), 148–9, 168 ('Living Theater in New Guinea's Highlands', by Gillian Gillison, photographs by David Gillison); 155/1 (Jan. 1979), 66 ('Man in the Amazon: Stone Age Present Meets Stone Age Past', by W. Jesco von Puttkamer); 188/2

(Aug. 1995), 107 (Ghana; 'The African Roots of Voodoo', by Carol Beckwith and Angela Fisher).

21. Photographic manipulation, whether of plates or negatives, or in the posing of subjects and arranging of backgrounds, is nowadays well recognized. For an indignant account, see Virginia-Lee Webb, 'Manipulated Images: European Photographs of Pacific Peoples', in Elazar Barkan and Ronald Bush (eds.), *Prehistories of the Future: The Primitivist Project and the Culture of Modernism* (Stanford, Calif., 1995), 175–201, 410–16 nn. Among the illustrations are several (esp. figs. 6, 12) which belong to the stereotype I am describing, though that stereotype is not itself discussed or said to have been a specific object of manipulation, beyond occasional remarks about the posing of 'non-European women as though they were sexually available ... for the pleasure of European males' (p. 187). The matter is presumably more complicated, since some examples, from de Bry to Lévi-Strauss, do not seem self-evidently directed at anyone's 'pleasure', though prurience may take some non-'pleasurable' forms, and there is no reason to assume that the detailing of breasts was any more exempt from falsification than any other features of a composition.

22. Claude Lévi-Strauss, *Tristes Tropiques* (Paris, 1955), plates 12, 31, 41, 54, 62; *Saudades do Brasil* (Paris, 1994), 90, 96, 106, 108, 129, 135, 139, 174–7, 188; for Nambikwara young girls, 138–55; puppies, 140, 149; monkeys, 141, 154; on charm and bad reputation, 42.

23. Bucher, *Icon and Conquest*, 135–6 and plates 20–1.

24. Vespucci, *Letters from a New World*, ed. Luciano Formisano, trans. David Jacobson (New York, 1992), 49–50, 63–4, 71, esp. 50, 64. These two published works were drafted by another hand on the basis of original letters by Vespucci, and cannot be regarded as fully authentic, but they were the only Vespuccian texts published in the sixteenth century, and by which his views were in the main known. There is some dispute as to whether they should be described as 'pseudo-Vespuccian' or 'para-Vespuccian'. For simplicity of reference I shall be referring to them as by Vespucci. This discussion is not concerned with Vespucci's own views, which are impossible to determine in any detail, but with what was reported in his name. For different emphases on the authorship question, see Formisano, Introduction, pp. xix–xxxv, and Antonello Gerbi, *Nature in the New World: From Christopher Columbus to Gonzalo Fernández de Oviedo*, trans. Jeremy Moyle (Pittsburgh, 1985), 45–6.

25. *Vespucci 'Discovering' America*, engraving by Theodor Galle, after Stradanus (Jan van der Street), in British Museum (pl. 3), reproduced as fig. 81 in Hugh Honour, *The New Golden Land: European Images of America from the Discoveries to the Present Time* (New York, 1975), 88 (for other blonde Americas, see p. 89, figs. 82 and 83, 1594 and 1644), and in *Letters from a New World*, after p. 118.

26. Daniel Defoe, *A New Voyage Round the World* (1725), 70.

27. Johann Reinhold Forster, *Observations Made During A Voyage Round the World* (1778), ed. Nicholas Thomas, Harriet Guest, and Michael Dettelbach (Honolulu, 1996), 181.

28. (pls. 4–5) Webber, see Bernard Smith, *Imagining the Pacific* (New Haven, 1992), 192, 199, plates 175, 179, and, in fuller detail, Rüdiger Joppien and Bernard

Smith, *The Art of Captain Cook's Voyages* (New Haven, 1988), iii (Text), 67–8 and plate 79; iii (Catalogue), 275 and figs. 3.13 and 3.13*a*.

29. For Prado de Tovar, see William Eisler, *The Furthest Shore: Images of Terra Australis from the Middle Ages to Captain Cook* (Cambridge, 1995), 48–9, figs. 20–2 (and *Furthest Shore*, 106–7, figs. 49–50; including one father); Albert Eckhout, see pls. 6–7, and Honour, *New Golden Land*, 80–1, fig. 70, 72, 73; George Shelvocke, *Voyage Round the World* (1726), facing p. 404, in Smith, *Imagining the Pacific*, 58, plate 50.

30. (pl. 7) Honour, *New Golden Land*, 80, fig. 70; Eisler, *Furthest Shore*, 107, plate 50. Compare the sexy blonde America welcoming Vespucci in Theodore Galle's engraving, with its cannibals in the background, Honour, *New Golden Land*, 88–9, fig. 81 (see pl. 3).

31. Graham Greene, *Journey Without Maps* (Harmondsworth, 1971), 46, 61, 53.

32. Barry Unsworth, *Sacred Hunger*, chs. 39, 24 (London, 1992), 435, 200, 205–8.

33. Ligon, *True and Exact History*, 51, 15–6, cited in Jennifer L. Morgan '"Some Could Suckle over their Shoulder": Male Travelers, Female Bodies, and the Gendering of Racial Ideology, 1500-1700', *William and Mary Quarterly*, 54 (1997), 167–9, 190; Forster, *Resolution Journal*, iii. 546 (30 June 1774); Patrick White, *Letters*, ed. David Marr (Chicago, 1996), 37 (23 Jan. 1941).

34. Elizabeth Bishop, *Complete Poems 1927–1979* (New York, 1995), 159–61. The poem cites the issue of Feb. 1918, which contains a long article about volcanoes but not the other items. Bishop talks about this in a letter of 27 July 1971: 'I did go to the library in N.Y. and look up that issue of the *National Geographic*. Actually—and this is really weird, I think—I had remembered it perfectly, and it was all about Alaska, called "The Valley of Ten Thousand Smokes." I tried using that a bit but my mind kept going back to another issue of the *National Geographic* that had made what seemed like a more relevant impression on me, so used it instead. Of course I was sure *The New Yorker* would "research" this, or "process it" or something—but apparently they are not quite as strict as they used to be—or else are sure that none of their present readers would have read *National Geographics* going back *that* far' (*One Art: Letters*, ed. Robert Giroux (New York, 1994), 545–6). In one sense, Bishop's faulty recollection is an index of how the motif of hanging breasts was taken for granted as *National Geographic* material. Another poem by Elizabeth Bishop, 'Pink Dog' (1979), about a beggar-woman in Rio de Janeiro '(A nursing mother, by those hanging teats)', is discussed in Chapter 3. See *Complete Poems*, 190.

35. Ploss, Bartels, *et al.*, *Woman*, i. 394–449, 454–6; for a summary version, see Paula Weideger, *History's Mistress: A New Interpretation of a Nineteenth-Century Ethnographic Classic* (Harmondsworth, 1986), 57–60. For wine-cups, see Marilyn Yalom, *A History of the Breast* (New York, 1997), 68.

36. *Faerie Queene*, i. viii. 47; *Orlando Furioso*, VIII. 69–74; Baudelaire, 'Don Juan aux enfers', ll. 5–8; on hags, see Marina Warner, *From the Beast to the Blonde: On Fairy Tales and their Tellers* (London, 1994), 43 ff.; on Veronica Franco, see Yalom, *History of the Breast*, 55–6; for visual examples see Hans Baldung Grien, *The Ages of Man and Death*, Prado Museum, Madrid (pl. 8); compare a seventeenth-century portrayal of *Old Age* in Yalom, *History of the Breast*, 57.

37. Swift, *Poems*, ii. 582; Fielding, *Amelia*, I. iii, ed. Martin C. Battestin (Oxford, 1983), 28; there are other examples in each of Fielding's novels of characters with comparable attributes: Mrs Slipslop (*Joseph Andrews*, I. vi, IV. xiv), Laetitia Snap (*Jonathan Wild*, I. ix), and Mrs Partridge (*Tom Jones*, II. iv: in the latter case, Fielding answered in favour of the breasts the question asked about natives in Woodes Rogers's book, 'whether the Women's Hair or Breasts be longest'); compare the bawd in John Cleland's *Memoirs of a Woman of Pleasure* (1749), ed. Peter Sabor (Oxford, 1985), 24; White, *Letters*, 25.

38. Lithgow, *Totall Discourse*, 378; Lithgow also spoke of the idleness of the Irish (373, 374), much as European writers dwelt on the idleness of Hottentots: see J. M. Coetzee, *White Writing: On the Culture of Letters in South Africa* (New Haven and London, 1988), 21, 16–35, and Chapter 3.

39. Hilary Mantel, *The Giant, O'Brien*, ch. 4 (London, 1998), 42; Schiebinger, *Nature's Body*, 163, cites Blumenbach on the large breasts of Irish women; *Modest Proposal, Works*, xii. 112.

40. Compare Crouch, *English Acquisitions*, 6, on natives of the Guinea coast: 'they give them the breast over their shoulders, and this may be the reason of the flatness of their Noses by their knocking them continually against the Back and Shoulders of the Mother'; Buffon, *History of Man*, ch. 9, 'Of the Varieties in the Human Species', *Natural History*, iv. 282.

41. See Frantz, 'Swift's Yahoos and the Voyagers', esp. 53–7; Daniel Eilon, 'Swift's Yahoo and Leslie's Hottentot', *Notes and Queries*, 228 (1983), 510–12; MacKinnon, 'The Augustan Intellectual', 55–63, esp. 59–62 (J. A. Bakker *et al.* (eds.), *Essays on English and American Literature . . . Offered to David Wilkinson* (Amsterdam, 1987)).

42. For urinating rituals and non-language, see Merians, 'What They Are', 26, 28, 30, 34; for corrupted flesh, *Encyclopédie*, new edn., xviii (1778), 786, art. 'Hottentots'; for poisoned arrows, Georges Cuvier, 'Extrait d' observations faites sur le cadavre d'une femme connue à Paris et à Londres sous le nom de Vénus Hottentotte', *Mémoires du Muséum d'Histoire naturelle*, iii (1817), 259–74, p. 262; I. Norwich, 'A Chapter of Early Medical Africana', *South African Medical Journal*, 45 (1971), 503; Stephen Jay Gould, 'The Hottentot Venus', *Natural History*, 91/10 (Oct. 1982), 22; Badou, *Énigme*, 29, 36 (citing Diderot).

43. Crouch, *English Acquisitions*, 109.

44. Lithgow, *Totall Discourse* 373, 374; Coetzee, *White Writing*, 16–35.

45. Lithgow, *Totall Discourse*, 378; Herbert, *Some Yeares Travels*, 18; for early assimilations, see also Merians, '"Hottentots"', 130–2.

46. W. J. Fitzpatrick, *Ireland Before the Union; with Extracts from the Unpublished Diary of . . . [the] Earl of Clonmell* (2nd edn., 1867), 32–3.

47. Torchiana, 'Jonathan Swift, the Irish, and the Yahoos', 201; L. P. Curtis, Jr., *Anglo-Saxons and Celts: A Study of Anti-Irish Prejudice in Victorian England* (Bridgeport, Conn., 1968), 63, 102–3.

48. Swift to James Stopford, 26 Nov. 1725 (the same day as a famous letter to Pope about *Gulliver's Travels*), to Charles Wogan, ?1736, and to Francis Grant, 23 Mar. 1734, *Correspondence*, iii. 116, iv. 468, 230 (posthumously reprinted as *A Letter on the Fishery, Works*, xiii. 112).

49. *Modest Proposal, Works*, xii. 116; Sheridan, *Intelligencer*, No. 2, c.18 May 1728, 52.

50. See Chapter 1, p. 75 and n. 124.

51. Bucher, *Icon and Conquest*, plates 8a, 14; Columbus, *Journal*, 9 Jan. 1493, cited in Tzvetan Todorov, *La Conquête de l'Amérique* (1982; Paris, 1991), 26.

52. Columbus, letter to Santangel, Feb.–Mar. 1493, cited in Todorov, *Conquête*, 26.

53. Todorov, *Conquête*, 27. On Amazons, see also Ploss, Bartels, *et al.*, *Woman*, i. 464–74; Frank Lestringant, *L'Atelier du cosmographe, ou l'image du monde à la Renaissance* (Paris, 1991), 114–29, 224–8. For some English perceptions, mainly Ralegh's, see Louis Montrose, 'The Work of Gender in the Discourse of Discovery', in Stephen Greenblatt (ed.), *New World Encounters* (Berkeley, 1993), 201 ff. and references 217 n. 42.

54. C. Lombroso and E. G. Ferrero, *La Donna delinquente: la prostituta e la donna normale* (Turin and Rome, 1893), 339, and see 341–3, 348, 423, 492–3 and plates and illustrations; the English translation, *The Female Offender* (London, 1895), is heavily abridged (the passage cited is at 91).

55. (pl. 9) Lombroso and Ferrero, *La Donna delinquente*, plate II, *Polisarcia in Abissina* (not in *Female Offender*); 342 and plate V (*Female Offender*, 95–6 and plate III, 102); Ploss, Bartels, *et al.*, *Woman*, iii. 344, plate 952 (his caption, in the Dingwall translation, is *Abyssinian matron* whereas Lombroso's, acknowledging Ploss, is *Ballerina o prostituta Abissina*); ii. 114–16, i. 156–61. Lombroso (14) cites an 1887 edition of *Das Weib*, where this picture does not appear; but in the 1905 edition (661), it appears as fig. 647, captioned *Abyssinierin im Matronenalter*.

56. See Chapter 1, pp. 28ff., 85ff.

57. BM 9178, Feb. 1798.

58. Joseph Campbell, *The Way of the Animal Powers*, i: *Historical Atlas of World Mythology* (London, 1983), 46–7, 66–73, fig. 66, 109, 118–24, 128; see also Ploss, Bartels, *et al.*, *Woman*, i. 308–9 and fig. 281.

59. Joseph Campbell, with Bill Moyers, *The Power of Myth* (New York, 1988), 164; on African art, see Susan Vogel (ed.), *For Spirits and Kings: African Art from the Paul and Ruth Tishman Collection* (New York, 1981), Nos. 9, 21, 34, 43, 69, 74, 96; Susan Vogel and Mario Carrieri, *African Aesthetics: The Carlo Monzino Collection* (New York, 1986), 1, 2, 3, 4, 58, 74, 96, 97, 172, 173, 202, 209.

60. In addition to poems and plays by Stephen Gray, Elizabeth Alexander, Suzan-Lori Parks, and others (some discussed below) see Gould, 'The Hottentot Venus'; Paul Edwards and James Walvin, *Black Personalities in the Era of the Slave Trade* (Baton Rouge, La., 1983), 171–82 (a useful collection of contemporaneous comments); Sander L. Gilman, 'Black Bodies, White Bodies: Toward an Iconography of Sexuality in Late Nineteenth-Century Art, Medicine, and Literature', in Henry Louis Gates, Jr. (ed.), *'Race', Writing, and Difference* (Chicago, 1986), 232–9, 258–60 nn., which appeared in the journal *Critical Inquiry* in Autumn 1985, and may be Gilman's first treatment of the subject, recycled at least twice in *Difference and Pathology: Stereotypes of Sexuality, Race, and Madness* (Ithaca, NY, 1985), 85–92, and *Sexuality: An Illustrated History* (New York, 1989), 292–6; Mielke, *Laokoon und die Hottentotten*, 225 ff., and 'Contextualizing the "Hottentot Venus"' esp. 159–61; Schiebinger, *Nature's Body*, esp. 160–72; Anne Faustino-Sterling, 'Gender, Race, and Nation: The Comparative Anatomy of "Hottentot" Women in Europe, 1815–1817', in Jennifer Terry and Jacqueline

Urla (eds.), *Deviant Bodies: Critical Perspectives on Difference in Science and Popular Culture* (Bloomington, Ind., 1995), 19–48; for interest in perceptions of Hottentot physique and way of life in general, see Merians, 'What They Are', and '"Hottentot"', and Bassani and Tedeschi, 'The Image of the Hottentot', already cited.

61. Ploss, Bartels, *et al.*, *Woman*, i. 327–53.

62. Gilman, 'Black Bodies', 232, 258.

63. (pl. 10) It accompanied a reprint of the autopsy report of 1817 by Georges Léopold Cuvier, 'Femme de race Boschismanne', in Étienne Geoffroy-Saint-Hilaire and Frédéric Cuvier, *Histoire naturelle des mammifères*, 2 vols. (Paris, 1824), i. 1–7; Hugh Honour, *The Image of the Black in Western Art*, iv. *From the American Revolution to World War I*, 2 vols. (Cambridge, Mass., 1989), ii. 52, 255 n. 27, 281. The image reproduced in Gilman, 'Black Bodies', 213, fig. 5, is wrongly said to have appeared with Cuvier's autopsy report in 1817, a mistake corrected in *Sexuality*, 292, plate 298.

64. Coetzee, *White Writing*, 1 n.

65. Richard D. Altick, *The Shows of London* (Cambridge, Mass., 1978), 268–73. Baartman was succeeded in 1822 by a 'Venus of South America', who exhibited a hundred or so scars for each act of adultery she was found to have committed (105 purportedly carried the death penalty among the Botocudo people of Brazil).

66. Altick, *Shows of London*, 268.

67. Ibid.

68. (pls. 11–12) See M. Dorothy George, *Catalogue of Political and Personal Satires Preserved in the Department of Prints and Drawings in the British Museum*, vols. viii–x, photolithic edn. (London, 1978), Nos. 11577, 11578, 11578A, 11580, 11602, 11748, 11763, 11765, 11765A, 12636, 12702, 12749, 12799, 13249, 14449, 14637 (hereafter referred to as BM followed by number); see also Bernth Lindfors, 'The Bottom Line: African Caricature in Georgian England', *World Literature Written in English*, 24 (1984), 43–51 (for Lewis's poster, pp. 46, 51 n. 7). Rowlandson's *Sartgee, the Hottentot Venus*, a drawing of her face, is at the Menil Collection, Houston, Texas.

69. See Bernth Lindfors, '"The Hottentot Venus" and other African Attractions in Nineteenth-Century England', *Australasian Drama Studies*, 1 (1983), 83–104; Gilman, 'Black Bodies', 232, 234 and 258 n. 17; *Sexuality*, 293.

70. Edwards and Walvin, *Black Personalities*, 181–2. See pp. 138–9 and n. 152.

71. *Encyclopédie*, xvii (1778), 786 (art. 'Hottentots'); John Ogilby, *Africa: Being an Accurate Description of the Regions of Aegypt, Barbary, Lybia, and Billedulgerid, the Land of Negroes, Guinee, Aethiopia, and the Abyssines* (1670), 589–90.

72. E. A. Hooton, 'Some Early Drawings of Hottentot Women', *Harvard African Studies*, 2 (1918), 83–99 and plates.

73. Georges Cuvier, 'Extrait d'observations', see above, n. 42. Cuvier regarded her peculiarities as belonging to the Bushman rather than the Hottentot people (259–61), and his account is consistent with the description of the Bushmen in Laurens van der Post's *Lost World of the Kalahari* (1958; Harmondsworth, 1978), 13–14.

74. See Merians, 'What They Are', 24–8.

75. Cuvier, 'Extrait d'observations', 259; for seventeenth-century reports, see Merians, 'What They Are', 28; for theories of the 'Hottentot apron', including the question of whether it was fully congenital, or partly induced by manipulation, see Ploss, Bartels, *et al.*, *Woman*, i. 327–36.

76. 'Sur une femme de la race hottentote', *Bulletin des sciences, par la société philomatique de Paris* (1816), 187, 189–90, reporting an examination by M. de Blainville on 18 Mar. 1815. Gilman, 'Black Bodies', 232, 259 n. 18, and *Sexuality*, 292, bizarrely speaks of this live examination as the same 'autopsy' as that performed by Cuvier after her death; Cuvier, 'Extrait d'observations', 265 ff. Cuvier had also seen her alive, and reports her consent to being painted nude in the Jardin du Roi in Spring 1815 (262–3, 265). For the report of 1689, see John Ovington, *A Voyage to Suratt* (1696), 497, cited in Merians, 'What They Are', 28. For a list of medical studies of Baartman from Blainville onwards, see Faustion-Sterling, 'Gender, Race, and Nation', 43–4 n. 13.

77. *Encyclopédie*, art. 'Hottentots'; L. H. Wells, 'An English Buccaneer's Notes on the Cape Hottentots in 1686', *South African Journal of Science*, 57 (1961), 182; Ploss, Bartels, *et al.*, *Woman*, i. 327–8, reports a Bushwoman named Afandy who exhibited her apron in Central Europe; for other nineteenth-century exhibitions, both popular and 'scientific', of Cape women, see Badou, *Énigme*, 174–7.

78. Badou, *Énigme*, 187–92, including the information that Nelson Mandela asked François Mitterand for the remains to be returned to South Africa, and that diplomats still report negotiations to be at a 'delicate stage'.

79. Cuvier, 'Extrait d'observations', 266; Gould, 'The Hottentot Venus', 20. Elizabeth Alexander, *The Venus Hottentot* (Charlottesville, Va., 1990), 3–4. On the other hand, Stephen Gray's *Hottentot Venus* (Cape Town, 1979), 1, makes Baartman say: 'they wanted to . . . sink me in wax and decant my brain/and put me in a case in the Museum of Man/I stare out at the Eiffel Tower my hands covering/my vaginal flaps my own anomaly'. On Baartman's brain, Badou, *Énigme*, 156.

80. Blainville, 'Sur une femme', 187–8; Cuvier, 'Extrait d'observations', 260, 265 ff.; van der Post, *Lost World*, 13.

81. Blainville, 'Sur une femme', 187–8; Cuvier, 'Extrait d'observations', 265.

82. Alexander, *Venus Hottentot*, 5. The poem seems to confuse Baartman with the second Hottentot Venus who appears in the engraving, *The Ball of the Duchess du Barry* (1829 or 1830, reproduced in Gilman, *Sexuality*, 293, plate 299); see above, p. 115 n. 69; the story, if not apocryphal, presumably refers to the duchesse de Berry (Badou, *Énigme*, 127–8).

83. Suzan-Lori Parks *Venus* (New York, 1997); for Cuvier's elevation to the baronage, Dorinda Outram, *Georges Cuvier* (Manchester, 1984), 292; Graham Greene, *The Comedians* (Harmondsworth, 1968), 31.

84. *A Pair of Broad Bottoms*, by William Heath (pl. 11) (BM 11578); see also, *Prospects of Prosperity, or Good Bottoms Going in to Business*, by C. Williams (BM 11580), both reproduced in Altick, *Shows of London*, 271–2; another Broad Bottom print which included the Venus was Heath's *Love at First Sight: or a Pair of Hottentots, with an Addition to the Broad Bottom Family* (BM 11577).

85. (pl. 12) BM 11763.

86. BM 11765, 12702, 12749, 13249, 14637.

87. BM 11577, 11578, 11602, 11748, 11763, 11765, 12702, 13249, 14449, and the print *Fashionables Comparing Notes with the Hottentot Venus*, not in BM (Library of Congress, 1–182); for seventeenth-century images of Cape people, male and female, smoking pipes, evidently an early Hottentot stereotype, see Bassani and Tedeschi, 'Image of the Hottentot', 180, 183 (figs. 23, 26).

88. On smoking and 'savage people', see Sir Walter Ralegh, *The Discoverie of the Large, Rich and Bewtiful Empyre of Guiana* (1596), ed. Neil L. Whitehead (Manchesher, 1997), 55 n. 15; on Hottentots in particular, Schiebinger, *Nature's Body*, 162–3, and fig. 54; *dacha* was reported by Ten Rhyne in 1686 after a visit to the Cape in 1673, Norwich, 'Early Medical Africana', 503.

89. Lithgow on breasts, money-bags, and tobacco, *Totall Discourse*, 378–9 and see above, pp. 100, 107, and nn. 18, 35; for pipe-smoking caricatures, *Knavish Pat—A Tale* (1804), BM 10353; *Young Ireland in Business for Himself* (1846), R. F. Foster, *Paddy & Mr. Punch: Connections in Irish and English History* (London, 1995), 177; *The King of A-Shantee* (1882), the pun on Ashanti emphasizing the African–Irish parallel, L. P. Curtis, Jr., *Apes and Angels: The Irishman in Victorian Caricature* (Washington, 1971), 63.

90. Blainville, 'Sur une femme', 189; Cuvier, 'Extrait d'observations', 263. Blainville also (189) stressed her carnivorous taste in food.

91. Lithgow, *Totall Discourse*, 379; Fitzpatrick, *Ireland before the Union*, 32–3; the drunkenness of Indians was spoken of from the time of the *conquista*, notably in Bernal Díaz's comprehensive diatribe, in *True History of the Conquest of New Spain*, XVII. ccviii, ed. Genaro García, trans. A. P. Maudslay, 5 vols. (Nedeln, 1967), v. 263. Alcohol was often used to placate natives or render them dependent, or would be seen as a native response to suffering, see Philip P. Boucher, *Cannibal Encounters: Europeans and Island Caribs, 1492–1763* (Baltimore, 1992), 43, 47, 73, 101–3, 118, 122, etc., for examples of mostly French Caribbean practices and perceptions.

92. Blainville, 'Sur une femme', 188. Cf. Cuvier, 'Extrait d'observations', 264–5 on her 'teint fort basané' and 'brun-jaunâtre' (yellowish-brown).

93. 'A Ballad', in Edwards and Walvin, *Black Personalities*, 178-81.

94. Altick, *Shows of London*, 269–70.

95. 'Law Intelligence—Court of King's Bench, Saturday Nov. 24', *Morning Post*, 26 Nov. 1810, in Edwards and Walvin, *Black Personalities*, 174–5.

96. Edwards and Walvin, *Black Personalities*, 174, 180, 181.

97. Letter in *Morning Post*, 23 Oct. 1810, cited in Edwards and Walvin, *Black Personalities*, 172.

98. Another Irishman, who adopted the name of 'the legendary Irish giant, O'Brien', retired from exhibition in 1804 and was careful to avoid Byrne's posthumous fate; Altick, *Shows of London*, 42, 26 n. For Mantel's novel, which is a sophisticated exploration of several themes of this book, see above, n. 39.

99. Altick, *Shows of London*, 16, 35, 43, 286, 341.

100. 'Black Bodies', 238–9; *Difference and Pathology*, 92; *Sexuality*, 29.

101. (pl. 13) Richard Newton, *The Full Moon in Eclipse* (8 May 1797), in David Alexander, *Richard Newton and English Caricature of the 1790s* (Manchester, 1998), plate 56 and 135, 156.

102. Thomas Harris, *Hannibal* (1999), ch. 13 (New York, 2000), 106.

103. Gilman's source is stated in 'Black Bodies', 260 n. 29, *Sexuality*, 351 n. 29, to be a German translation of a work by John Grand-Carteret, *Die Erotik in der französischen Karikatur*, trans. Cary von Karwarth and Adolf Neumann (Vienna, 1909), 195. I have been unable to see the image in the only known publicly owned copy, in the Library of the Department of Prints and Drawings, British Museum, to which Professor Gilman kindly directed me (personal letter, 11 Mar. 1996). Since he saw the book there, some time before 1985, the image and surrounding text have been torn out. In *Sexuality* (1989), 296, Gilman cites a copy in a private collection in Ithaca. The French original of Grand-Carteret's book is presumably unpublished (see *Sexuality*, 351 n. 29). The identification of the image as referring to the Hottentot Venus occurs in a source five years earlier than Grand-Carteret, to which Gilman does not refer, Eduard Fuchs, *Das erotische Element in der Karikatur* (Berlin, 1904), 195, plate 145, who describes the image as a German caricature of the beginning of the nineteenth century (pl. 14).

104. Gilman, 'Black Bodies', 238-9, *Difference and Pathology*, 90-2; *Sexuality*, 295-6, still citing Grand-Carteret. On Fuchs, see previous note.

105. Andreas Mielke, personal letter of 5 Mar. 1997. Shakespeare's lines are from *Hamlet*, I. v. 166-7, German trans. in *Shakespeare's Dramatische Werke*, trans. A. W. von Schlegel and L. Tieck, ed. Richard Gosche and Benno Tschischwitz, 8 vols. (Berlin, 1889), iv. 128.

106. Among many caricatures commenting on, or catering to, a national taste for backsides and jokes about them, see the amusing seventeenth-century German print, *Der Weiber Flöhenplag*, in Fuchs, *Das erotische Element*, 135, fig. 103, with two of the flea-plagued women baring their backsides like self-consciously vulgarized Callipygian Venuses.

107. See Ronald Paulson, *Hogarth's Graphic Works* (rev. edn., New Haven, 1970), i, No. 337, ii. 314-16. The engraving was published in the first volume of Samuel Ireland, *Graphic Illustrations of Hogarth*, 2 vols. (London, 1794-9), i. 117-20. See also the 'Third Revised Edition', London, 1989, of *Hogarth's Graphic Works*, 36, where the work is not reproduced, and Paulson, *Hogarth* (New Brunswick, NJ, 1991-3), ii. 69, 113. A later German analogue, *The Greek Rebellion* (c. 1822), signed 'Gilray' and falsely pretending to be by James Gillray (d. 1815), shows Metternich with a telescope, viewing with satisfaction the Turkish Sultan's backside being licked by a British officer, much as a Yahoo herd leader is served by his official favourite (IV. vii. 262, see p. 143): see Mary Lee Townsend, *Forbidden Laughter: Popular Humor and the Limits of Repression in Nineteenth-Century Prussia* (Ann Arbor, 1992), 156, fig. 37.

108. *The Punishment inflicted on Lemuel Gulliver*, in Paulson, *Hogarth's Graphic Works*, 3rd rev. edn., No. 107.

109. *A Proclamation in Lilliput* (22 May 1792), see Alexander, *Richard Newton and English Caricature*, plate 5 and 30-1, 116-7 (Newton also produced twenty plates for an illustrated edition of *Tom Jones*, posthumously published in 1799, see 54); for some uses of *Gulliver's Travels* in caricature, see BM 10019 and variants A-C, 10227 and variants A-B, 10460, 10657; for a readily accessible example, see Altick, *Shows of London*, 259, fig. 82; for an erotic *In Lilliput* by or attributed to Vivan-Denon, representing Gulliver as

a giant phallus among Lilliputians, see Fuchs, *Das erotische Element*, 182, fig. 135.

110. Ploss, Bartels, *et al.*, *Woman*, i. 300–8.

111. Francis Haskell and Nicholas Penny, *Taste and the Antique: The Lure of Classical Sculpture 1500–1900* (New Haven, 1981), 39, 316–18, figs. 20, 21, 168; John Evelyn, *Diary*, 25 Jan. 1645, ed. E. S. de Beer (London, 1959), 162; for a reference to Baartman as a 'Vénus callipyge', see Badou, *Énigme*, 129.

112. (pl. 15) Joseph Grego, *Rowlandson the Caricaturist*, 2 vols. (London, 1880), ii. 217–8; A. P. Oppé, *Thomas Rowlandson: His Drawings and Water Colours* (London, 1923), 52; for Sade, as well as Diderot, on this statue, see Sade, *Œuvres*, ed. Michel Delon and Jean Deprun, 3 vols. (Paris, 1990–8), i. 574, 1267 n., iii. 92, 466, 843, 1448 n., 1516 n.

113. On Cuvier and his artists, see Honour, *Image of the Black*, iv. *From the American Revolution*, ii. 52–5 (and figs. 35, 36), 255 nn. 21–7, 281.

114. Cuvier, 'Extrait d'observations', 265; Blainville, 'Sur une femme', 187.

115. Blainville, 'Sur une femme' 189.

116. Cuvier, 'Extrait d'observations', 263–4, 268–70; Blainville, 'Sur une femme', 183–6.

117. Gilman, *Sexuality*, 293–4.

118. Blainville, 'Sur une femme', 189; Cuvier, 'Extrait d'observations', 263–4, 268–70; Alexander, *Venus Hottentot*, 5–6; Gould, 'The Hottentot Venus', 22; Cuvier specified, however, that the genital apron distinguished her from monkeys, whose nymphae are generally barely visible (268), and he dwells more than Blainville does on some features which resemble human (Negro and Mongol) rather than simian races (264), and he also compared and contrasted her with other races (270 ff.); for other views of the resemblance to simians, see Ploss, Bartels, *et al.*, *Woman*, i. 335. On the other hand, Cuvier also said some features of both Bushmen and Negroes were close to those of female apes and he reported on her animal characteristics ('caractères d'animalité'), and noted that her 'muzzle' was more salient even than that of Negroes (269, 271). Blainville also spoke of her muzzle (183).

119. On earlier theories of the human relationship to apes, see Stepan, *Idea of Race*, 7 ff., 15 ff.

120. See Frantz, 'Swift's Yahoos and the Voyagers', 52, 55–7; Merians, 'What They Are', 21, 29, '"Hottentot"', 123; Ovington, *Voyage to Suratt*, 489; for Herbert and Wafer, see nn. 158, 161. An alternative example of the 'missing link', proposed in Edward Tyson's *Orang-Outang, Sive Homo Sylvestris: or The Anatomy of a Pygmie compared with that of a Monkey, an Ape, and a Man* (1699), was the 'pygmy' (here in the sense of an Angolan chimpanzee). Perceived analogies between Africans and 'the great apes which came out of Africa, and which Europeans encountered at the same time they met the Negro' (Stepan, *Idea of Race*, 8), became a staple of 'scientific' interest, giving rise to a long tradition of anatomical measurements of skull sizes and shapes, facial angles, and brain development (Stepan, *Idea of Race*, 8 ff. and *passim*). On 'missing link' theories, involving Hottentots and Amerindians, and the importance of the 'great chain' (which had formed the basis of Tyson's thought) in the work among others, of the *Encyclopédistes*, see P. J. Marshall and Glyndwr Williams, *The*

Great Map of Mankind (Cambridge, Mass., 1982), 215. But the concept of a 'great chain' 'was not typical of racial science in the late eighteenth century and the early nineteenth century' and Blumenbach, Cuvier, and others repudiated what Prichard called attempts '"to find in the Negro an intermediate link"'; Cuvier called the concept of the great chain '"detrimental to the progress of natural history"' (Stepan, *Idea of Race*, 7–12). It was, however, reactivated in a variant form in later race science, and even its opponents did not dispute the principle of racial gradation, in which comparative relationship to apes played an important part (Stepan, *Idea of Race*, 12–19). For the 'Irish Yahoo' as missing link, see Curtis, *Apes and Angels*, 100.

121. Gould, 'The Hottentot Venus', 22; Buffon, 'Nomenclature of Apes', and 'Orang-Outang', ix. 109—10, 168. A similar story, without racial implications, is told in *Grande sertão: veredas* (1956), by the Brazilian novelist João Guimarães Rosa: a group of starving men capture and eat a monkey whom they subsequently discover to be a naked man (*Ficção completa* (Rio de Janeiro, 1994–5), ii. 40).

122. Cuvier, 'Extrait d'observations', 270–1, 273.

123. Cuvier, 'Extrait d'observations', 270; *Encyclopédie*, xvii (1778), 786, art. 'Hottentots'.

124. Ploss, Bartels, *et al.*, *Woman*, i. 300–8, figs. 268–80; van der Post, *Lost World of the Kalahari*, 30, 34–5; see Stepan, *Idea of Race*, 104, 208 n. 58, on the geographical dispersal of steatopygous features, explained either by migration or, after Edmund Leach, by the hypothesis that morphological similarities might be '"the result of a local adaptation to a similar set of selective pressures"'. For 'La Polichinelle', see Campbell, *The Way of the Animal Powers*, i. 71, fig. 121.

125. Cuvier, 'Extrait d'observations', 269, 271.

126. Cuvier, 'Extrait d'observations', 263–4; see Claude Rawson, 'Gulliver and the Flat-nosed People', *Order from Confusion Sprung* (1985; rptd. London and Atlantic Highlands, NJ, 1992), 68.

127. Cuvier, 'Extrait d'observations', 263; Blainville, 'Sur une femme', 187.

128. Cuvier, 'Extrait d'observations', 264; Swift, 'On the Death of Mrs. Johnson', *Works*, v. 227.

129. *La Donna delinquente*, 10, 331–2, and *passim*. Gilman 'Black Bodies', 248–9; the Ploss compendium cites de Blasio to make the more neutral point that 'semi-steatopygous cases occur in women of Mediterranean race', mentioning two prostitutes in Naples in a discussion of geographical distribution, *Woman*, i. 304–5.

130. Compare the naked profile of de Blasio's steatopygous prostitute ('Black Bodies', 249, fig. 15) with the notional contours of a dress, *c.* 1745–50, on a tailor's dummy in Zillah Halls, *Women's Costumes 1600–1750* (London, 1969), 27, plate 19. On the history of the hoop-petticoat in England (roughly 1709–1820), and its English and European prehistory and afterlife (including the Elizabethan farthingale and the Victorian crinoline), see Kimberly Chrisman, '*Unhoop* the Fair Sex: The Campaign Against the Hoop Petticoat in Eighteenth-Century England', *Eighteenth-Century Studies*, 30 (1996), 5–24. This useful account brings out the paradox of an 'artificial' or 'mechanical' contrivance acting as a mimicry or even as an enhancement of the passional and primitive,

a constraint and sexual barrier, which in its own ways abetted lewdness and drew attention to nudity. On the hoop-petticoat, or panier, see also François Boucher, *20,000 Years of Fashion: The History of Costume and Personal Adornment* (expanded edn., New York, 1987), 295–9, esp. 95–6 and figs. 713–24.

131. Erin Mackie, 'Lady Credit and the Strange Case of the Hoop-Petticoat', *College Literature*, 20/2 (June 1993), 27–43, esp. 36; examples from Fielding, see Claude Rawson, 'Henry Fielding', in *Cambridge Companion to the Eighteenth-Century Novel*, ed. John Richetti (Cambridge, 1996), 124.

132. (pl. 16) *A New Authentic, and Complete Collection of Voyages Round the World Undertaken and Performed by Royal Authority. Containing a … Complete Historical Account of Captain Cook's First, Second, Third and Last Voyages*, ed. George William Anderson (London, 1784), 491–2, fig. facing p. 491, reproduced in a variant form in Mackie, 'Hoop-Petticoat', 28–9; for various versions by Webber, William Ellis, and de Loutherbourg (1777–85), see *Art of Captain Cook's Voyages*, iii (Text), 57, 59, plate 67; iii (Catalogue), 362–5, figs. 3. 106–8, and William Eisler and Bernard Smith (eds.), *Terra Australis: The Furthest Shore* (Sydney, 1988), 142–3, 194–5. For English and French fashionable analogues, see pl. 17, and C. W. and P. Cunnington, *A Handbook of English Costume in the Eighteenth Century* (London, 1957), 114–17, figs. 30, 31; Natalie Rothstein (ed.), *Four Hundred Years of Fashion* (London, 1984), 26–7, fig. 19.

133. Boucher, *20,000 Years of Fashion*, 373 (the French text, *Histoire du costume en occident de l'antiquité à nos jours* (Paris, 1965), 372, reads 'la jupe plus ample dans le dos', i.e. 'back' in the dorsal sense, not the buttocks; programme note, *Venus*, by Suzan-Lori Parks, Yale Repertory Theatre, 14–30 Mar. 1996.

134. See Diana Donald, *The Age of Caricature: Satirical Prints in the Reign of George III* (New Haven, 1996), 84, 94, 100, 103, figs. 91, 103, 109, 112.

135. *Repertorio Americano*, in Pratt, *Imperial Eyes*, 176, fig. 32; on this journal see 172–4.

136. (pls. 18a–c) Horace Walpole, letters to Countess of Upper Ossory, 27 Jan. and 10 Feb. 1786 (Horace Walpole, *Correspondence*, ed. W. S. Lewis *et al*. 48 vols. (New Haven, 1937–83), xxxiii. 512–13, 516–17, where the two drawings are reproduced, as they are, together with the print of 1786, in Donald, *Age of Caricature*, 91, fig. 98. The print is BM 8257, and see 7100). Both the drawings and the print are preserved in Walpole's album of caricatures, now in the New York Public Library. See also Joan Sussler, 'Walpole's "Bosom Friends": Enhancing the Figure of the Mid-1780's', *Essays in Arts and Sciences*, 22 (Oct. 1993), 19–49, esp. 24–30.

137. Sussler, 'Walpole's "Bosom Friends"', 27 ff.; Donald, *The Age of Caricature*, 90–1. On the pouter-pigeon look, see Sussler, 'Walpole's "Bosom Friends"', 35.

138. Sussler, 'Walpole's "Bosom Friends"', 27.

139. Walpole to Sir Horace Mann, 4 May 1786, *Correspondence*, xxv. 641, cited in Sussler, 'Walpole's "Bosom Friends"', 23–4. Compare Lawrence Stone, *The Family, Sex and Marriage in England, 1500–1800* (New York, 1977), 536: 'Elegant women resembled the callipygous [!] statues of prehistoric art.'

140. Sussler, 'Walpole's "Bosom Friends"', 45 n. 14. For Hogarth's composition, see Paulson, *Hogarth's Graphic Works*, 3rd rev. edn., 75–6, 287 (fig. 120). On Diana of Ephesus, see Ploss, Bartels, *et al.*, *Woman*, iii. 218.

141. (pls. 19–20) BM 7112, 7111, 6874. On these prints, see Sussler, 'Walpole's "Bosom Friends"', 24–35, 45 n. 16, 46 n. 23, 47 n. 43, and figs. In *The Bum-Bailiff Outwitted; or the Convenience of Fashion*, also by Stubbs, the entire armature comes off in the bailiff's hands, enabling the lady to escape the law by crawling out from under (BM 7102; Sussler, 'Walpole's "Bosom Friends"', 33–5); for further examples, see references in the entry on BM 7099, a companion print to *The Bum Shop*. Max Beerbohm, *The Iconoclast's One Friend*, in N. John Hall, *Max Beerbohm: Caricatures* (New Haven, 1977), 99, plate 82.

142. 'Beautiful Young Nymph', ll. 21–6, *Poems*, ii. 582.

143. Stone, *Family, Sex and Marriage*, 536; Aileen Ribeiro, *The Art of Dress: Fashion in England and France 1750 to 1820* (New Haven, 1995), 91–4, 150; *Revolution in Fashion: European Clothing, 1715–1815* (New York, 1989) (catalogue of exhibition held at Fashion Institute of Technology), 116, 133–4 and *passim*.

144. *Fashionables Comparing Notes*, see above, n. 87.

145. Mrs Charles Matthews, *Memoirs of Charles Matthews*, cited in Richard Altick, *The Shows of London*, 269.

146. e.g. *McGraw-Hill Nursing Dictionary* (New York, 1979); *International Dictionary of Medicine and Biology* (New York, 1986).

147. Mielke, 'Contextualizing the "Hottentot Venus"', 165.

148. (pl. 9) Lombroso and Ferrero, *La Donna delinquente*, plate II, *Polisarcia in Abissina*; Abyssinian women are evidently the examples of choice for Italians: Ignazio Silone's novel, *Pane e Vino* (Lugano, 1937), 245–6, describes a placard in front of a barber-shop showing Abyssinian women with long breasts coming down to their knees.

149. For an excellent summary account of attitudes to maternal breast-feeding, see Ruth Perry, 'Colonizing the Breast: Sexuality and Maternity in Eighteenth-Century England', *Journal of the History of Sexuality*, 2 (1991), 204–34, esp. 213–24; see also Felicity A. Nussbaum, *Torrid Zones: Maternity, Sexuality and Empire in Eighteenth-Century English Narratives* (Baltimore, 1995), 25–6.

150. Mantel, *The Giant, O'Brien*, ch. 4, pp. 42, 41–51.

151. *Poems*, ii. 721.

152. Badou, *Énigme*, 50; *Neptune's Last Resource*, BM 11748, *Love and Beauty*, BM 14449; Edwards and Walvin, *Black Personalities*, 181–2, citing T. E. Crispe, *Reminiscences of a KC* (1909).

153. Vespucci, *Letters from a New World*, 50, 71; Cuvier, 'Extrait d'observations', 263–4; Forster, *Observations*, 174; Greene, *Journey Without Maps*, p. 53; Unsworth, *Sacred Hunger*, ch. 24, p. 208; Cleland, *Memoirs*, 24; Sade, *Cent Vingt Journées de Sodome*, I.i. *Aline et Valcour*, letter xxxv, in *Œuvres*, i. 47–8, 51–2, 555 and n., 557 and commentary, 1261–2 n.2.

154. Boucé, 'Rape of Gulliver', 103–4.

155. Ploss, Bartels, *et al.*, *Woman*, iii. 340–1.

156. (pl. 2) Ploss, Bartels, *et al.*, *Woman*, iii. 343–6 and figs. 951–2.

157. Herodotus, IV. clxxx; Strabo, VII. iii. 4; Pliny, V. viii. 45. For the people of Seba, see Gilman, 'Black Bodies', 228, 258 n. 10; for a general indictment of the sexual depravities of Amerindians, see Díaz, *Conquest of New Spain*, XVII. ccvii, trans. Maudslay, V. 263–4.

158. Herodotus, IV. clxxx; Herbert, *Some Yeares Travels*, 17, 18.

159. *Encyclopédie*, new edn., xxvi (1779), 620, art. 'POLYGAMIE (*Jurispr.*)'.

160. *A Treatise of Brasil*, from Purchas, xvi. 454, cited in Passmann, '*Full of Improbable Lies*', 201, 434 n. 19; for a fictional example of the interest in the rituals of kingship, see Sade, *Aline et Valcour*, letter xxxv, in *Œuvres*, i. 583 and Delon's note, p. 1269. There is a whole chapter on such rituals across the world in Jean-Nicholas Démeunier, *L'Esprit des usages et des coutumes des différents peuples*, 3 vols. (1776), 1785 edn., I. 293–317.

161. On Hottentots, see Merians, nn. 13, 42, 74 above; on monkeys, *Gulliver's Travels*, ed. Turner, 363 n. 17; Lionel Wafer, *A New Voyage and Description of the Isthmus of America* (1699), 108; 3rd edn. (1729), in *A Collection of Voyages*, 4 vols. (1729), iii. 330, 400; Passmann, '*Full of Improbable Lies*', 193–4 and nn. 30–2; on King Bolo, see T. S. Eliot, *Inventions of the March Hare: Poems 1909–1917*, ed. Christopher Ricks (New York, 1996), 316.

162. Pliny, *Natural History*, VII. xi. 48; Ploss, Bartels, *et al.*, *Woman*, ii. 344, 442–5, 466. Similar restraints are often imposed during lactation, iii. 219–20.

163. See, for example, M. de Cuneo (a member of Columbus's second expedition), in Gerbi, *Nature in the New World*, 33–4; Vespucci, *Letters from a New World*, 32, 49–51, 63–4.

164. On monogamy and sexual abstinence among the Houyhnhnms, see Chapter 1, p. 60.

165. See *Works*, I. 172 and xii. 116. See J. H. Rowe, 'Ethnography and Ethnology in the Sixteenth Century', *Kroeber Anthropological Society Papers*, 30 (1964), 5: 'For most sixteenth century Europeans the classic "savages" came to be the Tupinambá.' It is evident that this continued beyond the sixteenth century. See also Chapter 1, p. 83 and nn. 153–5.

166. Vespucci, *Letters from a New World*, 31, 49 (and see 181 n. 10 on Columbus, contrasting his 'Cannibals' with the Tainos of Hispaniola).

167. Thomas Phillips, 'Journal of a Voyage', cited in Marshall and Williams, *Great Map*, 232.

168. Marshall and Williams, *Great Map*, 280.

169. H. Rider Haggard, *She*, ed. Daniel Karlin, ch. 6 (Oxford, 1991), 80–82; on the kiss of the early Christians, see 325 n. 81, citing Romans 16: 16 and 1 Peter 5: 14.

170. *She*, chs. 20, 7–8, pp. 227, 87–100. Later, She punishes the cannibals, ch. 15, pp. 174–6.

171. Vespucci (pl. 3) *Letters from a New World*, 68; Honour, *New Golden Land*, 88–9; on Eckhout's young woman, see above, p. 104 and n.30, and pl. 7.

172. See *Bougainville et ses compagnons autour du monde 1766–1769*, ed. E. Taillemitte, 2 vols. (Paris, 1977), i. 314 n. 2, 315, ii. 87–8; J. R. Forster, *Resolution Journal*, ii. 302–3, 356–7; Neil Rennie, *Far-Fetched Facts: The Literature of Travel and the Idea of the South Seas* (Oxford, 1995), 86.

173. Bronwen Douglas, 'Science and the Art of Representing "Savages": Reading "Race" in Text and Image in South Seas Voyage Literature', *History and Anthropology*, 11 (1999), 157–201, esp. 180–1; on Dumont d'Urville's and others' discriminations between racial groups, see Bronwen Douglas, 'Art as Ethno-historical Text: Science, Representation and Indigenous Presence in Eighteenth and Nineteenth Century Voyage Literature', in Nicholas Thomas and

Drake Losche (eds.), *Double Vision: Art Histories and Colonial Histories in the Pacific* (Cambridge, 1999), 65–99.

174. Marshall and Williams, *Great Map*, 280, 282–3. A dispute arose after the publication of Bougainville's *Voyage* as to whether syphilis had been introduced to Tahiti by the French, or by the English expedition under Samuel Wallis, which landed in Tahiti in June 1767, several months before Bougainville. See Howard M. Smith, 'The Introduction of Venereal Disease into Tahiti: A Re-Examination', *Journal of Pacific History*, 10/1 (1975), 38–45, which concludes that 'the guilt lies with [Wallis's] crew and with England', and Greg Dening, *Mr. Bligh's Bad Language: Passion, Power and Theatre on the Bounty* (Cambridge, 1992), 267–8: the 'venereals' were a recurrent worry on board ship, subject to a 15s. fine for the surgeon's costs (renewable, since there was no cure), but not, like other transgressions, to flogging, though statistically men with venereal diseases were 'twice as likely to be flogged' as others (27, 63, 116, 122, 126).

175. For wigwams, used of primitive housing outside North America, see *OED*, wigwam, *sb.* b, quotations for 1743 (South Seas), 1793 (Tierra del Fuego); Bernard Smith, *European Vision and the South Pacific*, 99, and, in Australia, *Journal of Arthur Bowes Smyth, . . . 1787–1789*, ed. P. G. Fidlon and R. J. Ryan (Sydney, 1979), 21 Jan. 1788, p. 57, cited in Hughes, *Fatal Shore*, 86.

176. *Bougainville et ses compagnons*, ed. Taillemitte, i. 316, see Chapter 1, p. 83.

177. Vespucci, *Letters from a New World*, 50–1 (*Novus Mundus*), 64, 71 (*Letter* to Soderini).

178. Vespucci, *Letters from a New World*, 11, 32 (first and third letters, 1500 and 1502).

179. Vespucci, *Letters from a New World*, pp. xxi–xxii, 49–50, 63–4.

180. Bucher, *Icon and Conquest*, 10; John Ogilby, *America: Being the Latest, and Most Accurate Description of the New World* (1671), 656–7, cited in Passmann, '*Full of Improbable Lies*', 193, 432 n.29.

181. For literary and folkloric sources or analogues to Gulliver's experiences with giants, see W. A. Eddy, *Gulliver's Travels: A Critical Study* (1923; New York, 1963), 116–44. For the general incidence of giants in books which were or might have been associated with *Gulliver's Travels*, see Passmann, '*Full of Improbable Lies*', 157, 162, 166–82 and 422–8 nn.

182. Giants were a staple not only of Odyssean mythology, but of more modern travel-writing. What Gulliver refers to as the belief 'that there must have been Giants in former Ages' (II. vii. 137) goes back to the Old Testament (Genesis 6: 4; Numbers 13: 32–3). Swift treats it as more or less discredited, though it survived as a *façon de parler*, as in Dryden's 'Theirs was the Gyant Race, before the Flood' ('To my Dear Friend Mr Congreve', 1694, l. 5, *Works of John Dryden*, 20 vols., ed. H. T. Swedenborg *et al.* (Berkeley, 1956–), iv. 432). For Homeric and more recent versions of the belief, see *Gulliver's Travels*, ed. Turner, 336 n. 14. Useful information on sightings of giants in Renaissance travel-writing is found in Gerbi, *Nature in the New World*, 43–4, 47–8, 108–11; for eighteenth-century debates about Patagonian giants, see Gerbi, *The Dispute of the New World: The History of a Polemic, 1750–1900* (1955), trans. Jeremy Moyle (Pittsburgh, 1973), index, s.v. Giants. Travel-writing stimulated the belief in giants distant in space rather than time, especially in Patagonia (land of giants, from Spanish *patagon*,

large foot), about which a mythology developed that outlived Swift's lifetime. For giants in Purchas, of which Swift owned a copy, and elsewhere, see Sherbo, 'Swift and Travel Literature', 116, 123, 127 n. 8. Patagonian giants (making a roaring noise) were sighted recurrently from the time of Magellan to that of John Byron ('grand-dad' of the poet—*Don Juan*, II. cxxxvii), and became a matter of debate in the reign of George III, and the subject of Gulliverian analogy, notably by Horace Walpole, in the 1760s: see Rennie, *Far-Fetched Facts*, 77–8, 83–4; Marshall and Williams, *Great Map*, 261, 268, and 296 n. 20; and 191, for 'giant' Indians in Virginia in Richard Blome's *America* (1687). As early as 1752, Maupertuis made it clear that the issue of Patagonian giants was thought of in France as needing to be examined, alongside the location of *Terra Australis*. Bougainville took a strong stand against John Byron, saying the stature of Patagonians was no more than ordinary. Some giant bones he examined with Commerson turned out in his view to be those of elephants. Observing Patagonians at first hand, he found many of them no taller than himself. Bougainville's scientist Commerson wrote in 1766 of his desire to see giant-sized men uncorrupted by society. The belief in good-natured giants, sometimes coloured with Rousseauistic rather than strictly Brobdingnagian elements, seems to have died hard (see *Bougainville et ses compagnons*, ed. Taillemite, i. 7, 88, 104–5, 118, 250, 268–9 and n. 3; ii. 62). Johnson took a similar view to Bougainville's, from an armchair perspective. Remarking that the age was one 'in which . . . the giants of antiquated romance have been exhibited as realities', he added: 'If we have not searched the Magellanick regions, let us however forbear to people them with Patagons' (*Journey to the Western Islands of Scotland*, ed. Mary Lascelles (New Haven, 1971), 119). For Patagonian giants see also Passmann, *'Full of Improbable Lies'*, 162, 169–73, 423–4 nn.

183. Vespucci, *Letters from a New World*, 13, 82–4, and commentary 174 nn. 31–2, 192 nn. 37–8.

184. *Bougainville et ses compagnons*, ed. Taillemite, i. 88, 268–9 n. 3; for Pigafetta's giantesses, see Gerbi, *Nature in the New World*, 110; Passmann, *'Full of Improbable Lies'*, 174; see 180–1 for an example of a 'first Race of Mortals, which . . . were all Gyants', from whose dimensions and virtues later men were said to have declined.

185. For sexual analogues or near analogues from Cyrano de Bergerac's *Histoire comique de la lune* and from the *Arabian Nights*, see Eddy, *Gulliver's Travels*, 128, 130–1.

186. On Spanish behaviour in this regard, as reported by M. de Cuneo, Bernal Díaz, and others, see Gerbi, *Nature in the New World*, 30, 34; Todorov, *Conquête*, 65–6, 78, 114, 132, 306–7; in eighteenth-century Tahiti, on the other hand, Spaniards were liked because of their 'abstention from sexual commerce', a matter on which Cook was 'sensitive', see Bridget Orr, '"Southern Passions Mix with Northern Art": Miscegenation and the *Endeavour* Voyage', in Jonathan Lamb *et al.* (eds.), *The South Pacific in the Eighteenth Century: Narratives and Myths, Eighteenth Century Life*, NS 18/3 (Nov. 1994), 212–31, esp. 217.

187. Cuneo, see Gerbi, *Nature in the New World*, 34; Bartolomé de Las Casas, *A Short Account of the Destruction of the Indies*, trans. Nigel Griffin (London, 1992), 74, discussed in Chapter 1, p. 87 and n. 164.

188. Pocahontas, see Bucher, *Icon and Conquest*, 10; Ralegh, *Discoverie*, 51–2, 100–1 (165, 199); on Spaniards trading in young girls for large profits, 33–4 (153).

189. A replay of several Gulliverian motifs occurred when Governor Arthur Phillip's fleet landed at Botany Bay in January 1788, where the Aborigines were mystified by the breeches worn by his men and took them for women (their beards not being grown) until one of them 'undeceived' them and received, like Gulliver in Lilliput (I. iii. 42), 'a great shout of Admiration'. The native women, 'all in puris naturalibus', and of course 'with infant children on their shoulders', were offered to the visitors. Lieutenant Philip King, whose journal reports this, and who himself later became Governor, tersely adds 'however I declined' (*Journal of Philip Gidley King*, ed. P. G. Fidlon and R. J. Ryan (Sydney, 1980), 34–5, entry for 20 Jan. 1788, cited in Hughes, *Fatal Shore*, 85, 618 n. 4).

190. Henry Reynolds, *The Other Side of the Frontier: An Interpretation of the Aborigine Response to the Invasion and Settlement of Australia* (Townsville, 1981), ch. 5, 'The Politics of Contact', esp. 108–10. For customs and rituals involving the offer of wives to white men as well as some intertribal exchanges of wives among Australian aborigines, see A. P. Elkin, *The Australian Aborigines* (rev. edn., Sydney, 1979), 159–62, cited in Hughes, *Fatal Shore*, 16, 613 n. 25.

191. Lilliputian intimations, mainly involving the size of Gulliver's phallus and the fact that Lilliputians are themselves six inches tall, occur at I. iii. 42, vi. 57, 65–6; see Boucé, 'Rape of Gulliver', 101–2.

192. For Plato's eugenics, see *Republic*, V. 458D–461C.

193. The relevant *OED* definitions of race, *sb*², 2c, 'A group of several tribes or peoples, regarded as forming a distinct ethnical stock', and 2d, 'One of the great divisions of mankind, having certain physical peculiarities in common', give first recorded usages of 1842 and 1774 respectively. Sense 2b, 'A tribe, nation, or people, regarded as of common stock', first recorded in 1600, is used by Swift to refer to 'the whole Race' of Houyhnhnms, twice on the same page as the one in which he uses the more limited sense, 6a, 'Denoting the stock, family, class, etc. to which a person . . . belongs', which dates from 1559, to refer to the specific social group known as 'the Race of inferior *Houyhnhnms* bred up to be Servants', presumably one of the various colour-coded classes (IV. viii. 268). For an important discussion, see Nicholas Hudson, 'From "Nation" to "Race": The Origin of Racial Classification in Eighteenth-Century Thought', *Eighteenth-Century Studies*, 29 (1996), 247–64.

194. For some interesting perspectives on this, see the career of Cabeza de Vaca, who spent years of captivity, practised starvation cannibalism, and returned to high office and social respect, though his closing years were clouded by unrelated litigation, Rolena Adorno and Patrick Charles Pautz, *Álvar Núñez Cabeza de Vaca: His Account, His Life, and the Expedition of Pánfilo de Narváez*, 3 vols. (Lincoln, Neb., 1999), i. 14–279 (*Relación*, 1542), and 293–413 (biography); on the much fabularized case of Gonzalo Guerrero, the subject of a famous account by Bernal Díaz (*Conquest of New Spain*, II. xxvii, xxix, liv, trans. Maudslay, i. 95–6, 102, 195), see Hugh Thomas, *Conquest of Mexico* (London, 1993), 57, 163–4, 180–1, and, for a strong contention that Guerrero

was a mythologized but invented figure, Rolena Adorno, 'La Estatua de Gonzalo Guerrero en Akumal: Íconos Culturales y la Reactualización del Pasado Colonial', *Revista Iberoamericana*, 62 (1996), 905–23; for discussion of these and other cases, see Todorov, *Conquête*, 130–1, 246–53, 275–6, and the chapter on the *métissage* of Diego Durán, 254–74, esp. 264–6, 274; on the twinned figures of Jeronimo de Aguilar, who allowed himself to be reabsorbed, and Guerrero, who, if he existed, did not, see 130, 146–7, and Stephen Greenblatt, *Marvelous Possessions: The Wonder of the New World* (Chicago, 1991), 140–1.

195. See Frank Lestringant, 'Going Native in America (French-Style)', *Renaissance Studies*, 6 (1992), 326–35.

196. Montaigne, *Essais*, i. 214, 205 (159, 151–2); see also Janet Whatley, introduction and commentary to Jean de Léry, *History of a Voyage to the Land of Brazil*, trans. Janet Whatley (Berkeley, 1990), pp. xix, xxxi, 235 n. 3, and index, s.v. Interpreters; where strong disapproval is expressed, it tends to be on grounds of apostasy, and much use was made of these men; see also Lestringant, 'Going Native', 331 ff.

197. For a recent discussion of this aspect, see Rennie, *Far-Fetched Facts*, 141–80; on aspects of the contemporaneity of the *Bounty* affair and the French Revolution, see also Dening, *Mr. Bligh's Bad Language*, 39, 247 ff.

198. Rennie, *Far-Fetched Facts*, 177 ff.

199. Dening, *Mr. Bligh's Bad Language*, 48, 250.

200. Dening, *Mr. Bligh's Bad Language*, 8, 83, 311, 217–18, 319 (and documentation, 390–5); on the matter of shipboard grievances, Dening reports with strong statistical support that floggings on the *Bounty* were much more infrequent than on any other British ship in the Pacific (*Mr. Bligh's Bad Language*, 62 ff., 381 ff.).

201. Dening, *Mr. Bligh's Bad Language*, 257–62, esp. 258, 260–1; on Heywood's connections and pardon, see 40–6.

202. Coetzee, 'Blood, Taint, Flaw, Degeneration: The Novels of Sarah Gertrude Millin', *White Writing*, 136–62, esp. 143 ff.

203. Coetzee, *White Writing*, 143 (citing Stepan, *Idea of Race*, 105–7), 158, 160–1. Sarah Gertrude Millin, *King of the Bastards* (New York, 1949), 26; *God's Stepchildren* (New York, 1924), 16–17.

204. Coetzee, *White Writing*, 157, 153.

205. Coetzee, *White Writing*, 150 ff., 156, 151 n.

206. On these verbal slippages, see Rawson, *Gulliver and the Gentle Reader*, 19 ff.

207. Jacques Ramin, *Le Périple d'Hannon/The Periplus of Hanno*, British Archaeological Reports, Suppl. Ser. 3 (Oxford, 1976), 120; Will Robinson, reproduced in Smith, *Imagining the Pacific*, 62, plate 55.

208. Paul Scarron, *Roman Comique*, I. iii, in *Romanciers du XVIIe Siècle*, ed. Antoine Adam (Paris, 1958), 536.

209. Edward Long, *Candid Reflections upon the Judgement ... On What is Commonly Called the Negroe-cause* (1772), 48–9; Sharp's copy, Yale Ntg45 G 772 L.

210. *Roman Comique*, I. iv, in *Romanciers du XVIIe siècle*, 540.

211. Voltaire, *Candide*, ch. 16; on this episode, see Claude Rawson, 'Savages Noble and Ignoble', in Jonathan Lamb *et al.* (eds.), *The South Pacific in the Eighteenth Century*, 194.

212. See Curtis, *Apes and Angels, passim*; Stepan, *Idea of Race*, 100, 208 n. 45.

213. Stepan, *Idea of Race* 7 ff. On the Locke–Stillingfleet controversy, see Rosalie L. Colie, 'Gulliver, the Locke–Stillingfleet Controversy, and the Nature of Man', *History of Ideas Newsletter*, 2 (1956), 58–62.

214. Stepan, *Idea of Race*, 59. Monboddo, *Of the Origin and Progress of Language*, i (2nd edn., Edinburgh, 1774), 188, 254–5, 270–361 *passim*.

215. Stepan, *Idea of Race*, 1–4, 29.

216. Léon Poliakov, *The Aryan Myth: A History of Racist and Nationalist Ideas in Europe*, trans. Edmund Howard (New York, 1974), 7–8; for a penetrating account, stressing the post-biblical character of efforts to identify the three brothers with specific continents and to justify the enslavement of descendants of Ham, see Benjamin Braude, 'The Sons of Noah and the Construction of Ethnic and Geographical Identities in the Medieval and Early Modern Periods', *William and Mary Quarterly*, 54 (1997), 103–42.

217. Henry Gee, 'How Humans Behaved before they Behaved like Humans', *London Review of Books*, 31 Oct. 1996, 36.

218. Marshall and Williams, *Great Map*, 35, 249, 136; for the prevalence of the monogenetic view, and the impulse to challenge it, in the eighteenth century, see 35–7, 136, 187–8, 241–50, 281.

219. Marshall and Williams, *Great Map*, 35–7, 242–50.

220. Buffon, 'Nomenclature of Apes', ix. 137; Marshall and Williams, *Great Map*, 248–50; Laura Brown, *Ends of Empire: Women and Ideology in Early Eighteenth-Century English Literature* (Ithaca, NY, 1993), 189–95; Long, *History of Jamaica*, ii. 365; on Himmler, Robert Jay Lifton, *The Nazi Doctors* (New York, 1986), 279 n.

221. Forster, *Observations* (1996), 174; Long, *History of Jamaica*, ii. 371.

222. Long, *History of Jamaica*, ii, 351–83, esp. 359–60, 364, 370, 383; Marshall and Williams, *Great Map*, 248–9.

223. *Encyclopédie*, xxii (1779), 841. It is apposite to recall that the word *mulatto* is derived from *mule*, an interesting example of the assimilation of an arguably cross-specific into a cross-racial category. Mules, the offspring of a he-ass and a mare, are 'ordinarily incapable of procreation' (*OED*). For the idea that people of different race could not interbreed, or only imperfectly, or that the half-breed products of such unions were infertile, see Stepan, *Idea of Race*, 95, 105–6.

224. On this, and on the decline of 'scientific racism' in the twentieth century, see Stepan, *Idea of Race*, and Elazar Barkan, *The Retreat of Scientific Racism: Changing Concepts of Race in Britain and the United States between the World Wars* (Cambridge, 1992).

225. See Stepan, *Idea of Race*, and Barkan, *Retreat of Scientific Racism, passim*; for eighteenth- and early nineteenth-century examples, see Stepan, *Idea of Race* 37–8.

226. Francis Leguat, *New Voyage* (1708), 189; cited in MacKinnon, 'The Augustan Intellectual', 61, 63 n. 13.

227. Lady Mary Wortley Montagu, *Complete Letters*, ed. Robert Halsband, 3 vols. (Oxford, 1965), i. 427, iii. 15 (letters to Abbé Conti, 31 July 1718, and Countess of Bute, 22 July 1752, in MacKinnon, 'The Augustan Intellectual', 56, 62. nn.).

228. Long, *History of Jamaica*, ii. 377, cited in Brown, *Ends of Empire*, 192.

229. Aphra Behn, *Oroonoko*, ed. Joanna Lipking (New York, 1997), 52.

230. See Gilman, 'Black Bodies', *passim*.

231. Lombroso and Ferrero, *La Donna delinquente*, 554.

232. Brown, *Ends of Empire*, p. 47, and *passim*; Lévi-Strauss, *Saudades do Brasil*, 140 (lapdog), 141, 154 (monkeys); for an early image, see Honour, *New Golden Land*, 14, plate 9*a*, from Hans Burkmair, *The Triumph of Maximilian I* (1526).

233. See Carol J. Adams and Josephine Donovan (eds.), *Animals and Women: Feminist Theoretical Explorations* (Durham, NC, 1995), *passim* (65–7 on forced couplings); *Times Literary Supplement*, 7 June 1996, 16 (NB column, by D.S.); for reflections on racism and speciesism in J. M. Coetzee, *The Lives of Animals* (Princeton, 1999), see below, chapter 4, n. 11.

234. Juvenal, XV. 1–6, 70 ff., 159 ff.

235. Lévi-Strauss, *Saudades do Brasil*, 149.

236. There are interesting discussions of 'nursing', with a psychobiographical emphasis, in Carol Houlihan Flynn, *The Body in Swift and Defoe* (Cambridge, 1990), 100–9, and Boucé, 'Rape of Gulliver', 102–3.

237. Brown, *Ends of Empire*, 183–6, 172–4, 182, 196–8.

238. Brown, *Ends of Empire*, 195–8, 188. *Purchas His Pilgrimes*, 5 vols. (1625), i. 77–9; Long, *History of Jamaica*, ii. 364 (also 359–60, 383), but Long also spoke of 'amorous intercourse' between Negroes and orann-outangs without specifying that the traffic was only one way (ii. 370). The *Code noir . . . concernant les esclaves nègres des isles françaises de l'Amérique*, promulgated by Louis XIV in 1685, and still cited almost a century later in the *Encyclopédie*, makes a slave-owner liable to a fine of 2,000 lb. of sugar and confiscation of the slave and children, if he fathers children on a female slave, unless he marries her; a free man, if not the owner, pays the fine only; the idea of a transaction in the opposite direction is so disconnected from reality that it does not even rate a mention, though marriages between slaves and non-slaves are provided for, presumably assuming both parties to be of the same race, *Code noir*, arts. IX, XIII (Paris, 1743), 6–8; *Encyclopédie*, new edn., xxii (1779), 846–7, art. 'NEGRES, considérés comme esclaves dans les colonies d'Amérique'. Stories of white ladies and Moors have an established ancestry, but carried an atmosphere of the exotic. They represent common anxieties rather than social facts; see Eldred Jones, *Othello's Countrymen: The African in English Renaissance Drama* (London, 1965); A. G. Barthelemy, *Black Face, Maligned Race: The Representation of Blacks in English Drama from Shakespeare to Southerne* (Baton Rouge, La., 1969); and Elliot H. Tokson, *The Popular Image of the Black Man in English Drama, 1550–1688* (Boston, 1982). The traditional anxieties about black sexuality led to familiar codes of representation: e.g. Honour, *Image of the Black*, iv. *From the American Revolution to World War I*, ii. 182: 'Black men were . . . seldom shown in physical contact with white women in nineteenth-century art', and films were forbidden to show 'equivocal situations' between white women and non-white men in cinemas throughout the British Empire until the 1950s.

239. Brown, *Ends of Empire*, 198, 183, 186.

240. *Works*, i. 77.

241. The conscientious evenhandedness as between male and female occurs also in less charged passages, including the account of 'the small Collection of Rarities' Gulliver had assembled in Brobdingnag to bring back to England. It was clearly impracticable in this instance to attempt to bring back whole natives, as he wished to do in Book I, and his list includes the comb made from the king's beard, and another using the queen's thumbnail, a corn from 'a Maid of Honour's Toe ... about the Bigness of a *Kentish* Pippin', from which he made a cup set in silver, and a footman's tooth, 'about a Foot long, and four Inches in Diameter' (II. viii. 146–7).

242. Gilman, 'Black Bodies', 238, *Sexuality*, 295–6; for an almost identical case of tendentious misreading, similarly overlooking a white man's simian features in order to represent his perspective as authorial, see Daniel Karlin's introduction to Haggard's *She*, pp. xxiii–xxvi.

243. Marjorie Perloff, 'Tolerance and Taboo: Modernist Primitivisms and Postmodernist Pieties', in Barkan and Bush (eds.), *Prehistories of the Future*, 340 (see the whole essay, 339–54).

244. Marshall Sahlins, in 'Cannibalism: An Exchange', *New York Review of Books*, 22 Mar. 1979, 47; Pierre Vidal-Naquet, *Assassins of Memory: Essays on the Denial of the Holocaust*, trans. Jeffrey Mehlman (New York, 1992), 7–8.

245. *Tale of a Tub*, IX, *Works*, i. 109–10.

Chapter 3. Killing the Poor: An Anglo-Irish Theme?

1. Oscar Wilde, *The Soul of Man Under Socialism* (hereafter *SMS*), in *The Artist as Critic: Critical Writings of Oscar Wilde*, ed. Richard Ellmann (New York, 1969), 256 (all quotations are from this edition). The occasion may have been, as Stanley Weintraub suggests, a lecture by Walter Crane on 'Prospects of Art Under Socialism' on 6 July 1888, at which Wilde and Shaw both spoke. According to *The Star*, 7 July 1888, 'Mr. Oscar Wilde, whose fashionable coat differed widely from the picturesque bottle-green garb in which he appeared in earlier days, thought that the art of the future would clothe itself not in works of form and colour but in literature ... Mr. Shaw agreed with Mr. Wilde that literature was the form which art would take', Bernard Shaw, *The Diaries 1885–1897*, ed. Stanley Weintraub (University Park, Pa., 1998), i. 392. Nearer the time of Wilde's essay, on 19 Sept. 1890, Shaw himself gave a Fabian lecture on 'Socialism and Human Nature' which seems to me also to contain material germane to Wilde's work, though Shaw does not report Wilde's presence on that occasion, *Diaries*, i. 650–1; the text of this lecture is reproduced in Bernard Shaw, *The Road to Equality: Ten Unpublished Lectures and Essays, 1884–1918*, ed. Louis Crompton and Hilayne Cavanaugh (Boston, 1971), 89–102. That the occasion was a lecture on Socialism by Shaw himself (not Crane), moreover, is suggested by Shaw's later recollection of 'a meeting somewhere in Westminster at which I delivered an address on Socialism, and at which Oscar turned up and spoke. Robert Ross surprised me greatly by telling me, long after Oscar's death, that it was this address of mine

that moved Oscar to try his hand at a similar feat by writing The Soul of Man Under Socialism' ('Oscar Wilde: A letter to Frank Harris, published by him in his Life of Wilde, 1918', in *Pen Portraits and Reviews* (London, 1931), 300).

2. Bernard Shaw, *The Intelligent Woman's Guide to Socialism, Capitalism, Sovietism and Fascism* (London, 1937), ii. 455 (ch. 86, originally 84, 'Peroration', dated 16 Mar. 1927, though the book was first published in 1928).

3. *Prose Works of Jonathan Swift*, ed. Herbert Davis *et al.* (Oxford, 1939–1974), xiii. 139, referred to as *Works*; Swift's *Proposal for Giving Badges to the Beggars* is abbreviated as *PBB* in page references to this volume.

4. Wilde, 'The Critic as Artist, II', *The Artist as Critic*, 386.

5. Elizabeth Bishop, *Complete Poems, 1927–1979* (New York, 1995), 190, she speaks of the 'ghastly' in this poem in two letters (*One Art: Letters*, ed. Robert Giroux (New York, 1994), 629, 632.

6. Ezra Pound, *Personae: Collected Shorter Poems* (London, 1952), 93; the phrase about the poor being always with us presumably originates in John 12:8.

7. Irvin Ehrenpreis, *Swift: The Man, His Works, and the Age*, 3 vols. (London, 1962–83), iii. 815. Swift very seldom signed his writings. Much earlier, on 27 May 1713, Swift referred to his *Proposal for Correcting... The English Tongue* (1712), as 'the only thing I ever published with my name' (*Correspondence*, i, ed. David Woolley (Frankfurt, 1999), 497). See *Works*, iv. 21.

8. Laws prescribing that an idle beggar should be whipped and sent 'to the place where he was borne, or where he last dwelled before the same punysshement by the space of iij yeres' existed as far back as the sixteenth century, 22 Hen. VIII, c. 12 (1530–1), 27 Henry VIII. c. 25 (1535–6), and 39 Eliz., c. 4 (1597–8), *Statutes of the Realm: Printed by Command of His Majesty George the Third* (Buffalo, NY, 1993), III. 329, 558; IV. ii. 899.

9. *A Modest Proposal*, in Swift, *Works*, xii. 114, subsequently abbreviated *MP*; Harriet Beecher Stowe, *Uncle Tom's Cabin*, ch. 10, New American Library (New York, 1966), 113–14: 'tol'able fast, ther dying is... so as to keep the market up pretty brisk.'

10. Fielding, *Covent-Garden Journal*, No. 11, 8 Feb. 1752, ed. Bertrand A. Goldgar, Wesleyan Edition (Oxford, 1988), 79–84.

11. 'Maxims Controlled in Ireland', *Works*, xii. 135–6.

12. Bernard Mandeville, 'An Essay on Charity and Charity-Schools', *Fable of the Bees*, ed. F. B. Kaye (Oxford, 1924), i. 253–322 and introduction, i. pp. lxix–lxxi; ed. Phillip Harth (Harmondsworth, 1970), 261–325 and introduction, 34–9; for Swift's less robust reservations, see *Works*, ix. 129–30, 136, 202–5; on maximizing the servant population, and the education of those destined for servant roles, see *Gulliver's Travels*, I. vi. 62–3, IV. vi. 256, viii. 268. For Hannah More, see William Roberts, *Memoirs of the Life and Correspondence of Mrs. Hannah More* (London, 1834), iii. 133, iv. 173–6.

13. *Works*, ix. 195.

14. James Boswell, *No Abolition of Slavery; or the Universal Empire of Love: A Poem* (London, 1791), esp. 21–4; for a later comparison of the joys of slavery and of amorous enslavement, see Jean Paulhan, 'Le Bonheur dans l'esclavage', introduction to 'Pauline Réage', *Histoire d'O* (Paris, n.d.), pp. v–xxvii. Carlyle, a thinker close to Shaw on some issues discussed in this chapter, offers perhaps

the most extravagant version, in an angry fantasia, 'The Nigger Question' (1849), which, as we shall see, shares preoccupations with poverty, idleness, Ireland, race, and the work ethic: 'In regard to West-Indian affairs, . . . Lord John Russell is able to comfort us with one fact, indisputable where so many are dubious, That the Negros are all very happy and doing well. A fact very comfortable indeed. West-Indian Whites, it is admitted, are far enough from happy' (*The Works of Thomas Carlyle*, Centenary Edition, 30 vols. (London, 1896–99), xxix. 349).

15. The phrase, widely publicized at the time of Rhodesia's unilaterally declared independence, seems an ironically unwitting echo of William Burchell's account in 1812 of the South African Hottentots as apparently 'the happiest of mortals'. Burchell's description is quoted and discussed by J. M. Coetzee, 'Idleness in South Africa', *White Writing: On the Culture of Letters in South Africa* (New Haven, 1988), 32–3. In the prose poem 'Assommons les pauvres', Baudelaire speaks with contempt of once reading books by promoters of public happiness who advise the poor to become slaves, or who assure them they are all unthroned kings: *Œuvres complètes*, ed. Y.-G. Le Dantec, rev. Claude Pichois (Paris, 1968), 304–5.

16. Oscar Wilde, *Plays, Prose Writings and Poems*, introd. Terry Eagleton (London, 1991), p. xxii.

17. See *OED*, Individualism 2 and quotations; *An Unsocial Socialist* (1884), introd. Michael Holroyd (London, 1980), ch. 12, p. 165. See also Upton Sinclair, *The Jungle* (1906), ch. 30, introd. Ronald Gottesman (New York, 1985), 386–7. Sinclair's novel appeared in time to be mentioned in the Preface to *Major Barbara* (1905; Preface, June 1906), in *The Bodley Head Bernard Shaw* (London, 1970–4), iii. 36, 38, 52, and obviously had an impact on Shaw, as well as Brecht. See p. 242. Quotations from *Major Barbara* and its Preface are from this edition, abbr. *MB* and *MBP*.

18. *An Unsocial Socialist*, 164–5. See *Everybody's Political What's What*, ch. 21 (London, 1944), 173–4, where sentiments and emphases are expressed to the effect that poverty extinguishes genius, where, as in Wilde, a list of geniuses is provided (which includes 'my astonishing self'), but where the statement that 'the notion of educating every Jack and Jill to be a genius remains too silly to be discussed' may conflict with Wilde's assertion that every man has his own perfection.

19. 'Our Lost Honesty', in *Road to Equality*, pp. xv, 1–17.

20. *Road to Equality*, 90. The king is cited again on 93.

21. For Shaw's interest in and admiration for Swift, see the many references in the *Collected Letters*, ed. Dan H. Laurence (London, 1972–88), as well as in many of his published writings. On the King of Brobdingnag, in addition to the passage from 'Socialism and Human Nature', see *John Bull's Other Island* (1904), Act III, where Larry alludes to 'making two blades of wheat [*sic*] grow where one grew before', *Bodley Head Bernard Shaw*, ii. 951–2; *Intelligent Woman's Guide*, ch. 40, i. 157–8; letter to Laurentia McLachlan, St Patrick's Day, 1931, *Collected Letters*, iv. 233–4; *Everybody's Political What's What*, 1. Wilde's Swiftian connections, on the other hand, seem slight. Ellmann says his maternal great-great-grandfather, Dr Kingsbury, was a friend of Swift, and Wilde's father, Sir William

Wilde, 'published a short, valuable book to prove that the great satirist in his last years was not insane but physically ill' (*Oscar Wilde* (London, 1988), 6, 10).

22. Quoted by Michael Holroyd, *Bernard Shaw* (New York, 1988–92), iii. 40, from the *Clarion*, 17 July 1914, 4; letter to Mrs Pakenham Beatty, 11 Sept. 1886, *Collected Letters*, i. 160.

23. *PBB* 135, and 'Causes of the Wretched Condition of Ireland'; 'On the Poor Man's Contentment' (*Works*, ix. 206, 191).

24. Wilde, 'The Critic as Artist, II', *The Artist as Critic*, 386.

25. 'Doing Good: A Sermon', *Works*, ix. 232–3.

26. 'Causes of the Wretched Condition of Ireland', *Works*, ix. 209.

27. e.g. *Works*, ix. 206–7, v. 233.

28. Flaubert to Louise Colet, 9 Dec. 1952, *Correspondance*, ed. Jean Bruneau (Paris, 1973–), ii. 203.

29. Holroyd, *Bernard Shaw*, ii. 104–5.

30. Martin Esslin, *Brecht: A Choice of Evils* (4th edn., London, 1985), 50.

31. *An Unsocial Socialist*, ch. 5, pp. 68–77, Appendix, 254–9, esp. 257.

32. *Socialism for Millionaires* (1896–1901), *Essays in Fabian Socialism* (London, 1932), 113–15.

33. *OED* Sturdy *a.* and *sb.*, A.II. 5c, with quotations from 1402 onwards; see also Beggar *sb.*, 1b, Valiant *a.*, 1b, and quotations.

34. See above, n. 8; 39 Eliz., c. 4 (1597–8), 'An Acte for punyshment of Rogues Vagabonds and Sturdy Beggars', in *Statutes of the Realm*, IV. ii. 899–902, esp. 900. The latter is cited by Robert Hughes, *The Fatal Shore* (New York, 1988), 40, as the origin of the transportation system. The distinction of Tudor legislators between the 'able-bodied' and 'impotent' unemployed remained active, with more humane lineaments, in later times, and the Whately Commission for an Irish Poor Law in the 1830s contemplated 'systematic emigration at the public expense for families willing to go to America. For men convicted of vagrancy, stern measures were proposed, including national penitentiaries and compulsory deportation to a new country' (Sidney and Beatrice Webb, *English Poor Law History. Part II: The Last Hundred Years* (1929; Hamden, Conn., 1963), ii. 1027.

35. 'As one reads history . . . one is absolutely sickened, not by the crimes that the wicked have committed, but by the punishments that the good have inflicted; *and a community is infinitely more brutalised by the habitual employment of punishment, than it is by the occurrence of crime*' (*SMS* 267). Cf. Charles's comment in the Epilogue to Shaw's *Saint Joan* (1923), *Bodley Head Bernard Shaw*, vi. 197, 'it is always you good men that do the big mischiefs'.

36. Bernard Shaw, *Imprisonment* (1922), in *Doctors' Delusions, Crude Criminology and Sham Education* (London, 1932), 231–2.

37. Bernard Shaw, *How to Settle the Irish Question* (Dublin and London, 1917), Introductory Note, 5; ch. 1, p. 9, reprinted in *The Matter with Ireland*, ed. Dan H. Laurence and David H. Greene (New York, 1962), 142, 145.

38. Shaw, *How to Settle the Irish Question*, ch. 1, p. 10. Shaw goes on (10–11; *Matter*, 146) to advise the arming of police stations and other displays of force. If anyone doubts Shaw's exact sentiments, the following anecdote may be cited, about 'the Scottish officer who said to me impatiently the other day, "Oh, let us

give the wretched place [Ireland] its independence, and make it a foreign Power. Then we can conquer it and treat it as a conquered country..." That Scot was a man after my own heart' (ch. 3, p. 31; *Matter*, 162).

39. *Saint Joan*, Preface, 59–60. On the Irish subtexts of *Saint Joan*, see Declan Kiberd, *Inventing Ireland* (Cambridge, Mass., 1996), 418–39.

40. *Everybody's Political What's What*, ch. 32, pp. 289–90.

41. *Everybody's Political What's What*, 291.

42. In the Fabian lecture, 'Socialism and Human Nature' (19 Sept. 1890), which may have been the immediate trigger for Wilde's *Soul of Man Under Socialism* (see above, n. 1), Shaw offered the canine analogy with a different spin: 'If all dogs were constantly chained, there would be a great prevalence of the opinion that all dogs were fierce brutes, only fit to be shot. Living, as I do, among chained men, I am not surprised to find the same opinion rife as regards mankind. And just as the ferocity of the chained dog makes people afraid to let him loose; so the ferocity of the chained man makes us similarly dubious of the wisdom of unchaining him.' Shaw proposes instead a Social Democracy in which we do not shrink from or suppress the selfish instincts, 'the pressure of self-interest', but make use of them in what may be described as a species of neo-Hobbesian accommodations, in which the oppressed make clear to their masters, as one does to a child, that they cannot have everything their own way, 'simply refusing to put up any longer with the Arrogance, the Covetousness, the Lust, the Anger, the Gluttony, the Envy, and the Sloth of their present masters'. Interestingly, Shaw took as his text the King of Brobdingnag's little odious vermin speech, agreeing with the king that the human vices were bad, but claiming that the human virtues, 'fraternity, truth, justice, love, self-sacrifice, duty, religion, and chastity,...do a great deal more harm...since the virtuous malefactors are praised and encouraged, whereas the vicious ones are punished and made infamous' (*Road to Equality*, 89–102, esp. 93, 96, 99–100, 90, and Introduction, pp. xviii–xix).

43. Anne Crowther, 'Penal Peepshow: Bentham's Prison that Never Was', *TLS* 23 Feb. 1996, 4; see *The Panopticon Writings*, ed. Miran Božovič (London, 1995).

44. Holroyd, *Bernard Shaw*, ii. 115–16, 263; citing Shaw, 'What I Think of the Minority Report', *Christian Commonwealth*, 29 (30 June 1909), 685.

45. Holroyd, *Bernard Shaw*, ii. 263.

46. *Essays in Fabian Socialism*, 115.

47. Baudelaire, *Œuvres complètes*, 304–6, 1618 nn. In a related, and even more ambivalent, prose poem, 'Les yeux des pauvres' (1864), a man and two children, dressed in rags, gaze in wonder at the new corner café in which Baudelaire and his mistress are sitting. The poet feels pity and looks for a corresponding sentiment in her eyes, but she says she finds these people insufferable, with their eyes gaping like gates, and asks for them to be moved away. The poet is shocked, by this and by his lack of communication with his lover. The story is told to explain why Baudelaire hates the woman that day: she is the finest example one could ever meet of female imperviousness ('le plus bel exemple d'imperméabilité féminine'), though his own shocked sense of this imperviousness carries a note of appreciation which competes with his moral feelings (268–9, 1611–12 nn.)

48. 'Pen Pencil and Poison', in *The Artist as Critic*, 339, 324, and Richard Ellmann's introduction, pp. xxi–xxiii.

49. Seamus Heaney, *An Open Letter* (Derry, 1983), 9.

50. *The Letters of Oscar Wilde*, ed. Rupert Hart-Davis (New York, 1962), 332, 339 (23 Feb. and 9 May 1893).

51. *Collected Letters*, i. 210, 222–3, 480 (letters of 9 May and 31 Aug. 1889, and 30 Jan. 1895); Holroyd, *Bernard Shaw*, iii. 191 (citing notice of *An Ideal Husband*, in *Saturday Review*, 12 Jan. 1895).

52. Holroyd, *Bernard Shaw*, iii. 191; see iii. 189–94 for a lively portrait of relations between the two.

53. Shaw, *Collected Letters*, iv. 499. On the subject of Wilde's 'Irish charm', see the more measured, as well as more affectionate, comment in 'Oscar Wilde: A Letter to Frank Harris', *Pen Portraits and Reviews*, 303–4: 'I was in no way predisposed to like him: he was my fellow-townsman, and a very prime specimen of the sort of fellow-townsman I most loathed: to wit, the Dublin snob. His Irish charm, potent with Englishmen, did not exist for me; and on the whole it may be claimed for him that he got no regard from me that he did not earn.

'What first established a friendly feeling in me was, unexpectedly enough, the affair of the Chicago anarchists, whose Homer you constituted yourself by your story called The Bomb. I tried to get some literary men in London, all heroic rebels and sceptics on paper, to sign a memorial asking for the reprieve of these unfortunate men. The only signature I got was Oscar's. It was a completely disinterested act on his part; and it secured my distinguished consideration for him for the rest of his life.' For an even more unequivocal tribute to Wilde, which appeared in the *Neue Freie Presse*, Vienna, 23 Apr. 1905, see *The Matter with Ireland*, 28–32.

54. Bernard Shaw, 'Irish Nonsense about Ireland', *New York Times*, 9 Apr. 1916; 'The Children of the Dublin Slums', *The Star*, 4 June 1918; both in *The Matter with Ireland*, 103, 163, 166.

55. On the special usage in 'Black English vernacular', see *OED*, s.v. Negro 1a; compare the use of *négraille* and *négrerie* in the Martiniquian novels of Patrick Chamoiseau and Raphaël Confiant, roughly equivalent to the contemptuous use of 'Irishry': e.g. Confiant, *Le Nègre et l'amiral* (1988; Paris, n.d.), 10, 114.

56. See Noel Ignatiev, *How the Irish Became White* (New York, 1995), 4–5.

57. *Road to Equality*, 101.

58. Yeats's antithesis cuts out the 'middle' figure of the merchant, who, neither too poor nor too rich, was a potent model for many. The great apologists of that more burgherly ideal in the eighteenth century included Robinson Crusoe's father, and Edward Gibbon, who asserted the value of a middle station against *his* father's deplorable predilection for the high and the low. See *Robinson Crusoe*, ed. Donald J. Crowley (Oxford, 1983), 4; Edward Gibbon, *Autobiographies*, ed. John Murray (London, 1896), 160, 292; and Claude Rawson, 'Gibbon, Swift and Irony', in David Womersley (ed.), *Edward Gibbon: Bicentenary Essays* (Oxford, 1997), 183–4.

59. Kiberd, *Inventing Ireland*, 449.

60. David Englander, *Poverty and Poor Law Reform in Britain: From Chadwick to Booth, 1834–1914* (London, 1998), 43–4. See Sidney and Beatrice Webb, *English Poor Law History. Part II*, i. 163–4. I owe this information to Dr Shelagh Hunter.

61. Cormac Ó Gráda, *Ireland Before and After the Famine: Explorations in Economic History, 1800–1925* (2nd edn., Manchester, 1993), i, 6–8, 41; Donald Winch, *Riches and Poverty: An Intellectual History of Political Economy in Britain, 1750–1834* (Cambridge, 1996), 341–3.

62. Joseph Conrad, *Youth, Heart of Darkness, The End of the Tether* (1902; London, 1956), 118.

63. L. P. Curtis, Jr., *Anglo-Saxons and Celts: A Study of Anti-Irish Prejudice in Victorian England* (Bridgeport, Conn., 1968), 71–3, 136–7; Elazar Barkan, *The Retreat of Scientific Racism* (Cambridge, 1992), 22–6. Ireland does not appear in Beddoe's map of the 'Index of Nigrescence of West-Central-Europe', in *The Races of Britain* (Bristol and London, 1885), between 202–3. For his main comments on the Africanoid Irish, and discriminations linking class and race, see also 11, 261–8 (262 on upper and lower classes in Ireland).

64. *A Letter to the Lord Chancellor Middleton, Works*, x. 103.

65. Henry Reynolds, *The Other Side of the Frontier: An Interpretation of the Aborigine Response to the Invasion and Settlement of Australia* (Townsville, 1981), 121.

66. See J. H. Elliott, *The Old World and the New 1492–1650* (Cambridge, 1996), 83–4.

67. J. M. Coetzee, 'Idleness in South Africa', *White Writing*, 12–35, esp. 21, 23.

68. Coetzee, *White Writing*, 22. One or two details differ from the Yahoos; the Hottentots 'wear skins' and 'live in the meanest of huts'.

69. *Letters of Sidney and Beatrice Webb*, ed. Norman MacKenzie, 3 vols. (Cambridge, 1978), i. 437. The question of Home Rule was one on which the Webbs differed, but it was partly bound up with the issue of resources being wasted on 'the relief of tramps'. The phrase is from the report of a British trade union originally opposed to Home Rule in 1837, which came to support it in 1840 on the grounds that the Irish would not properly manage funds placed at their disposal 'until they are thrown more on their own resources' (Sidney and Beatrice Webb, *Industrial Democracy* (new edn., 1902, 88 n. 1, 84)). For a fuller account of the Irish–Hottentot analogy, see Chapter 2, pp. 108–11.

70. For English writers on exterminating the Irish, see pp. 232–55; on Nazi 'manufactures', see n. 73 and Chapter 4, pp. 275–87 and nn. 51–62, 65, 78.

71. See Claude Rawson, *Order From Confusion Sprung* (1985; Atlantic Highlands, NJ, and London, 1992), 131, 143 n. 25. Variations on this black-humorous theme, in which Gulliver makes objects of Yahoo skin, occur in *Gulliver's Travels*, IV. iii, x. 236, 281.

72. André Breton, *Anthologie de l'humour noir* (1939–1966); rev. edn., Paris, 1966), 9–21, esp. 13–14, 19–21; extracts from *A Modest Proposal* are on pp. 26–32. I first pointed out the pertinence of Breton's observations in *Gulliver and the Gentle Reader* (1973; Atlantic Highlands, NJ, and London, 1991), 34–5, 59, 158 n. 5.

73. The extent of Nazi 'industrialization' in this sphere is in considerable doubt, not only among Holocaust deniers but reputable historians. Evidence does on the other hand exist of smaller-scale manufacture, laboratory experiments, and perhaps unsuccessful attempts at industrial production: see Chapter 4.

74. Fynes Moryson, *An Itinerary* (1617; Glasgow, 1908), iv. 185.

75. Oliver W. Ferguson, *Jonathan Swift and Ireland* (Urbana, Ill., 1962), 20–2 and *passim*.

76. See David Harkness, 'Ireland', in *The Oxford History of the British Empire, v. Historiography*, ed. Robin W. Winks (Oxford, 1999), 115; for an extended

sociological discussion, see Michael Hechter, *Internal Colonialism: The Celtic Fringe in British National Development, 1536–1966* (London, 1975).

77. Jorge Luis Borges, 'The Argentinian Writer and Tradition', in Donald A. Yates and Jane E. Irby (eds.), *Labyrinths* (Harmondsworth, 1970), 218 (citing also Thorstein Veblen).

78. *Industrial Democracy*, 697–8 n. 1, 687, 744 n. 1.

79. Beatrice Webb to Sir William Beveridge, 17 Nov. 1938, *Letters*, iii. 424.

80. Niall Ferguson, *The House of Rothschild*, cited in Robert Skidelsky, 'Family Values', *New York Review of Books*, 16 Dec. 1999, 26.

81. See the screen version, *Major Barbara* (London, 1954), 134; *Collected Screenplays of Bernard Shaw*, ed. Bernard F. Dukore (Athens, Ga., 1980), 106, 330–1. A variant of this comment is made by the Nobleman in *Saint Joan*, Scene iv, p. 127: 'The Jews generally give value. They make you pay; but they deliver the goods. In my experience the men who want something for nothing are invariably Christians.' It is an odd coincidence of history that Hitler seems to have entertained similar sentiments in his early years, relying on Jewish friends 'for loans and other help in his worst times. He always preferred to sell his watercolors to Jewish dealers, because he thought they were more honest and gave him better prices' (Gordon A. Craig, 'Working Toward the Führer', *New York Review of Books*, 18 Mar. 1999, 35, reviewing Brigitte Hamann, *Hitler's Vienna: A Dictator's Apprenticeship*, and other books).

82. Götz Aly, Peter Chroust, and Christian Pross, *Cleansing the Fatherland: Nazi Medicine and Racial Hygiene*, trans. Belinda Cooper (Baltimore, 1994), *passim* (on beggars, etc.); Kant, cited by Léon Poliakov, *The Aryan Myth*, trans. Edmund Howard (New York, 1974), 172. Adolf Hitler, *Mein Kampf*, trans. Ralph Manheim (Boston, 1971), 309 ff. For Shaw's views on the unproductive rich, not Jewish, and the contribution of the poor to that status, see *Intelligent Woman's Guide*, ch. 18, 'The Idle Rich', i. 74–5: 'But when every possible qualification of the words Idle Rich has been made, and it is fully understood that idle does not mean doing nothing (which is impossible), but doing nothing useful, and continually consuming without producing, the term applies to the class, numbering at the extreme outside one-tenth of the population, to maintain whom in their idleness the other nine-tenths are kept in a condition of slavery so complete that their slavery is not even legalized as such: hunger keeps them sufficiently in order without imposing on their masters any of those obligations which make slaves so expensive to their owners. What is more, any attempt on the part of a rich woman to do a stroke of ordinary work for the sake of her health would be bitterly rejected by the poor because, from their point of view, she would be a rich woman meanly doing a poor woman out of a job.'

83. Jean-Paul Sartre, *Réflexions sur la question juive* (10th edn., Paris, 1954), 83.

84. Dermot Keogh, *Jews in Twentieth-Century Ireland: Refugees, Anti-Semitism and the Holocaust* (Cork, 1998), 21, citing an article of 1893. For recurrent perceptions of Jews as moneylenders and usurers, see also 23, 28, 29, 42, 46, 50, 53, 133, 166, 169, 235, and *passim*. Official responses to such accusations in Ireland usually exonerated the tiny Jewish minority from charges of improper financial dealings. A Moneylenders Act, designed to ensure proper practice in the trade,

was sponsored by Robert Briscoe, the Dáil's only Jewish member, in 1929, and passed into law in 1933 (89–90).

85. See Pierre Vidal-Naquet, *Assassins of Memory: Essays on the Denial of the Holocaust*, trans. Jeffrey Mehlman (New York, 1992), 9–11; Vidal-Naquet goes on to discuss how this 'explanation' developed into an 'inverse explanation...', denying the genocide'.

86. Michael Rogin, 'Magician Behind Bars', *London Review of Books*, 2 July 1998, 10, reviewing David Mamet, *The Old Religion*.

87. David Mamet, *The Old Religion* (New York, 1997), 100–1; also 103.

88. In Mamet's *The Old Religion*, 11, the leader of a lynch mob says, '*Lord*, Mr. Weiss,... not *you*. You're *our* Jew...', a status not uncommon in Jew–Gentile relationships, sometimes socially formalized, as in the institution of the tolerated Jew, in eighteenth-century Prussia: see Paul R. Mendes-Flohr and Jehuda Reinharz (eds.), *The Jew in the Modern World: A Documentary History* (Oxford, 1980), 20–5. For Vercors, *Le Silence de la mer* (1942), see *The Silence of the Sea/Le Silence de la mer*, ed. James W. Brown and Lawrence D. Stokes (New York, 1991), 72 and n. 3. For Vercors's sense of the 'real' underlying character of 'good' Germans during the Occupation, see *La Bataille du silence: Souvenirs de minuit* (1967; Paris, 1992), 179 ff., esp. 184–5 (*The Battle of Silence*, trans. Rita Barisse (New York, 1968), 147 ff., 150–1).

89. Mamet, *The Old Religion*, 95; Harriet Beecher Stowe, *A Key to Uncle Tom's Cabin*, III. i (1854; New York, 1964), 242–3.

90. Eric Lott, *Love and Theft: Blackface Minstrelsy and the American Working Class* (New York, 1993), 229.

91. Lott, *Love and Theft*, 67, 70–1, 75, 94–6, 148–9, 154, 237, 249 n. 26, 253 n. 18, 257 n. 13. On *Punch*, see Fintan O'Toole, 'Venus in Blue Jeans: Oscar Wilde, Jesse James, Crime and Fame', in Jerusha McCormack (ed.), *Wilde the Irishman* (New Haven, 1998), 80.

92. Ignatiev, *How the Irish Became White*, 76.

93. Bernard Shillman, *A Short History of the Jews in Ireland* (Dublin, 1945), 33, 49–50, 75–6; Keogh, *Jews in Twentieth-Century Ireland*, 6–7. An interesting speculation on the idea of Jews as a counterweight was proposed by Swift, who generally regarded Dissenters as a greater danger than Catholics, and wrote ironically in *Examiner*, No. 36, 12 Apr. 1711, of the Dissenters' supposed willingness to ally themselves against the Church with collaborators from groups they were supposedly hostile to, like Papists and profligates, adding: 'what if the *Jews* should multiply and become a formidable Party among us? Would the *Dissenters* join in Alliance with them likewise, because they agree already in some general Principles, and because the Jews are allowed to be a *stiff-necked and rebellious People*?' (*Works*, iii. 130). The remarks are not evidence of any notable degree of anti-semitism, but Swift's sense of the outlandishness of the idea seems itself to imply that the prospect is far-fetched even in England.

94. Keogh, *Jews in Twentieth-Century Ireland*, 6–7, 19, 20, 31–2; endorsements of this perception were made by various rabbis, including Chief Rabbis of London and of Ireland (32, 113, 201, 227). Anti-Semitic feelings achieved a high profile in the 1930s and during the Second World War, and found expression in notoriously illiberal immigration policies for Jewish refugees, despite many examples of

good will and the marked but not wholly reliable sympathy of Eamon de Valera (88–223).

95. James Joyce, *Ulysses*, introd. Declan Kiberd (London, 1992), 44, 41.

96. For pre-1946 population statistics and related information see Keogh, *Jews in Twentieth-Century Ireland*, 6–25, esp. 9–10; for later figures, 224–7. Jakobovits, cited in Keogh, 226. For a summary account, see *Encyclopaedia Judaica*, viii. 1463–6. The *Encyclopaedia*'s decennial supplements for 1973–82 (322–3), and 1983–92 (187–8) record a steady decline from 2,633 in 1971 to 1,400 on 'current estimates' (*c*.1994). The later *Decennial Book* reports that 'Anti-Semitism was very low-key' (188). Earlier history suggests figures of 3 or more Jews in Dublin around 1660, about 200 in 1746, dwindling to 9 in 1821 (Shillman, *Short History*, 16, 28–9, 33, 63, 69–70).

97. Though there were African troops in Roman Britain, there seems little evidence of any significant black presence in Ireland at any period. For scattered instances of Blacks in Ireland from the Middle Ages to the present, see Paul Edwards, 'The Early African Presence in the British Isles', in Jagdish S. Gundara and Ian Duffield (eds.), *Essays on the History of Blacks in Britain* (Aldershot, 1992), 9–29, esp. 11–14, 16; Peter Fryer, *Staying Power: The History of Black People in Britain* (London, 1984), 84. The *Oxford Companion to Irish History*, ed. S. J. Connolly (Oxford, 1998), s.v. immigration, reports some 600 (Asian) Indians living in the Irish Republic in the 1980s and makes no mention of African immigrants. Responses to a recent wave of asylum seekers from Nigeria include repeated statements that Ireland was not used to seeing black people: see, for example, *New York Times*, 8 July 2000, A1, 8. The paper reports that as late as 1992 'only 39 people applied for asylum in Ireland', as compared to a heavy recent increase (A8).

98. Roddy Doyle, *The Commitments* (1987), in *The Barrytown Trilogy* (London, 1995), 13; in her role as President of the Irish Republic, Mary Robinson visited Somalia, telling the Somalis 'that they were the Irish of Africa'; both passages cited by Kiberd, *Inventing Ireland*, 611, 579. Ms Robinson later defended her acceptance of a UN appointment which Third World leaders did not wish to confer on a European by insisting on her Irishness, *New York Times*, 6 Oct. 1997, A10.

99. In Ned Ward, 'The Character of an *Irishman*', *London Spy*, February 1700, 12, also cited in Edward D. Snyder, 'The Wild Irish: A Study of Some English Satires against the Irish, Scots, and Welsh', *Modern Philology*, 17 (1920), 700 and n. 4; for some later uses of 'white negro' and comparable phrases, see L. P. Curtis, Jr., *Apes and Angels: The Irishman in Victorian Caricature* (Washington, 1971), 1–2, 13–15, 107; Lott, *Love and Theft*, 49–55 and 248–9 n. 26; Ignatiev, *How the Irish Became White*, esp. ch. 2, 'White Negroes and Smoked Irish', 34–59 (for Blacks as 'smoked Irish', see also Lott, *Love and Theft*, 95); for analogies between Irish and Blacks, beginning with scattered examples in the sixteenth and seventeenth centuries, see D. B. Quinn, *The Elizabethans and the Irish* (Ithaca, NY, 1966), 23–7; Curtis, *Anglo-Saxons and Celts*, 72 and 136 n. 12, 119, 121, and 149 n. 7. Some of these analogies pretended to be based on racial factors such as the 'nigrescence' of 'black Celts'. In America, Irish people were sometimes referred to as 'niggers turned inside out' (Ignatiev, *How the Irish Became White*, 41).

100. On this matter, see Chapter 1.

101. See R. B. Cunninghame Graham, 'Bloody Niggers' (1897), later 'Niggers' (compare Carlyle's reverse switch in 'The Nigger Question', p. 235 below), in Graham's *Thirty Tales & Sketches*, ed. Edward Garnett (London, 1929), 3–15, denouncing the term, and its indiscriminate application to Brahmins, Bengalis, Malays, Sioux, Comanches, Araucanos, Turks, Levantines (12–13); 'Niggers are niggers, whether black or white' (13). For Greenlanders, see Joseph Conrad and Ford Madox Hueffer (Ford), *The Inheritors* (1901; London, 1941), 42; Robert Burns, 'The Ordination', ll. 30–1, in *Poems and Songs*, ed. James Kinsley (London, 1969), 171; see *OED*, s.v. Nigger 1a, Negro 1, and Black sb. 6.

102. Frederick Douglass, cited as epigraph to Ignatiev, *How the Irish Became White*, p. vii. Douglass seems to have felt a close bond with Irish responses to oppression. Writing on at least two occasions of the slave-songs of his youth that 'I have never heard any songs like those anywhere since I left slavery, except when in Ireland... during the famine of 1845–6', *My Bondage and My Freedom* (1855; New York, 1968), 98, and see *Life and Times of Frederick Douglass* (1881; facsimile edn., Secaucus, NJ, 1983), 43.

103. Honoré Daumier, *Irlande et Jamaïque—Patience!...*, *Charivari*, 11 Apr. 1866, in Loÿs Delteil, *Honoré Daumier (IX)*, in *Le Peintre Graveur Illustré*, 20–9 (Paris, 1925–30), 28 (1926), No. 3494; see also N.-A. Hazard and Loÿs Delteil, *Catalogue raisonné de l'œuvre lithographique de Honoré Daumier* (Paris, 1904), 655, No. 3165. It is one of several satires by Daumier on the British in Ireland and elsewhere during this period: see also Nos. 3616, 3657, and, in volume 29 (*Daumier X*), 3818, 3835–7 (all dating from 1867–71).

104. O'Toole, in McCormack (ed.), *Wilde the Irishman*, 78; Ignatiev, *How the Irish Became White*, 3.

105. Cited in Curtis, *Anglo-Saxons and Celts*, 81.

106. Mark Storey, *Robert Southey: A Life* (Oxford, 1997), 117 (letter of 27 June 1798); Louis-Ferdinand Céline, *Bagatelles pour un massacre* (Paris, 1937), 316–17. A *Times* editorial of 1865 (no date supplied) is said to have reported 'contentedly', apropos of Irish emigration, that 'A Catholic Celt will soon be as rare on the banks of the Shannon as a Red Indian on the shores of the Manhattan', another variation (whether or not authentic) on this play of fearful symmetries: cited, not directly, by Liz Curtis, *Nothing but the Same Old Story: The Roots of Anti-Irish Racism* (London, 1984), 58, and by O'Toole, in McCormack (ed.), *Wilde the Irishman*, 78, from Liz Curtis.

107. Joseph Conrad, 'An Outpost of Progress', *Tales of Unrest* (1898; London, 1947), 108.

108. Curtis, *Anglo-Saxons and Celts*, 58.

109. Joyce, *Ulysses*, 427, 421.

110. Curtis, *Anglo-Saxons and Celts*, 84.

111. 'How to Restore Order in Ireland', *The Matter with Ireland*, 259–60, 258.

112. On blackface minstrelsy, see Lott, *Love and Theft*, 35, 67, 71, 94–6, 148–9, 154, 249 n. 26, 253 n. 18, 257 n. 13. For Irish composers, performers, and audiences of blackface songs and routines, see 35, 75, 95, 249 n. 26; for Irish stereotypes in blackface acts, with friendly or hostile analogies with Blacks, 71, 95, 253 n. 18. See also Ignatiev, *How the Irish Became White*, 42 and 196–7 nn. 30–1; for

jokes about Oscar Wilde derived from blackface minstrel routines, see O'Toole, in McCormack (ed.), *Wilde the Irishman*, 80. On Jews and black entertainment, Jeffrey Melnick, *A Right to Sing the Blues: African Americans, Jews, and American Popular Song* (Cambridge, Mass., 1999).

113. M. F. Burnyeat, 'Letter from Sofia', *TLS* 16 Apr. 1999, 17; Curtis, *Anglo-Saxons and Celts*, 46.

114. See Ó Gráda, *Ireland Before and After the Famine*, 41–2. As a son of Sir John Parnell, William Parnell was related both to Thomas Parnell, the poet and friend of Swift, and to Charles Stewart Parnell.

115. 'Ain't We Got Fun' (1921), song by Gus Kahn and Raymond B. Egan.

116. Swift, 'Maxims Controlled in Ireland: The Truth of Some Maxims in State and Government, Examined with Reference to Ireland', *Works*, xii. 136, 129–37; better-known expressions of the same idea are *A Short View of the State of Ireland* (1728) and *A Modest Proposal* itself (1729), *Works*, xii. 3–12 *passim*, 107–18, esp. 116–18. And see Louis Landa, 'Swift's Economic Views and Mercantilism', and, esp., '*A Modest Proposal* and Populousness', in his *Essays in Eighteenth-Century English Literature* (Princeton, 1980), 13–48.

117. On the badging of Jews, which has a long history in Islamic and Christian countries, see *Encyclopaedia Judaica*, iv. 62–73.

118. Summaries of the various categories may be found in Robert Jay Lifton, *The Nazi Doctors: Medical Killing and the Psychology of Genocide* (New York, 1986), 153, and Gregory Woods, *A History of Gay Literature: The Male Tradition* (New Haven, 1998), 249–50, 408–9 nn. There is a substantial literature on pink triangles.

119. See Raul Hilberg, *The Destruction of the European Jews* (rev. edn., New York, 1985), ii. 589; *Documents of Destruction: Germany and Jewry 1933–1945*, ed. Raul Hilberg (Chicago, 1971), 147.

120. Ian McEwan, *The Child in Time* (London, 1988), 8, 27, 39, 101–2, 192.

121. McEwan, *The Child in Time*, 8.

122. 'Upon Giving Badges', *Works*, xiii. 172–3, and see Introduction, xiii, pp. xxxviii–xxxix; and Ehrenpreis, *Swift: The Man, his Works, and the Age*, iii. 813–16.

123. Ferguson, *Jonathan Swift and Ireland*, 183–4 n. 10.

124. See also 'Upon Giving Badges', *Works*, xiii. 172.

125. Fielding, *Amelia*, I. iv, Wesleyan Edition, ed. Martin C. Battestin (Oxford, 1983), 33.

126. McEwan *The Child in Time*, 8–9, 192–3; there is a replay of this scene in Mantel, *The Giant, O'Brien*, ch. 8, p. 120, where the Giant gives money to a woman he thinks is the beautiful young mother whose story is noted in Chapter 2, p. 137 and n .150.

127. *Works*, ix. 208, xiii. 134–5, 172.

128. *Works*, xiii. 173, 132.

129. Owen Dudley Edwards, 'Impressions of an Irish Sphinx', in McCormack (ed.), *Wilde the Irishman*, 53; Jane Francesca Elgee, Lady Wilde, *Poems by Speranza* (Dublin, n.d.), 10–12.

130. Edwards, in *Wilde the Irishman*, 52, 55 ('The Great Famine and its revelation of human responsibility... were probably the greatest individual legacies in creative response which Wilde inherited from his parents', an overstatement in my view); Ó Gráda, *Ireland Before and After the Famine*, 3–4.

131. Snyder, 'Wild Irish', 697, citing William Camden, *Britannia* (1722 edn.), ii. 1419; see also William Lithgow, *The Totall Discourse of the Rare Adventures and Painefull Peregrinations of Long Nineteene Yeares Travayles* (1632; Glasgow, 1906), 375–81.

132. The *OED* gives examples from 1702 and 1744, as well as another use by Swift (1725).

133. W. E. H. Lecky, *A History of Ireland in the Eighteenth Century*, new edn., 5 vols. (London, 1892), i. 162–3. For a vivid account of the legal disabilities suffered by Catholic priests in Ireland, see 160–5. Lecky is eloquent on the injustices suffered by Irish Catholics but reminds us that they were often exceeded by restrictive laws against Catholics in other Protestant countries (including England), or Protestants in Catholic ones. In particular 'persecution in Ireland never approached in severity that of Lewis XIV [against the Huguenots], and it was absolutely insignificant compared with that which had extirpated Protestantism and Judaism from Spain' (i. 137).

134. *New York Times*, 27 Nov. 1996, A22.

135. Lecky, *History of Ireland,* i. 162–3 n. 3, 163.

136. Ferguson, *Jonathan Swift and Ireland*, 16.

137. Lecky, *History of Ireland,* i. 163: constitutionally, 'a Bill which had been returned from England might be finally rejected, but could not be amended by the Irish Parliament'; Ferguson, *Jonathan Swift and Ireland*, p.16.

138. Lecky, *History of Ireland*, i. 164–5.

139. Lecky, *History of Ireland*, i. 163 and n. 2: an anonymous paper printed in Dublin in 1725 recommended the castration of criminals.

140. In the internal chronology of *Gulliver's Travels*, the fourth voyage takes place in the years 1710–15, so that the castration debate in its fictional time would actually precede the Irish Privy Council's recommendation.

141. On castration and sterilization, see Lifton, *Nazi Doctors*, 22–44, 269–302 (castration, 269, 278–84); Lore Shelley (ed.), *Criminal Experiments on Human Beings in Auschwitz and War Research Laboratories: Twenty Women Prisoners' Accounts* (San Francisco, 1991), *passim*; *Documents on the Holocaust: Selected Sources on the Destruction of the Jews of Germany and Austria, Poland, and the Soviet Union*, ed. Yitzhak Arad, Yisrael Gutman, and Abraham Margaliot (Jerusalem and Oxford, 1987), 272–3; for Wannsee, see the Reich Secret Document, restricted to 30 copies, 'Protocol of the Wannsee Conference, January 20, 1942', in *Documents of the Holocaust*, 260; limited sterilization plans were adopted for some classes of mixed birth, 258.

142. Edmund Spenser, *View of the Present State of Ireland* (1596), in *Works of Edmund Spenser: A Variorum Edition, x. Spenser's Prose Works*, ed. Rudolf Gottfried (Baltimore, 1949; rpt. 1966), 158 and (for different interpretations) commentary 381–2; *View of the Present State of Ireland*, ed. W.L. Renwick (Oxford, 1970), 104.

143. *Spenser's Prose Works*, 381; *View*, ed. Renwick, 185 ff; R. F. Foster, *Modern Ireland: 1600–1972* (London, 1989), 34.

144. *Brief Note*, in *Spenser's Prose Works*, 233–45, esp. 244, and commentary, pp. 430–40.

145. *Brief Note*, 240.

146. For the gesture of moderation, in Swift's scaled-down context, see *PBB* 133: 'What shall we do with the Foreign Beggars? Must they be left to starve? I answered No; but They must be driven or whipt out of Town'; for Southey, see p. 221 and n. 106; Thomas Carlyle, 'Repeal of the Union', *Examiner*, 29 Apr. 1848, cited in James A. Davies, 'The Effects of Context: Carlyle and the *Examiner* in 1848', *Yearbook of English Studies*, 16 (1986), 58–9.

147. Thomas Carlyle, *Chartism* (1839), ch. 4, in *Works*, xxix. 136–40; for vignettes of beggary, see xxix. 138–9, and Fred Kaplan, *Thomas Carlyle: A Biography* (Berkeley, 1993), 339–44.

148. Carlyle, *Chartism*, 139.

149. Carlyle, 'The Nigger Question', *Works*, xxix. 353; for the original version with the less inflammatory title, see *Fraser's Magazine*, 40 (1849), 670–9.

150. Mamet, *The Old Religion*, 11, 95.

151. Kaplan, *Thomas Carlyle*, 489, 589 n. 124; Thomas Carlyle, *Letters to his Wife*, ed. Trudy Bliss (London, 1953), 388.

152. Kaplan, *Thomas Carlyle*, 370–1; see also John Sutherland, 'Black Electricities', *London Review of Books*, 30 Oct. 1997, 31–4.

153. Sidney and Beatrice Webb, *English Poor Law History. Part II*, ii. 1025.

154. Lynn Hollen Lees, *The Solidarities of Strangers: The English Poor Laws and the People, 1700–1948* (Cambridge, 1998), 179, 217–29, 357.

155. Colm Tóibín, *The Irish Famine* (London, 1999), esp. 10 ff., 23–5, 65–6.

156. Ó Gráda, *Ireland Before and After the Famine*, 138.

157. *Works*, xiii. 174–7, 176.

158. *Works*, xiii. 174, 176 (for knavery).

159. Ehrenpreis, *Swift*, iii. 816.

160. *Intelligent Woman's Guide*, ch. 86, ii. 455.

161. James Joyce, *Portrait of the Artist as a Young Man* (New York, 1975), 203.

162. Sinclair, *The Jungle*, ch. 12, p. 145; Thomas Harris, *Hannibal*, ch. 9 (New York, 2000), 59–60.

163. Klaus Völker, *Brecht: A Biography*, trans. John Nowell (New York, 1978), 152–9; Esslin, *Brecht: A Choice of Evils*, 50.

164. Sinclair, *The Jungle*, ch. 29, 376–7 (cf. Tolstoy, *Resurrection*, III. xix, trans. Rosemary Edmonds (Harmondsworth, 1966), 529); Sinclair's novel flirts variously with cannibal issues, as when Jurgis, the victimized hero, bites off the cheek of Connor, one of his exploiters, chs. 15, 26, 183, 332, a situation reproduced in Ian McEwan's *The Innocent*, chs. 16, 17 (London, 1990), 156–9.

165. J. M. Coetzee, *The Lives of Animals*, ed. Amy Gutmann (Princeton, 1999), 53.

166. Jean de Léry, *Voyage*, 228–9 (132). See Chapter 1, pp. 40–1, and n. 55.

167. See Claude Rawson, 'Henry Fielding', in *The Cambridge Companion to the Eighteenth-Century English Novel*, ed. John Richetti (Cambridge, 1996), 124–7.

168. *Works*, i. 109.

169. William Frost, 'The Irony of Swift and Gibbon: A Reply to F. R. Leavis', *Essays in Criticism*, 17 (1967), 44.

170. *Works*, i. 109–10.

171. *Gulliver and the Gentle Reader*, 33–7.

172. Curtis, *Anglo-Saxons and Celts*, 62, 134 n.; also 53, 54, 61. See Gunnar Myrdal, *An American Dilemma: The Negro Problem and Modern Democracy*, 2 vols.,

introd. Sissela Bok (New Brunswick, NJ, 1996), ii. 1073–8 ('A Parallel to the Negro Problem').

173. *A Letter to the Lord Chancellor Middleton* (1724), in *Drapier's Letters*; see also *A Letter Concerning the Sacramental Test* (1709; *Works*, x. 104, ii. 120). Deprivation of social and legal status, though not always to the specific disadvantage of women, was also variously an issue in the slavery culture of the American South and elsewhere: see Edmund S. Morgan, 'Plantation Blues', *New York Review of Books*, 10 June 1999, 32.

174. Ferguson, *Jonathan Swift and Ireland*, 17.

175. Breton, *Anthologie de l'humour noir*, 19.

176. *Works*, xiii, pp. vii ff., 1–65.

177. For some statistics of executions, see Douglas Hay, 'Property, Authority and the Criminal Law', in Douglas Hay, E. P. Thompson, *et al.*, *Albion's Fatal Tree: Crime and Society in Eighteenth-Century England* (London, 1988), 22–3.

178. *Works*, xiii. 8, 40.

179. Breton, *Anthologie de l'humour noir*, 20.

180. Breton, *Anthologie de l'humour noir*, 13.

181. Henry Fielding, *Jonathan Wild* (1743), IV. xv (IV. xiv in edition of 1754), in *Miscellanies by Henry Fielding*, iii, ed. Bertrand A. Goldgar and Hugh Amory, Wesleyan Edition (Oxford, 1997), 186–9. In II. xiii (xii), Wild is saved from drowning because he was born to be hanged, a destiny also alluded to in IV. i and IV. xiii (xii), iii. 86–9, 138, 176–7, and see Claude Rawson, *Henry Fielding and the Augustan Ideal Under Stress* (1972; Atlantic Highlands, NJ, and London, 1991), 126. Also, *Tom Jones*, III. ii, ed. Martin C. Battestin and Fredson Bowers, Wesleyan Edition (Oxford, 1974), i. 118. For other examples, see Shakespeare, *The Tempest*, I. i. 32–8; Morris P. Tilley, *A Dictionary of the Proverbs in England in the Sixteenth and Seventeenth Centuries* (Ann Arbor, 1950), B139.

182. Henry Fielding, *An Enquiry into the Causes of the Late Increase of Robbers* (1751), pp. x, viii, ed. Malvin R. Zirker, Wesleyan Edition (Oxford, 1988), 166, 164, 157.

183. Breton, *Anthologie de l'humour noir*, 14.

184. On Artaud see Martin Esslin, *Antonin Artaud* (New York, 1977), 32, 116, 123–4; on Céline, Milton Hindus, *Céline: The Crippled Giant* (1950; New Brunswick, NJ, 1997), 19; for some comments on Céline's 'aestheticism', see Irving Howe 'Anti-Semite and Jew', in *Celebrations and Attacks: Thirty Years of Literary and Cultural Commentary* (New York, 1979), 68–71 esp. 69.

185. Allen Ginsberg, 'Encounters with Ezra Pound' (1967), in his *Composed on the Tongue*, ed. Donald Allen (Bolinas, Calif., 1971), 8.

186. Herbert Lottman, *The Left Bank* (Boston, 1982), 228; Céline seems to have played a small part in denouncing or attempting to denounce Jews to the Nazis, see Nicholas Hewitt, *Life of Céline* (Oxford, 1999), 212 (see 207 ff. for an account of his 'collaboration').

187. Liz Curtis, *Nothing but the Same Old Story*, 70–9, reference made to *Irish News*, 12 June 1984 and *Irish Times*, 30 May 1984.

188. Swift, *Sentiments of a Church-of-England Man* (1708), *Works*, ii. 13.

189. Ian McEwan, *Enduring Love*, chs. 13–14 (London, 1998), 117, 119.

190. Immanuel Wallerstein, 'The Albatross of Racism', *London Review of Books*, 18 May 2000, 11–14, 12.

191. Wallerstein, 'Albatross of Racism', 13.
192. Wallerstein, 'Albatross of Racism', *passim*, esp. 12, 14, explores the demographic context of complaints of underclass behaviour, and the 'sanitised racism' which often underlies them, in a familiar interpenetration of class and race.
193. Cited in Kiberd, *Inventing Ireland*, 37.

Chapter 4. God, Gulliver, and Genocide

1. See the preceding chapter for some aspects of this species of rhetoric.
2. *Prose Works*, ed. Herbert Davis *et al.* (Oxford, 1939–74), xii. 116–17.
3. George Orwell, 'Politics vs Literature: An Examination of *Gulliver's Travels*', *Collected Essays, Journalism and Letters*, ed. Sonia Orwell and Ian Angus, 4 vols. (Harmondsworth, 1970), iv. 241–61, 255. Orwell's probing, subtle, and controversial essay, a classic of Swift criticism, is a model of responsible and suggestive enquiry, whether or not one shares his opinions. At the other extreme, a flood of confused and undigested associations between Swift and the Nazis seems to persist in the popular mind. Professor Donald Mell has passed on to me the results of a Netscape search, made in November 1999, under 'Nazis and Jonathan Swift', which threw up 165 entries.
4. After the castration option is proposed to the Assembly, 'This was all my Master thought fit to tell me at that Time, of what passed in the Grand Council' (IV. ix. 273). Gulliver goes on to say the Master 'was pleased to conceal one Particular, which related to myself', namely Gulliver's own expulsion. The first sentence may refer to that, but the reader has no means of knowing, and is naturally poised to hear the outcome of the substantive debate. Either way, this is not revealed.
5. For the first, see Anthony Stewart, 'The Yahoo and the Discourse of Racialism in *Gulliver's Travels*', *Lumen*, 12 (1993), 35–41: an attack on Swift's critics, apparently implicating Swift himself, for suppressing the African presence in *Gulliver's Travels*; for the second, Clement Hawes, 'Three Times Round the Globe: Gulliver and Colonial Discourse', *Cultural Critique*, 18 (1991), 187–214, esp. 206, 208. For a more nuanced view of Houyhnhnmland as a slave society (though 'no direct evidence can be found in Book IV to support this view'), see Ann Cline Kelly, 'Swift's Explorations of Slavery in Houyhnhnmland and Ireland', *Publications of the Modern Language Association of America*, 91 (1976), 846–55, 846. Perhaps the best and most sophisticated reading of Houyhnhnmland as a slave-owning tyranny is Michael Wilding, 'The Politics of *Gulliver's Travels*', *Studies in the Eighteenth Century, ii. Papers Presented at the Second David Nichol Smith Memorial Seminar*, ed. R. F. Brissenden (Canberra, 1973), 302–22, esp. 315–21.
6. See James L. Clifford, 'Gulliver's Fourth Voyage: "Hard" and "Soft" Schools of Interpretation', in Larry S. Champion (ed.), *Quick Springs of Sense: Studies in the Eighteenth Century* (Athens, Ga., 1974), 33–49.
7. See Orwell, 'Politics vs Literature', esp. 249–55; Kelly, 'Swift's Explorations of Slavery', 846–55; Wilding, 'Politics of *Gulliver's Travels*', esp. 315–21.
8. On Swift's 'extraordinarily clear prevision of the spy-haunted "police State"', referring more especially to Laputa, see Orwell, 'Politics vs Literature', 249.

9. The Houyhnhnms' Platonic derivation, clearly related to the listing of both Socrates and Sir Thomas More in the famous 'Sextumvirate to which all the Ages of the World cannot add a Seventh' (III. vii. 196), has often been discussed: e.g. J. Churton Collins, *Jonathan Swift* (London, 1893), 39–40 n. 2; John F. Reichert, 'Plato, Swift, and the Houyhnhnms', *Philological Quarterly*, 47 (1968), 179–92; M. M. Kelsall, '*Iterum* Houyhnhnm: Swift's Sextumvirate and the Horses', *Essays in Criticism*, 19 (1969), 35–45; Irene Samuel, 'Swift's Reading of Plato', *Studies in Philology*, 73 (1976), 440–62, esp. 459–60; Jenny Mezciems, 'The Unity of Swift's "Voyage to Laputa": Structure as Meaning in Utopian Fiction', *Modern Language Review*, 72 (1977), 1–21, esp. 5–7, 12–16; Hoyt Trowbridge, 'Swift and Socrates', *From Dryden to Jane Austen: Essays on English Critics and Writers, 1660–1818* (Albuquerque, N. Mex., 1977), 81–123, esp. 87–93.

10. Wilding, 'Politics of *Gulliver's Travels*', 319, 321, blurs an important distinction when he says Swift sees the relation 'as one of a different species, a different race, a different nation' (321), since the tension created by Swift rests on opposite and contending perceptions of difference of species and racial difference within the same species. Orwell's view that the Houyhnhnms' 'caste system . . . is racial in character' is based on the perception that Houyhnhnms themselves come in different colours, some deemed fit only for menial work, while Wilding oddly rules out 'class oppression' among them (Orwell, 'Politics vs Literature', 251, Wilding, 'Politics of *Gulliver's Travels*', 319).

11. J. M. Coetzee, *The Lives of Animals*, ed. Amy Gutmann (Princeton, 1999), 20–2, 49–50, 55 ff. (including somewhat unfocused remarks on *Gulliver's Travels* and *A Modest Proposal*), and remarks by Amy Gutmann and other commentators, 6–10, 81–3, 86 (Peter Singer on 'the parallel between racism and speciesism'), 86–91.

12. See Ian Higgins, 'Swift and Sparta: The Nostalgia of *Gulliver's Travels*', *Modern Language Review*, 78 (1983), 513–31, esp. 515–18.

13. See *Gulliver's Travels*, ed. Paul Turner (Oxford, 1994), 373 n.1, citing W. H. Halewood, 'Plutarch in Houyhnhnmland: A Neglected Source for Gulliver's Fourth Voyage', *Philological Quarterly*, 44 (1965), 185–94, esp. 191; see also Higgins, 'Swift and Sparta', 517–8. For the best-known episode, see Thucydides, IV. lxxx. 4; Plutarch, *Lycurgus*, XXVIII. 3–4. The Earl of Orrery seems first to have suggested a connection between *Gulliver's Travels* (specifically the educational system of Lilliput, I. vi) and 'the institutions of LYCURGUS' (*Remarks on the Life and Writings of Dr. Jonathan Swift* (1752), ed. João Fróes (Newark, Del., 2000), 180.

14. For Plato's qualified admiration for Sparta, and the influence of the Spartan ideals on More and the Renaissance Utopian tradition, see Elizabeth Rawson, *The Spartan Tradition in European Thought* (Oxford, 1969), 61–72, 170–6; Thomas More, *Utopia*, in *Complete Works of St. Thomas More*, iv, ed. Edward Surtz, S.J., and J. H. Hexter (New Haven, 1965), pp. clx–clxi. Plutarch, *Lycurgus*, XXVIII. 1, thought the *krupteia* may have led Plato to think of Spartan institutions as producing efficacy rather than righteousness. He may be alluding to *Laws*, I. 630D ff.

15. Plato, *Laws*, VI. 776C–77D.

16. Thucydides, IV. lxxx. 1–4; Xenophon, *Hellenica*, III. iii. 6–7; Pierre Vidal-Naquet, *Assassins of Memory: Essays on the Denial of the Holocaust*, trans. Jeffrey Mehlman (New York, 1992), 99–102.

17. On Hecuba, and Amerindian warriors, see above, Chapter 1, pp. 29–32.
18. Plutarch, *Lycurgus*, XXVIII. 1–6, *Lycurgus and Numa*, I. 5–6; on the Utopian writers, Frank E. and Fritzie P. Manuel, *Utopian Thought in the Western World* (Oxford, 1979), 96–9, esp. 97.
19. Swift's main expressions of praise are for the balanced constitution of Sparta, and occur in the *Contests and Dissentions in Athens and Rome* (1701; *Works*, i. 195–236, esp. 196–200; also ed. Frank H. Ellis (Oxford, 1967), 84–8), and in the *Sentiments of a Church-of-England Man* and the *Fragment of the History of England* (*Works*, ii. 16; v. 36).
20. Elizabeth Rawson, *Spartan Tradition*, 351 and n. 1; see also 308 n. 2.
21. *Correspondence*, ed. Harold Williams (Oxford, 1963–5), iii. 117–18.
22. See Vidal-Naquet, *Assassins of Memory*, 100, 101.
23. On this question, see Chapter 1, p. 89 and n. 169.
24. See *Gulliver's Travels*, ed. Turner, n. 3 to IV. ix. In general, however, Swift's mind seems more on Genesis than on Milton, and James V. Falzarano, 'Adam in Houyhnhnmland: The Presence of *Paradise Lost*', *Milton Studies*, 21 (1985), 179–97, traces Miltonic allusion to improbable lengths, though it is worth consulting on some points of detail.
25. Among recent critics who have registered this evocation is Laura B. Kennelly, 'Swift's Yahoo and King Jehu: Genesis of an Allusion', *English Language Notes*, 26 (1989), 43.
26. *Works*, xi. 322 (textual notes) to IV. xii. 295.
27. See A. K. Easthope, 'The Disappearance of Gulliver: Character and Persona at the End of the *Travels*', *Southern Review* (Adelaide), 2 (1967), 264–5.
28. See *Gulliver's Travels*, ed. Turner, n. 20 to IV.xii, who also says that the original passage's attack on the English may have 'seemed dangerous to publish in Ireland', hardly a likely reason from an author who had recently published the *Drapier's Letters*, but possible as an act of caution, as Turner suggests, by the publisher Faulkner.
29. *Correspondence*, iii. 102.
30. Citations from Genesis, unless otherwise noted, are from the Authorized Version, which is the one best known to Swift as well as the most familiar in English literary tradition. In ensuing discussions of the stories of Noah and Lot, I take no account of theories of multiple authorship. These were not known to Swift, and do not affect my argument, which is based on the composite and integral versions appearing in Genesis as we have it. For convenient introductions to the several authors known as J, E, and P, and for references to alternative or unitary readings, see Norman C. Habel, 'Two Introductions to the Flood Stories', reprinted from his *Literary Criticism of the Old Testament* (Philadelphia, 1971), 29–42, in Alan Dundes (ed.), *The Flood Myth* (Berkeley, 1988), 13–28 (Dundes's headnote, 13–15, is a particularly informative summary); see also Enid B. Mellor, *The Making of the Old Testament* (Cambridge, 1972), 60 ff., and the introduction to *Genesis*, trans. Robert Alter (New York, 1996), xl–xlii. On the 'text as it stands' reading of the story of Lot, see the introduction to R. I. Letellier, *Day in Mamre Night in Sodom: Abraham and Lot in Genesis 18 and 19* (Leiden and New York, 1995), esp. 7 ff.
31. *Correspondence*, iii. 117, 104; *Works*, ix. 238.

32. See also Wisdom of Solomon, 10: 4–8; Dundes (ed.), *The Flood Myth*, 170, 'The Lot story is typologically and structurally similar to the Noah story'; Claus Westermann, *Genesis 12–36: A Commentary*, trans. John J. Scullion S. J. (Minneapolis, 1985), 314. For other parallels between Lot and Noah, see Dundes (ed.), *The Flood Myth*, 175–6; H. Hirsch Cohen, *The Drunkenness of Noah* (University, Ala., 1974), 9–12, 15, 34–5; on Noah and Lot, see Letellier, *Day in Mamre*, 233–4; and especially Robert Alter, 'Sodom as Nexus: The Web of Design in Biblical Narrative', in Jonathan Goldberg (ed.), *Reclaiming Sodom* (New York and London, 1994), 35–6, and *Genesis*, trans. Alter, 88, n. to 19: 24. On their wives, Francis Lee Utley, 'The One Hundred and Three Names of Noah's Wife', *Speculum*, 16 (1941), 437–8 n. 14.

33. See Alan Ford, *The Protestant Reformation in Ireland, 1590–1641* (Dublin, 1997), 176.

34. For a challenge, not in my opinion persuasive, to the prevailing view that *Gulliver's Travels* is a work of mainly secular rather than religious interest, see Martin Kallich, *The Other End of the Egg: Religious Satire in Gulliver's Travels* (Bridgeport, Conn., 1970).

35. For some other Old and New Testament parallels or allusions, see Roland M. Frye, 'Swift's Yahoos and the Christian Symbols for Sin', *Journal of the History of Ideas*, 15 (1954), 201–17 *passim*, esp. 216, 210. One of the oddest conclusions of recent scholarship in this field is C. A. Beaumont's sense of the 'total absence' of the Bible from *Gulliver's Travels*, *Swift's Use of the Bible: A Documentation and a Study in Allusion* (Athens, Ga., 1965), 53, 53–63, 66. On the other hand, L. J. Morrissey, *Gulliver's Progress* (Hamden, Conn., 1978), displays an extravagant overpreoccupation with a multiplicity of scriptural allusions, mainly non-existent.

36. See James L. Kugel, *The Bible as It Was* (Cambridge, Mass., 1997), 99–100. For interpretations of this wickedness, see 99–114. For the righteousness or otherwise of Noah, 112–17.

37. Antonia Fraser, *Cromwell: Our Chief of Men* (London, 1974), 327; Paul Johnson, *Ireland: Land of Troubles* (London, 1980), 43.

38. On the other hand, the God of Genesis does not sound wholly guilt free himself, and promises never to visit such punishments on humankind again (Genesis 8: 21–22, 9: 8–17), though these verses are also read as expressive of God's mercy and care for human life: see P. J. Harland, *The Value of Human Life: A Study of the Story of the Flood* (Leiden, 1996), 114–24, 130–40. But God's Mesopotamian analogue Enlil is sometimes actually blamed. See *Atra-Hasis: The Babylonian Story of the Flood* (II. viii. 35), ed. W. G. Lambert and A. R. Millard (Oxford, 1969), 87, and introduction, 12–13; see also *The Gilgamesh Epic*, Tablet XI, ll. 166 ff., in Alexander Heidel, *The Gilgamesh Epic and Old Testament Parallels* (Chicago, 1963), 87–8, 226–7. Other good general accounts of the relationship of the Genesis Flood to Mesopotamian versions may be found in articles by Lambert (1965) and Millard (1967), reprinted in Richard S. Hess and D. T. Tsumura (eds.), *'I Studied Inscriptions from before the Flood': Ancient Near Eastern, Literary, and Linguistic Approaches to Genesis 1–11* (Winona Lake, Ind., 1994), 96–128, esp. 121–5; and Claus Westermann, *Genesis 1–11: A Commentary*, trans. John J. Scullion, S. J. (Minneapolis, 1984), 398 ff.

39. On these topics, see Chapter 2.
40. See Claude Rawson, *Gulliver and the Gentle Reader* (1973; Altantic Highlands, NJ, and London, 1991), 28, citing John Traugott on the last point.
41. On Mary Gulliver, see Dick Taylor, Jr., 'Gulliver's Pleasing Visions: Self-Deception as Major Theme in *Gulliver's Travels*', *Tulane Studies in English*, 12 (1962), 10; see also 'the much-neglected Mrs. Gulliver' in Laura Brown, *Ends of Empire: Women and Ideology in Early Eighteenth-Century English Literature* (Ithaca, NY), 176. On Noah's and Lot's wives, see Alan Dundes (1986), reprinted in Dundes (ed.), *The Flood Myth*, 170; Utley, 'One Hundred and Three Names', 426–52, which not only records a hundred and three names conferred on Noah's wife by later tradition, but several dozen names for the wives of Noah's three sons (438–43) and names for Lot's wife, sometimes confused in Moslem tradition with Noah's wife under the name Wahêla (437–8 n. 14, 450). Later rabbinical writers sometimes gave Mrs Noah the name of Naamah (432 n. 5, 445).
42. On Mrs Noah's later career, including her relations with the Devil, and her character as the shrewish wife in English mystery plays, see Francis Lee Utley, 'Noah, his Wife, and the Devil', in Raphael Patai, Francis Lee Utley, and Dov Noy (eds.), *Studies in Biblical and Jewish Folklore* (Bloomington, Ind., 1960), 57–91; Utley, 'One Hundred and Three Names', 426; V. A. Kolve, *The Play Called Corpus Christi* (Stanford, Calif., 1966), 146–50, 262–3; Rosemary Woolf, *The English Mystery Plays* (Berkeley, 1980), 136–45, 375–77 nn.
43. Utley, 'One Hundred and Three Names', 445: 'there are only four women named in the Bible before the Flood'. One of Lot's daughters acquired the name Pelotit in a Midrashic text, cited in Kugel, *The Bible as It Was*, 188.
44. Rawson, *Gulliver and the Gentle Reader*, 27, 27–32.
45. See n. 32 above.
46. See pp. 298–9 and n. 104. On the *minyan* or quorum of ten, see *Encyclopaedia Judaica*, xii. 67.
47. For Plato on knowledge, opinion, and controversy, *Republic*, V. 476D–480E, VI. 499A, 506B–D; the distinction as between 'something that is or is not' at V. 476E may be part of the background to the Houyhnhnm locution about the thing which is not (IV. iv. 240); see also Reichert, 'Plato, Swift, and the Houyhnhnms', 180–2; Trowbridge, 'Swift and Socrates', 91–3.
48. See Westermann, *Genesis 1–11*, 393.
49. On the Madagascar plan, see *Documents on the Holocaust:Selected Sources on the Destruction of the Jews of Germany and Austria, Poland, and the Soviet Union*, ed. Yitzhak Arad, Yisrael Gutman, and Abraham Margaliot (Jerusalem and Oxford, 1987), 216–18.
50. An order of 23 Oct. 1941 decreed that the emigration, as distinct from evacuation, 'of individual Jews can only be approved *in single very special cases*' (*Documents on the Holocaust*, 153–4).
51. *Documents on the Holocaust*, 349.
52. Circular to concentration camp commanders by SS Brigadeführer Richard Glücks, 6 Aug. 1942. The full text, in a different translation, with precise operational instructions on an industrial scale, is given in *Concentration Camp Dachau: 1933–1945*, Dachau Memorial Museum Catalogue (Brussels, 1978), 137; see also Raul Hilberg, *The Destruction of the European Jews* (rev. edn.,

New York, 1985), iii. 954 and n. 26. On the industrial collection and use of women's hair, see iii. 971, 976. For Robert Harris's version, see *Fatherland* (London, 1993), 327 (see also 325), a novel citing historical documents. For another novelistic replay, see Thomas Keneally, *Schindler's List*, ch. 16 (Harmondsworth, 1982), 136 ('something special for U-boat crews'); also chs. 18, 26, pp. 155, 243, the latter passage cited from Glücks's directive; see also Gerald Reitlinger, *The Final Solution* (2nd edn., London, 1968), 160–1, on 'dentures and hair' as 'strategic materials'.

53. *Encyclopaedia Judaica*, v. 86 (s.v. Camps).

54. See Yehuda Bauer, letter in *Jerusalem Post*, 29 May 1990, 4; *Encyclopaedia Judaica*, xiii. 761–2 (s.v. Poland); on this factory, see also Hilberg, *Destruction of the European Jews*, iii. 967 n. 27; for a balanced survey of the 'soap rumor' in general, see Hilberg, *Destruction of the European Jews*, ii. 520–1, 737–8, 955 n. 26 ('the use of human fat for soap cannot be established as a fact'), 966–7, 1118 n. 22; Walter Laqueur, *The Terrible Secret: Suppression of the Truth about Hitler's 'Final Solution'* (1980; New York, 1993), 82. It seems that soap manufacture proved technologically impractical (Gitta Sereny, *Into that Darkness: An Examination of Conscience* (1974; New York, 1983), 141 n.); see also letter from Yehuda Bauer, dated 9 Jan. 1991, to editor of the *Jewish Standard* (Hackensack, NJ), reproduced in Nizkor Project website, 'Deceit & Misrepresentation: The Techniques of Holocaust Denial', 'The Soap Allegations', Appendix 5, http://www.nizkor.org/features/techniques-of-denial/soap-01.html; Vidal-Naquet, *Assassins of Memory*, 64, 161 n. 131 (11, 59 ff., on more general attempts to play down evidence of industrial killing). Attacking the Holocaust denier Robert Faurisson's view that the idea was scientifically 'absurd', Vidal-Naquet nevertheless says that 'as far as he knows' ('pour autant que je sache') this particular example was in fact a 'myth' ('légende'), a view expressed more tentatively in the French original than in the English translation: *Les Assassins de la mémoire* (Paris, 1987), 91 n. 11.

55. John Thornton, *Africa and Africans in the Making of the Atlantic World, 1400–1800* (2nd edn., Cambridge, 1998), 161.

56. Yehuda Bauer, letter to *Jewish Standard*, 9 Jan. 1991; *Trials of War Criminals before the Nuremberg Military Tribunals* (Washington, 1947–53), viii. 624; Vercors, *La Bataille du silence: Souvenirs de minuit* (1967; Paris, 1992), 315–16 (*The Battle of Silence*, trans. Rita Barisse (New York, 1968), 259).

57. Gitta Sereny, *Albert Speer: His Battle with Truth* (London, 1995), 309–10. In Coetzee's fictionally structured Tanner lectures, which include the narrative of a novelist called Elizabeth Costello giving lectures on the slaughter of animals, Costello imagines a comparable scene: 'as if I were to visit friends, and to make some polite remark about the lamp in their living room, and they were to say, "Yes, it's nice, isn't it? Polish-Jewish skin it's made of . . ."' (*Lives of Animals*, 69).

58. Inga Clendinnen, *Reading the Holocaust* (Cambridge, 1999), 94–5.

59. Sereny, *Albert Speer*, 310. Somebody commented 'the swine', to which Bormann replied: 'To call those people swine is an insult to swine'.

60. *Encyclopaedia Judaica*, viii. 856 (s.v. Holocaust); Primo Levi, *The Drowned and the Saved*, trans. Raymond Rosenthal (New York, 1989), Preface, 10–11; see also Simon Wiesenthal, *The Murderers Among Us* (New York, 1967), 335.

61. Hilberg, *Destruction of the European Jews*, iii. 1118 n. 22.
62. See *The Buchenwald Report*, trans. David A. Hackett (Boulder, Colo., 1995), 43 n., 64, 224, 338, 'a translation of *Bericht über das Konzentrationlager Buchenwald bei Weimar*, prepared in April and May of 1945 by a special intelligence team from the Psychological Warfare Division, SHAEF, assisted by a committee of Buchenwald prisoners'. The Nizkor Project's website on 'Deceit & Misrepresentation: The Techniques of Holocaust Denial' includes an article by Jamie McCarthy on 'Frau Ilse Koch, General Lucius Clay, and human-skin atrocities'. This cites newspaper reports of court findings, including one of a German court which convicted Ilse Koch of incitement to murder and other charges. It 'found no proof that anyone at Buchenwald had been murdered for his tattooed skin, but... expressed no doubt that skin lampshades had been made and that human heads had been shriveled and preserved at the camp' (*New York Times*, 16 Jan. 1951, 1, 8). Also cited is a memorandum of 25 May 1945 to the 'Commanding General, Third U.S. Army' by a Major Reuben Cares, Chief of Pathology, Seventh Medical Laboratory, APO403, New York, to the effect that 'three tanned pieces of skin... from Buchenwald Camp' were tested and found to be 'tattooed human skin' (http://www.nizkor.org/features/techniques-of-denial/clay-koch-01-html).
63. André Breton, *Anthologie de l'humour noir* (1939; rev. edn., Paris, 1966), Preface and headnotes to Swift and Sade, 9–16, 19–21, 38–42; for other expressions of Breton's interest in Swift, see the extract from *Manifeste du surréalisme* (1924) in *Jonathan Swift: A Critical Anthology*, ed. Denis Donoghue (Harmondsworth, 1971), 129–30; on Artaud, see Claude Rawson, 'Cannibalism and Fiction. Part II: Love and Eating in Fielding, Mailer, Genet, and Wittig', *Genre*, 11 (1978), 241, 279 n. 117, 292.
64. Breton, *Anthologie*, 43–8; for the full original episode, see *Histoire de Juliette*, Parts 3 and 4, in Sade, *Œuvres*, ed. Michel Delon (Paris, 1990–), iii (1998), 700 ff., esp. 701–7. For the lamp of skulls, not in Breton, see 709. For analogues of human furniture in Rétif de La Bretonne and Lamartine, see the note to 706 on 1490.
65. *Buchenwald Report*, 64.
66. Breton, *Anthologie*, 47, Sade *Œuvres*, iii. 706; see Vidal-Naquet, *Assassins of Memory*, 109: 'concentration camp labor... had the characteristic of being indefinitely replenishable'.
67. Breton, *Anthologie*, 40.
68. On Queneau see Roger Shattuck, 'Farce & Philosophy', *New York Review of Books*, 22 Feb. 2001, 24; on Flaubert's early discovery of Sade, see references in Claude Rawson, 'Cannibalism and Fiction: Reflections on Narrative Form and "Extreme" Situations. Part I: Satire and the Novel (Swift, Flaubert and others)', *Genre*, 10 (1977), 691 n. 37; for Sade's influence on Flaubert, Artaud, Breton, and others, see 667–711 *passim*, esp. 685 ff., 691–711; Apollinaire, cited in Breton, *Anthologie*, 38.
69. Breton, *Anthologie*, 46–7, 45; Sade, *Œuvres*, iii. 701–7.
70. Breton, *Anthologie*, 19, 13.
71. Flaubert understandably found Sade wanting in that quality; see *Souvenirs, notes et pensées intimes*, introd. Lucie Chevalley Sabatier (Paris, 1965), 73–4, cited in Rawson, 'Cannibalism and Fiction, I', 691 n. 37. Flaubert also missed cannibals

and wild beasts, and presumably had not read this episode (for wild beasts in the Minski story, *Œuvres*, iii. 722), not to mention several other Sadeian works.

72. Breton, *Anthologie*, 20.

73. Breton, *Anthologie*, 30, omitting four paragraphs corresponding to *Works*, xii. 112–13. The 'other Expedients' Swift had hopelessly recommended are at xii. 116–17.

74. Thomas Harris, *The Silence of the Lambs*, chs. 19, 34, 39 (New York, 1990), 130, 217, 255.

75. Harris, *Silence of the Lambs*, chs. 26, 53, 59, pp. 172, 322, 359.

76. Herodotus, IV. lxiv, lxv; Strabo, VII. iii. 6, 7; for Amerindian analogues, see Chapter 1, n. 157.

77. On the Scythian–Irish connection, much harped on by Swift, see Chapter 1, pp. 79 ff. and nn. 137 ff.

78. See *Encyclopaedia Judaica*, xvi. 1332 (s.v. Gassing), which reports that brains of euthanasia victims were 'secured for "medical research"', as well as their gold teeth, and those ('and other valuables') of Holocaust victims; for gold teeth and women's hair at Auschwitz, see iii. 855 (s.v. Auschwitz). See also Joseph Borkin, *The Crime and Punishment of I.G. Farben* (New York, 1978), 126, on 'gold teeth for the Reichsbank, hair for mattresses, and fat for soap' being 'recycled . . . into the German war economy' by I.G. Auschwitz. For the use of human flesh for culture media in medical experiments, see Robert Jay Lifton, *The Nazi Doctors: Medical Killing and the Psychology of Genocide* (New York, 1986), 289; Lore Shelley (ed.), *Criminal Experiments on Human Beings in Auschwitz and War Research Laboratories: Twenty Women Prisoners' Accounts* (San Francisco, 1991), 69, 308–9. For the use, and sale, of body parts and skulls of euthanasia victims for medical research, see Götz Aly, Peter Chroust, and Christian Pross, *Cleansing the Fatherland: Nazi Medicine and Racial Hygiene*, trans. Belinda Cooper (Baltimore, 1994), *passim*, esp. 141–55, 144 n., 149. For 'industrial' analogies with the human body in the fantasies of the anatomist Hermann Voss, see 146–7.

79. *Works*, i. 111–13.

80. Lifton, *Nazi Doctors*, p. xii.

81. *Gulliver's Travels*, II. vii. 134; IV. v.247, xii. 294.

82. Cited by Vidal-Naquet, *Assassins of Memory*, 12, from a speech of 6 Oct. 1943, in Himmler's *Geheimreden 1933 bis 1945 und andere Ansprachen*, ed. B. F. Smith and A. F. Peterson (Frankfurt, 1974), 169. The divine phrasing in Luther's Bible is 'Ich will die Menschen . . . vertilgen von der Erde'. It is well known that no written document survives over Hitler's signature ordering the extermination of the Jews, but the vocabulary of his recorded conversation includes frequent use of the words *Vernichtung* (annihilation), *Ausrottung* (rooting out), and *Eliminierung* (elimination): see Dan Jacobson, 'The Downfall of David Irving', *Times Literary Supplement*, 21 Apr. 2000, 14–15.

83. The man–horse reversal seems the main point, but it was said specifically of the Scythians 'that they castrate their horses to make them easy to manage' (Strabo, VII. iv. 8), and the phrasing, together with the Scythian–Irish connection, might suggest a subtextual evocation.

84. Elizabeth Rawson, *Spartan Tradition*, 342, 341–3, 365. See p. 1: 'admiration for Sparta reached a fantastic conclusion under the Nazis.' For an amusing

contemporaneous (1937) perspective, see R. H. S. Crossman, *Plato Today* (rev. 2nd edn., London, 1971), 150–4.

85. See *Encyclopaedia Judaica*, v. 86–7 (s.v. Camps); xiii. 701 (s.v. Pohl); Lifton, *Nazi Doctors*, 156–7, 188; *Documents on the Holocaust*, 246–9, 394–400; Vidal-Naquet, *Assassins of Memory*, 109; on factories, Martin Gilbert, *The Holocaust: A History of the Jews of Europe during the Second World War* (New York, 1985), 353, 425, 673.

86. Paul Berben, *Dachau 1933–1945: An Official History* (London, 1975), 89, 94, 95; for an important discussion of this question, too recent to be fully taken into account here, see Christopher R. Browning, *Nazi Policy, Jewish Workers, German Killers* (Cambridge, 2000), esp. 58–115.

87. See Pross, in *Cleansing the Fatherland*, 9; Reitlinger, *Final Solution*, 186–92, 362–3; Hilberg, *Destruction of the European Jews*, ii. 420–5, 494, 589–90, 608, iii. 940–5; Lifton, *Nazi Doctors*, 22–44, 269–302 (on castration specifically, 269, 278–84; Shelley, *Criminal Experiments*, 7, 14, 36–7, 94, 139, 278, 367 n. 13 and *passim*. Shaw's statement is in *Everybody's Political What's What*, ch. 32 (London, 1944), 290.

88. See Francis D. Adams and Barry Sanders, *Three Black Writers in Eighteenth-Century England* (Belmont, Calif., 1971), 3.

89. Stewart, 'The Yahoo and the Discourse of Racialism', 38, citing Adams and Sanders, *Three Black Writers*, 3, who do not report castration in this connection. Their source, W. R. Aykroyd, *Sweet Malefactor: Sugar, Slavery and Human Society* (London, 1967), 34–5, does not report this either. On the age of twelve in *Gulliver's Travels*, however, see Chapter 2, p. 93 and nn. 2–3.

90. Hans Sloane, *A Voyage to the Islands of Madera, Barbados, Nieves, S. Christophers and Jamaica*, 2 vols. (1707), i, p. lvii, cited in Aykroyd, *Sweet Malefactor*, 52; Jerome S. Handler, 'Slave Revolts and Conspiracies in Seventeenth-Century Barbados', *Nieuwe West-Indische Gids/New West Indian Guide*, 56 (1982), 24; Hilary Beckles, *Black Rebellion in Barbados: The Struggle Against Slavery, 1627–1838* (Bridgetown, 1984), 47.

91. *Documents on the Holocaust*, 260 (and 258), 272–3; Lifton, *Nazi Doctors*, 275, 280 n.; on preserving the workforce in this way, see also Shelley, *Criminal Experiments*, 49–50.

92. Orwell, 'Politics vs Literature', 249.

93. Report of Lublin division, 26 Sept. 1942, in Hilberg, *Destruction of the European Jews*, ii. 494.

94. See above pp. 279 ff. nn. 63 ff.

95. *Works*, xii. 113.

96. Rabelais, I. xvii. For similar episodes of urinary prowess in Rabelais, see also I. xxxviii, II. xxxiii; Freud, *Interpretation of Dreams* (1900), VI (H), in *Standard Edition of the Complete Psychological Works*, trans. James Strachey *et al.*, 24 vols. (London, 1975), v. 469; *Civilization and its Discontents* (1930), *SE* xxi. 90 n. 1. For the wider thinking about fire and urination to which Freud's note belongs, see 'The Acquisition and Control of Fire' (1932), *SE* xxii. 185–93; on Otto Rank's and other urinary theories of the Flood, and theories related to fantasies of fertility and sexuality, see Norman Cohn, *Noah's Flood: The Genesis Story in Western Thought* (New Haven, 1996), 131–3; on 'the urinary cast of…many

flood myths', see Alan Dundes 'The Flood as Male Myth of Creation' (1986), reprinted in *The Flood Myth*, 167–82, esp. 174, 171 ff., and references to Stith Thompson's *Motif-Index of Folk-Literature*, rev. edn., 6 vols. (Bloomington, Ind., 1955), esp. Nos. A923.1, A1012.2.

97. On blinding and castration, see Freud, *Totem and Taboo* (1913), IV. 3; 'The "Uncanny"' (1919); *SE* xiii. 130, xvii. 231.

98. *Works*, ii. 13.

99. See Chapter 3, pp. 230–2.

100. Montaigne, I. xxxi, *Essais*, ed. Pierre Villey, rev. V.-L Saulnier (Paris, 1988), i. 208; *Complete Essays*, trans. Donald M. Frame (Stanford, Calif., 1965), 154.

101. See the parallel passages in Bernard Weinberg, 'Montaigne's Readings for *Des Cannibales*', in George Bernard Daniel Jr. (ed.), *Renaissance and other Studies in Honor of William Leon Wiley* (Chapel Hill, NC, 1968), 270–1; André Thevet, *Singularités*, in *Le Brésil d'André Thevet* (Paris, 1997), 147.

102. On female circumcision, and its ancient history (reported by Strabo and others), see Hermann Heinrich Ploss, Max Bartels, *et al.*, *Woman: An Historical, Gynaecological and Anthropological Compendium* (1885–1927), trans. Eric John Dingwall, 3 vols. (London, 1935), i. 341–53.

103. See Robert A. Greenberg, '*A Modest Proposal* and the Bible', *Modern Language Review*, 55 (1960), 568–9, refuting in advance an assertion by C. A. Beaumont that the *Modest Proposal* 'ignores the Bible' (*Swift's Use of the Bible*, 66). There may also be a patristic model for Swift's use of the cannibal formula (see Claude Rawson, *Order from Confusion Sprung* (1985), rptd. London and Atlantic Highlands, NJ, 1992), 143 n. 28).

104. Jack P. Lewis, *A Study of the Interpretation of Noah and the Flood in Jewish and Christian Literature* (Leiden, 1968), 124–5 and n. 1. See Westermann, *Genesis 12–36*, 292: 'The reason Abraham stops at the number ten is that this represents the smallest group (so B. Jacob and L. Schmidt). If there are fewer than ten in the city, then these are individuals and as such they can be saved from the city as happens in ch. 19. Abraham's query reaches its natural limit with the number ten.' *Genesis*, trans. Alter, 83, n. to 18: 32, explains that ten is 'the minimal administrative unit for communal organization in later Israelite life'. See also J. A. Loader, *A Tale of Two Cities: Sodom and Gomorrah in the Old Testament, early Jewish and early Christian Traditions* (Kampen, 1990), 30–1: 'The fact that Abraham stops here, does not mean that righteous individuals will have to perish if they number less than ten, but that they can be saved as individuals, which is evident in the rest of the story.' For yet another, somewhat inconclusive, view, see Gerhard von Rad, *Genesis: A Commentary*, trans. John H. Marks (3rd rev. edn., London, 1972), 214. Cf. Robert Davidson, *Cambridge Bible Commentary: Genesis 12–50* (Cambridge, 1979), 70: 'Why the argument stops at ten is not clear. The narrative which follows makes it clear that Sodom was destroyed because there was not a single innocent man in the city. The attack on Lot's guests is carried out by "everyone without exception" (19.4)'.

105. Von Rad, *Genesis*, 214–15; Davidson, *Genesis 12–50*, 69: Westermann, *Genesis 12–36*, 292–3.

106. On Lot's wife and daughters, see Kugel, *The Bible as It Was*, 191–4.

107. See Kugel, *The Bible as It Was*, 182; and see von Rad, *Genesis*, 224, Davidson, *Genesis 12–50*, 78–9; Westermann, *Genesis 12–36*, 312–14. The names Moab and Ammon are said to have been etymologized to suggest incestuous origins: see *Genesis*, trans. Alter, 90 n. 30–8, and Alter, 'Sodom as Nexus', 34–6, esp. 36 on the '(folk-)etymology' of the names.

108. Westermann, *Genesis 12–36*, 312, declares baldly that 'there is no discernible connection between the drunkenness of Noah and that of Lot'.

109. For what Ham did, or what happened between Noah and Ham, see Westermann, *Genesis 1–11*, 487–8, the simplest and most authoritative statement, arguing that being seen naked is, as elsewhere in the Old Testament, a disgrace, and that Ham not only disgraced his father in that sense, but failed to cover him and revealed the shameful fact to his brothers; for this and other views, including a variety of suggested sexual transgressions, see also Steven L. McKenzie, in *Oxford Companion to the Bible*, ed. Bruce M. Metzger and Michael D. Coogan (Oxford, 1993), s.v. Ham/Canaan; Robert Graves and Raphael Patai, *Hebrew Myths: The Book of Genesis* (New York, 1964), 120–4; Lewis, *Interpretation of Noah*, 153–4; Lloyd R. Bailey, *Noah: The Person and the Story in History and Tradition* (Columbia, SC, 1989), 161–2; Cohen, *Drunkenness of Noah*, 13 ff. Also Robert Davidson, commentary on Genesis 9: 18–29, *Cambridge Bible Commentary: Genesis 1–11* (Cambridge, 1973), 94–7; for Renaissance interpretations of Noah's curse, and whether or not it was justified, see Don Cameron Allen, *The Legend of Noah: Renaissance Rationalism in Art, Science, and Letters* (Urbana, Ill., 1949), 77–8.

110. McKenzie, *Oxford Companion to the Bible*, s.v. Ham/Canaan.

111. For an account of historical-political interpretations, see Westermann, *Genesis 1–11*, 490–4, and his own robustly independent discussion of the alternative readings of the curse and its geographical reach; his view is that the enslavement visited on Canaan by the curse at 9: 25 is 'pre-political' (492), a local matter of servitude to one's brothers for committing an outrage, and that there is at this point no 'coherent notion of three peoples or groups of peoples' (494). On the story of Ham having his skin turned black, and the fact that Canaanites were not negroid, see Graves and Patai, *Hebrew Myths: Genesis*, 114, 115 n. 12, 118, 121. For Renaissance treatments of Ham's progeny, including Negroes and chimpanzees, see Allen, *Legend of Noah*, 118–20, noting also that Jean de Léry thought Amerindians were descended from Canaanites. For fuller treatments of Ham's progeny in the Table of Nations of Genesis 10, see Westermann, *Genesis 1–11*, 495–530, esp. 510 ff., and articles by J. Simons (1954) and D. J. Wiseman (1955) in Hess and Tsumura (eds.), '*I Studied Inscriptions . . .*', 234–65, esp. 237 ff., 259 ff.; for the history of the identification of the three sons with distinct continents or races, and the use of the curse of Ham to justify slavery, both of which are forcefully described as late, non-biblical developments, see Benjamin Braude, 'The Sons of Noah and the Construction of Ethnic and Geographical Identities in the Medieval and Early Modern Periods', *William and Mary Quarterly*, 54 (1997), 103–42. For another account of the 'post-Deluge dispersion', with particular references to the history of Ham and his portrayal, see Jean Devisse, *The Image of the Black in Western Art*, ii. *From*

the Early Christian Era to the 'Age of Discovery', trans. William Granger Ryan, 2 vols. (New York, 1979), ii. 55 ff.

112. Robert Burns, 'The Ordination', ll. 30 –1, in Poems and Songs, ed. James Kinsley (London, 1969), 171; Graham, Thirty Tales & Sketches, ed. Edward Garnett (London, 1929), 3, 14.

113. Oxford Companion to the Bible, s.v. Cush; James Luther Mays, Amos: A Commentary (Philadelphia, 1969), 156–60; Hans Walter Wolff, Joel and Amos, trans. W. Janzen, S. D. McBride, Jr., and C. A. Muenchow, Jr. (Philadelphia, 1977), 347–8, argues that the passage is not necessarily disdainful to the Cushites.

114. See Allen, Legend of Noah, 113–37; J. H. Elliott, The Old World and the New 1492–1650 (Cambridge, 1996), 49–50; Pagden, European Encounters with the New World from Renaissance to Romanticism (New Haven, 1993), 43.

115. John Beddoe, Races of Britain (Bristol and London, 1885), 11; for the honorific version, see Ahmed and Ibrahim Ali, The Black Celts: An Ancient African Civilization in Ireland and Britain (3rd edn., Cardiff, 1994), 12–15. For the 'town in Ireland called Cush' (not specified by the authors), the Census of Ireland: General Alphabetical Index to the Townlands and Towns, Parishes, and Baronies of Ireland (Dublin, 1861), 351, lists four places called Cush, in the counties of Kildare and Limerick and (two) in King's County (now Co. Offaly). A village called Cush in County Wexford appears in Colm Tóibín's novels, The Heather Blazing (1992) and The Blackwater Lightship (1999). Other theories of prehistoric African presence in Ireland are reported, and found questionable, by Paul Edwards, 'The Early African Presence in the British Isles', in Jagdish S. Gundara and Ian Duffield (eds.), Essays on the History of Blacks in Britain (Aldershot, 1992), 9.

116. Ovadiah Yosef, reported Guardian Weekly, 10–16 Aug. 2000, 2.

117. Two earlier uses, in Genesis 4: 11, 14, refer to the punishment of Cain. The Hebrew original of 6: 7 translates literally into English as: 'I will wipe off...man...from [upon] the face of the ground' (Joseph Magil, The English-man's Hebrew–English Old Testament (Grand Rapids, Mich., 1974), 13), as does the Septuagint, a translation by Jews into Greek. The Vulgate has 'Delebo...hominem...a facie terrae', which carries the connotations both of 'erase' and 'destroy', the latter being adopted by the King James version. See above, Chapter 1, n. 3. For some examples of the more general sweep, see Genesis 7: 3–4, 23; Proverbs 2: 22; Jeremiah 25: 26; Ezekiel 38: 20; for the Jews, Deuteronomy 6: 15; Amos 9: 8; for enemies, Exodus 9: 15; Deuteronomy 7: 1–10; 1 Samuel 20: 15; Psalms 21: 10. For more circumscribed cases, beginning with Cain being driven from the earth, see Genesis 4: 14; 1 Kings 13: 34; Jeremiah 28: 16. For some early non-biblical uses of the phrase, alluding to the destructive or purifying Flood, see Kugel, The Bible as It Was, 119.

118. Noah's invention of viticulture was frequently perceived as an agricultural breakthrough and an important 'advance in civilization', extending the technology of farming, catering to the human need for 'joy and celebration', and making possible that 'festal drinking' which is associated with 'the blessed life in the messianic era' (Westermann, Genesis 1–11, 487–88); see also Jancis Robinson, Oxford Companion to Wine (Oxford, 1994), 112, s.v. Bible; Bailey, Noah, 158–63, esp. 162 on viniculture 'presented as an advance in the history of

civilization'. Bailey also offers in these pages some undeveloped hints on the relation between Noah's invention of wine-making and 'the political and/or social relationships' between the ethnic groups represented by Noah's three sons (159). Noah's drunkenness, on the other hand, frequently aroused disapproval, and elicited defences (Allen, *Legend of Noah*, 73, 78, 116 and n., 143; for portrayals in art, see 155–73). In particular, there was much rabbinic disapproval of Noah's vine-growing and drunkenness (Lewis, *Interpretation of Noah*, 151–2). For a balanced modern account, in the context of a wider consideration of Noah's 'righteousness', see Harland, *Value of Human Life*, 45–69, esp. 55–7. Cohen, *Drunkenness of Noah*, 7–8, says the inebriation was wholly laudable: Noah, anxious to obey the divine command to 'be fruitful, and multiply' (9: 1), and, conscious of his age (600 at the time), felt he needed wine to reinforce his sexual powers. Cohen mounts a defence of Lot and his daughters, on similar grounds, and sees Lot as conniving in his daughters' admirable project of renewing the race (9–10: on Lot, see also Letellier, *Day in Mamre*, 235–6). By contrast with Genesis, the Babylonian Flood myth of *Atrahasis*, where the emphasis is on repopulation, represents the Flood as a solution to overpopulation (see Tikva Frymer-Kensky in Dundes (ed.), *The Flood Myth*, 65–7; for a Syrian analogue to the story of Noah's drunkenness, see Eleanor Follansbee, ibid. 76–7). In the Greek analogue to the story of Noah, vine-stock was planted in the reign of Deucalion's son Orestheus, 'probably the earliest Greek wine myth'. Deucalion's sons, like Noah's, were ancestors of the world's peoples. 'The entire Hellenic race', for example, was descended from Hellen (Robert Graves, *The Greek Myths*, 2 vols. (Harmondsworth, 1955), i. 142, 158 ff., Nos. 38.7, 9; 43).

119. On Amos 4: 11, see Loader, *Tale of Two Cities*, 65–6; on 4: 11 and 9: 7–15, see Mays, *Amos*, 77, 80, 156–68.

120. Allen, *Legend of Noah*, 74–5, 84–112, 135, etc. There was a pagan claim that Noah's Flood was a Jewish version of a Mesopotamian Deluge long before modern scholarship began to explore the *Gilgamesh* parallels. Favourite locations for it at various times included Palestine, or even specifically Judea (97); Syria (86); Mesopotamia (86); and 'Asia' (89). For recent coverage of Flood myths throughout the world, see Westermann, *Genesis 1–11*, 398 ff. *passim*, 475 ff.; Dundes (ed.), *The Flood Myth, passim*; on the debate between theories of universality and non-universality (and incidentally, their bearing on the issue of monogenesis vs. polygenesis), see Dundes's headnote to the extract from Frazer, 113–16, esp. 115). On confrontations between biblical universalism and geological science, see the discussions by Rhoda Rappaport, James R. Moore, and Stephen Jay Gould, 383–437. For a brief popular survey, see Cohn, *Noah's Flood*, 41–6.

121. William Ryan and Walter Pitman, *Noah's Flood: The New Scientific Discoveries about the Event that Changed History* (New York, 1998), a more serious book than its title suggests.

122. Allen, *Legend of Noah*, 86; for the Deucalion story, see Ovid, *Metamorphoses*, I. 253 ff., and for the perception of it as local, *Legend of Noah*, 74; for views of the equivalence of, or analogies between, Noah and Deucalion, 83, 188. On the various mountains on which Deucalion is supposed to have landed,

suggesting 'that an ancient Flood myth has been superimposed on a later legend of a flood in Northern Greece', and on Aristotle's view 'that Deucalion's Flood took place "in ancient Greece (*Graecia*), namely the district about Dodona and the Achelous River"', see Graves, *Greek Myths*, i. 142, Nos. 38.5, 10. On the local (Anatolian) origins of another Ovidian story of a Flood and its righteous survivors, Philemon and Baucis (*Metamorphoses*, VIII. 611–724), see an essay of 1922 by W. M. Calder, 'New Light on Ovid's Story of Philemon and Baucis', in Dundes (ed.), *The Flood Myth*, 101–11. For the latter story, like that of Lot, as a hospitality parable, see Graves and Patai, *Hebrew Myths: Genesis*, 169.

123. Roddy Doyle, *The Commitments*, in *The Barrytown Trilogy* (New York, 1995), 13. See Chapter 3, p. 219 and n. 98.

124. Jean-Paul Sartre, *Réflexions sur la question juive* (10th edn., Paris, 1954), 83–4, 159, 176, 181, and *passim*; *Saint Genet: comédien et martyr* (1952; Paris, 1969), 21, 63–88., and *passim*; Sartre's analysis of Genet is partly based on the latter's *Journal du voleur* (1949) and his 'autobiographical' novels, but Archibald's call in *Les Nègres* (1959; Paris, 1967), 76, 'Que les Nègres se nègrent. Qu'ils s'obstinent jusqu'à la folie dans ce qu'on les condamne à être . . .', may in turn be influenced by Sartre's writings on racial matters. For Genet on his pariah status, see Claude Rawson, 'Cannibalism and Fiction. Part II: Love and Eating in Fielding, Mailer, Genet, and Wittig', *Genre*, 11 (1978), 227–313, esp. 272–5.

125. See Chapter 3 n. 99, on descriptions of the Irish, especially that by Ned Ward, c. 1700; Chamfort, *Maximes et pensées* (1795), ch. 8, No. 519, in *Maximes et pensées, Caractères et anecdotes*, ed. Geneviève Renaux, Pref. Albert Camus (Paris, 1970), 148; Dostoevsky, cited in Michael Holroyd, *Bernard Shaw* (New York, 1988–1992), i. 69; Rimbaud, *Une Saison en enfer*, in *Œuvres complètes*, ed. Antoine Adam (Paris, 1972), 97, 94. See 957 n. 5 for a different use of the idea of the white Negro.

126. Verlaine, 'À Arthur Rimbaud, sur un croquis de lui par sa soeur' (1893), *Œuvres poétiques complètes*, ed. Y.-G. Le Dantec (Paris, 1954), 432; Rimbaud, *Saison*, in *Œuvres complètes*, 94; for an extended recent account of Rimbaud's African years, with some Conradian resonances, see Charles Nicholl, *Somebody Else: Arthur Rimbaud in Africa 1880–91* (London, 1997), *passim*; Conrad, *Youth, Heart of Darkness*, 117 (Conrad was very determined to emphasize this cosmopolitanism, which is adumbrated in Carlier in 'An Outpost of Progress', *Tales of Unrest*, 88; see *Collected Letters*, ed. Frederick R. Karl and Laurence Davies, 8 vols. (Cambridge, 1983–), iii. 94).

127. Westermann, *Genesis 12–36*, 297.

128. Westermann, *Genesis 12–36*, 297–9; also Davidson, *Genesis 12–50*, 68–9, and von Rad, *Genesis*, 217–18; Kugel, *The Bible as It Was*, 185–9; Westerman, *Genesis 12–36*, 298, says 'no event in the whole of Genesis . . . is mentioned so frequently in the Old Testament as the destruction of Sodom', and cites almost two dozen references from both the Old and New Testaments; for the full range of these, to which are added passages from the Apocrypha and from some patristic sources, see Loader, *Tale of Two Cities*, 49–138. Loader, *Tale of Two Cities*, 37, argues that the emphasis in Genesis is 'on the social [hospitality] aspect of their sin and not on the sexual aspect itself'; on questions of hospitality and sexual sin, see further Letellier, *Day in Mamre*, 154 ff.;

Weston W. Fields, *Sodom and Gomorrah: History and Motif in Biblical Narrative* (Sheffield, 1997), 41–2, 54–85; on sexual transgression, see 116–33.

129. Westermann, *Genesis 12–36*, 301.

130. On myths of sexual transgression before the Flood, see Kugel, *The Bible as It Was*, 107–12.

131. Westermann, *Genesis 12–36*, 311. For further insights into the interplay of particular, tribal, and universal, with further analogies to the Flood story, see 311–15 *passim*. For the belief of Lot's daughters that they and their father 'are the sole survivors of humankind', see *Genesis*, trans. Alter, 88 n.; also Davidson, *Genesis 12–50*, 78.

132. Michael D. Coogan, in *Oxford Companion to the Bible*, s.v. Lot; for early interpretations of Lot, see Kugel, *The Bible as It Was*, 179–95.

133. Letellier, *Day in Mamre*, 185 ff.; *Genesis*, trans. Alter, 85, n. to 19: 8; Alter, 'Sodom as Nexus', 33; Westermann, *Genesis 12–36*, 301–2.

134. *Oxford Companion to the Bible*, s.v. Lot; A. E. Harvey, *The New English Bible Companion to the New Testament* (Oxford and Cambridge, 1979), 753. For rabbinical and other traditions disapproving of Lot, and for a defence, see Cohen, *Drunkenness of Noah*, 9 –10.

135. Westermann, *Genesis 12–36*, 314–15, is scornful of the use of terms like 'incest' and 'incestuous' in the story of Lot and his daughters, which belong to 'a distant past on which we cannot impose our criteria' (314–15); for a Midrashic suggestion that the daughters were not only not guilty, but actually aided by God, see Graves and Patai, *Hebrew Myths: Genesis*, 172; Davidson, *Genesis 12–50*, 78, says the daughters 'are being commended for taking the only possible course open to them to ensure the future'; see also Letellier, *Day in Mamre*, 234–5.

136. See F. R. Tennant, *The Sources of the Doctrines of the Fall and Original Sin* (Cambridge, 1903), esp. ch. 4, pp. 89–105; Herbert Haag, *Is Original Sin in Scripture?*, trans. Dorothy Thompson (New York, 1969); Paul Rigby, *Original Sin in Augustine's Confessions* (Ottawa, 1987).

137. Deane Swift, *An Essay upon the Life, Writings, and Character of Dr. Jonathan Swift* (1755), 220; T. O. Wedel, 'On the Philosophical Background of *Gulliver's Travels*', *Studies in Philology*, 23 (1926), 441; Frye, 'Swift's Yahoos and the Christian Symbols for Sin', 202–3.

INDEX